Shared Encounters

Computer Supported Cooperative Work

For other titles published in this series, go to
www.springer.com/series/2861

Katharine S. Willis · George Roussos
Konstantinos Chorianopoulos · Mirjam Struppek
Editors

Shared Encounters

Editors

Katharine S. Willis
University of Siegen
Germany
willis@locatingmedia.uni-siegen.de

George Roussos
University of London
UK
g.roussos@bbk.ac.uk

Konstantinos Chorianopoulos
Bauhaus University of Weimar
Germany
choko@ionio.gr

Mirjam Struppek
Interaction Field
Germany
struppek@interactionfield.de

Computer Supported Cooperative Work ISSN 1431-1496
ISBN 978-1-4471-2528-0   e-ISBN 978-1-84882-727-1
DOI 10.1007/978-1-84882-727-1
Springer Dordrecht Heidelberg London New York

British Library Cataloguing in Publication Data
A catalogue record for this book is available from the British Library

Printed on acid-free paper

Springer is part of Springer Science + Business Media (www.springer.com)

Foreword

Paul Dourish

In the early 1990s, Mark Weiser published his landmark paper on ubiquitous computing. Partly a manifesto and partly a progress report, it anticipated a world in which increasing miniaturization of computational devices and the pervasive availability of wireless networking would allow for a radical reconfiguration of the relationship between people and computation. Freed from the confines of conventional devices, computation could move beyond the PC and "off the desktop." However, if computing is moving off the desktop, where is it going? One of the challenges of the reconfiguration that Weiser anticipated is to understand something of the spaces into which computation is moving. The contributions in this volume reflect just this sensitivity.

Arguably, the fundamental character of ubiquitous computing research is not technological, but spatial. Certainly, ubiquitous computing poses significant technological challenges, but in many ways these are simply the extrapolation and intensification of trends that predated the arrival of ubiquitous computing as a topic. Power management, decentralized software architectures, multiagent systems, interlayer processing, sensor fusion are all active areas of research, but they reflect concerns that manifest themselves too in others areas of computer science and engineering research. On the other hand, the spatial character of ubiquitous computing systems is one of their intrinsic properties and a crucial area for analysis and design. By "spatial" here, I do not mean merely geometric. Instead, I am focused on the fact that they inhabit the same space as we do, and that they structure it and organize it in much the same way as our own activities and movements do. Here, the concerns of computer science and technological design intersect with those of cultural geography and urban studies to produce an immensely generative new research area.

The city, and the urban experience, has long been a site of social inquiry, in the writings of cultural critics such as Walter Benjamin and sociologists such as Georg Simmel. At this point, though, in the early twenty-first century, we are rapidly

Paul Dourish
Donald Bren School of Information and Computer Sciences, The University of California,
6210 Donald Bren Hall, Irvine, CA, 92697-3425, USA
e-mail: jpd@ics.uci.edu

approaching the point at which more than 50% of the world's population are urban dwellers for the first time in our history. It is a particularly apposite moment, then, to examine the relationship between technology and urban experience.

It is not that the urban experience is becoming a technological one, because cities depend critically upon technologies for their very existence. The city is a product of infrastructure of many sorts – transportation, communication, sanitation, power, and more (including, of course, the information infrastructures of urban management and regulation). The technologies associated with mobile and ubiquitous computing, then, are being deployed in environments already heavily technological. However, some significant new issues arise around the personal – and interpersonal – aspects of these technologies.

Some of the most interesting questions arise around topics of ownership, management, stewardship, and control over technology and information. If the mobile phone is a critical tool of urban infrastructure in contemporary cities, then it differs from those other pieces of urban infrastructure in that it is individually owned, operated, and to an extent, controlled. Ubiquitous and mobile computing forges systems out of ad hoc coalitions of devices and services, but, critically, it does so across administrative boundaries. When urban dwellers use public transport to get around, they do so entirely as "users" of a system over which they have little control and no direct ownership. On the other hand, when mobile phone owners use location-based services to locate each other and exchange information, the "system" that they employ is one that depends on public and private infrastructures, technologies that they own, and technologies that they encounter. Mobile technologies connect people to each other in ways that both depend upon, and transcend, public or commercial infrastructures, offering services that are "personal" in ways that public infrastructures never can. In doing so, they create new forms of technologically mediated social relations, not only among people, but between people, corporations, and states.

That said, it is important not to be blinded by the rhetoric of revolution that so often attends discussion of new technologies, the sense that new technologies and new technological practices have radically destabilized the old order, and that everything is up for grabs. It is all too easy to allow our fascination for genuine innovation and novelty to blind us to the ways in which new technologies are firmly enmeshed in preexisting contexts. Doreen Massey uses the term "power geometries" to draw attention to the ways in which encounters with urban space are structured by complex power dynamics and that questions of accessibility, mobility, representation, and regulation are means by which power is exercised and power relations maintained. So, alongside the "flaneur" – the urban wanderer, for whom the city becomes a sensory feast and a place of pleasure, whose discretionary time, money, and mobility are these days supplemented by any number of location-aware devices and services – we must also consider those for whom mobility is not a choice but a necessary mode of living, or those for whom it is not available at all, or those excluded from participation due to the barriers of all sorts – technological, economic, linguistic, physical, and more. The urban experience is heterogeneous, not simply in the sense that cities vary from one to another, but also in the sense that there are many simultaneous experiences of any given urban space. There are those who move through it and those who are imprisoned by it, those who consume it and those charged with its upkeep, those for whom it is a site of freedom and those for whom it is a site of regulation, and more. While Michel de Certeau has written of the ways in which urban residents can take possession of the city, producing their experience of it through their own tactical appropriations, they do so only within limits and bounds.

In the image of the informated urban resident, we have the fusion of technology and urbanism, two major components of the image of modernity. It is exactly this opportunity to examine the cultural imaginary of modernism and its contemporary manifestations that makes the topics explored in this volume so generative. The "encounters" that animate are at once personal and cultural, physical and conceptual – and of ever-increasing relevance to our daily lives.

The contributions to this volume reflect the diversity of work in this research area. They are drawn from disparate disciplines, including computer science, cultural studies, anthropology, sociology, urban design, and architecture; they span the globe, including studies in Europe, Asia, Australia, and the United States); and they reflect a wide range of concerns, including those in working, domestic, professional, and entertainment settings. What ties them together, though, is the common concern with encounters both with and through information technology as a site for the production of social and cultural life. Mobile blogging, urban games, and academic conferences, among others, provide sites for examining the lived phenomena of shared encounters.

Above all, the theme that pulls these contributions together is an understanding of the mutuality of technological opportunity and social practice. The significance of emerging mobile technologies, such as those explored here, cannot be understood purely in their own terms. Rather, they must be understood in the context of social practices that render them meaningful in particular settings. The material and fabric of every space have always constrained and enabled social relations and reflected historical circumstances and the interests of those who have shaped it, responding to human needs but also opening up a space of possibilities. When mobile technologies are considered in this light, our focus moves to the encounters that arise and the forms of collective practice that make up the social glue, in the words of the final section here, by which people are connected. Understanding the social organization of spatial settings, the appropriation afforded by forms of playful interaction, and the complexities of sharing – the topics, in turn, of the other sections of this collection – is critically important in pushing the research agenda forward.

As location-enabled services are increasingly deployed on mobile devices, the topics explored here will become even more important, and the blend of social, technological, theoretical, and design elements that this volume encompasses will become even more necessary. The contributions collected here not only provide evidence of the richness of this domain, but also point toward its future directions.

Preface

This book is intended to offer insights and knowledge on the topic of shared encounters. It is introduced by Paul Dourish, a highly respected thinker in this area, who offers his distinctive viewpoint on the topic. The main section of the book opens with a chapter, contributed by the book editors, in which the different themes and methodologies of shared encounters are discussed in detail.

The book is then divided into four sections; each section presenting a different facet of the topic of shared encounters. Each section is introduced by a text from a key author in the field and presents an overview on the sub-topic in order to offer the reader a way into each collection of chapters; Barry Brown discusses shared experience, George Roussos outlines playful encounters, Malcolm McCullough introduces the section spatial settings and Elisabeth Churchill provides an introduction of the topic of social glue. The individual chapters that follow offer a particular perspective on the main topic and also provide insights from the author's own research background. The contributions are interdisciplinary in nature and the authors have a range of research backgrounds; among them computer scientists, architects, sociologists and artists.

Overall, the intention of the book is to introduce the range of empirical and theoretical approaches in the study of shared encounters and to highlight the multi-faceted nature of shared experience in our everyday experience of space. It is by no means exhaustive, but we hope that it opens up new ways of thinking about the subject and stimulates a wider understanding of the value of shared encounters in our everyday lives.

Acknowledgments

This book is the result of a workshop held as part of the CHI 2007 conference that took place on April 29, 2007. There were 16 attendees of the workshop and it is their involvement that made the day a valuable experience and aslo contributed to the development of the topic: Cheryl Cole, Joan DiMicco, Eric Gilbert, Connor Graham, Maria Hakannson, Anthony Jameson, Greet Jans, Pamela Jennings, Omar Khan, Christian Licoppe, Karen Martin, Mark Rouncefield, Christine Satchell, Ava Fatah gen. Schieck, Heather Vaughan, and Michael Voong. The members of the scientific committee of the original workshop (excluding those who have written for this volume) also provided expert review and guidance on the workshop submissions: Stefan Agamanolis, Louise Barkhuus, Barry Brown, Laura Colini, Panos Markopoulos, Sara Price, Carlo Ratti, Mark Shepard, Norbert Streitz, and Anthony Townsend. We also thank Laura Colini and Karen Martin for their assistance in the workshop organization.

However, this book is the outcome of many contributions, and many people have supported and assisted us in shaping of this work. During its making, Paul Dourish, Barry Brown, Malcom McCullough, and Elizabeth Churchill have made invaluable contributions to the individual chapters.

We are also grateful for the support of various funding bodies during the preparation of this book. Katharine S. Willis and Konstantinos Chorianopoulos benefited from the support of the EU Marie Curie funded MEDIACITY project at the Bauhaus University of Weimar.

Finally, our special thanks to Beverley Ford and her colleagues at Springer for their invaluable guidance on the book development.

Contents

Contributors

Barry Brown
Department of Communication, University of California, San Diego, CA, 92093-0503, USA
barry@ucsd.edu

Dimitris Charitos
Laboratory of New Technologies in Communication, Education, and the Mass Media, Department of Communication and Media Studies, National and Kapodistrian University of Athens, 5 Stadiou street, 105 62 Athens, Greece
vedesign@otenet.gr

Konstantinos Chorianopoulos
Bauhaus University of Weimar, Bauhausstrasse 7b, 99423 Weimar, Germany
k.chorianopoulos@archit.uni-weimar.de

Elizabeth F. Churchill
Yahoo! Research, 2821 Mission College Blvd, Santa Clara, CA 95054, USA
churchill@acm.org

Katerina Diamantaki
Laboratory of New Technologies in Communication, Education, and the Mass Media, Department of Communication and Media Studies, National and Kapodistrian University of Athens, 5 Stadiou street, 105 62 Athens, Greece
knd@hol.gr

Marcus Foth
Institute for Creative Industries and Innovation, Queensland University of Technology, Creative Industries Precinct, Brisbane QLD 4059, Australia
m.foth@qut.edu.au

Nicole Garcia
Institute for Creative Industries and Innovation, Queensland University of Technology, Creative Industries Precinct, Brisbane QLD 4059, Australia
picoloska@yahoo.com

Thierry Giles
K3 The School of Arts and Communication, Malmö University, SE-205 06
Malmö, Sweden
thejimiworld@gmail.com

Connor Graham
Computing Department, Lancaster University, Lancaster LA1 4YW, UK
c.graham@lancaster.ac.uk
and
Department of Information Systems, University of Melbourne, Parkville,
Victoria 3010, Australia

Andrea Grimes
School of Interactive Computing, Georgia Institute of Technology,
85 5th St. NW Atlanta, GA 30332, USA
agrimes@cc.gatech.edu

Kenton O'Hara
Microsoft Research Cambridge, 7 J J Thomson Avenue, Cambridge, UK
v-keohar@microsoft.com

Greg Hearn
Institute for Creative Industries and Innovation, Queensland University of
Technology, Creative Industries Precinct, Brisbane QLD 4059, Australia
g.hearn@qut.edu.au

Yoriko Inada
Department of Social Science, Telecom Paristech, Institut Telecom,
46 rue Barrault 75013 Paris, France
yoriko.inada@telecom-paristech.fr

Giulio Jacucci
Helsinki Institute for Information Technology HIIT, Helsinki
University of Technology TKK, P.O. Box 9800, FIN-02015 TKK, Finland
giulio.jacucci@hiit.fi

Pamela L. Jennings
Computer & Information Science & Engineering Directorate,
Information and Intelligent Systems Division, National Science Foundation,
2100 Wilson Blvd., Arlington, VA, U.S.A.
pljenn@gmail.com

Nikos Kaimakamis
Laboratory of New Technologies in Communication, Education, and the Mass
Media, Department of Communication and Media Studies, National and
Kapodistrian University of Athens, 5 Stadiou street, 105 62 Athens, Greece
nikaimakam@yahoo.com

Omar Khan
Center for Architecture and Situated Technologies, chool of Architecture and
Planning, University at Buffalo, 3435 Main Street, Buffalo, NY 14214, USA
omarkhan@buffalo.edu

Masaru Kitsuregawa
University of Tokyo, 4-6-1, Komaba, Meguro-Ku, Tokyo 153-8505, Japan
kitsure@tkl.iis.u-tokyo.ac.jp

Shin'ichi Konomi
University of Tokyo, 4-6-1, Komaba, Meguro-Ku, Tokyo 153-8505, Japan
konomi@iis.u-tokyo.ac.jp

Vassilis Kostakos
Department of Mathematics & Engineering, University of Madeira,
Funchal 9000-319, Portugal
vassilis@cmu.edu

Esko Kurvinen
Elisa Oyj, P.O. Box 1, 00061 Elisa, Finland
esko.kurvinen@elisa.fi

Christian Licoppe
Department of Social Science, Telecom Paristech, Institut Telecom,
46 rue Barrault 75013 Paris, France
christian.licoppe@telecom-paristech.fr

Mike Marianek
Bauhaus University of Weimar, Bauhausstrasse 7b, 99423 Weimar, Germany
redmike@spiritofspace.com

Karen Martin
The Bartlett School of Graduate Studies, University College London,
1-19 Torrington Place, London WC1E 6BT, UK
karen.martin@ucl.ac.uk

Malcolm McCullough
Taubman College of Architecture and Urban Planning, University of Michigan,
2000 Bonisteel Boulevard, Ann Arbor, MI, 48103, USA
mmmc@umich.edu

Ann Morrison
Helsinki Institute for Information Technology HIIT Helsinki University
of Technology TKK, P.O. Box 9800, FIN-02015 TKK, Finland
ann.morrisson@canterbury.ac.nz

Antti Oulasvirta
Helsinki Institute for Information Technology HIIT Helsinki University
of Technology TKK, P.O. Box 9800, FIN-02015 TKK, Finland
antti.oulasvirta@hiit.fi

Peter Peltonen
Helsinki Institute for Information Technology HIIT Helsinki University
of Technology TKK, P.O. Box 9800, FIN-02015 TKK, Finland
peter.peltonen@hiit.fi

Alan Penn
The Bartlett School of Graduate Studies, University College London,
1-19 Torrington Place, London WC1E 6BT, UK
a.penn@ucl.ac.uk

Tim Rieniets
Institut für Städtebau, Wolfgang-Pauli-Str. 15, ETH Hönggerberg,
HIL H 47.1, CH-8093 Zürich, Switzerland
rieniets@nsl.ethz.ch

Charalampos Rizopoulos
Laboratory of New Technologies in Communication, Education, and the Mass
Media, Department of Communication and Media Studies, National and
Kapodistrian University of Athens, 5 Stadiou street, 105 62 Athens, Greece
c_rizopoulos@media.uoa.gr

Mark Rouncefield
Computing Department, Lancaster University, Lancaster LA1 4YW, UK
m.rouncefield@lancaster.ac.uk

George Roussos
School of Computer Science and Information Systems, Birkbeck College,
University of London, Malet Street, London WC1E 7HX, UK
g.roussos@bbk.ac.uk

Antti Salovaara
Helsinki Institute for Information Technology HIIT, Helsinki University
of Technology TKK, P.O. Box 9800, FIN-02015 TKK, Finland
antti.salovaara@hiit.fi

Christine Satchell
Department of Information Systems, University of Melbourne,
Parkville, Victoria 3010, Australia
christine.satchell@qut.edu.au
Institute for Creative Industries and Innovation, Queensland
University of Technology, Kelvin Grove, Brisbane 4059, Australia

Ava Fatah gen. Schieck
The Bartlett School of Graduate Studies, University College London,
1-19 Torrington Place, London WC1E 6BT, UK
ava.fatah@ucl.ac.uk

Kaoru Sezaki
University of Tokyo, 4-6-1, Komaba, Meguro-Ku, Tokyo 153-8505, Japan
sezaki@iis.u-tokyo.ac.jp

Mirjam Struppek
Interactionfield, Rheinbergerstr. 68, 10115 Berlin, Germany
struppek@interactionfield.de

Maria N. Stukoff
The Manchester Digital Development Agency (MDDA) and the Manchester
Institute for Research and Innovation in Art and Design (MIRAD), Manchester
Metropolitan University (UK), Righton Building, Cavendish Street, Manchester
M15 6BG, UK
mstukoff@yahoo.co.uk

Katharine S. Willis
Locating Media Graduate School, US 236, 57072 University of Siegen, Germany
willis@locatingmedia.uni-siegen.de

Chapter 1
Shared Encounters

Katharine S. Willis, George Roussos, Konstantinos Chorianopoulos, and Mirjam Struppek

Introduction

The approach often adopted by Human Computer Interaction (HCI) focuses on exchanges between a person and the interface of a device situated within a specific context of use. This view is increasingly challenged by the complex and dynamic world of the physical and social environment integrated with ubiquitous technologies, which requires an alternative view that sees people creating settings which frame and structure their encounters. As a result, in recent years, HCI researchers have recognized the need for social and physical data to be gathered and interpreted, but have often been frustrated in their attempts to codify and make sense of the complex and dynamic nature of the real world of human experience. Developments in the early 90s such as the emergence of the field of Computer Supported Cooperative Work (CSCW), the introduction of the concept of social navigation (Hook et al. 2003), work on ambient environments, the UbiComp conference series as well as more theoretical positions on embodied or situated interaction (Dourish 2001, McCullough 2005) have all lead the way to a new understanding of HCI.

Another driver for this change in emphasis in HCI is the emergence of mobile and ubiquitous computing that has brought significant changes in social and cultural practices in spatial settings. Interactions through and with ubiquitous technologies no longer require physical co-presence and have broadened the range of possible interactions as well as the range of settings in which these interactions can unfold. The basis for this lies in the fact that physical distance no longer prevents many of the types of interactions and encounters that had previously been confined to face-to-face contact. As a result, there has been much discussion on the role of spatial setting and interaction mediated through technologies such as that on the role of space and agency in the quality of the interaction (Dourish and Harrisson 1996) and also the broader concept of the situated behavior and actions (Suchman 1987).

K.S. Willis (✉)
Locating Media Graduate School, US 236, 57072 University of Siegen, Germany
e-mail: willis@locatingmedia.uni-siegen.de

K.S. Willis et al. (eds.), *Shared Encounters*, Computer Supported Cooperative Work,
DOI 10.1007/978-1-84882-727-1_1, © Springer-Verlag London Limited 2010

1

A good deal has also been written on the subject of social collaboration among individuals using communication devices and the conditions or features that are required to enable such activities (Gaver 1992; Paulos and Goodman 2004; Hook et al. 2003; Churchill et al. 2004). Further discussion has focused on the technologies themselves, assessing the social impact of the emerging forms of behavior, such as the activities of ad hoc communities enabled through mobile technologies (Rheingold 2002), or the patterns of mobile phones' use (Katz and Aakhus 2002). Finally, numerous applications and locative media projects (e.g., Harle and Hopper 2005) which explore interactions through realization have been developed. These projects and research offer many useful insights, but there still remain many questions about how to create the conditions for meaningful and persisting shared interactions in public space. The challenge is not only to build systems that respond to rich and dynamic social and physical events, but also to provide a structure for sustainable participation and sharing.

If we are to design for such changes in social practice then we need to understand them in the actual context in which they occur in everyday life. Methodologies, particularly ethnographic studies, have started to become popular means by which one can analyze the qualitative as well as the quantitative aspects of user behavior and interaction in everyday settings (e.g., Ito et al. 2006). Yet, several challenges lie ahead before it is possible to fully capture and interpret the multiple and diverse interactions of people on the move in urban places. We believe that to address these challenges, it is necessary to build on contributions from fields outside of HCI to inform both theoretical and empirical work; with sociology, architecture, anthropology, and urban planning providing valuable perspectives that can offer us new insights and solutions.

In this chapter, we address the topic of shared encounters in two stages; first by discussing in depth the characteristics and features of shared encounters and how they are enacted in our everyday lives. The second half of the chapter then focuses on reviewing appropriate methodologies for the study of shared encounters in public space.

Background

The topic of shared encounters derives from the conversations at the Shared Encounters workshop held as part of CHI 2007 (Willis et al. 2007). In our discussions during the workshop, we investigated the nature of interaction in public space as mediated through new technologies and in particular we questioned "what is the glue that creates links between people in public spaces?" Interestingly, it turned out that one of the most provocative questions during the workshop was the most obvious; what constitutes a shared encounter and what sets it apart from other experiences? In particular, when does an interaction between a person and another or between members of a group become a shared encounter? A further core question was to identify the ways in which the physical setting affects the nature of an encounter.

In the development of the topic, we respond to these questions by first outlining an explanation of what we mean when we talk about shared encounters. We then continue by differentiating shared encounters into four sub topics; shared experience, playful encounters, spatial settings, and social glue. These subtopics reflect not just the range of contributions in this volume, but also outline the multifaceted nature of shared encounters.

Characterizing a Shared Encounter

The way we behave when we encounter others is differentiated by many diverse factors; whether our encounters are in a public or private place, with an individual or a group, planned or by chance. Our encounters are therefore situated or defined by the particular set of available background information that we make use of to structure our interactions. According to Goffman, the physical setting in which an encounter takes place is not insignificant, but rather acts as a frame for how people interact and helps define the nature of the situation (Goffman 1963). Goffman referred specifically to face-to-face encounters, but communication technologies have allowed for many types of interaction to occur where we are not necessarily physically sharing the same space with those we encounter. This fundamentally affects the nature of presence in an encounter, since we may experience a sense of shared space, yet be acting on different signals from the distinct settings in which we find ourselves. In such situations, we still manage to act differently with different people, but our encounters are no longer so strongly framed by the physical setting (Meyrowitz 1986). Communication technologies, like physical places, create structures which include and exclude participants and in so doing they can create social boundaries equivalent to the walls and windows in physical space. These boundaries define the nature of social access to situations, and also help to frame awareness among individuals of whether an encounter is accessible to them or not. Put simply, this affects whether someone can clearly identify and develop a role for themselves and others in the interaction, a factor that is often necessarily based on existing social conventions. Once the basis for an encounter has been established, the subsequent process of exchange also needs to have a dynamic quality with a system of feedback, where participants can mediate their interaction and develop a sense of persistent, shared space (Mynatt et al. 1997). This shared setting does not need to be explicit and it can be passive as well as actively experienced, but it will involve some negotiated factors; for instance there will be a shared sense of "being there" or co-presence even when participants are quiet or absent.

In the study of encounters in everyday settings, it is also important to consider the role that performance plays in the interaction. This concept was outlined by Goffman, who uses the term performance to refer to activities of an individual before a set of observers, whether these are friends or strangers (Goffman 1959). In order to give an action of coherency those participating need to agree upon a definition of the situation and this involves playing a "role." However, this is rarely a conscious behavior since the conception of role becomes second nature and is infused into an individual's personality. Through this process, interaction can be defined as the reciprocal influence of individuals on one another's actions, when in one another's immediate physical presence. In sharing an experience, individuals co-operate to enact a goal-oriented performance. This is very significant for our understanding of shared encounters since peoples' behaviors are performed through a filter of an unspoken negotiation of social roles and terms of the situation in which the individuals find themselves. In addition, the terms of the situation are not just socially constructed, but are also framed by the physical setting of the interaction which acts as a stage.

We therefore define a shared encounter as:

"the interaction between two people or within a group where a sense of performative co-presence is experienced and which is characterised by a mutual recognition of spatial or social proximity"

Fundamental to this whole discussion is the concept of sharing, which extends a notion of an interaction to one that is experienced on some common level. This sees technology as affording a background to what is the most important interaction; that between one person and another.

Shared Experience

We experience many encounters in our daily life, but the ones that tend to make an impression on us are those in which we are aware of some form of shared experience. Although the human-to-human interaction is still the key aspect, ubiquitous technologies can provide a valuable background to such encounters and can reinforce levels of connectivity since they lend themselves to content sharing. For instance the use of mobile phones, which have been readily adopted by youth cultures, reinforces and extends existing social networks and drives them toward a higher level of networked sociability. In these interactions, face-to-face interaction is equated with mobile phone-based communication and a "full-time intimate" community develops (Castells et al. 2006). Other technologies allow alternative modes of communication; for example, Bluetooth enables people to engage in more intimate and timely information exchanges dependent on proximity, whereas WiFi can provide the infrastructures for neighborhood-wide communication (Rheingold 2002). A theoretical approach to this subject is introduced by Diamantaki et al. (this volume) who explored the social implications of using locative media in the context of urban everyday life. Although technology may appear to augment shared experiences and the types of ad hoc encounters practiced through the use of mobile technologies are widespread, this sharing is often limited or "minimal sharing" (Wellman 2001) such as showing off on-screen photos within a peer group. Sharing practiced within a context can be referred to as "selective sociality" (Ito et al. 2006); since it occurs within small, selectively insular social groups. To explore this topic, Konomi (this volume) discusses the advantages and drawbacks of data mining into historical data in order to reveal existing patterns of subtle social relationships.

Ubiquitous technologies such as situated interactive public displays in the city enable an interplay between large displays and mobile end-user terminals, which brings shared experiences into a public setting. These media offer a different model of sharing; joint and widespread reception of media content. Screen-based content, such as Television, has often been criticized not only due to the quality of the content and on the passive nature of the watching activity, but also on a social level, the shared viewing of content creates a strong mutual experience (Kubey and Csikszentmihalyi 1990). In fact, shared viewing and discussion about mass media content can provide a valuable common reference point in everyday life. The possibility of rethinking fixed screens in ubiquitous contexts lies in the use of content-enriched communication to enhance awareness and human connectedness in public spaces. By connecting large outdoor screens with experiments in online worlds, the culture of collaborative content production and networking could be brought into a wider context (Struppek 2006). The nature of such collaborative experience is discussed by Chorianopoulos and Rieniets (this volume), who describe an interactive video installation that allows participants to explore a map narrative and engage in group interactions through a shared screen. Jacucci et al. (this volume) also study behavior around a public screen and found that key practices could be observed where social roles were played out. One practice observed was that of turn-taking, which formalized roles in the transient social space that was created by the screen.

Playful Encounters

The concept of play has at its very core the need for shared experience. During play, a shared space is created, which establishes the medium for collective activity between participants and their informational environment. Social games structure defines the context of action and distribution of roles, expectations, and responsibilities in the framework of the activity that is taking place. They contribute to making encounters meaningful and shape the conventions governing the course of interactions. To explore this further, Licoppe and Inada (this volume) evaluate the features of situated and mediated encounters in a location-aware game called Mogi and found that players played not just within the game format, but also were playful in the way that they sought to exploit "gaps" they discovered within the game structure. A key practice was that of "cara-gattai" or achieving co-presence, where players deliberately froze their icons at a particular space and sought to create an overlap of their icon with another player's icon. Thus, the playful encounters that occurred were not always those that were designed into the game experience, but also those where the players had fun within the game format itself.

This new generation of locative games, such as Mogi, brings mediated play out of online spaces into urban public settings. They develop the social potential of location-aware devices, which seek to extend and reappropriate the functions of locative technologies, through exploring ways in which the game format can be socially constructive and facilitate new dynamics within everyday life. Stukoff (this volume) describes the development and features of one such project that supports the creation of emotional, cohabitable spaces that facilitate urban play with public screens. This study found that play occurred on a number of levels; unconscious, conscious, as well as dynamic play. However, the key aspect that motivated people to become playful was that of "social infection" where onlookers felt more at ease with getting involved when they heard other people talk about it or observe what is expected of them before they joined in.

Jennings (this volume) highlights a further useful characteristic of playful experience, which is the desire for tangible or tactile experience. Although, locative gaming may involve moving through a space, the bodily engagement through playfully manipulating is an aspect of play that many of us have been familiar with since childhood. This way of playing brings face-to-face interaction back into the frame of playful encounters, and can therefore appeal to less technically minded individuals or people in transit.

Spatial Settings

The way in which we communicate with others also bears a strong relationship with space, and our interactions with others can be considered as situated in that they are shaped by both the physical setting (Goffman 1963) and the social situation. Consequently, we behave differently in different situations depending on both where one is and who one is with, and this is influenced by the degree to which they are present in the situation. Yet, Meyrowitz points out that communication technologies undermine influence of the physical setting on the situation so that where one is in space has less and less to do with what one knows and experiences (Meyrowitz 1986). McCullough underlines this by stating that that ubiquitous technologies require new ways of grounding digital information in order that they do not undermine ways of acting in the physical world (McCullough 2005). One such example of how behavior is changed is that space enacted through such technologies conforms to a different concept of boundedness (Willis 2008). Instead of some form of definable extent, space is instead experienced more in terms of regions that are not only defined by spatial extents, but also by patterns of informational or social access. Consequently, collectively defining boundaries becomes part of the pattern of communication, such as the common practice of asking for and reporting location at the beginning of a mobile phone call (Laurier 2001). This highlights the fact that shared experiences are still framed not only by the spatial setting but through patterns of connectivity enabled through technology rather than by physical boundaries. Therefore, it is critical to find ways of spatializing ubiquitous technologies and thus reconnecting them to spatial settings. This requires new views on the interconnectedness of location and behavior in public space.

Schieck et al. (this volume) study how the deployment of two prototypes that augment face-to-face social communication affects the manner in which people act in public space. They point out the importance of creating settings for encounters and introduce the concept of a digital stage that can facilitate and encourage different types of social interactions. Through proactive staging of encounters, they create an urban performance that unfolds over time and the authors report that in order for this kind of public display to be engaging, the viewer needs to be able to construct a socially meaningful relationship of which the display and the human observer form a part. Garcia et al. (this volume) also observe encounters in public space, but over a more extended timeframe and in a specific physical setting. They discuss an approach that utilizes methods from archaeology to analyze the social encounters between residents, visitors, creative content, and the built and natural elements of the environment in an urban village. They found that the built environment creates stages for encounters, but that sometimes the features of built space can actually hinder rather than allow these shared experience, and that media can be used to replace the advantage lost in the spatial setting.

Khan introduces (this volume) the concept of underspecification, and describes two artistic projects that provide ways for participants to participate in collaborative behavior in public space. He claims that people need to be able to continually negotiate their own sense of place as they confront one another in a dynamic public sphere, and only when this process is facilitated can the conditions for a collective public come into being. Both Khan and Schieck et al. highlight how everyday ubiquitous technologies have the potential to create powerful shared connections in public space. It is just these types of mediated situations that can overcome the "lost advantage" of the physical spatial setting.

Social Glue

Social spaces emerge through multiple one-to-one interactions and by participation in groups. These encounter spaces can disperse as rapidly as they are created, but some can become more established and exist for a period of time. For most people, the sense of identity which they draw from their interaction in such shared social spaces is the key to the way they relate to the world. Social spaces are developed around communities, such as those described by Packard:

> " a social network of people of various kinds, ranks and ages who encounter each other on the streets, in the stores, at sports parks, at communal gatherings. A good deal of personal interaction occurs... all recognize it as a special place with ongoing character. It has a central core and well understood limits. Most members base most of their daily activities in or near the community" (Packard 1972).

New communication technologies exacerbate the network effect where access and membership is defined not by entering and leaving a physically bounded space, but instead by the making and breaking of nodes and links. Inhabitants of such communities are separated physically and interact strictly through computer systems, such that users are aware that their virtual lives will rarely intersect with their real lives. The question is therefore, how to enable bridges between online communities and patterns of behavior in physical settings. In attempting to understand the nature of everyday online activities, Graham et al. (this volume) provide a literature review of blogging and sharing practices in order to suggest directions in future research of mobile blogging in the context of everyday life.

Martin (this volume) discusses empirical findings from a long-term research program that involved local communities in developing content about their neighborhood through ubiquitous applications. She discusses the complex issues associated with the motivation for participation by members of existing place-based communities, and highlights how researchers may need to overcome participants' reluctance to engage due to pressures of time or lack of perceived relevance. She also points out that access to an "authentic context of use" often requires facilitation from a third-party organization and consequently researchers' relationship to some portion of the community may be indirect. Grimes (this volume) found that, working within a similar local community setting, a system for sharing experiences about healthy eating facilitated a sense of community empowerment. This highlights the fact that technology introduced into an existing local community infrastructure needs to be carefully facilitated and that community gatekeepers need to be involved from the outset. Grimes proposes the terms "deeply local" to describe this, which refers to both the geographic and social qualities of involvement.

This aspect of locality further underlines the fact that studies of practices around the topic of shared encounters often encounter issues when the social scene is not closely linked to a static physical setting (such as a neighborhood or workplace). The use of mobile media often incurs such problems, since the community is no longer defined by a shared physical setting. Instead the community is more transient, collaboration is ad hoc and the core interaction is not necessarily face-to-face. Bardren and Bossen term this "local mobility," which is the intermediate space between working together over distance on the one hand and working face-to-face on the other (Bardrem and Bossen 2003). These spaces of collaboration show a fine balance between remote interaction and face-to-face meeting, a practice that has also been referred to as "zooming with the feet" (Bertelsen and Bødker 2001). This practice of acting remotely, but then coming together for a specific purpose is also highlighted by Ito in the context of use of mobile media, who terms it a "flesh meet" (Ito et al. 2006). Interestingly Ito points out that although the physical co-presence among friends is seen as a heightened experience, it is also often augmented by the presence of others through mobile media and it is this constant nonphysical contact that creates a feeling of intimacy and closeness between people in a social group.

Studying Shared Encounters: Some Methodological Challenges

The primary focus of much HCI in terms of methodology to date has been on designing and measuring the performance of new ICT in terms of usability. Yet, the development of ubiquitous and pervasive computing technologies has seen the context of the digital task extend beyond the desktop toward an ambiguity of activities in the public space and in everyday life. In this context, it has become practically difficult and sometimes inappropriate to use many of the established techniques (interviews, direct observation, and questionnaires). A number of alternative methodological frameworks for studying shared encounters have therefore started to be developed and implemented. Early works in CSCW involved video-conferencing being installed in researchers' offices or in student dormitories which was used to link distant offices of the same organization (Jancke et al. 2001, Karahalios and Donath 2004). However, these early innovative systems were only evaluated for technical feasibility and basic user acceptance. In addition, the effects on behavior and attitudes were not formally evaluated over a longer period of time. However, longitudinal evaluation of ICT has been established as a worthwhile data collection technique during the adoption phase (Kraut et al. 2002).

The topic of shared encounters covers a broad spectrum of disciplines; such as computer science, sociology, architecture, and art which, in itself, presents significant methodological challenges. A further issue is that the topic responds to an inherently intangible concept; the nature, motivation, and outcomes of shared experience. For instance, everyday social interactions are not necessarily either explicit or even consciously recognized and they usually leave no tangible trace. Furthermore, they are not planned events. Even when media afford such shared interaction, encounters can happen either unexpectedly or on an entirely different level from that which is expected. For example, O'Hara et al. found that children using a mobile information system in a zoo type of environment were far more motivated to collect and keep location-based content, rather than the expected interaction with it in-situ (O' Hara et al. 2007).

A key methodological priority in understanding such encounters is that it is preferable to study them in natural or real-world settings and as part of peoples' daily activities. This also presents challenges, since real-world situations pose a number of practical problems for data gathering and analysis. First, it is often difficult to meaningfully document a shared experience between people without the researcher themselves becoming part of the situation and thus affecting it in some way. Second, users are usually mobile, and activities can take place over long time-scales, which can make it difficult to frame and document their actions. Finally, the focus on often a small number of people and the interpretation of gathered data can make analysis and evaluation a lengthy process, a factor that can be at odds with early responses and rapid prototyping required in a design process.

Data Gathering, Design and Evaluation

Due to the multidisciplinary aspects of the theme of shared encounters (e.g., novel technology, social aspects of ICT, and physical space considerations) the contributors to this volume have employed a broad set of methodological approaches. Although, in studying a topic such as shared encounters there is no general methodological approach, ethnography, with its focus on the situated nature of interaction and the social character of use, has been shown to be a valuable method for understanding how shared encounters occur and the characteristics of such interactions. The overall approach of such methodologies is still user-centered, where the user is regarded to have many roles, such as casual passersby, or author of content. However, the aims of an ethnographic study are much broader than traditional user-centered design and involve identifying routine practices, problems, and possibilities for development within a given activity or setting. Wolcott further extends this idea and distinguishes ethnography as more than just a set of field methods and practices, but instead as a way of seeing "through the lens of culture" (Wolcott 2008). This highlights the fact that ethnography is motivated by a need to understand the social and cultural qualities of people's actions.

In the context of situated technologies, ethnographic methods have been further adapted for system evaluation, in addition to requirements gathering, which was their initial role in CSCW. In particular, cultural probes are considered to be a lightweight' and nonintrusive data collection method (Gaver et al. 1999). In terms of analysis, cultural probes data usually can be analyzed and visualized with affinity diagrams (Beyer and Holtzblatt 1999), and additional data collection techniques include data logging. However, the data collection and analysis generally needs be performed continuously over long periods of time in order to record the temporal and social effects. The analysis of the data focuses not only on differences due to age, gender, culture, but also on differences related to socioeconomic background as well as differences of attitudes toward the alternative modalities of the situated computation. For example, text vs. abstract video representations, or shared vs. solitary use. The final stage of ethnographic methodology is the interpretation of gathered data. These results are generally in the format of text or visual (e.g., photos) descriptions, records, and explanations. Therefore the outcomes are by necessity subjective and qualitative.

Situating Ethnographic Methods

A number of researchers have successfully engaged with ethnographic approaches to understand the nature of shared experiences. All these approaches use participant observation as a core method. However, the situation in which the observed group can be studied varies, and this has implications both for the exact methods used, for how the outcomes can inform the design process, and also for the particular challenges undertaken during the fieldwork. These settings can be termed as cultural scenes, which are defined as "the information shared by two or more people that define some aspect of their experience….and closely linked with recurrent social situations" (Spradley and McCurdy 1989). In the following text, we review existing work where ethnographic methods have been employed to study shared encounters and consider this within the framework of the particular "scene" in which the research is undertaken.

Technology Scene

Ito et al.'s study of Japanese teenagers, which discusses how social relationships develop through the use of mobile technology, is a prime example of how beneficial ethnographic study can be in understanding emerging practices within a certain cultural group (Ito et al. 2006). A similar social group to that of Ito et al. is studied by Licoppe and Inada (this volume); their detailed evaluation of communication in the Mogi game reveals a set of definable practices that is hard to imagine being discovered through any other methodological approach. In studying mobile subjects, Licoppe and Inada benefited from the fact that, although the community was physically disparate and interactions took place all over Japan, the technology platform created a trace of both the user's location and the corresponding social interaction. This aspect of data logging with GPS or similar location-based sensing provides a valuable method for capturing the interlinked social and spatial aspects of mobile experience.

Barkhuus et al. took the approach of using a specially designed application to capture data documenting everyday usage. They created a mobile diary application, which automatically constructed questions based around the users' own activities with the phone, such as the incoming and outgoing calls they made that day and text messages they may have sent (Barkhuus et al. 2008). This was followed by focused interviews to elicit more specific information. Graham et al. took advantage of an everyday blogging application to observe the interactions within a small group of participants of their experiences of giving up smoking. The blog format became the site of focus, and the particular uses of the technology revealed characteristics and practices among the participants. Both of these studies benefited from the fact that they focused on one primary application. Such analysis of behavior is far more complex and time consuming when interaction is distributed across different applications and devices.

Social Scene

A useful approach to understanding the nature of shared encounters within a social group is to cite the study in an existing community, and to study any changes in practices that occur due to the introduction of technology. For example, Grimes (this volume) worked within an African–American social group, where even though the participants had never met before they were aware that they were people living in the same community. The critical aspect of this approach is the ability of participants to identify and empathize with others using the system, and thus the sense of shared experience is heightened. In the social setting studied by Grimes, the use of a narrative method was found to be particularly useful, which Miskelly et al. also established in a series of workshops that were held in an existing community in Bristol, United Kingdom (Miskelly et al. 2005). In this research, the participants were encouraged to create mediascapes documenting their experience of places as a way of formalizing shared experience.

Running workshops within existing community settings can help to elicit specific requirements of the social group. For example, Williams et al. used a series of workshops where children aged 9 and 10 years old were encouraged to think about their use of an outdoor space before their introduction to the technology (Williams et al. 2005). Martin (this volume) also documents how workshops were run among residents of a housing estate to identify issues and concerns about everyday local environment. However, the author raises questions about the sustainability of such methods, since they may initially yield useful outcomes, but tend to be difficult to integrate as a method into longer-term ethnographic studies.

Spatial Scene

In this volume, Schieck et al., Jacucci et al., and Stukoff undertook their studies in urban public spaces, such as streets and open-public spaces, in order to investigate collaboration around interactive screens and spaces. In these studies, screens or interactive stages were installed into existing public spaces and the changes in behavior of passersby was observed. The studies identified the fact that two layers of interaction needed to be observed; those who participated actively, and bystanders who watched the activities, but tended not to join in. Public squares also present useful sites for study since they not only have a highly mobile population, but also reveal common practices. Paay and Kjeldskov undertook a survey of interactions at Federation Square, Melbourne with participants they recruited, but were then interviewed and observed undertaking everyday socializing experiences in the setting (Paay and Kjeldskov 2008).

Laurier et al. present an alternative approach by undertaking their fieldwork in an interior spatial setting; a local café. The researchers conducted the study primarily through observation; since it was a fixed place it was possible for them to simply "hang-out" and watch people. The authors report that they "learnt a great deal about the life of our café by becoming regulars, thereby following the ordinary paths through which a person becomes a regular and finding ourselves with the particular rights and obligations that go along with this mundane identity" (Laurier et al. 2001). The café environment had the benefit that it was possible for the researchers to observe behavior in a way that they were unobtrusive, and thus they did not significantly shape the activities they were documenting. In fact, through this ethnographic approach Laurier et al. highlight a valuable method for studying shared encounters in public space; that of choosing a specific physical setting and simply observing in detail patterns of behavior over time. The performative and public characteristics of shared encounters that are enacted in such spaces lend themselves particularly well to study in this way.

Future Directions

In this chapter we discussed the topic of shared encounters, and highlighted the fact that such encounters are a crucial ingredient of everyday social life. In a discussion of methodologies, we considered the use of ethnographic research as a valuable way to both understand and evaluate such encounters. In HCI, such methods are becoming increasingly widespread and yet there remains the issue of whether the design for such interactions is sustainable. In this volume, Martin highlights the concerns of the researchers on a community project who found that creating long-term integration of technologies that support shared encounters, particularly within existing community scenes, is often difficult to achieve. Therefore, a critical aspect of future research is to investigate how sharing through media can provide ways for people to communicate and engage with others in networked communities, whether these are on or offline. The fields of HCI and CSCW are evolving and the implied dichotomy created between humans and technology is no longer a useful metaphor. Cooperation and sharing within everyday situations provoke a research agenda that demands that these fields reassess the approach of providing solutions through technology to perceived social "problems" in what is often an isolated research environment. As ubiquitous technologies are now entirely interwoven in everyday life, the challenge is to find ways of integrating research fieldwork within everyday infrastructures and practices. This will require an approach that is already starting to emerge, where computer scientists team with professionals such as ethnographers and partners in the community to take a long-term view of how changes can be made to the way in which shared experiences are facilitated in these social scenes. This can only be achieved when all parties focus not on creating quick solutions, but on building for learning and change in the design process. Only in this manner can such work become integrated into what Lave and Wenger term a "community of practice" (Lave and Wenger 1991).

A parallel agenda for future research and one that we have sought to clarify in this chapter is the importance of also understanding how encounters are enacted within the physical setting. Public space is experienced with and through media, whether this is fixed screens and routers or mobile technologies, and finding ways to merge these experiences is critical, if social activities in these spaces are to be sustained. In this way, the field of HCI needs to address the issues of working with designers and users of urban-public space in order to gain with a longer-term view. The form and use of physical-public space changes slowly; buildings tend to take more time to design and build than a software application and in order to create a synergy between built space and media space it will require the field of HCI to reassess both its working methods, and also what can be defined as a successful outcome.

Summary

Our everyday encounters are increasingly mediated by communications technologies that free up our social interaction from fixed spatial settings. We propose that content sharing through mobile and ubiquitous technologies, consciously situated in public space is a valuable new social practice. It can contribute toward redefining boundaries of access between communities and contribute to more fulfilled sustained encounters in spatial settings. In this context, we discussed how it is necessary to acquire a clearer idea of the diverse types of encounters that can occur and gain a better understanding of the specific characteristics of situations that influence these encounters. We highlighted how this can only be achieved by the use of methodological frameworks that can evaluate and respond to everyday interactions in natural settings and proposed that ethnographic approaches have great potential in this area. We discussed the challenges of studying shared encounters through ethnographic research and summarized with a review of settings or scenes in which such studies can be usefully undertaken. In conclusion, we proposed some areas of future research, with a focus on HCI reaching out to other fields and working with a long-term vision of how sustainable relationships can be afforded within existing social frameworks.

References

Bardram JE & Bossen C (2003) Moving to get ahead: local mobility and collaborative work. In: Kuutti K, Karsten EH, FitzpatrickJ , Dourish P & Schmidt K (eds) Proceedings of ECSCW 2003, 355-374. Kluwer Academic Publishers, Massachusetts

Barkhuus L, Brown B, Bell M et al. (2008) From awareness to repartee: sharing location within social groups. In: Proceeding of CHI '08, 497-506. ACM, New York. DOI= http://doi.acm.org/10.1145/1357054.1357134

Bertelsen OW & Bødker S (2001) Cooperation in massively distributed information spaces. In: Prinz W, Jarke M, Rogers Y, Schmidt K & Wulf V (eds) Proceedings of CSCW 07, 1-17. Klüver Academic Publishers, Netherlands

Beyer H & Holtzblatt K (1999) Contextual design. Interactions 6(1): 32-42

Castells M, Qui JL, Ardero MF & Bey A (2006) Mobile communications and society. MIT Press, Massachusetts

Churchill EF, Girgensohn A, Nelson L & Lee A (2004) Information cities: blending digital and physical spaces for ubiquitous community participation. Commun. ACM 47, 2 (Feb. 2004), 38-44. ACM Press, New York. DOI= http://doi.acm.org/10.1145/966389.966413

Dourish P & Harrisson S (1996) Re-place-ing space: the roles of place and space in collaborative systems. In: Ackerman MS (ed) Proceedings of CSCW 96, 67–76. ACM Press, New York. DOI= http://doi.acm.org/10.1145/240080.240193

Dourish P (2001) Where the action is: the foundations of embodied interaction. MIT Press, Massachusetts

Gaver W (1992) The affordances of media spaces for collaboration. In: Proceedings of CSCW '92, 17-24. ACM Press, New York. DOI= http://doi.acm.org/10.1145/143457.371596

Gaver B, Dunne T & Pacenti E (1999) Design: cultural probes. Interactions 6(1): 21-29

Goffman E (1959) The presentation of self in everyday life. Doubleday, New York

Goffman E (1963) Behavior in public places; notes on the social occasion of gatherings. The Free Press, New York

Harle RK & Hopper A (2005) Deploying and evaluating a location-aware system. In: Proc Mobisys, 219 – 232. ACM Press, New York. DOI= http://doi.acm.org/10.1145/1067170.1067194

Hook K, Benyon D & Munro A (eds) (2003) Designing information spaces: the social navigation approach. Springer, London

Ito M, Okabe D & Matsuda M (2006) Personal, portable, pedestrian: mobile phones and japanese life. MIT Press, Massachusetts

Jancke G, Venolia GD, Grudin J, Cadiz JJ & and Gupta A (2001) Linking public spaces: technical and social issues. In: Proceedings of CHI '01, 530-537. ACM, New York. DOI= http://doi.acm.org/10.1145/365024.365352

Karahalios K & Donath J (2004) Telemurals: linking remote spaces with social catalysts. In: Proceedings of CHI'04, 615-622. ACM Press, New York. DOI= http://doi.acm.org/10.1145/ 985692.985770

Katz JE &Aakhus MA (eds) (2002) Perpetual contact: mobile communication, private talk, public performance. Cambridge University Press, Cambridge

Kraut R, Kiesler S, Boneva B, Cummings J, Helgeson V & Crawford A (2002) Internet paradox revisited. Journal of Social Issues 58: 49-74.

Kubey R and Csikszentmihalyi M (1990) Television and the quality of life: how viewing shapes everyday experiences. Lawrence Erlbaum, New jersey

Lave J & Wenger E (1991) Situated learning: legitimate peripheral participation. Cambridge University Press, New York

Laurier E (2001) Why people say where they are during mobile phone calls. Environment and Planning D: Society and Space 19(4), 485 – 504

Laurier E, Whyte A, Buckner K (2001) An ethnography of a neighbourhood café: informality, table arrangements and background noise. Journal of Mundane Behavior 2(2)

McCullough M (2005) Digital ground. MIT Press, Massachusetts

Meyrowitz J (1986) No sense of place: the impact of the electronic media on social behaviour. Oxford University Press Inc, USA

Miskelly C, Cater K, Fleuriot C, Williams M & Wood L (2005). Locating Story. In: Proceedings of the 4th Media in Transition conference - The Work of Stories. MIT, Boston

Mynatt E, Adler A, Ito M & O'Day V (1997) Design for network communities. In: Pemberton S (ed) Proceedings of CHI 97, 210 – 217. ACM Press, New York. DOI= http://doi.acm. org/10.1145/258549.258707

O'Hara K, Kindberg T, Glancy M, Baptista L, Sukumaran B, Kahana G & Rowbotham J: (2007) Social practices in location-based collecting. CHI 2007: 1225-1234. ACM, New York. DOI= http://doi.acm.org/10.1145/1240624.1240810

Paay J & Kjeldskov J (2008) Understanding situated social interactions: a case study of public places in the city. In: Proceedings of CSCW17, 275-290. DOI= http://dx.doi.org/10.1007/ s10606-007-9072-1

Packard V (1972) A nation of strangers. McKay, New York

Paulos E & Goodman E (2004) The familiar stranger: anxiety, comfort and play in public places. In: Proceedings of ACM CHI 2004, 223-230. ACM, New York. DOI= http://doi.acm.org/ 10.1145/985692.985721

Rheingold H (2002) Smart mobs: the next social revolution. Perseus Book Group, Cambridge

Spradley, J & McCurdy D (1989) Anthropology: the cultural perspective. Waveland Press, Prospect Heights

Struppek M (2006). The social potential of urban screen. screens and the social landscape. Visual Communication 5(2): 173-188

Suchman L (1987) Plans and situated actions: the problem of human machine communication. Cambridge University Press, Cambridge

Wellman, B (2001) Physical place and cyber-place: changing portals and the rise of networked individualism. International Journal for Urban and Regional Research 25 (2): 227-52

Williams M, Jones O, Fleuriot C & Wood L (2005) Children and emerging wireless technologies: investigating the potential for spatial practice. In: Proceedings of CHI '05, 819-828. ACM, New York. DOI= http://doi.acm.org/10.1145/1054972.1055088

Willis K, Chorianopoulos K, Struppek M, Roussos G (2007). Shared encounters. In: Proceedings of CHI'07, 2881-2884. ACM, New York. DOI= http://doi.acm.org/10.1145/1240866.1241101

Willis KS (2008) Spaces, settings and connections. In: Aurigi A & De Cindio F (eds) Augmented urban spaces: articulating the physical and electronic city. Ashgate Press, Reading

Wolcott HF (2008) Ethnography: A way of seeing. Altamira Press, Lanham

Section 1
Sharing Experience

Introduction: Sharing Experience

Barry Brown

The social life of technology is something frequently rediscovered in our investigations of technology. In the early 1980s, it was Kling in his article on the social contexts of technology use (Kling 1980). In the early 1990s, it was the field of computer-supported collaborative work that took on the challenges of understanding technology's many faceted place in social life. Most recently, the advent of collaborative Internet technologies – Facebook and its like has brought the social use of technology to public attention and broadened the number of research fields seeking to understand the increasingly intertwined issues of social life and technology.

Perhaps the biggest change in research interests on this topic has been the shift from considering solely work contexts, to understanding activities that take place outside what we would normally think of as work. While we are used to the over-powering importance of the workplace in our discussions and investigations, leisure demands as much attention. Indeed, it is interesting to reflect that the average American over his/her whole life will spend more time watching television in his home than spend time in the workplace. Moreover, television watching is some-thing that is increasingly mediated through a computer in some form – be it a set top box, tivo, or bittorrrent (Barkhuus and Brown 2008).

Our social engagements outside work take two dominant forms, those involving family and friends. And for both of these, technology has always played a major role. In 1885, Bertha Benz used an early car to drive 80 km to visit her parents–the first documented social use of the car (Urry 2007). Nowadays, many social relationships would be near impossible without modern communication and transport systems to maintain contact. With the advent and extensive use of social networking sites, dating websites, and online gaming, we find that new friendships are increasingly forming online, alongside the incorporation of these technological systems in how friendships develop and are maintained, particularly amongst teenagers.

Yet, the dominant way in which social relationships and their mediation through technology has been documented has been social network analysis (Degenne and

B. Brown (✉)
Department of Communication, University of California, San Diego, CA, 92093-0503, USA
e-mail: barry@ucsd.edu

Forsé 1999; Wellman and Berkowitz 2006). Social network analysis has its roots in the so-called "small world" problem–the attempt to analyze how well-connected individuals are and to explore the nature of these connections. In Millgrams' classic small world experiment, he explored if individuals could forward on a letter to an ambiguously described individual, with each forwarding of the letter being taken as a probe into individuals' social connections (Milgram et al., 1977). These sort of connections have been used to analyze social connections using the graph theory–where social connections are reduced to a relationship between two nodes of a graph. The graph theory can then predict the importance of certain relationships to preserve the cohesion of the graph and presumably the social network.

Much of this work, however, relies upon removing the contents of relationships–their reduction to pair-wise relationships. This may prove to be important for some kinds of activities (e.g., finding a new job), but the broader implication for our social lives is questionable. Finding a job is a very specific economic activity, not as often undertaken as other activities. Focusing on job searches as an activity is representative of an overly economic approach to social life, one that ignores the importance of our face-to-face interactions, in contrast to individualistic notions of asocial calculating actors. If we consider what social relationships mean the most to us emotionally, we would be unlikely to pick any from the large number of relatively lightweight connections. Whatever the role of these relationships in certain highly circumscribed activities (such as finding a new job, vs. getting promoted in one's own job) they are much less important than, say, getting a mate.

It is the contents of relationships and in particular what we do with our families or our friends that skips out of consideration in these analyses. Friends do very different things together than families, with different rights, responsibilities, and the like. Social relations show a huge variety and take many different forms. One form we have is the light connections between friends, how we might guess what a friend is doing at some point in time, our ongoing awareness of each others' activity. This was one application area that we explored with the "connecto" system, where friends could share with each other an awareness of where they were and their current activity (Barkhuus et al., 2008). We see this echoed in the use of status messages in Facebook. At the other extreme, we have close face-to-face intimate relationships. For example, the experience of going on holiday with a friend or family member, where we spend much time sharing just about everything we do for a short period of time.

The experience of those on holiday is very different from that of two friends sharing a text message during the working day. It is the contents of relationships then – what people do together– that is crucial to understanding shared interactions. It is particularly in the building of technology that these questions come to the fore. If one is interested in building technology for shared encounters, it is important that we build for real activities that sit within the world of friendship and family interactions. As the chapters in the next section show, for technology we must reflect in original ways on how to bring people together through their shared interactions and exchanges.

Jacucci et al. discuss the opportunities for collocated user interactions in public displays, both mobile and situated. In Konomi et al.'s chapter they explore how technology can bring the history of different places into the engaged interactions in conference settings. For Diamantaki et al. the exploration is more the way in which locative media can support and engage with our shared interactions. Lastly, Chorianopoulos et al. explore the different ways in which interactions around maps can be supported and the range of different engagements technology might support.

All these four chapters demonstrate an interest in supporting situated face-to-face shared interactions – and moving beyond a reduction of our social exchanges to mere lines on a graph. The growing interest in leisure activity is just one facet of this, but there is still much work to be done–attempting to understand and design for shared interactions.

References

Barkhuus L & Brown B (2008) Unpacking the television: user practices around a changing technology. Transactions of Computer Human Interaction (TOCHI) In Press.

Barkhuus L, Brown B, Bell, M et al. (2008) From awareness to repartee: sharing location within social groups. In: Proceeding of CHI'08, 497-506. ACM, New York. DOI= http://doi.acm.org/10.1145/1357054.1357134

Degenne A & Forsé M (1999) Introducing social networks. Sage, London

Kling R (1980) Social analyses of computing: theoretical perspectives in recent empirical research. Computing Surveys 12(1): 61-110

Milgram S, Sabini J, Silver M (1977) The individual in a social world: essays and experiments. McGraw-Hill, New York

Urry J (2007) Mobilities. Polity Press, London

Wellman B & Berkowitz SB (2006) Social structures: a network approach. Cambridge University Press, Cambridge

Chapter 2
Ubiquitous Media for Collocated Interaction

Giulio Jacucci, Peter Peltonen, Ann Morrison, Antti Salovaara, Esko Kurvinen, and Antti Oulasvirta

Introduction

Has ubiquitous computing entered our lives as anticipated in the early 90s or at the turn of the millennium? In this last decade, the processing of media combined with sensing and communication capabilities has been slowly entering our lives through powerful smartphones, multimodal game consoles, instrumented cars, and large displays pervading public spaces. However, the visionary formulations (Weiser 1991) and updated scenarios (Abowd and Mynatt 2000) have not been realized, despite the fact that the technology has become increasingly accessible.

Abowd and Mynatt (2000) identify three interaction themes for ubiquitous computing: natural interfaces, context-aware computing, and automated capture and access to live experiences. They also posit everyday computing as an area of development focusing on supporting the user with a continuously present interface, also addressing the periphery of the user's attention and connecting the physical and virtual worlds. While recent advances in mobile telephony and web technologies have been driven by social usage, exactly how this could affect ubiquitous computing has yet to be defined. Earlier views have considered social implications rather than making social use the target of the design (Abowd and Mynatt 2000), or has focused on remote and mediated social interactions in mixed reality (Buxton 1997; Benford et al. 2005; Grudin 2002; Crabtree and Rodden 2008).

The ubiquitous user seems to be characterized as someone who needs situated and continuous assistance, access to media and the recording of experiences, or the provision of mediated interaction in mixed reality. In our constructive and field-oriented research, we have found it useful to characterize the ubiquitous user as an active user who opportunistically and skillfully uses technology rather than being assisted; a user for whom technology is a resource in constructing experiences rather than just using it to record them. Finally and most importantly, our studies promote

G. Jacucci (✉), P. Peltonen, A. Morrison, A. Salovaara, E. Kurvinen, and A. Oulasvirta
Helsinki Institute for Information Technology HIIT, Helsinki University
of Technology TKK, P.O. Box 9800, FIN-02015, TKK, Finland
e-mail: giulio.jacucci@hiit.fi

K.S. Willis et al. (eds.), *Shared Encounters*, Computer Supported Cooperative Work, DOI 10.1007/978-1-84882-727-1_2, © Springer-Verlag London Limited 2010

the view of the ubiquitous user as engaged in the social usage and sense-making of media, thereby integrating its use into their everyday lives (Jacucci et al. 2007a, b; Salovaara et al. 2006).

In this spirit, we want to enrich the understanding of the development of *ubiquitous media* systems: technologies providing users with digital multimodal content through ubiquitous computing devices. We want to explore new "artifacts," where the technologies are embedded and become a part of the architecture of our urban environments. We also focus on materiality that ties together the physical artifacts and embodied interaction and discuss how digital objects and interfaces become props in our social environment, rather than just media to be consumed.

Through our constructive and field-oriented work, the contribution of this chapter is to outline aspects of the *public availability* of ubiquitous media and its relationship to collocated interaction. Robertson (2002) provides an account of how we begin to negotiate the public availability of artifacts and embodied actions. Through concepts such as the reversibility of perception (the body as an object in the world that we and others perceive and also "the sentient body as it is lived by a particular person" (Robertson 2002), it is possible to explain how we can act and create meaning in an existing social and physical world. While this work points out the fundamental mechanisms of the availability of artifacts and actions in a social and physical world, implications that are relevant to the design of experiences in virtual spaces are also drawn.

Our focus is on the capacity of ubiquitous media to support embodied interaction, in particular via natural interfaces. The central features are how the "public availability" of ubiquitous media provides *common stages* and opportunities for *performative interaction*. Common stages are configured by users utilizing features of ubiquitous media and provide a scene for social interaction. Performative interactions further indicate how media objects and interfaces are used as props in embodied and expressive acts.

We present two cases and report our observations from extensive user trials:

City Wall: In a study of interactions at a large multitouch display, we detail how the public availability of media supports embodied interaction and performative encounters. Here, shared experience is constructed in embodied performances elicited by the interface and supported by the architectural configuration. Public availability emerges thanks to the multitouch interface, since it encourages users to interact with the media, and is produced out of mobile posting and web harvesting.

MapLens: We present how the physical–digital configurations of maps and media viewed in combination with the lens of a mobile phone support group interaction. Here, navigation and coordination tasks are carried out collaboratively and the mixed media configurations provide common ground and place-making as important aspects of shared experiences.

Studies of Collocated Interactions in Public Spaces

User studies of collaboration around large public displays constitute a major part of the research on social interaction in collocated settings. In their study, Russell et al. (2002) observed the benefits of visible physical actions (that facilitate learning from others), difficulties in developing clear turn-taking practices, and varying emerging ways to collaborate without anyone taking a leading role, while participants were using a touch-screen display designed for small-group collaborative use.

Before users can start interacting with a public display, they have to withdraw from other activities they are engaged in. Hornecker et al. (2007) have noted the central role of access and entry points for publicly available technology. Entry points invite and entice people into engagement, provide an overview of the system, and draw observers into the activity. Access points are the characteristics that enable users to interact and join a group's activity. All these factors produce the *shareability* of the system, which refers to how a system engages a group of collocated users in shared interactions around the same content. Brignull and Rogers (2003) have suggested positioning public displays along traffic thoroughfares, and describe the ways in which the interaction principles are communicated to bystanders.

Tangible interfaces are a key element for supporting face-to-face social interaction, as the physical interaction objects (such as touch-screens) eliminate the need for restricted and often singular input devices such as keyboards (Hornecker et al. 2006). Arias et al. (1997) have also highlighted the importance of interacting with physical objects in a world that is becoming more and more virtual. Both aspects of reality – physical and virtual – have their strengths and weaknesses, and future systems should provide a flexible way to move in both worlds freely.

Collocated interaction has also been studied in the context of media sharing. Digital media archive studies on PC's have presented new collaborative methods for sharing media, such as the manipulation of content with gestures (e.g., Morris et al. 2006; Rogers et al. 2004; Wu and Balakrishnan 2003) and the visualization of content for shared use (Shen et al. 2002). A study by Frohlich et al. (2002) provides a useful distinction between collocated media use practices by differentiating *storytelling*, which is mostly a single-person endeavor, from *reminiscing talk*, which is more a collaborative project where many people participate in sharing their experiences of the same photograph with the others.

Studies on the collocated creation of media with mobile devices are, however, surprisingly few, probably because gathering data from this kind of use is difficult because of the personal nature of the devices. We organized a number of field trials at large-scale events such as a world championships rally, music festivals, and a national festival day analyzing usage of group media applications through observations and systems logs (Jacucci and Salovaara 2005; Jacucci et al. 2005, 2007a, b; Salovaara et al. 2006). The studies highlight the aspect of *active spectatorship* (Jacucci et al. 2007a, b) in participation in large-scale events. We observed users performing different expressive activities with the media: staging, arranging impromptu competitions, storytelling, joking, communicating their presence, and portraying others. With regard to remote others, the collocated users could engage in activities such as reporting what was going on onsite and making plans. All these expressive forms contain creative elements such as joking, exaggeration, deception, and so on. The collocated use of ubiquitous media is thus a constructive activity and not a passive endurance of events. Similarly, the active role of visitors to a museum has been noted by Heath et al. (2002), who studied how people construct the meaning of objects and artifacts together during museum visits. The creation and use of ubiquitous media in public is an eventful social activity, but the research is only starting to grasp its possibilities.

Another potential application area for ubiquitous media is tourism. Brown and Chalmers (2003) presented an ethnographic study of city tourists' practices describing how tourists work together in groups and collaborate around maps and guidebooks, which are used in combination to plan and create a setting providing an opportunity to spend time with friends or family. For this purpose, the authors recommend systems that support sociality and, for example, combine a physical map with an electronic version of a guidebook.

City Wall: Multiuser Interaction at an Urban Multitouch Display

One of the visions of ubiquitous computing has been to render media accessible on large displays integrated into the environment. City Wall is a large multitouch display installed in a central location in Helsinki, Finland. It acts as a collaborative and playful interface for the ever-changing media landscape of the city. The main features of the City Wall technology are: (1) multiple hand tracking capable of identifying uniquely as many fingers and hands as can fit onto the screen; (2) hand posture and gesture tracking; (3) high-resolution and high-frequency camera processing up to 60 FPS and (4) computer vision-based tracking that works in changing light conditions. The main motivation behind implementing City Wall in Helsinki was to support interactions for any user, from a child to a senior citizen that did not require special skills or previous knowledge. The four technological features create the conditions for a multiuser and multitouch installation that is appropriate for a public space. Technologically, the setup is similar to HoloWall (Matsushita and Rekimoto 2003). With this setup, all the expensive equipment can be placed indoors out of the public space and after the addition of a semi-opaque thin coating, normal safety glass in a shop window can be used as a touch screen.

City Wall shows media content (pictures) about the events taking place in the city, photographed by Flickr users or by users sending them directly by email or phone. It gathers this content by querying pictures tagged with certain keywords ("Helsinki" and the selected large-scale event in our case). By this means, City Wall attempts to provide a sense of awareness to its users and the passersby about both ongoing and past urban events and a place for exploring these in a public site. Figure 2.1 shows a screenshot from City Wall with Flickr content displayed on it. The bottom part (B) of the screen has a timeline with thumbnail-sized pictures. It is navigated by panning it horizontally, and it can also be compressed or expanded to show the contents retrieved during a full day or just a couple of minutes. This has been found to be important as the frequency of media may vary greatly.

Interaction with the top part (A) of City Wall follows two interaction paradigms. The moving, scaling, and rotation of content (C) follow direct manipulation principles:

Fig. 2.1 Screenshot of CityWall with Flickr content

the user can grab an image by putting their hand on it. The photo follows the hand movements when the user moves her hand. Rotation and scaling are possible by grabbing the photo at more than two points (e.g., with two hands or two fingers of the same hand), and then either rotating the two points around each other or altering the distance between them.

For a user study, City Wall was installed in a central location in Helsinki, Finland for the summer of 2007. The site was a 2.5-m-wide shop window between the main bus and train stations (see Fig. 2.2).

The analysis presented here is an extension of our earlier findings (Peltonen et al. 2007, 2008), based on the analysis of 8 days of use, during which 1,199 persons interacted with the system in various social configurations. The data constituted webcam-quality video footage shot from a corner of the shop window's sunshade and interaction logs based on users' touch-based interactions. Selected parts of encounters were examined qualitatively. In this data, only 18% of the users were using City Wall alone. At other times, groups of users were present at the display, or people were watching others using the display and awaiting their turn. This made the usage a social experience.

While our earlier work has focused on social interaction and turn-taking in general (Peltonen et al. 2008), in the following section we specifically address the findings related to collocated interaction at the display.

Fig. 2.2 CityWall installation in Helsinki, Finland

Turn-Taking Management at the Display

To be able to browse the content together with others, people needed ways to manage turn-taking. Typically, the people who were present negotiated with those who had the right to use the display in a discrete manner. Sometimes this also led to game-like activities and competitions, especially between friends.

In multiuser situations, two basic settings exist. In *parallel use,* people occupy an area of the screen and focus on their own task, irrespective of the activities around them. In doing this they consider the display space in front of them as theirs and assume that the others are doing the same in their part. In this way, all the users have an equal chance to manipulate the content; however, they are not able to make use of the whole width of the display. Figure 2.3 shows an extreme case of this, with seven users interacting with the display in parallel. In a few cases, the users also engaged in teamwork, by teaming up to do the same task together, as when resizing the same photo together.

The other pattern of collocated interaction consisted of alternating *collaborative interaction.* For example, when the space in front of the display was crowded, members of a group (usually a pair) could organize themselves so that only one user used the display, while others contributed to the interaction by suggesting what to

Fig. 2.3 An extreme example of parallel use

do next, being prepared to take the floor at transition relevant places (Sacks et al. 1974) such as idle breaks or verbally negotiated moments. Figure 2.4 provides a sequence that shows examples of both teamwork (a–b) and alternation (c–e). In Fig. 2.4a, the girl in a white top is experimenting with resizing and rotation, assisted by her friend who feeds her more photos from the right. In Fig. 2.4b, the girls are rotating one photo together, employing three hands in this task. In contrast, in Figs. 2.4c–e, the girl in the black top has the floor (c), but gives it to her friend (d), who then uses the display alone (e).

In order to hold the floor, people did not only occupy the space in front of them. They could employ "pondering grips" (holding a picture steady and keeping their fingers on it) and "grandiose gestures" (large hand movements that act as an equivalent of shouting in verbal communication) to make clear that their interaction is still underway.

The activities of different groups are likely to collide at some point. We observed conflicts that were mostly related to the ownership of photos and their immediate surroundings, that is, areas that may be needed for rotating, scaling, and sorting the set of photos being worked on. Occasionally, the UI causes people to break these territorial borders. For example, photos can be accidentally blown-up, or the timeline can be used without the other participants being considered. This was found to be the most disturbing conflict by the users interviewed. Although conflicts take place, they can also have positive consequences for the social organization at the display. Figure 2.5 shows a sequence that starts with polite negotiation of space, but turns into an impromptu game-like interaction between the parties present. The girl in a white top waits for her opportunity to interact with the display (a) and, after occupying a space, engages in alternating interaction with her friend to her right (b).

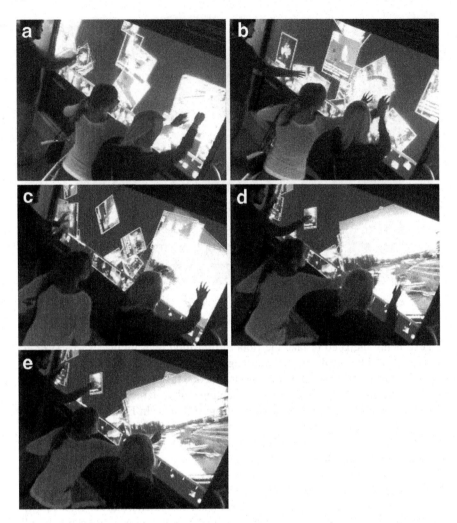

Fig. 2.4 Teamwork (**a–b**) and alternating collaborative interaction (**c–e**)

After the girls have enlarged one photo to a very large size accidentally (c), the boy to their left manages the conflict by withdrawal (d), but later finds another space (e). A man, having observed the conflict and its resolution and been inspired by it, steps in and turns the conflict about the display space into a game, first claiming one photo as his by shouting "It's mine, don't touch!" (f), after enlarging it to take up all the space in the display (g and h). In addition to screen estate competitions, we also observed games such as Pong or soccer, which consisted of photos being thrown horizontally across the screen.

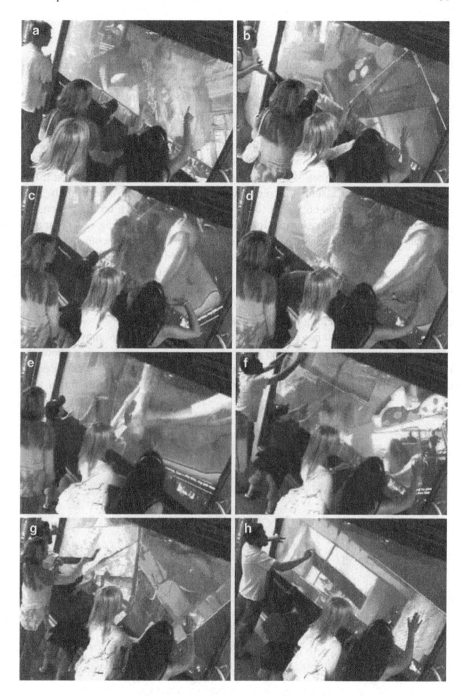

Fig. 2.5 A sequence of negotiated interaction, conflict resolution and game-playing

The Display as a Stage

In the previous section, we analyzed the interaction between peers who assumed equal roles in interaction with the display. When people team up at the screen, individuals in groups may also gravitate toward complementary roles or social configurations. The most common social configuration of that kind was the teacher–apprentice setting (see Fig. 2.6). For instance, one or more users could take the role of an experienced user and others attended to their presentation and demonstration of what City Wall was capable of doing.

In other cases, a member of a group could use City Wall to seek attention from others in the group, or assume the role of a *comedian* to make the others laugh. The user would, for example, enlarge a funny picture to a large size on the screen, or demonstrate difficult-to-master manipulations to others. Role-taking was naturally important in game-like activities. Such roles – teacher, apprentice, comedian etc. – can naturally change during the course of interaction. In the case of City Wall, this, however, happened rarely because of the relatively short time that people spent at the display. For instance, a median duration of interaction for a pair of users was just 60 s in our data. In other cases, when users interact with different kinds of content, more role-switching may take place.

Shop windows and other places and objects in urban settings may enable or require people to interact with each other (e.g., when queuing or asking about an empty chair in a café). City Wall brought people together by making them interact collaboratively or with respect to each other in a space that was both digital and physical.

Fig. 2.6 A teacher-apprentice setting

Fig. 2.7 Using City Wall as a stage for performance

Ubiquitous technology in public space concretizes Goffman's (1956) metaphor of social interaction as theatre. For instance, consider the situation in Fig. 2.7. The man in a white shirt enters the display (a), enlarges one of the photos to its maximum size, in this way occupying the whole screen and taking the floor from the woman to his left (b). When rotating the photo, he shouts theatrically "the world is mine" (c) and leaves the screen laughing (d).

Conflicts between the parallel tasks of two or more users or teams were the main reason for the interactions between strangers that were observed. Users did try to avoid interfering with parallel activities, but the system did not support *the norm of social segregation* between the unacquainted and instead made photos accidentally expand or fly across the screen. This forced the users to engage in conflict management with each other. The positive outcome was that the system made strangers interact with each other.

The photos displayed on City Wall were downloaded from public forum on the web. Therefore, the average user had no personal relationship with the content of the photos that happened to be on the screen when she appeared on site. The user's attention was thus turned from content to aspects of the interface. There were also users that seemed to take the content of the photos seriously, but the vast majority seemed to focus on playing with the interface.

MapLens: Place-Making with a Map-Based as Application

Ubiquitous media can be interwoven with everyday environments through different types of natural interfaces (Abowd and Mynatt 2000). An example is the use of mobile devices for augmenting everyday objects, such as a map. MapLens is an application that allows users to read a standard nonmarked paper map in tandem with a mobile phone. The application uses a *natural feature tracking method* (Wagner et al. 2008) to identify the map area visible beneath the phone's screen, augmenting the location with additional digital information displayed on the screen. Users click on icons to access larger versions of images or text (Fig. 2.8). Additionally, user-taken photographs are uploaded to the database, placed as per a set of GPS coordinates and shared on-screen between all the users. The system allows for a distance of 15–40 cm between the printed map and the camera and a tilt tolerance of up to 30°. The paper map was printed onto an A3 size foam-core card, which was carried and used in tandem with the mobile device.

For the sake of comparison, we added a digital version called DigiMap (Fig. 2.9). DigiMap is a digital 2D map akin to Google Maps Mobile, with standardized joystick phone navigation for scrolling across the map and using two buttons to control zoom in and out. It shows the same information as MapLens and uses the same digital map, but it is fully digital. Both systems use the same virtual map and augmented information. To evaluate the technology, we devised an environmental awareness location-based game requiring players to complete 12 varied tasks (some sequential), negotiate roles, and coordinate the task order. The game was trialled over three Sundays in 2008 in the centre of Helsinki. Each trial was incrementally larger in size, with the final trial including DigiMap. We wanted to see if there were differences in how people used the two systems for the same tasks.

We enlisted professionals, early adopters, environmental researchers, a scout group, and their friends and families. Thirty-seven people, 20 females and 17 males

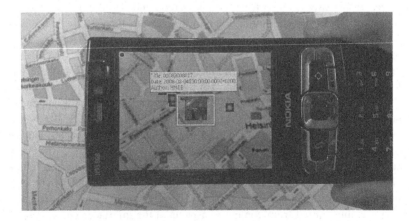

Fig. 2.8 MapLens in use with a paper map, overlaying digital information on-screen. The highlighted square (*centre*) is used to select augmented icon

Fig. 2.9 DigiMap version, Google Map with icons. Used by the control group in the trial

Fig. 2.10 Kits contained seven items that needed to be managed: sunlight photographs, map, phone, water testing kits, voucher for internet use, clue booklet and pen

aged 7–50 years participated. Twenty-one had owned five or more mobile phones, with 22 familiar with the brand being trialled, and there was one nonphone user. Players were grouped into teams and, using the technology, followed clues and completed given tasks within a 90-min period. Each team managed the coordination of a kit of artifacts (see Fig. 2.10). One connected series of game tasks included: find a leaf in the museum; find the same leaf outside the museum; take a sunlight photo of the leaf using water to develop it (supplied in the kit; see Fig. 2.10); test pond water; test sea water for chlorine, alkalinity, and pH balance (supplied in the kit), and record all the readings (upload photos or enter the results in the clue booklet).

To encourage friendly competitiveness, we included three prizes, awarded for speed and accuracy, the best photograph, and the best environmental task design. The game promoted internal and external group activities: the negotiation of tasks and artifacts; "noticing" and awareness of the environment; higher-level task management and physicality, proximity, embodiment, and physical configurations around the artifacts. There was particular emphasis on the mix of digital and augmented objects, with overtly tangible and tactile ones that were included to encourage physical proximity and team bonding and to "jolt" users away from small-screen absorption.

In our observations, we noted the joint efforts of the users and present a discussion of our findings. In this section, we label figures and name groups with M when referring to MapLens and with D when referring to DigiMap.

The Mobile Device and Bodily Configurations

MapLens users (hereafter "M users") typically held the device with their arms stretched out because the camera needed to be held at a range of 15–40 cm away from the paper map. The best light to view by was with sunlight on the map and the lens in shade. Importantly, with the device placed in this way, with one's arm stretched out, others could see what part of the map was being examined and, at times, the contents of the display.

In contrast, DigiMap users (hereafter "D users") users typically held the device lower and closer to their body, as with a conventional phone. However, this rendered the phone more private (see Fig. 2.11 right), as others could not directly see the contents of the screen. Shading from the sun with the use of one hand and, generally, one-handed use of the device was possible with D.

Handing over of the phone occurred more with M groups than with D ones. When difficulties were encountered, it was common for the phone to be passed on. The D user roles were defined earlier in the game and one user tended to "own the use" of the phone, while others managed parts of the kit.

We observed teams negotiating together in all parts of the trial. The discussions concerned not only the task at hand and what the team should do next, but also how best to use the technology (see Fig. 2.12 centre). In many instances, M users gathered

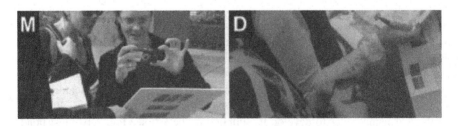

Fig. 2.11 MapLens (M) was held in such a way that it could be shared with the group, whereas DigiMap (D) users held the device more privately

Fig. 2.12 Walking while using and bodily configurations. *Left*: Girls walk in front while one tries to read off MapLens (M). *Center*: MapLens (M) team negotiate where next. *Right*: One DigiMap (D) user reads the system while the other navigates

together around the physical map to use M. The group members who did not have the phone gave instructions to the one holding M about where to look. Needing to hold the map steady restricted movement (Fig. 2.12 centre), unlike the case of D, where often one person was the "navigator" of the group, searching for things from the mobile, while others observed the environment and led the way (Fig. 2.12 right). The bodily configuration around the use of D was separate and individual. The smaller screen and lower visibility meant that less sharing occurred and the division of roles took place earlier in the game.

Turn-Taking

Corresponding to the ease of handing over the phone, turn-taking, switching, and transiting back and forth between roles occurred more spontaneously with M. In Fig. 2.13 left, we see Player A holding the map level, while Player B looks through the lens. Player C, close by, is listening and interjecting while looking at the environment for clues. In Fig. 2.13 centre, Player B is still holding the phone, but the focus is on Player A and C is looking at clues, reading instructions, and determining the location and the ordering of the clues. In Fig. 2.13, right, the team is posing barefoot on the grass (a game task). Player A is using the device as a camera, Player C is advising on camera use, and Player C is arranging their shoes in order to compose the shot optimally. The natural ease with which the passing of the phone and artifacts between the players occurred was reflected in the ease with which role-switching, turn-taking, and coordinating occurred.

Establishing Common Ground

Given that the typical way of using M involved a team gathering around and gesturing at the physical map with the device, establishing common ground was easier for M groups. We noted a shared understanding around the objects that were the focus

Fig. 2.13 Turn-taking: *Left*: PlayerA holds map as Player B looks through MapLens, Player C (out of picture) looks at environment. *Centre*: Player C looks at one clue while Player A looks at another and Player B holds device. *Right*: group poses for team photo barefoot on grass; Player A uses device to take photo, Player C points to device, Player B composes the shot

Fig. 2.14 The physical map as a common ground, established by showing with MapLens (M) and pointing with finger

Fig. 2.15 DigiMap (D) Users experienced difficulties while attempting to share the map as common ground

of the co-conversants' attention (Costabile et al. 2008). The location of M on the paper map and the contents revealed to others on its display helped everyone to understand the points under discussion without explicitly needing to ask. In Fig. 2.14, a young woman browses the map by using M. After finding a place, she suggests it to her father by pointing to it with her finger. The father proposes a nearby location and points to it by using the corner of a clue booklet.

The D teams were not able to share the map in such a fluent way (see Fig. 2.15). A young boy tries to identify a place by pointing to a relevant location on the screen and glancing around. After this he gestures toward the direction he suspects is correct and hands the device over to his uncle.

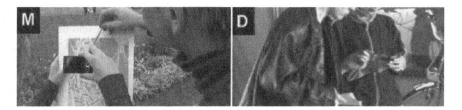

Fig. 2.16 Referring to objects by pinpointing. *Left*: pointing with a pen while using MapLens (M). *Right*: pointing with a finger from the DigiMap (D) screen

The physical paper map supported the players better in establishing a common understanding of the area and referring to different locations. The combination of MapLens and the paper map provided a means to be collaborative in a more physical way with other objects: fingers, clue booklets, pens, and other components from the kit (see Fig. 2.16 left). However, some M players found it challenging to identify the location on the map through the focus of the lens, especially while it was in use by another player. The D players often referred more directly by pointing at their surroundings. For one D team, we observed constant pointing at the mobile screen, establishing common ground. In another D team, one looked at the screen behind the "navigator's" shoulder (see Fig. 2.16 right), but with other D teams this did not occur.

Place-Making

Stopping, holding out MapLens and the paper map, and gathering around for a short time created an ephemeral opportunity, isolated from the surroundings by the physical map and the team members' bodies, to momentarily focus on a problem as a team. The phenomenon of place-making with the mobile use of technology has been raised previously in the literature (Kristoffersen and Ljungberg 1999), and here we encounter a special multiuser form of it. The physical map, as a tangible artifact, acted as a meeting point; a place where joint understandings could be more readily reached and participants were able to see, manipulate, demonstrate, and agree upon the action. In pausing for discussion, the teams created a series of temporary spaces, places for collaboration where they "downed" bags, swapped or rearranged the objects they were carrying, stabilized the map, and looked through M again to ascertain their progress. At this rapidly made "place," tasks were again shared, the negotiation and switching of roles, artifacts and the device often occurred, and we noted a different kind of social usage in this temporary place, with other pedestrians walking around these "places." Conversely, D teams only needed to stop at the places that the tasks themselves dictated; the rest of the action, decision-making, and way-finding was mainly done on the move or while stationary and completing tasks.

As a general overview, it becomes clear through observation, interviews, the results of the game, and observations that the MapLens users concentrated more on the interface, but not the environment around them. Additionally, the MapLens users were more concentrated on the combination of the technology and the game – which involved problem-solving via negotiation and physical and social interaction. The way in which place-making affects attention on the task and technology, as opposed to the surroundings, is a plausible explanation for this observation.

Discussion and Conclusions

The case studies described above presented our understanding of ubiquitous media by providing observations from real-world use. Nearly a decade ago, Abowd and Mynatt (2000) recognized that the evaluation of ubicomp systems was difficult. Since then, numerous proofs-of-concepts have been presented, but empirical studies in real settings are rare. Neither have conceptual work for tangible interaction (e.g., Hornecker and Buur 2006) or shareability (Hornecker et al. 2007) been systematically informed more by anecdotal evidence than by empirical, prototype-driven field trials (e.g., see Huang et al. 2007). While most of the previous work on ubiquitous media has focused on distributed and mediated interactions, this chapter looked at collocation. We presented two examples: in the City Wall study, usage included mostly playful interaction and engagement with others, while users were less engaged with the content (pictures and text concerning the city). In the MapLens case, the interaction was more collaborative; the users focused more on the content and interacting with each other. The trial included a control condition where a nonaugmented version (DigiMap) was utilized. Although the DigiMap users were faster in completing their tasks, the MapLens users were more thorough in their execution and more engaged in the game and their solution process was more collaborative. Behind the two designs, we can observe two concepts of how ubiquitous media renders media publicly available for others. We conclude this chapter with discussion of these concepts, with the purpose of informing future design work.

Common Stages

In the MapLens case, collocated interaction took place mostly while on the move. Mobility is characterized by the uncertainty of events and courses of action (Perry et al. 2001). At its best, ubiquitous media can provide open and flexible support for groups that, in the face of unexpected events, need to coordinate their joint activities. Maps and guidebooks can provide this support, as was found by Brown and Chalmers (2003). The key question for designers is how technology comes in between people, segregating or connecting them in ways inconsistent with the prevalent orderliness of social action in urban space.

Ubiquitous computing technology provides novel means to establish and become drawn into *face engagement*, where a sense of *mutual activity* is formed

(Goffman 1963). Furthermore, after being drawn in, since it is largely unclear to people how to behave in this new situation, people rely on each other to learn about the possibilities and constraints of the setting. The metaphor of a *stage* (Goffman 1956) is the most descriptive of the ways in which the public availability of media in a physical space can create areas inside which the actions of individuals turn into a *performance*, with people assigning *roles* to themselves, as well as to others and swapping them on the fly. In both cases, we observed how the ubiquitous media contributed to the formation of a common stage for collocated interaction.

In the case of City Wall, common stages were facilitated by the public availability of the media, with passersby being able to easily learn how to use the stage by watching others interacting with the display and with each other. The stage was framed by the architectural solution, the large size of the display, and the space in front of it. More importantly, the stage was framed by people approaching, negotiating, and using the display. On this common stage people could adopt roles such as being teachers, apprentices, clowns, or members of the audience. In some cases, multiple activities were taking place at the same time. Such asymmetric participation patterns have not been reported to this extent before. This stage provided an opportunity for encountering "the other" (Schutz 1967) with the possibilities of being in possession or control of the ubiquitous media and its interactivity. In particular, the single timeline provided a strong feature for encountering others through coordination or conflict.

In the MapLens study, the map and mobile device as tangible objects provided a common ground to perform fine gestural communication movements allowing reference points during collocated interaction. This contrasted with DigiMap, where the tasks were carried out with more divided roles and without a common support as a reference. The awkwardness of the map and mobile device also led the users to place-making. The map and mobile device became the place around which to gather, acting as a pretext to appropriate a bench or a space in the park. The paper-card map was also used as if it was a miniature stage. All in all, the casual approach to the environment, the "throwing-down" of kits and artifacts and "owning the space," supported rapid place-making. The kit of lo-fi tangible objects – a muslin bag, expandable paper clue booklet, biro, and a map on foam-core card – contributed to the informality of the use (Ehn and Kyng 1992). We observed how interactions and bodily configurations made the teams unaware of their surroundings and others in the environment, for example., other pedestrians needing to walk around their rapidly made "place," which could also be viewed – in Goffman's sense of the word – as an informally established stage.

Performative Interaction

An important aspect of collocated interaction is the shared experiencing of media. Heath et al. (2002) observed how the meaning of works of art was reflexively constituted in collaboration by museum visitors. Experiences are lived through, constructed, and interpreted as a group rather than as an individual

(Forlizzi and Battarbee 2004). This aspect was particularly accentuated in the City Wall examples through bodily expressions and role-taking, causing the ubiquitous media to take on the role of a "prop" in *performative interactions*. Here we refer to the idea of "interaction as performance" (Jacucci 2004), originating from pragmatic and anthropological views of experience and performance. For these views, performance implies at the same time experience and expression, action and representation, consciousness of the act and, like an event, an initiation and consummation.

For the MapLens users, holding and looking through the lens and "showing" the other group members' possible solutions on the paper-card map forced a form of performative interaction, where the phone became a physical interface and prop; it became an AR lens used to negotiate the floor, orient attention, and access information collaboratively. Crabtree et al. (2005) argue that technology-assisted playful activities rely on the participants' ability to manage, diagnose, and repair interruptions. Conversely, we have shown how playful and jocular activities help people not only to account for mistakes they make, but also deal with system-generated problems. In consequence, the collaborative learning process becomes more enjoyable and hence more sustainable over time.

In City Wall, the content on the wall and the features of the interface were used as resources to coordinate the activity and to create events or interactions, so they were meaningful in front of others. For example, interactions such as photo-moving and scaling turned into games such as playing Pong. Some gestures were made salient to others. "Grandiose gestures" and "pondering grips" were used to manifest the extent of the user's actions and her intentions toward others, while also marking the boundaries of the workspace that the user felt she had claimed as her own. The presence of strangers – all the other people walking past the installation, sometimes stopping by to observe what the users are doing – also has an effect on one's activities at City Wall, which can be perceived as a public performance in a city space. It is clear that the use of City Wall provided richer instances of performative interaction than that of MapLens. This is also because of the explorative and casual setting of City Wall, and because the use of MapLens took place in a game with goals and tasks.

It is not only about the interface being *big enough* to be used in parallel by several people (the case of City Wall). An impromptu stage for performative interaction can also be formed around smaller items, such as smartphones or printed maps (the case of MapLens). Paper, just like public displays, can also configure spaces and surfaces (Rogers et al. 2004) in support of social interaction. Both our prototypes were able to support expressive gestures that helped the participants in coordinating, communicating, and acting out different roles.

Interaction Design Issues

To conclude, we would like to reflect on two design issues. Addressing these in the future would strengthen collocated interaction as an aspect of ubiquitous media.

Effort and common stages: The size and other aspects of the materiality of ubiquitous media facilitate or hamper collocated interaction. Surprising aspects, such as architecture and positioning in a physical space, affect use. Similarly, combining an artifact such as a map with dynamic media provided opportunities for social interaction. In the MapLens case, effort was needed for technical and ergonomic reasons, such as illumination issues constraining the orientation of the map and the orientation of the device to the map, or the position of participants so that they could view and access the interface. This effort and awkwardness provided a pretext for place-making and common stages. The approach of natural interfaces, such as multitouch on the one hand and augmenting physical objects on the other, also provided parallel access to media and shared experience. Challenges included the effort needed by the users to manage this availability. As an example, common features, such as the timeline in City Wall or the map and the mobile device in MapLens, need to be negotiated through coordination and conflict, which provides opportunities for shared encounters. The challenges are therefore to solve the trade-off between effortless operation and the sociality of the system.

Performative interaction for immediate, but superficial use: In the case studies, ubiquitous media was successful in collocated interaction in the way it provided props for interaction. We see the mobile device in MapLens used as a physical lens or the media objects in City Wall used for playful and expressive interactions. Embodied and expressive interactions were easy to learn, playful, and immediate. At the same time there was the problem that the encounters relied heavily on the immediacy of the interface and its playfulness. The success of the usage, for example, of City Wall seems to rely on the novelty of the technology. Moreover, the immediacy and playfulness of the system attracted more attention than the media that were provided.

Acknowledgment   We thank Tommi Ilmonen and John Evans, who worked on the City Wall. MapLens and DigiMap were developed in cooperation with the University of Oulu, Graz University of Technology and the University of Cambridge, within the IPCity project funded by the 6th Framework Research Programme of the EU. We thank Saija Lemmelä and Jaana Juntunen for their contribution in the analysis of MapLens trials.

References

Abowd GD & Mynatt ED (2000) Charting past, present and future research in ubiquitous computing. ACM Transactions on Computer-Human Interaction, 7(1), 29–58. DOI= http://doi.acm.org/10.1145/344949.344988

Arias E, Eden H & Fisher G (1997) Enhancing communication, facilitating shared understanding and creating better artifacts by integrating physical and computational media for design. In: Proceedings of the 2nd Conference on Designing interactive Systems: Processes, Practices, Methods and Techniques,1–12). ACM Press, New York

Benford S, Magerkurth C. & Ljungstrand P (2005) Bridging the physical and digital in pervasive gaming. Communications of the ACM, 48(3), 54–57. DOI= http://doi.acm.org/10.1145/1047671.1047704

Brignull H & Rogers Y (2003) Enticing people to interact with large public displays in public spaces. In Proceedings of INTERACT 2003, 17–24. IOS Press, Amsterdam

Brown B & Chalmers M (2003) Tourism and mobile technology. In Kuutti K, Karsten EH, Fitzpatrick G, Dourish P & Schmidt K (Eds) Proceedings of ECSCW 2003, 335–355. Kluwer Academic Publishers, Norwell

Buxton W (1997) Living in augmented reality: ubiquitous media and reactive environments. In Finn K, Sellen A & Wilber S (eds). Video mediated communication, 363–384. Lawrence Erlbaum Associates, Hillsdale

Costabile MF, De Angeli A, Lanzilotti R, Ardito C, Buono P & Pederson T (2008) Explore! possibilities and challenges of mobile learning. In: Proceedings of the SIGCHI Conference on Human Factors in Computing Systems (CHI'08, pp. 145–154). ACM Press, New York. DOI= http://doi.acm.org/10.1145/1357054.1357080

Crabtree A, Rodden R & Benford S (2005) Moving with the times: IT research and the boundaries of CSCW. Computer Supported Cooperative Work, 14, 217–251

Crabtree A & Rodden T (2008) Hybrid ecologies: understanding cooperative interaction in emerging physical-digital environments. Personal and Ubiquitous Computing 12(7), 481–493

Ehn P & Kyng M (1992) Cardboard computers: mocking-it-up or hands-on the future. In: Greenbaum J & Kyng M (eds) Design at work: cooperative design of computer systems, 169–196. Lawrence Erlbaum Associates, Hillsdale

Forlizzi J & Battarbee K (2004) Understanding experience in interactive systems. In: Proceedings of the 5th Conference on Designing interactive Systems: Processes, Practices, Methods and Technique, 261–268. ACM Press,New York. DOI= http://doi.acm.org/10.1145/1013115.1013152

Frohlich D, Kuchinsky A, Pering C, Don A & Ariss S (2002) Requirements for photoware. In: Proceedings of the 2002 ACM Conference on Computer Supported Cooperative Work, 166–175. ACM Press, New York. DOI= http://doi.acm.org/10.1145/587078.587102

Goffman E (1956) The presentation of self in everyday life. Anchor Books, New York

Goffman E (1963) Behavior in public places. Free Press, New York

Grudin J (2002) Group dynamics and ubiquitous computing. Communications of the ACM 45(12): 74–78. DOI= http://doi.acm.org/10.1145/585597.585618

Heath C, Luff PK, vom Lehn D, Hindmarsh J & Cleverly J (2002) Crafting participation: designing ecologies, configuring experience. Visual Communication 1(1): 9–34

Hornecker E Jacob Buur (2006) Getting a Grip on Tangible Interaction: A Framework on Physical Space and Social Interaction. Proc. of CHI 2006. Montreal, Canada. ACM Press pp. 437–446

Hornecker E & Buur J (2006) Getting a grip on tangible interaction: a framework on physical space and social interaction. In: Grinter R, Rodden T, Aoki P, Cutrell E, Jeffries R & Olson G (Eds) Proceedings of the SIGCHI Conference on Human Factors in Computing Systems , 437–446. ACM Press, New York. DOI= http://doi.acm.org/10.1145/1124772.1124838

Hornecker E, Marshall P & Rogers Y (2007) From entry to access - how shareability comes about. In: Proceedings of the 2007 Conference on Designing Pleasurable Products and interfaces, 328–342. ACM Press, New York. DOI= http://doi.acm.org/10.1145/1314161.1314191

Huang, E.M., Mynatt, E.D. & Trimble, J.P. (2007). Displays in the wild: understanding the dynamics and evolution of a display ecology. Personal and Ubiquitous Computing 11 (7): 537–547

Jacucci G (2004) Interaction as performance. cases of configuring physical interfaces in mixed media. Doctoral Thesis, University of Oulu. Oulu: Acta Universitatis

Jacucci G & Salovaara A(2005). Mobile media sharing in large-scale events – beyond MMS. Interactions 12(6): 32–35

Jacucci G, Oulasvirta A, Salovaara A & Sarvas R (2005) Supporting the shared experience of spectators through mobile group media. In: Proceedings of the 2005 international ACM SIGGROUP Conference on Supporting Group Work, 207–216. ACM Press, New York. DOI= http://doi.acm.org/10.1145/1099203.1099241

Jacucci G, Oulasvirta A & Salovaara A (2007a) Active construction of experience through mobile media: a field study with implications for recording and sharing. Personal and Ubiquitous Computing 11(4): 215–234

Jacucci G, Oulasvirta A, Ilmonen T, Evans J & Salovaara A (2007b) CoMedia: mobile group media for active spectatorship. In: Proceedings of the SIGCHI Conference on Human

Factors in Computing Systems, 1273–1282. ACM Press, New York. DOI= http://doi.acm.org/ 10.1145/1240624.1240817

Kristoffersen S & Ljungberg FL (1999) "Making place" to make IT work: empirical explorations of HCI for mobile CSCW. In: Proceedings of the international ACM SIGGROUP Conference on Supporting Group Work (SIGGROUP 1999, 276–285). ACM Press, New York. DOI= http://doi.acm.org/10.1145/320297.320330

Matsushita N & Rekimoto J (2003) HoloWall: designing a finger, hand, body and object sensitive wall. In: Proceedings of the 10th Annual ACM Symposium on User interface Software and Technology (UIST 2003, 159–168). ACM Press, New York. DOI= http://doi.acm.org/ 10.1145/263407.263549

Morris MR, Huang A, Paepcke A & Winograd T (2006) Cooperative gestures: multi-user gestural interactions for colocated groupware. In: Grinter R, Rodden T, Aoki P, Cutrell E, Jeffries R & Olson G (Eds) Proceedings of the SIGCHI Conference on Human Factors in Computing Systems '06, 1201–1210. ACM Press, New York. DOI= http://doi.acm.org/ 10.1145/1124772.1124952

Peltonen P, Salovaara A, Jacucci G, Ilmonen T, Ardito C, Saarikko P & Batra V (2007) Extending large-scale event participation with user-created mobile media on a public display. In: Proceedings of the 6th international Conference on Mobile and Ubiquitous Multimedia '07, 131–138. ACM Press, New York. DOI= http://doi.acm.org/10.1145/1329469.1329487

Peltonen P, Kurvinen E, Salovaara A, Jacucci G, Ilmonen T, Evans J, Oulasvirta A & Saarikko, P (2008) "It's mine, don't touch!": interactions at a large multi-touch display in a city centre. In: Proceeding of the Twenty-Sixth Annual SIGCHI Conference on Human Factors in Computing Systems '08, 1285–1294. ACM Press, New York. DOI= http://doi.acm.org/ 10.1145/1357054. 1357255

Perry M, O'Hara K, Sellen A, Brown B & Harper R (2001) Dealing with mobility: understanding access anytime, anywhere. In: ACM Transactions on Computer-Human Interaction (TOCHI) 8(4): 323–347. DOI= http://doi.acm.org/10.1145/504704.504707

Robertson T (2002) The public availability of actions and artefacts. Computer Supported Cooperative Work 11(3–4): 299–316

Rogers Y, Hazlewood W, Blevis E & Lim Y-K (2004) Finger talk: collaborative decision-making using talk and fingertip interaction around a tabletop display. In: Proceedings of the SIGCHI Conference on Human Factors in Computing Systems (CHI'04, 1271–1274). New York: ACM Press.

Russell DM, Drews D & Sue A (2002) Social aspects of using large public interactive displays for collaboration. In: Borriello G & Holmquist LE (eds) Proceedings of the 4th international Conference on Ubiquitous Computing, 229–236). Springer, London

Sacks H, Schegloff EA & Jefferson G (1974) A simplest systematics for the organization of turn taking in conversation. Language 50(4): 696–735

Salovaara A, Jacucci G, Oulasvirta A, Kanerva P, Kurvinen E & Tiitta S (2006) Collective creation and sense-making of mobile media. In: Grinter R, Rodden T, Aoki P, Cutrell E, Jeffries R & Olson G (Eds) Proceedings of the SIGCHI Conference on Human Factors in Computing Systems '06, 1211–1220. ACM Press, New York. DOI= http://doi.acm.org/10.1145/ 1124772.1124954

Schutz A (1967) The phenomenology of the social world. Northwestern University Press, Chicago

Shen C, Lesh N, Vernier F, Forlines C & Frost J (2002) Sharing and building digital group histories. In Proceedings of the 2002 ACM Conference on Computer Supported Cooperative Work, 324–333. ACM Press, New York. DOI= http://doi.acm.org/10.1145/587078.587124

Wagner D, Reitmayr G, Mulloni A, Drummond T & Schmalstieg D (2008) Pose tracking from natural features on mobile phones. In Proceedings of IEEE International Symposium on Mixed and   Augmented   Reality,   125–134.   Available: http://dx.doi.org/10.1109/ ISMAR.2008.4637338

Weiser M (1991) The computer for the 21st century. Scientific American 265(3): 94 –104

Wu M & Balakrishnan R (2003). Multi-finger and whole hand gestural interaction techniques for multi-user tabletop displays. In Proceedings of the 16th Annual ACM Symposium on User interface Software and Technology, 193–202. ACM Press, New York. DOI= http://doi.acm. org/10.1145/964696.964718

Chapter 3
History-Enriched Spaces for Shared Encounters

Shin'ichi Konomi, Kaoru Sezaki, and Masaru Kitsuregawa

Introduction

Today, people create and interact with the digital media in various places using mobile phones, digital cameras, notebook computers, public displays, and so on. In addition, historical data about people, places, and physical objects are increasingly captured and accumulated in various forms. We can use such data to effectively support verbal and nonverbal communications in encounters if we can provide the "right" information at the "right" time, at the "right" place, in the "right" way, and to the "right" people.

We discuss the uses of historical data to support shared encounters based on our experience of deploying social network displays that respond to RFID conference badges. When people introduce themselves to strangers at social events such as academic conferences, they sometimes reveal their historical information by narrating brief stories about past experiences. Historical data can similarly be revealed on personal devices or public displays to support existing practices such as self-introduction. Historical data may in addition, support awareness about opportunities of meaningful conversations before people engage in face-to-face communications with strangers, thereby supporting the process of shifting from unfocused to focused interactions (Goffman 1963).

Historical data, such as academic publication databases, blog archives, web and email log files, product purchase records, music playlists, and location tracking data, may collectively reflect temporal patterns of social relations that influence the risks and meaningfulness of encounters. However, extracting human relationships from all kinds of historical data would cause serious privacy problems. Privacy is a complex issue as people have the simultaneous need to disclose their information and protect their privacy, and privacy implications of historical data change when they are processed and presented in different ways, in different contexts. One may disclose one's personal data if there is a clear value proposition. However, it is generally difficult to control privacy-sensitive data once they are digitally captured.

S. Konomi (✉), K. Sezaki, and M. Kitsuregawa
University of Tokyo, 4-6-1, Komaba, Meguro-Ku, Tokyo, 153-8505, Japan
e-mail: konomi@iis.u-tokyo.ac.jp

K.S. Willis et al. (eds.), *Shared Encounters*, Computer Supported Cooperative Work,
DOI 10.1007/978-1-84882-727-1_3, © Springer-Verlag London Limited 2010

Instead of dealing separately with privacy, we explore a holistic view (Dourish and Anderson 2006) of shared encounter practices to understand everyday contexts in which people disclose and acquire information. We first take a closer look at spatial patterns of social practices in public spaces, and argue that naive uses of historical data could undermine "the power of constraints" (Erickson and Kellogg 2000) that physical spaces provide. The richness of people's spatial patterns suggests that supporting shared encounters is more than just detecting people in proximity and establishing digital communication links. It also concerns the process in which individuals become "accessible, available, and subject to one another" (Goffman 1963), and technologies of course should not force people to be friends with each other.

Weakly involved interactions are an important element of public spaces in which shared encounters take place. Strangers act in awareness of others even when they are not talking with each other. For example, without engaging in face-to-face interactions, people could improve a sense of belonging through a means to increase awareness of familiar strangers (Paulos and Goodman 2004). Wear and tear of library books and black streaks on guardrails are collective, incrementally accumulated information that informs and influences people.

Based on these considerations, we also discuss an approach to designing a history-rich awareness tool for pedestrians, and describe our prototype that utilizes mobile blogs and an RFID-based distance sensing mechanism.

Supporting Social Encounters in Academic Conferences: A Case Study

Encounters take place in different physical and social settings. Some settings, such as a busy sidewalk, are full of strangers who rarely talk with each other. In other settings, such as a conference banquet, people are more likely to meet and begin relationships.

Different settings provide a different amount of information about the people in them. For example, we may know more about strangers at a conference banquet than about strangers on a busy sidewalk. What physical and social spaces inform us about their people is an important resource for *assessing* the interactions with strangers (Karp et al. 1991).

By blending digital information with physical and social spaces, we can make more resources available for such assessment. Digitally augmented spaces could in effect reduce some uncertainties in interacting with strangers. They could also increase clues for discovering opportunities of meaningful encounters.

An important challenge then is to blend the "right" information in the "right" spaces in the "right" way, and thereby increase the "right" encounters in our everyday lives. Our first step toward addressing this challenge is to examine a system that supports shared encounters in academic conferences. We additionally discuss specificities and commonalities of encounters in different physical and social spaces.

DeaiExplorer

Academic conferences offer many benefits that virtual meeting tools cannot easily offer: rich, interactive presentations and demonstrations, various opportunities to socialize and make new friends, serendipitous discoveries of relevant ideas, people, and projects, and so on. *DeaiExplorer*[1,2] is a system that enhances conference experiences using the data accumulated through a research community's history (Konomi et al. 2006). The system allows colocated conference participants to easily display and examine relevant social networks (see Fig. 3.1), which is derived from DBLP (Digital Bibliography & Library Project) (Ley 2007), a publication database covering major computer science journals and proceedings. It responds to RFID conference badges, automatically displaying relevant social networks for individuals and groups.

DeaiExplorer was first deployed at the Twenty-first International Conference on Data Engineering (ICDE 2005) that took place in Tokyo during the second week of April 2005. We used this opportunity to conduct a user study (Konomi et al. 2006) and iteratively improved the system by additionally deploying and testing it at the following conferences: the Sixth International Conference on Web Information Systems Engineering (WISE 2005), the Seventh International Conference on Mobile

Fig. 3.1 People using *DeaiExplorer* at the 21st International Conference on Data Engineering (ICDE 2005). Two RFID readers are connected to each public display, which responds to RFID conference badges and shows relevant social networks

---

[1] *Deai* is a Japanese word for encounter.

[2] http://www.tkl.iis.u-tokyo.ac.jp/socialnet

Data Management (MDM 2006), and the Ninth International Conference on Asian
Digital Libraries (ICADL 2006).

As shown in Fig. 3.2, the latest version of the software additionally displays
research keywords using a tag-cloud format. When an individual uses the system,

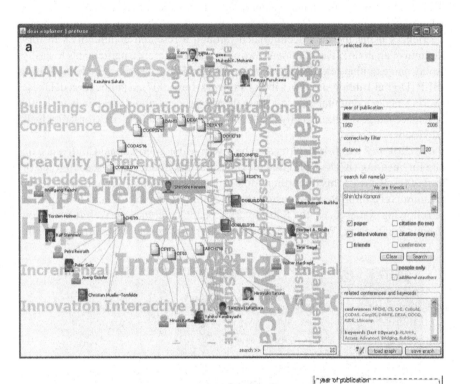

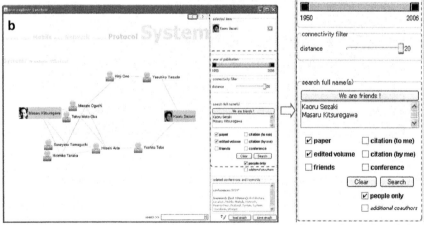

Fig. 3.2 Sample screenshot of *DeaiExplorer*. (**a**) *Personal view* showing an egocentric social
network and (**b**) *Small-world view* showing a "group-centric" social network including the
connecting paths of the two users, one on the *left* and the other on the *right*

it computes a *personal view* (Fig. 3.2a) that combines her research keywords and egocentric social network. Likewise, when a group uses the system, it computes a *small-world view* (Fig. 3.2b) that visually combines the group's common research keywords and "group-centric" social network showing the shortest paths between its members.

Users can passively view or actively explore the social network visualization. Using simple mouse operations, one can zoom in and out, navigate the networks, display additional information in a popup window, and search the web for more information. Moreover, users can examine historical evolution of their academic social networks by using the range slider labeled "year of publication." Figure 3.3 shows a sample use of the range slider. The social network became increasingly dense and connected during the period between 1995 and 2006.

Publication databases may not embody certain social relations including people who rarely publish together but chat with one another a lot, or people who just made friends with one another during a conference. The "We are friends!" button (see Fig. 3.2b) allows people to explicitly declare a "friend" relation. This may sound similar to "adding friends" on social network websites such as MySpace and Facebook.

The system provides various options for customizing social network computation. The check boxes (see Fig. 3.2b) allow users to specify the relationship types that must be considered in deriving social networks: "paper" (coauthoring papers), "edited volume" (co-editing books or proceedings), "friends" (declaring "We are friends!" relations), "citation" (citing other researchers' papers), and "conference" (publishing in the same conference proceedings). The "people only" check box hides document icons in the visualized network.

During the second, the third, and the fourth deployments, we provided the service without using RFID conference badges. Therefore, the cost of these three deployments was much lower than the first deployment. The largest drawback was that users had to manually input their names using a keyboard. This did not seem to put off users so much in our particular settings (i.e., technical conferences in computer science); however, it could be problematic in other settings.

Issues of Supporting Social Encounters

In our experiences with *DeaiExplorer*, some issues emerged around the quantity and quality of contents as well as the complexity of social processes. We summarize how these issues came into play based on our data from the first deployment (Konomi et al. 2006) and anecdotal evidences from the other three deployments. Moreover, we discuss similarities and differences between academic conferences and other public settings.

Quantity and Quality of Contents

We appropriated a publication database as the contents for supporting shared encounters. Publication databases of course do not embody all kinds of human

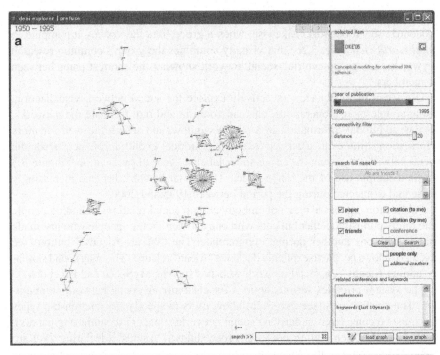

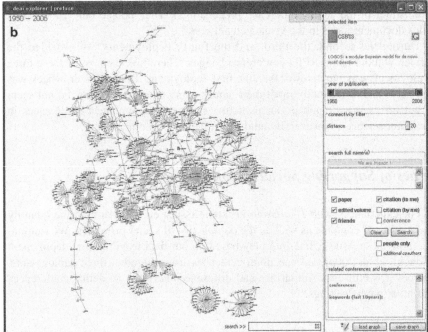

Fig. 3.3 Exploring historical patterns of a social network: (**a**) social network derived from the 1950–1995 data and (**b**) social network derived from the 1950–2006 data

relations; however, they describe certain types of relations very well, such as the ones based on coauthoring and citing. These relations are often of interest to conference participants, and therefore their visual representations could complement physical and social spaces of a conference.

Contents are indeed critical for successfully supporting social encounters in our service. Quantity of contents alone can substantially influence user experiences. For example, since *DeaiExplorer* computes social networks based on each user's publication records, it may display small, rather trivial networks for newcomers of a research community, and large, overwhelmingly complex networks for highly experienced researchers. Since too little or too much information can disappoint or frustrate users, we added certain features to improve user experiences. For example, the system now allows people to use the "We are friends!" button so that newcomers can immediately populate their networks without writing papers.[3]

It should be easy for users to make sense of the visualized relations. The current version of the system is implemented by using the *prefuse* visualization toolkit[4] (Heer et al. 2005), and allows users to interactively explore and make sense of complex social networks using animated effects as well as various mouse and keyboard operations. It displays "group-centric" social networks using a force-directed layout algorithm, and egocentric social networks using a radial layout algorithm (Ka-Ping et al. 2001). Also, users often asked which journals and conferences our system incorporates so that they can correctly interpret the displayed social networks. It was not too difficult for us to answer such questions since the system uses a well-structured publication database, rather than arbitrary information on the web.

We have to think carefully about what people might feel about sharing their contents in public spaces. This is undoubtedly a critical issue when we talk about sharing what users normally consider private. From our experiences, we learned that this can also be an issue when we talk about sharing *public* data. Privacy implications change when information is processed, aggregated, or presented in different ways. Even though we only used publicly available data from a publication database, the way the system visualizes the data clearly shows the amount of papers one has published. Anecdotal evidences suggest that some people could feel intimidated or might be unwilling to use the system, especially when the information is presented on a public display. It is not only the contents, but also the uses and the context that influence privacy perceptions. Given the diversity of public spaces and the social encounters that take place in them, general-purpose solutions would be quite limited in terms of preserving privacy and supporting encounters.

Complexity of Social Processes

Settings can facilitate or inhibit social encounters. It is uncommon that someone overhearing strangers' conversations in a crowded elevator easily joins the con-

---

[3] The system visualizes different types of relations by using colors and icons.

[4] http://www.prefuse.org

versations even if he is interested in the topics. People are more likely to break in and interact with strangers at a party or the coffee break of an academic conference. Also, extraordinary events such as an earthquake are likely to facilitate strangers to interact with each other.

Settings help define the meanings of behaviors. They may also provide some information about the identities and biographical details of people in them. They can then reduce perceived risks in social encounters, and indeed *some settings may reduce substantially the uncertainties normally accompanying interactions with strangers* (Karp et al. 1991). Digital contents can augment physical and social spaces and enhance settings of social encounters in terms of time and space. However, digitally augmented settings may not effectively support encounters, unless it is integrated with human interaction processes and social conventions.

We can easily capture, store, retrieve, and use a large amount of historical data in digitally augmented spaces. For example, *DeaiExplorer* accumulates and uses historical data to support social encounters, that is, the system uses historical social networks in a publication database as well as the "We are friends!" button that incrementally captures social relations during conferences. These mechanisms can enhance people's presentation of self and communication in social encounter processes. Moreover, historical data may influence the meaning and atmosphere of a setting through aggregation and collective visualization.

Digital media allow for communication across distances. Though this statement may invoke the image of geographically distributed people using email or video communication tools, we would like to examine digital media's impact around much smaller distances, such as the ones across which people can talk, walk, and identify others. In particular, ubiquitous computing technologies change our "abilities" in the space that immediately surrounds us. For example, Bluetooth technology may allow people to "see" everyone in a crowded room and search the best people to speak to, and mobile social networking tools such as *dodgeball.com* may allow one to announce one's presence to "friends" at a walking distance.

As humans, we develop our abilities to use various physical and social distances in the real world (Hall 1966). Therefore, we can view digital technologies as something that can not only remove some distances, but also extend and complement distances. Our experiences with *DeaiExplorer* suggest the importance of *social translucence* (Erickson and Kellogg 2000) in supporting social encounter processes. For example, in our user study, some people stood at a distance and passively observed others using *DeaiExplorer*. We could extend the system by installing a video camera so that observers can view the screen anywhere. Alternatively, we could support the passive observers so that they can eventually be involved (or not involved) in social interactions by developing mechanisms that exploit their familiar distances.

After gaining information from the setting, people may decide to interact with one another. They often begin with nonverbal gestures to interactively probe others' willingness to respond. Then, there could be ritualized verbal exchanges about unimportant issues so as to again probe others' willingness to engage in conversations on more important issues. When strangers use *DeaiExplorer* without RFID conference badges, they sometimes say things like: "How does this work?," "Let's try together, shall we?," or "May I ask your name?" With RFID conference badges, the system allows people to display social networks without such verbal exchange. Strangers can exchange useful data to make informed decisions on whether or not to engage in conversation. When they come to decline, their reluctance can be communicated without discrediting or embarrassing others. However, informed decisions may not always be the best decisions if the information is not "right" (e.g., erroneous, irrelevant, or incomplete information) or users don't have the "right" skills to use the information.

Using RFID badges, we could potentially keep track of familiar strangers (Paulos and Goodman 2004) as well as friends. However, a question remains about how much details we should remember about them. Besides privacy implications, digital traces may create unbalanced situations in terms of familiarity. Suppose users can use their personal computers to redisplay the (egocentric) social networks of everyone they use *DeaiExplorer* with. User A may not display B's information even when B displays A's information many times, which makes A familiar to B, but B unfamiliar to A. If users can only display collective familiarity levels of a place using anonymous historical traces (Paulos and Goodman 2004), such discrepancy might not be exacerbated as much. This seems to be one of the points where digital- and physical-based social spaces diverge. The question about what we should remember about past encounters (and how we should use it) suggests a critical design parameter when we must carefully consider the ramifications of a key issue of shared encounters: lack of coherency and fragmentation in the sense of a shared space of community.

Toward History-Enriched Spaces

We now explore three complementary approaches to addressing the issues of supporting social encounters: (1) embedding historical data in embodied interactions, (2) designing for weakly involved interactions such as social navigation, and (3) designing for privacy.

Embedding Historical Data in Embodied Interactions

Historical information is encoded in our everyday environments, influencing social encounters that take place in them. For example, interactions around greeting rituals allow one to express various feelings and thoughts while revealing some historical information. When we shake hands with elderly people, the tangible feeling of their hands may tell us something about the nature of their historical experiences. Simultaneously, we may mutually communicate willingness to engage in conversation by firmly shaking hands, making eye contact, and smiling. Note that interpretations of these actions depend on the cultural context.

Historical data reduce perceived risks and uncertainties in stranger encounters. However, we cannot easily increase historical data in our everyday environment because existing physically based media cannot store so much information. Digital media can remove such limitations, and also introduce the problems of information overload and privacy. We therefore need a framework to embed historical data in embodied interactions so as to provide integrated experiences that alleviate information overload and privacy problems. This embedding must reflect the use patterns of our immediate space and time, and it can exploit not only public, but also personal and intimate devices including body-worn sensors.

We acknowledge that successful social encounters require certain human skills. These skills include not only the ability to passively assess interactions with strangers, but also the ability to actively make interactions a success. We therefore consider learning as a critical element that makes history-enriched spaces meaningful. Critical agents (Fischer et al. 1990, 1993), who provide feedback and suggestions as users and go about their ordinary tasks, could potentially be useful for facilitating learning in situated embodied actions.

We could use the notion of distances (Hall 1966) and contexts to create a framework that blends relevant human, sensing, and computational mechanisms together. To build on human abilities to use various distances in different context, we could align sensing and computational mechanisms with these distances. If it is difficult to perfectly align distances of humans and machines, we can at least make people aware of the discrepancy.

Designing for Weakly Involved Interactions

The provision of historical data about people, things, and places can positively or negatively impact social encounters. Like wear-and-tear of library books or black streaks on guardrails, historical data can be collective, anonymous, and unintentional. Other historical data may be individual, traceable, and deliberate like resumes and pedigrees.

Interestingly, there are various weakly involved interactions, which are much less costly than making friends. It can be argued that such interactions could meaningfully be augmented with context-aware technologies and historical data. For example, history-rich tools (Hill et al. 1992; Waxelblat and Maes 1999) enable social navigation, which can be viewed as a type of lightweight interaction and is particularly useful for supporting newcomers to an environment. Without engaging in focused interactions, people could foster a feeling of community solidarity and a sense of belonging through a method used to create awareness of familiar strangers (Paulos and Goodman 2004).

Designing for Privacy

Privacy mechanisms define the boundaries of the self. Identity is a notion that is inseparable from privacy. Technology-mediated communication complicates regulation of the self/nonself boundary (Palen and Dourish 2003). It changes the ways we perceive who is receiving information, what is received, and how it is received.

People have simultaneous need to disclose their information and protect their privacy (Smith et al. 2005). Privacy implications of historical data change when they are processed and presented in different ways. People would not want their personal data collected without a clear value proposition. There are technologies for preventing unwanted data capture; however, it is extremely difficult to control how data are processed and used once they are captured. Privacy again is a critical issue and it could potentially conflict with the interest to build history-rich tools for supporting shared encounters.

Going Everywhere

Inspired by the experience of *DeaiExplorer*, we designed a history-enriched framework for supporting pedestrians' awareness about relevant things, people, and information in a reachable distance, and implemented a prototype awareness tool using mobile blogs and an RSSI[5]-based technique to sense simple copresence patterns.

We developed a few scenarios in which downtown pedestrians visit various shops of their interest, or look for a lost child. We then designed a proxemics-based (Hall 1966) awareness support framework that includes pedestrian devices and location markers. A pedestrian device has multiple communication ranges, each of which provides different visibility and controllability of relevant pedestrian-generated contents. Ranges can be defined by using radio coverage (and signal strengths), distance sensors, and positioning devices. Moreover, a pedestrian device can detect its movement by using these technologies. Pedestrians can exchange information, implicitly and explicitly, using ad hoc networks. One can access information about people, places, and things in her "social range" (<3 m). Her device supports awareness about people, places, and things in her public range (<10 m), through information filtering, summarization, and abstract visualization. Finally, the framework considers not only physical distance and movement patterns, but also cognitive and social patterns, which are embodied in location-relevant blogs and social networks, so as to support colocated pedestrians.

We developed a prototype awareness tool using an RFID-based technique for sensing simple copresence patterns. Our pedestrian device uses a small active RFID

---

[5]Received signal-strength indicator.

Fig. 3.4 Four co-presence patterns of two pedestrians

reader (RF Code™ Spider V Mobile Reader 303 MHz) that can be inserted into a PC card slot. Active RFID tags (RF Code™ Spider V) are used as location markers as well as RSSI-based range beacons for pedestrian devices. The software component uses Processing and Twitter API to detect pedestrians in the user's social and public ranges, and anonymously visualize their recent mobile blog messages. Messages from the public range are decomposed and aggregated into a tag-cloud format, allowing the user to "smell" things that are ahead of and behind her. Figure 3.4 shows two users passing by each other. Figure 3.5 shows sample screen shots of the prototype awareness tool. Messages from the social and public ranges are displayed in the inner and outer circles, respectively. The tool displays public-range messages in two different ways: (1) "pizza" is frequently mentioned ahead of the user; "coffee" and "raining" behind the user and (2) displays words using a revolving animation effect, and is used when pedestrians' orientations are unknown.

We are conducting a user study to improve and extend the framework. As our initial experience suggests a limitation of RSSI in stably detecting ranges, we might possibly test a hybrid tagging device that combines RFID, Motes, and/or WiFi, and explore distance sensor-based and location-based range demarcation techniques as well. We also envision a mobile phone-based awareness tool using GPS and Bluetooth. Continuous uses of a mobile awareness tool could produce historical data that can be used as resources for future services.

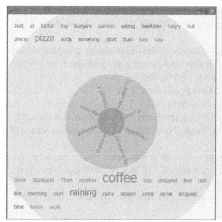 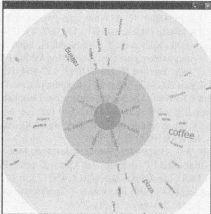

Fig. 3.5 Sample screenshots of the prototype awareness tool: (**a**) tag-cloud visualization and (**b**) animated visualization

Conclusions

We examined our experiences with *DeaiExplorer* and discussed the implications of historical data in supporting shared encounters. Of course, academic conferences are just one of the diverse settings of shared encounters. Therefore, our understanding of the geographical, social, and cultural diversity of encounter processes may still be limited. Moreover, it is not always the goal for people to socially encounter and develop relations. There are situations in which one wants to plausibly ignore others or talk with someone only once (e.g., when asking for directions). Another concern related to the use of historical data is that it could potentially reduce opportunities of surprising and inspiring encounters that existing data do not suggest.

To find the right way to capture, manage, and use historical data for supporting shared encounters, we must understand not only how people encounter today, but also how people could encounter with the support of pervasive context-aware technologies. As technologies and practices of shared encounters coevolve, new forms of social relations and ties could potentially emerge, greatly impacting fundamental mechanisms of our society.

References

Dourish, P and Anderson K (2006) Collective information practice: exploring privacy and security as social and cultural phenomena. Human-Computer Interaction, 21(3), 319–342
Erickson T, Kellogg WA (2000) Social translucence: an approach to designing systems that support social processes. In: Proceedings ACM TOCHI 7, 1: 59–83. DOI= http://doi.acm. org/10.1145/344949.345004

Fischer G, Lemke AC, Mastaglio T & Morch AI (1990) Using critics to empower users. In: In: Chew JC & Whiteside, J (eds) Proceedings of CHI'90, 337-347. ACM, New York. DOI= http://doi.acm.org/10.1145/97243.97305

Fischer, G., K. Nakakoji, J. Ostwald, G. Stahl & T. Sumner (1993) Embedding computer-based critics in the contexts of design. In: Ashlund S, HendersonA, Hollnagel E, Mullet K and White T (eds) Proc. of INTERCHI'93, 157-164. IOS Press, Amsterdam

Goffman E (1963) Behaviors in public places. The Free Press, New York

Hall ET (1966) The hidden dimension. Doubleday, New York

Heer J, Car SK, Landay JA (2005) Prefuse: a toolkit for interactive information visualization. In: Proceedings of CHI 2005, 421-430. ACM Press, New York. DOI= http://doi.acm.org/10.1145/1054972.1055031

Hill WC, Hollan JD, Wroblewski D & McCandles T (1992) Edit wear and read wear. In: Bauersfeld P, Bennett J & Lynch G (eds) Proceedings of CHI'92. ACM Press, New York. DOI= http://doi.acm.org/10.1145/142750.142751

ICADL (2006) 9th International Conference on Asian Digital Libraries, ICADL 2006, Kyoto, Japan, November 27-30, 2006

ICDE (2005). The 21st International Conference on Data Engineering (ICDE 2005). April 5-8 2005, Tokyo, Japan. http://icde2005.is.tsukuba.ac.jp/

Ka-Ping Y, Fisher D, Dhamija R & Hearst M (2001) Animated exploration of dynamic graphs with radial layout. In Proceedings of the IEEE Symposium on Information Visualization (INFOVIS), 43-50. INFOVIS. IEEE Computer Society, Washington

Karp DA, Stone GP & Yoels WC (1991) Being urban: A sociology of city life. Praeger, New York.

Konomi S, Inoue S, Kobayashi T, Tsuchida M & Kitsuregawa M (2006) Supporting colocated interactions using RFID and social network displays. IEEE Pervasive Computing 5, 3: 48-56. DOI= http://dx.doi.org/10.1109/MPRV.2006.60

Ley M (2007) DBLP Bibliography Website, http://www.informatik.uni-trier.de/~ley/db/. Retrieved 9 January 2009

MDM (2006) The 7th International Conference on Mobile Data Management (MDM'06) Nara, Japan, May 9-13, 2006. http://www.mdm2006.kddilabs.jp/

Palen L & Dourish P (2003) Unpacking "privacy" for a networked world. In: Proceedings of ACM Conference on Human Factors in Computing Systems (CHI'03), 129-136. ACM Press, New York. DOI= http://doi.acm.org/10.1145/642611.642635

Paulos E & Goodman E (2004) The familiar stranger: anxiety, comfort, and play in public places. In: Proceedings of ACM CHI 2004, 223-230. ACM, New York. DOI= http://doi.acm.org/10.1145/985692.985721

Smith I, Consolvo S, Lamarca A, Hightower J, Scott J, Sohn T, Hughes J, Iachello G & Abowd GD (2005) Social disclosure of place: from location technology to communication practices. In: Proceedings of Pervasive 2005, 134-151. Springer, Berlin

Waxelblat A & Maes P (1999) Footprints: history-rich tools for information foraging. In: Proceedings of CHI'99, 270-277. ACM Press, NY. DOI= http://doi.acm.org/10.1145/302979.303060

WISE (2005). Web Information Systems Engineering - WISE 2005 Workshops: WISE 2005 International Workshops, New York, NY, USA, November 20-22, 2005. http://www.cse.unsw.edu.au/~jas/wise05/

Chapter 4
Conceptualizing, Designing, and Investigating Locative Media Use in Urban Space

Katerina Diamantaki, Charalampos Rizopoulos, Dimitris Charitos, and Nikos Kaimakamis

Introduction

The recent proliferation of computer networks and mobile communication technologies has led to the emergence of new cultural media forms that significantly transform modes of communication and social connectedness. The novelty of "new media" rests not so much on the technological advancements they embody, but on their impact on human social activity; media use involves "the creation of new forms of action and interaction in the social world, new kinds of social relationship and new ways of relating to others and to oneself" (Thompson 1995). The association of digital content with real locations via location detection technologies has resulted in the concept of *locative media* (LM) (Tuters 2004), which offers unprecedented opportunities for anytime-anywhere communication, collaboration, and social interaction in shared interpersonal and group encounters, in accordance with Weiser's view (1991) that technology should be designed to fit into our natural human environment.

Additionally, LM brings human–computer communication and human–computer–human communication back into the context of our physical world. The design of location-based systems should therefore take into account (even more than traditional user-centered human–computer interaction approaches) the actual needs of individuals and groups as well as the social situations they find themselves in while using these media. For this purpose, it is important to study and comprehend the social, spatial, cultural, and interpersonal dimensions of LM use, in the context of modern urban settings.

This chapter documents part of the theoretical background of the interdisciplinary research conducted in the context of a project titled LOCUNET (LOcation-based Communication Urban NETwork) that aims to investigate the sociocultural potential

K. Diamantaki (✉), C. Rizopoulos, D. Charitos, and N. Kaimakamis
Laboratory of New Technologies in Communication, Education, and the Mass Media,
Department of Communication and Media Studies, National and Kapodistrian University of
Athens, 5 Stadiou street, 105 62 Athens, Greece
e-mail: knd@hol.gr

K.S. Willis et al. (eds.), *Shared Encounters*, Computer Supported Cooperative Work,
DOI 10.1007/978-1-84882-727-1_4, © Springer-Verlag London Limited 2010

of communication environments that emerge from the integration of mobile and location-aware technologies. More specifically, it focuses on the impact of the use of such systems on social interaction within urban public space.

The main research objective of LOCUNET was to explore the way users interact with one another (human–computer–human interaction) and with the location-based system itself (human–computer interaction), while focusing on the physical and social context in which this interaction takes place. Ultimately, LOCUNET aimed to investigate the social and environmental experience of the participants. As a means of accomplishing this objective, a system was designed and developed, and a specific application in the form of a location-based game was implemented.

In the following sections, part of the theoretical framework that directed our investigation of the social aspects of LM use in the city is described. We also highlight the manner in which this framework led to the design of the application and the implementation and evaluation of the system. To achieve this evaluation, both qualitative and quantitative techniques were employed, and some of the findings are presented here.

The Experience of Locative Media Use

Flew (2005) defines new media as forms of media that combine communication networks, computing, and information technology and content. In the case of LM, this conceptualization could be expanded to encompass location-awareness. Location-awareness enriches digital information with an additional layer of meaning which is dependent on the physical environment or its digital representations.[1]

LM contribute to the respecialization of digital information and the social and communicative practices associated with it, by making the user's actual location in a physical setting a condition for determining access and use of digital information. In a way, LM use may mitigate the phenomenon of "despatialized simultaneity," defined as the possibility of experiencing simultaneous events taking place at different places (Thompson 1995). The LM users may experience or navigate a shared spatiotemporal context, irrespective of whether they are physically co-present.

Green (2006) argues that throughout the twentieth century, individuals have been "dislocated" or "disembodied" from their common spatial and temporal context due to urban expansion and technologies that overcome the barriers of time and distance. For instance, computer-mediated communication (CMC) via the Internet has allowed physical meeting places to "immigrate" to a "virtual" spatial context, as in the case of various graphical online communities.

Souza e Silva (2003) advocated the social significance of mobile LM through which virtual worlds immigrate from the Internet to urban zones of cultural mediation.

---

[1] A broad definition of LM also includes systems that utilize digital representations of real spaces (such as city maps) that can be accessed remotely (e.g., over the Internet), and not necessarily via a mobile device.

Location awareness reintroduces the parameter of real location and corporeal presence in CMC, thus mapping the "virtual" mental space of communication to physical space inhabited by the real bodies of communicating participants. Using LM involves mapping the virtual spatial context of a communicative activity onto the physical world, thus producing a hybrid topography that includes elements from both real and virtual space. Such a communication environment affords the possibility of face-to-face interaction and brings back the "compulsion of proximity" (Boden and Molotch 2004) into CMC.

The CMC has so far been characterized by a lack of locality; the Internet and mobile telephony are often perceived as taking place in "an indeterminate space in which spatial difference is erased and is experienced as always elsewhere ... a place out of space and time, a placeless place" (Hemment 2005). Actual physical location was not very important compared to bandwidth, a phenomenon termed as "spaceless proximity" by Baym (2006). Furthermore, the decentralization of communication has encouraged communication between "atomized individuals" (Green 2006).

On the Internet, whatever is being transmitted and exchanged (e.g., data, interactions, expressions, feelings or symbolisms) has been abstracted away from physical location. Internet communication is fundamentally de-territorialized, occurring in the immaterial, boundless, and ever-expanding matrix of Internet connections. The LM, on the other hand, afford the possibility of relating part of this content and its associated activities to physical locations, resulting in a "spatialization" of part of the Internet (Charitos 2006). The Internet can be understood as a noncentralized network of communication (Briggs and Burke 2005). Through the combination of Internet access and mobility, the decentralized and "bottom-up" nature of the Internet passes on to mobile telephony, which has so far been a centralized communication network.

At the same time, the Internet obtains the status of city infrastructure, that is, mostly an imperceptible layer of technology which is superimposed over the physical environment and with which people interact implicitly on a regular basis (McCullough 2004). Such a layer of infrastructure may effectively support social activity and assist the creation of location-aware information storage spaces or repositories of knowledge and memories, accessible by means of a mobile device. In accordance with Embodiment Theory (ET) (Dourish 2001) technology is seamlessly integrated in the social context. Similarly, the city itself is imparted some of the versatility and fluidity that characterizes digital information. As a result of this fluidity, the structure and meaning of technologically mediated space are ever-changing, and users have to adapt accordingly.

The significance of utilizing actual physical location as a precondition for the communication interface (as defined by Biocca and Delaney 1995) to an information and communication technologies (ICT) system lies in its naturalness, since humans continuously use location-related information. Even the most mundane day-to-day activities (walking, commuting, meeting friends) involve a series of location-related activities and decisions. Context remains important even in aspects of CMC from where it is seemingly left out. Although it can be argued that CMC renders it irrelevant by removing the physical environment from the interaction process, context still plays a prominent role in many online and other kinds of interpersonal or community interaction, mainly through language and conventions established by the participants (asynchronous technologies require users to explicitly convey contextual information provided implicitly in the case of interpersonal communication).

In the case of LM, geography regains its importance. Consequently, modern cities become actual "technospaces," a novel type of spatial formation where technology meets human practice and the linkage between built environment and information is reaffirmed.[2] The LM seem to subvert the trend of the diminution of geographic space that may result in confusion and uncertainty in finding agency in a rapidly globalizing mediated social life. Because of their respatializing effect, LM also hold the potential of bringing forth not only the geographical but also the cultural contextuality, or rather the notion that spaces have a history and a material continuity that is a vital counterpoint to the illusion of abstract and deterritorialized communication which has suffused much of the discourse on cyberfutures. This clearly opens up the possibility for abstract and neutral spaces to turn into meaningful places.

This seemingly paradoxical convergence of the physical and the digital environment may undermine certain characteristics that are typical of Internet communication, such as the adoption of multiple identities, anonymity, and absence of visible social markers, such as age or sex. In doing so, multiuser and group-based LM may act to invigorate collective identities mainly by moderating the individualism that is characteristic, if not inherent, in a large part of CMC.

It is well-known that Internet users are free to adopt multiple, changing, and fictional identities, often to a liberating and self-enhancing effect (Turkle 1996; Baym 2006). However, this is no longer the case when the other party is only a short distance away as in the case of multiuser LM applications such as LOCUNET.

Likewise, it is significantly more difficult to remain anonymous during LM use due to the physical proximity to other users, although this would be conceivably easier in the case of LM being used outside a group context. For instance, someone who only leaves feedback (e.g., geotag) about a particular locale is more likely to remain anonymous than a user who participates in a collective activity that entails close and repeated contact with other users. Nonetheless, anonymity does not necessarily imply lack of or deterioration of interpersonal relations, given that CMC allows socialization to occur on the basis of shared interests and common goals rather than inherited identities and/or physical attraction based on fixed bodies (as is more often than not the case in face-to-face interaction) (Baym 2006).

The role of nonverbal social cues is another distinguishing point. Internet communication is by definition a "cues-filtered-out" means of communication (Kiesler et al. 1984), characterized by the absence of the body and the nuances and social meaning inherent in nonverbal communication (Argyle 1998). Although reduced social cues do not necessarily eliminate the potential for personalized

---

[2]In the words of Thackara (2003), we may be talking of a "post-spectacular city," where digital technologies are used for meaningful human interaction.

communication, they are significantly lower on "social presence" compared to face-to-face communication (Hine 2000). By specializing CMC, LM essentially combine both CMC and face-to-face interaction. While they bring nonverbal cues back to the communication process, in those cases where users do not come into direct contact, the standard strategies for compensating for the lack of social cues in CMC may also be present during LM use.

The frequency and intensity of interpersonal interaction during LM use may be largely determined by certain design choices, as well as by the specifications of the system itself. In brief, factors that may encourage or discourage interpersonal communication include:

- The degree of location awareness of communication via LM: if one can communicate with everybody from any location, the need for proximity and interpersonal communication is diminished.
- The limitations imposed by the device on the richness of communication: a device that supports multimodal communication may be more successful in narrowing the gap between CMC and interpersonal communication; thus, the need for proximity and interpersonal communication may also diminish.
- Whether LM use is part of a purposeful and structured activity involving several users (a location-based game for instance): if users participate in a multiuser activity, they are expected to engage in CMC or interpersonal communication more frequently. On the other hand, a purely informative application of LM, as for instance geo-tagged advertisements, will probably remain focused on the individual.
- The limitations resulting from the design of the application: it is possible to regulate by means of location detection the user's ability to access stored information, or communicate with one another. For instance, in the LOCUNET system a user must be a short distance away from a geo-tag in order to access it.

The Situated Character of Social Encounters

Social encounters of any sort are always situated. Since they take place in particular contexts, they are always to be understood as fundamentally contextualized. For Goffman, an encounter is fundamentally interpersonal, communicative, and intersubjective. Goffman (1967) defined an "encounter" or "face engagement" as a phenomenon in which two persons engage one another in focused interaction, which is also mutual and participative. Face engagements comprise all those instances of two or more participants in a situation who join each other openly in maintaining a single focus of cognitive and visual attention. An encounter with many participants may entail different degrees of individual engagement, and this defines whether the gathering is fully or partly focused. When there are only two participants in a situation, the encounter results in a fully-focused gathering. With more than two participants, there may be persons who are present in the situation but are officially excluded from the encounter. Such an encounter is partly focused.

If more than three persons are co-present, there may be more than one encounter taking place in the same situation (multifocused gathering).

As Goffman demonstrated, in social situations, activity and interaction are "framed"; they unfold within a frame, that is, they make sense within a particular spatiotemporal context. In social interaction, the frame is often constructed jointly by the participants, a phenomenon described by Goffman (1967, 1990) as "the common definition of the situation" referring to two or more people describing the situation they are in with a high level of agreement. Their recognition of the frame coincides, even if they are in disagreement with one another.

The idea of a frame is critical to the idea of interaction as performance, because participation in a social encounter necessitates knowledge of what is going on. Participants have to agree that they are part of the same "definition of the situation." When interacting with one another, they also interact with the physical and social context that contains them. Context influences our action, behavior, and understanding in numerous and complex ways. First of all, there are context-specific conventions, principles that govern the moves used to initiate, conduct (i.e., communicate), and end an encounter. Phatic expressions, for example, are familiar framing practices that help us conduct an encounter successfully. Additionally, sociotemporal conditions are a crucial dimension of any social encounter. Furthermore, there is the cultural and social context from which any type of social encounter or activity emerges.

In addition to interpersonal interaction, mediated communication may also be seen as "a contextualized social phenomenon" (Thompson 1995). As such, it is always embedded in social contexts which influence, and are influenced by the forms of communication occurring within them, in contrast with Robins' argument that new media have produced a knowledge/communication space, which is "de-referentialized," that is, disconnected from local, situated knowledge and experience (Lievrouw and Livingstone 2002). On a similar note, Lievrouw and Livingstone (2002) conceptualize new media as ICTs, and their associated social contexts which incorporate the artifacts and devices that "enable and extend our abilities to communicate" the communication practices and activities in which we use these artifacts and devices, and "the social arrangements or organizations that form around the devices and practices." In general, new media shape and are shaped by the social, economic and cultural contexts they are situated in.

"Situatedness" can be found at the interplay between agent, situation, and context. The concept of context can be further divided into outer context (society, urbanity, space-time), inter-context (interpersonal conventions) and intra-context (the habitus, individuality). The factor "agent" involves the individuals and the activities they are involved in. Agency[3] is the locus and starting point for any experience. "Situation" refers to the activity at hand. Activities are not pursued in isolation; factors that influence the outcome of an activity may include community

---

[3] Agency is a sociological concept that underlies user actions and activities. Agency involves intentionality and motive, as well as content (information) and a consciousness of the above. Both user experience and interaction are about agency (Berger and Luckmann 1966; Giddens 1984; Bourdieu 1990).

membership and role, sociocultural background, and the history of past practices (Rizopoulos 2007). "Context" is more complex. The "outer-context" is the social, cultural, institutional, and economic conditions under which a particular medium arises, and within which media use takes place. It also involves the time and place of a mediated activity as central determinants and mediators of human experience.

The "inter-context" comprises social interaction practices, resources, rules, conventions, and habits (e.g., how people communicate, how conversations open up, how decisions are made, and how interpersonal dynamics evolve). The "intra-context" or *habitus* (Bourdieu 1972) stands for the skills, institutions, and habits a person has made his or her own, in order to function in the different social fields and levels of context.

A Theoretical Framework of Communication Via Locative Media

Given the complexity, novelty, and multidisciplinary nature of the aforementioned forms of contextualized interaction, we have attempted to outline a theoretical framework for approaching LM use as a series of contextualized, situated social encounters. To that end, this chapter highlights possible connections among a number of theoretical approaches dealing with the uses and the impact of sociotechnological systems and derived from social sciences, philosophy of everyday life, communication theory, and social psychology. This theoretical structure can be depicted as a schema of three nested circles (Fig. 4.1) (Diamantaki et al. 2007).

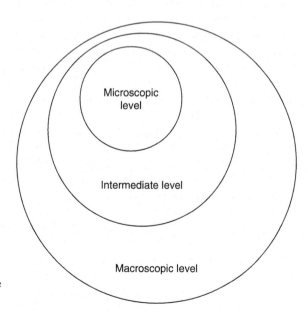

Fig. 4.1 The model of the three nested circles

The wider circle corresponds to the macroscopic level, the wider or "outer" context of contemporary urban culture, which forms the culturally and socially specific environment that surrounds all communication and media use.

The intermediate circle corresponds to an intermediate level of media use, approached from the perspective of Activity Theory, Actor-Network Theory (ANT) and ET. These three approaches offer compatible perspectives, which could be synthesized in order to form the background for understanding HCI and technologically mediated communication.

The inner circle is the microscopic level that focuses more specifically on user-to-user exchanges, acts, and relations. Here we focus on the interpersonal intra-group processes that define the communication system at hand.

These levels should be seen as inextricably linked. Thus, the use of new media and all new forms of communication arise from, and are conditioned by the wider urban culture in which they are embedded. On the other hand, no contemporary urban culture can be regarded as separate from the technologies, artifacts, actions, individualities, and experiences that continuously recreate its cultural content and meaning.

Locative Media Use and Communication in Urban Environments

The urban environment may be seen as the locus where the basic processes and forces of modernity are crystallized (Simmel 1971; Augé 1992). Urban studies have always depicted the city as a complex and highly ambivalent space, where the conflicting forces of modernity coexist in various and often unpredictable ways. Urbanity above all denotes a post-traditional order of mostly secondary, technologically mediated social relations evolving around the possibility of various associations, groupings, and social circles which are constantly multiplying, giving social integration new meanings. Augé (1992) appropriately describes the nature of urban space in post-industrial societies as an accumulation of "non-spaces" that people merely perceive or passively observe as a spectacle without paying them any real attention. In these spaces, city dwellers usually navigate without interacting with others, or relating to the environmental setting; they are mere passersby. These nonspaces are usually not experienced as places.

In order to investigate how and why locative communication media are used within the urban context, we have attempted to interweave three theoretical approaches that have been used in HCI, and present numerous similarities.

Activity Theory: Activity Theory is a theoretical framework that seeks to understand the relationship between consciousness and action. It considers consciousness "the product of an individual's interactions with people and artifacts in the context of everyday practical activity" (Kaptelinin and Nardi 2006). According to Activity Theory, "we are what we do," and what we do is strongly connected to the social world, which is complex and hybrid, consisting of humans and artifacts, tools, and technologies. Artefacts in Activity Theory are mediators of human activity that transform and are transformed by the user's perceptions, actions, motivations, and culture (Gay and Hembrooke 2004). Artefacts cannot be understood outside the context of human activity, that is, the needs they are supposed to satisfy, the way they are being used, and the history of their development.

In pursuing their goals, subjects appropriate tools and artifacts. Natural human capabilities are combined with external artifacts, forming functional organs. This allows humans to augment their preexisting abilities and to gain completely new ones (Kaptelinin and Nardi 2006). Functional organ formation is facilitated by the users' preexisting knowledge of the objects' operation (tool-related competencies) and their ability to determine the higher-level goals attainable through the use of the object and the means of accomplishing them (task-related competencies).

Actor-Network Theory: ANT (Latour 2005; Law 1992) is a distinctive constructivist approach known for its insistence on the agency of nonhumans. Certain sociotechnological hybrids are created by the combinations of actors and artifacts (Graham 2004). These hybrids are actor-networks which incorporate social activity and environmental conditions in a nonlinear and complex way. Humans and nonhumans are treated symmetrically and defined relationally as nodes in the same total network. An actor in ANT is anything made to act, whether human or nonhuman. There is no difference in the ability of technology, humans, animals and other nonhumans to act. By engaging with an actor-network, actors become part of the unified web of relations linking humans and nonhumans.

Embodiment Theory: As a model for HCI and one of the basic tenets of social computing, ET (Dourish 2001) views technology as situated in a social world. The ET provides a model for designing systems of technological interaction by taking into account social action and construction of social meanings that surround technologies.

"Meaning" is an important and recurring concept in ET. We interact with technological systems by constructing social meanings. Users construct meaningful events by "appropriating" the physical and the conceptual elements of the world around them. The ET emphasizes the context and the social situatedness of media use, in accordance with the view that interaction cannot be examined separately from the contexts within which it takes place, and discusses the concepts of "engagement" and "action."

Common Threads Among Theoretical Approaches

There are common conceptual and analytical threads that connect these theories and from which a set of basic premises and criteria can be derived and guide the design and evaluation of mobile LM.

Media use is a form of social action: Users act on the basis of personal (though culturally conditioned) intentionalities and motives and are perpetually engaged in meaning-production processes. Users "appropriate" and "construct" the media they use.

Technological media are integrated and embedded in the social world: Technological artifacts are not simply tools used to carry out various tasks; they are media which communicate human experience and are an integral part of the social world.

Media use involves meaning-making processes: Being engaged with technology involves not only material, but also semiotic and social dimensions. We are involved with technology through "practice," which is not mere action. Practice unites action with meaning. Actions produce meaning, and meanings produce actions. Therefore, a technological system is incorporated in a set of practices through which it acquires symbolic, individual, emotional value.

Media use is contextual and socially situated: Being an integral part of everyday life practices, technologies and media, which are all forms of social action, are context-specific, user-specific and socially-situated.

Space is practiced: Space may essentially be redefined as a construction of the actions of its inhabitants. De Certeau (1984) defines urban space according to the patterns of those who use it. Thus, "space is a practiced place." Walkers ascribe a logic to the city through their daily movements and intersections. In turn, space is delineated by their itineraries. This sense of practiced space is greatly enhanced by LM use.

The Case of LOCUNET: An Applied Approach

The design and evaluation of the LOCUNET experiment was based on the theoretical framework described so far, complemented by theories of intra- and inter-group interaction among both conventional and technologically mediated groups. These theoretical sources directed us toward a set of principles for the design (scenario, architecture) of the application itself and provided specific epistemological and methodological guidelines for its execution and evaluation.

The formulation of a comprehensive theoretical background resulted in a set of fundamental research questions which guided the research conducted for the LOCUNET project, and can be summarized as follows:

- How can this new technology be designed and used to facilitate technology-mediated group communication and enhance the experience of the group?
- What are the factors that should be taken into consideration to improve effectiveness, enjoyability and performance of mobile group communication engaged in social communication?
- How (and to what extent) does LM use affect the users' perception and experience of the environment they navigate?

The contextual and socially situated nature of media use should be regarded as a decisive factor for design and evaluation. Technology is always embedded in a specific cultural, environmental, and material milieu (the macroscopic or outer-context), such as urban space, which influences, and is influenced by technology use. The distinction between context and content was highlighted by Dourish (2001). Context is "the outcome of embodied practice." Technological artifacts are situated in a given context not only in terms of their design, but more so in terms of how they are being appropriated by the users for whom they were initially designed.

Practice is not just a task-oriented activity; it is a more complex meaning-making process enacted by conscious social actors who are always sociotemporally situated.

This understanding of context as enacted through practice led us to a user-centric approach and to a context-sensitive research methodology. Context sensitivity in this case refers to making observations, collecting data, and essentially conducting empirical research into the practices and meaning-making processes of real users (the intra-context or "microscopic" level).

Thus, we opted for a combination of "emic" and "etic"[4] research approaches in order to focus on real users' experiences, test the users' conceptions against our theoretical understandings, and vice versa. This choice was also dictated by our view of technology and media use as an essentially mundane embodied activity embedded into everyday life in the city. The LOCUNET project was essentially an experiment in navigation and group activity in a shared hybrid spatiotemporal context, effectively combining elements of both interpersonal interaction (which requires physical co-presence in a common spatiotemporal context) and CMC (which potentially transcends the limits of space and time). LOCUNET used part of the city of Athens "as a canvas" (Benford et al. 2006), a physically built environment merged with its digital representations, thereby producing a hybrid spatial context and bringing the rules of communication and social interaction into the public sphere of the urban environment. The digital representation of the urban environment was deliberately abstract with an appropriate use of color and form, so as to enhance certain environmental elements that could be significant to the activity (see Sect. 5.1). This approach was preferred to using satellite images or 3D representations of the environment due to the increased cognitive load they would impose on the user and their complexity, which was considered unnecessary for the activity in question.

The system we designed and the communicative experience it supported had to be assessed at the level of the individual user. The accumulation of individual evaluations and perceptions of the system, the activity and the external environment allowed us to draw certain conclusions and identify some strengths and weaknesses of the application and the system. However, social interaction is an essentially inter-subjective and interpersonal affair, necessitating a shift of focus from the

---

[4]The distinction between an "emic" and an "etic" level of analysis in the social sciences originates from linguistics and is analogous to the distinction between a "phonemic" and a "phonetic" approach to language (Pike 1967). According to linguistic and anthropologist Kenneth Pike, who invented the terms, there are two ways to approach a cultural or social system, as there are two ways to approach the phonemic system of language. We can either choose to see the object of our research "from within" (an emic approach), or "from outside" (an etic approach). The "emic" approach focuses on the meanings and understandings of the members that make up a given social group, whereas the "etic" approach is based on the use of concepts and categories that come from outside the group and which are meaningful to the scientists or observers. Although there has been much debate on which one of the two levels is the most appropriate for the study of social groups, in fact the "emic" and the "etic" approaches are neither antithetical nor mutually exclusive; in practice, they are proven to be complementary, since social research usually applies both emit and etic methods and interpretations in order to analyze social phenomena.

Fig. 4.2 A screenshot of the
LOCUNET mobile device
interface

strictly individual to a more interpersonal and collective level. Consequently, we
chose a group-based approach, applying the LOCUNET platform to the design and
implementation of a competitive communicative activity (which also functioned
as a test-bed for the validity of our theoretical framework). This choice was
compatible with the interactional potential of LM, but it was also dictated by realistic
reasoning. Research at the macroscopic level would require a more widespread and
mass-oriented usage of this medium, something which is planned, but has not yet
been realized.

In light of the above, we investigated:

- Group awareness and the sense of belonging to and being part of the group
- The presentation of personal identity and the perception of the identities of others
- The mechanisms of performativity, discourse, and team cooperation
- The observation of individual and team strategies

- The observation not only of the rules of the activity, but also of naturally occurring social protocols related to group formation when people are co-located in the context of a shared activity
- The environmental experience in hybrid (physical and virtual) space

These directions necessitated the use of various evaluation methods, (from interpretative-ethnographic to quasi-experimental approaches) derived from several disciplines including HCI, social, and environmental psychology, and cultural anthropology.

Data was mostly collected through questionnaires, group interviews, in situ observation, sketches of spatial knowledge, and open-ended post-activity reporting, in an attempt to explore how the users themselves perceived and framed new types of social presence. The collected data were subjected to qualitative and quantitative analysis. The content that users generated and exchanged, the actions they performed, and their navigational patterns (as derived from the system's log) also provided complementary information about the participants' levels of attention, interest, and participation. In brief, the multiplicity of the methods employed enabled us to investigate player experience by taking into account the situated, dynamic, and distributed nature of a location-based system (Fig. 4.2).

The LOCUNET System and Activity Scenario

Description of the Activity

As a means toward evaluating the theoretical framework presented in the earlier sections, a multiuser activity involving LM use was organized. The activity took place in a central area of Athens, Greece. The participants used GPS-enabled cell phones and formed two opposing "teams."

The setting: The selected area was largely off-limit to motor traffic and included several environmental features that promoted playful and exploratory navigational behavior (e.g., hiding places, bridges, footpaths, etc.) (Fig. 4.3).

The interface: A map of the selected area, with the user's avatar at its centre, was displayed on each mobile device. The avatar was essentially an emoticon depicting the user's emotional state (as set by the user himself). Totally there were four possible emotional states: "happy," "sad," "indifferent" and "confused" (e.g., requesting technical assistance). The user's navigational experience was egocentric, since the avatar remained at the centre of the screen while the map moved with the user.

The area map was designed so that certain elements that are generally considered particularly useful to pedestrians, such as bridges, gardens, parks, walls, etc., would be highlighted.

As users navigate the area, various digital "objects" appear on their screen in the form of suitcase icons (indicative of their mobility). Being entirely digital, these

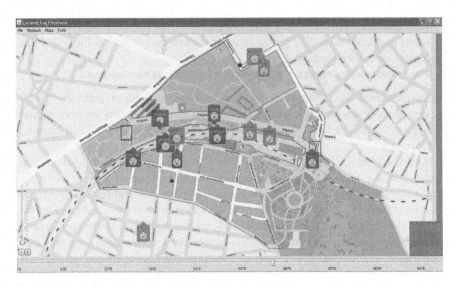

Fig. 4.3 A map of the area, where the LOCUNET activity takes place, as displayed on the playback tool

objects are accessible only via the mobile device. The activity's objective is to score more points than the opposing team. Points are scored through the collection of objects. A user who is sufficiently close to an object (within 5 m) can "collect" it. Upon collecting an object, the user's avatar changes to that of a suitcase-carrying emoticon, (reflecting the fact that the object is in the user's possession). An object may remain in the user's possession for 2 min, unless intentionally released sooner. When the 2-min time limit is reached, the object is automatically "dropped," wherever the user happens to be at that time. When dropped in this manner, the object cannot be immediately picked up again by the same player. More often than not, the distance between the object and the HQ will be too great for a user to travel given the 2-min time limit. Therefore, players will have to collaborate with one another in order to capture objects. When an object is dropped onto either of the special areas designated as "team headquarters," it is "captured" by the team to which the headquarters belong and this team's score increases by one point. The team with the highest score at the end of the activity wins.

In addition to objects, the game includes another type of digital elements, called "info-packs." These are containers of digital information in the form of text, sound, image, or video. Info-packs are associated with a physical location, and access to them is gained in the same way. Unlike objects, though, info packs are immovable. Info-packs are one way of asynchronous CMC provided by the LOCUNET system. A series of info-packs are created by the designers in order to guide players through the activity. In this way, the potential for embedding narrative within the activity by means of structuring and locating related content in physical space arises. Players can create info-packs by typing text or using the phone to record sound/video or take pictures. Once generated, an info-pack is placed at the user's location. Its contents can be useful (e.g., directions to various objects) or misleading (e.g., instructions aimed at delaying members of the opposing team). Another means of asynchronous communication is text messaging: users are able to send text messages to a single user, the members of a given team, or every user who participates in the game.

The authoring tool: An authoring tool was developed as part of the LOCUNET project for the purpose of creating any number of multiuser activities similar to the one described earlier. Several parameters of the activity, such as the number of teams, the number of users per team, the number of objects, object possession time limit, the "active area" around objects and info packs (wherein it is possible to manipulate them), and the overall duration of the activity, are fully adjustable. Additionally, a new version of the authoring tool offering the possibility of "object access prerequisites" (i.e., conditions that will regulate whether users may access an object or info-pack[5]) is currently under development.

The authoring tool's structure promotes a view of an activity scenario as modular, consisting of numerous distinct but interconnected parts. This modularity is expected to facilitate research on the different aspects of multiuser communicational activities via LM.

The playback tool: The users' movement and their exchange of content were recorded in a log file as the activity proceeded. This log file can be played back on a graphical interface so as to facilitate research into the users' spatial and communicative behavior during the activity.

The Technological Infrastructure

The system essentially consists of two components, the client (Nokia N95 phones) and the server. The GPS data and user commands (e.g., objects picked up or dropped) are transmitted by each client device to the server, which updates the game state accordingly, at 5-s intervals. All server–client communication (including text messages) was accomplished via mobile Internet.

The system generally operated in an efficient manner. The majority of problems noted were due to server crashes. Every content exchange was performed via the server; consequently, any problem that caused the server to crash also caused the activity to temporarily stop. Server crashes were observed relatively frequently at the initial stages of the activity, and depended partly on the overall amount of traffic on the mobile operator network. However, this problem was relatively easy to correct, since the client automatically attempted to reconnect once its

---

[5] For instance, users who belong to the Team A cannot access Object no. five unless a user who belongs to the same team has accessed info-pack No. 2 OR the team has already captured three objects.

connection with the server was broken. Another source of trouble was the variable accuracy of the GPS. Trial runs revealed that the Nokia N95's inbuilt GPS module was very inaccurate. Another factor that may have influenced the accuracy of the GPS is the area selected for the activity to take place. While some parts of it were flat and open, other parts were full of tall buildings. External modules were used as a solution to both problems, and only minor deviations were occasionally observed.

Despite these problems, the participants considered the system easy to use. This ease of use may be attributed to the fact that the rules were fairly simple and straightforward. Although this simplicity may have resulted in a less interesting experience, it is believed to have reduced cognitive load on the part of the users and rendered the system less prone to rules-related technical errors.

The User Testing Procedure

After a briefing session about the activity, participants were asked to fill a demographic questionnaire. After the activity (which lasted approximately one hour), participants filled questionnaires regarding the usability of the system they had just used (*Standard Usability Scale* – SUS proposed by Brooke 1996), the communicative acts they engaged in, their attitudes toward LM, and their perception of the environment. They were asked to produce sketches of the environment they had experienced during the activity for the purpose of investigating their spatial memory. Subsequently, they participated in two focus groups: one regarding the experience of using the system (which complemented the quantitative usability evaluation methods) and another one regarding group-based communication during the activity, as well as an evaluation of the overall experience. The overall process, including the activity itself, lasted for approximately 7 h.

Preliminary Findings and Conclusions

In this section, part of the findings of the LOCUNET project that deal with the users' conception of the communicative potential and implications of LM, as well as their influence on the users' spatial experience, are presented and discussed in light of the theoretical framework outlined in the earlier sections.

The LOCUNET experience was very much akin to what Goffman termed "social encounter"; it was a short-lived, bounded, and regulated focused interaction, a "multifocused multiparticipant gathering" during which participants had to make decisions and to cooperate with each other through social interaction. Although users acted as individual players, during the game they maintained a single and shared focus of cognitive and visual attention, bounded by the activity's rules.

Generally, LOCUNET participants were successful in defining and continuously reaffirming the "common definition of a situation" that is necessary for the effective pursuit of their teams' goals (Goffman 1967). Despite the short duration of the activity, there was an emergent sense of group identity, typically manifested as a sense of being an integral part of a group, sharing a set of common goals with other group members, a willingness to assist them during the course of the game, and a collective feeling of satisfaction or disappointment caused by the team's winning or losing the game, respectively. Certain participants decided to work in pairs, thus forming ad hoc subgroups within the basic unit of the group. In addition, the participants were willing to keep in touch with their fellow co-players outside the context of the activity. It can thus be suggested that if the duration of the activity had been longer, "true" group formation may have been observed. Thus, although the development of group feelings does not in any way equal collectivity or shared identity, we should not underestimate the prospects of group-building through these systems. The same can be said with respect to the adoption of roles. In the LOCUNET activity, the participants did not believe they had assumed distinct roles. However, the majority of the participants engaged in specific types of action that could, given time, coalesce to form distinct roles. Additionally, it could be suggested that, given enough time, such quasi-group formations may coalesce to full-fledged groups.

LOCUNET users held stable identities throughout the activity and they invoked them in their post-activity report. This is in sharp contrast to the anonymity and identity fluidity present in much of Internet CMC, where the vast number of users and their invisibility ensure that their anonymity can be retained (in contrast, LM users may be co-present at times). The co-presence of LM users allowed for spontaneous use of modalities typically used during face-to-face interaction, such as voice, gestures, eye contact, etc. (after all, the use of LM may entail aspects of interpersonal interaction). Users were found to simultaneously experience two different types of sense of presence: a *physical* sense of presence, which the human experiences when physically existing within or close by a mediated or nonmediated environment, and a *social* sense of presence, which relates to the sense of proximity or co-existence with a virtual and possibly remotely located social entity.

Participants of the LOCUNET activity experienced a "spatialized temporality" (a simultaneous or quasi-simultaneous temporality), rather than a de-located connectivity. The users attested to a space-embedded and situated proximity (echoing the respatialization thesis, central in our theoretical framework). Our research findings also testified to the crucial differences between LM and internet communication alluded to earlier in this chapter (see Sect. 4.2). LOCUNET participants perceived the spatial context of the activity as a hybrid environment. They confirmed the view that the activity took place within both the physical and the digital environment simultaneously. The majority reported having felt present in both these aspects of the environment at the same time, while others alternated between them. This hybrid character of the environmental experience during LM use was also reported as one of the most appealing elements of the entire activity.

The satisfaction users derive from LM use may also be related to their ability to attach meaning to specific locations in the physical environment as a result of their activity in this hybrid spatiotemporal context. The majority of the participants reported that elements of the environment within which the LOCUNET activity took place (and to which users were generally indifferent prior to the activity) had acquired a new meaning as a result of their experience. They "saw the familiar urban space under a new light," indicating that LM may have the potential to transform "empty" space into socially meaningful interaction spaces and thus alter the experience of urban public space as such.

Concluding Remarks and Future Work

The CMC tends to become the dominant paradigm for communication between groups in modern society. The widespread worldwide adoption of mobile communication and the advent of location-based services offer unprecedented opportunities for anytime-anywhere communication, collaboration, and social interaction in shared interpersonal and group encounters. The use of LM affords a hybrid spatial experience, as the mediated communication space is mapped onto the physical urban environment, allowing for new kinds of collaborative mediated interaction, while also offering the possibility of face-to-face interaction. Being present in this environment is itself a social situation capable of generating novel and meaningful forms of interaction.

Rheingold (2002) believes that the widespread use of mobile Internet will result in a new array of abilities: "mobile Internet, when it really arrives, will not be just a way to do old things while moving, it will be a way to do things that couldn't be done before." Thus, LM can act as Activity Theory's "functional organs" in augmenting human capabilities. Furthermore, new hybrid forms of communication and social behavior at various levels (individual, group, community) may emerge as a result of LM use. However, the research we have so far conducted does not allow for a definite answer to the question as to whether these new forms of social interaction will entail a strong sense of collective identity, and to what extent this sense of identity will be attributable to the nature and intrinsic characteristics of LM. In any case, mobile location-aware applications that involve a large enough number of users, and last long enough for such patterns to emerge are expected to allow for an in-depth investigation of social and cultural practices by means of suitable methodological approaches. Such an investigation is planned as the next step in our research.

Some other future developments are underway. The most significant of these is the design and development of a desktop interface that will allow remote users to participate in activities supported by the LOCUNET system. This desktop interface will feature a 3D representation of the urban area where the activity will be taking place. The degree of realism of this representation is, however, still under consideration. It is hoped that the combination of the mobile and the desktop interfaces will allow for a more in-depth investigation of the complex hybrid environmental experience of LM users and the significance of location-awareness as a parameter of mediated communication.

Acknowledgments The research project titled "LOCUNET" is supported by the Greek General Secretariat of Research and Technology under the framework of the Operational Program PEP Attikis, Measure 1.2. The Program is co-financed (70%) by the European Fund of Regional Development (EFRD), which aims to facilitate the reduction of the inequalities within the European Union regions.

References

Argyle M (1998) Bodily communication. Routledge, London

Augé M (1992) Non places: introduction to an anthropology of supermodernity. Verso, London

Baym N (2006) Interpersonal life online. In: Lievrouw LA & Livingstone S (eds). The handbook of new media (Updated Student Edition), 35–54. Sage, London

Benford S, Flintham M, Drodz A, Tandavanitj N, Adams M & Farr JR (2006) The design and experience of the location-based performance uncle roy all around you. Leonardo Electronic Almanac 14.03 2006, http://leoalmanac.org/journal/Vol_14/lea_v14_n03-04/roy.asp. Retrieved 7 June 2008

Berger PL & Luckmann T (1966) The social construction of reality: a treatise in the sociology of knowledge. Anchor Books, NY

Biocca F & Delaney B (1995) Immersive virtual reality technology. In: Biocca F & Levy, MR (eds). Communication in the age of virtual reality, 57–124. Lawrence Erlbaum Associates, Hillsdale

Boden D & Molotch H (2004) Cyberspace meets the compulsion of proximity. In: Graham, S (ed). The cybercities reader, 101–105. Routledge, London

Bourdieu P (1990) The Logic of Practice, Polity Press: Cambridge

Bourdieu P (1972) Outline of a theory of practice. Cambridge University Press, Cambridge

Briggs A & Burke P (2005) A social history of the media: from gutenberg to the internet. Polity Press, Cambridge

Brooke JSUS (1996) A "Quick and Dirty" usability scale. In Jordan PW, Thomas B, Weerdmeester BA & McClelland AL (eds), Usability evaluation in industry. Taylor & Francis, London

De Certeau M (1984) The practice of everyday life. University of California Press, Berkeley

Charitos D (2006) Spatialising the internet: new types of hybrid mobile communication environments and their impact on spatial design within the urban context. In: Bourdakis, V & Charitos D (eds) Communicating space(s): Proceedings of the 24th eCAADe Conference, 160-167. University of Thessaly, Volos

Diamantaki K, Charitos D, Tsianos N, Lekkas Z (2007) Towards investigating the social dimensions of using LM within the urban context. In: Proceedings of the 3rd IET International Conference on Intelligent Environments, pp. 53–60. Ulm, Germany

Dourish P (2001) Where the action is: the foundations of embodied interaction. The MIT Press, Massachusetts

Flew T (2005) New media: an introduction (2nd edition). Oxford University Press, Melbourne

Gay G & Hembrooke H (2004) Activity-centered design: an ecological approach to designing smart tools and usable systems. The MIT Press, Massachusetts

Giddens A (1984) The constitution of society. Polity Press, Cambridge

Goffman E (1967) Interaction ritual: essays on face-to-face behavior. Doubleday and Co., New York

Goffman E (1990) The presentation of self in everyday life. Penguin, London

Graham S (ed) (2004) The cybercities reader. Routledge, London

Green N (2006) On the move: technology, mobility, and the mediation of social time and space. In: Hassan R and Thomas J (eds). The new media theory reader, 249–265. Open University Press, Maidenhead

Hemment D (2005) The mobile effect. Convergence 11 (2): 32–39

Hine C (2000) Virtual ethnographer. Sage Publications, London

Kaptelinin V & Nardi B (2006) Acting with technology: activity theory and interaction design. The MIT Press, Massachusetts

80   K. Diamantaki et al.

Kiesler S, Siegel J, McGuire TW (1984) "Social psychological aspects of computer-mediated communication", American Psychologist, 39(10): 1123–1134

Latour B (2005) Reassembling the social: an introduction to actor-network theory. Oxford University Press, New York

Law J (1992) Notes on the Theory of the Actor Network: Ordering, Strategy and Heterogeneity. Centre for Science Studies, Lancaster University, http://www.comp.lancs.ac.uk/sociology/papers/Law-Notes-on-ANT.pdf

Lievrouw LA & Livingstone S (2002). Introduction to the First Edition. In: Lievrouw LA & Livingstone S (eds). The handbook of new media (Updated Student Edition), 15–32. Sage, London

McCullough M (2004) Digital ground: architecture, pervasive computing and environmental nnowing. The MIT Press, Massachusetts

Pike K (1967) Language in relation to a unified theory of structure of human behavior (2nd edition), Mouton, The Hague

Rheingold H (2002) Smart mobs: the next social revolution – transforming cultures and communities in the age of instant access. Basic Books, Massachusetts

Rizopoulos C (2007) An activity-based perspective of interacting with ambient intelligence systems. In: Proceedings of the 3rd IET International Conference on Intelligent Environments, 81–88. Ulm, Germany

Simmel G (1971) Metropolis and the mental life. In: Levine D (ed). Georg Simmel: on individuality and social forms (Selected Writings), 321–340. The University of Chicago Press, Chicago

Souza e Silva A (2003) Mobile networks and public spaces: bringing multi-user environments into the physical space. In: Ascott R (ed). Electronic proceedings of the 2003 consciousness reframed international conference. CaiiA STAR, University of Wales College, Newport

Thackara J (2003) "The post-spectacular city", lecture at Creativity and the City Conference, Amsterdam, 25 September 2003. http://www.doorsofperception.com/archives/2003/09/the_postspectac_1.php. Retrieved 17 September 2007

Thompson JB (1995) The media and modernity: a social theory of the media. Polity Press, Cambridge

Turkle S (1996) Life on the screen: identity in the age of the internet. Simon & Schuster, New York

Tuters M (2004) The locative commons: situating location-based media in urban public space. In: Electronic Proceedings of the 2004 Futuresonic Conference, Manchester, UK

Weiser M (1991) The computer for the twenty-first century. Scientific American 265 (3): 94–104

Chapter 5
Shared-Screen Interaction: Engaging Groups in Map-Mediated Nonverbal Communication

Konstantinos Chorianopoulos and Tim Rieniets

Introduction

In this chapter, we examine how mass communication can be extended with collaborative interactivity on a shared screen that facilitates and promotes cooperation between two opposing groups of people. In particular, a shared screen that displays a map narrative becomes a representation of a shared physical space, which is claimed by two conflicting groups. In our work, a double screen projection is used to portray dynamic graphics and narratives, which are made interactive through motion-tracking input from a camera.

In the 1970s and 1980s, early video-art installations explored the links between television, architectural space, and community identity. During the 1990s and later, the artistic inspiration caught on with research labs, which developed several systems for Computer Supported Cooperative Work (CSCW). In contrast to the traditional CSCW approach, we focus on nonverbal communication and we make an effort to bring together artistic and scientific aspects of earlier works. For this purpose we take the city of Jerusalem as a case study–a city of extraordinary historic and religious meaning.

The video installation depicts the Israeli-Palestinian struggle for territorial and demographic hegemony, which has transformed the city into a unique urban constellation. The resources and content of the interactive video installation are based on a book published on the same topic, titled "City of Collision: Jerusalem and the Principles of Conflict Urbanism" (Misselwitz and Rieniets 2006). The book presents a unique collection of essays, maps, and photographs, gathered by Israeli, Palestinian, and international authors (Fig. 5.1). However, it cannot provide the immediacy and engagement opportunities of a large-scale interactive video system, which is installed in a public space.

K. Chorianopoulos (✉)
Bauhaus University of Weimar, Bauhausstrasse 7b, 99423 Weimar, Germany
e-mail: k.chorianopoulos@archit.uni-weimar.de

K.S. Willis et al. (eds.), *Shared Encounters*, Computer Supported Cooperative Work, 81
DOI 10.1007/978-1-84882-727-1_5, © Springer-Verlag London Limited 2010

Fig. 5.1 A two-page spread from the book "City of Collision-Jerusalem and the Principles of Conflict Urbanism"

The interactivity with the video installation is considered to be complementary to the book, providing entirely new forms of conceptualization, mediation, and interaction. In order to realize this project, there was a need for close collaboration between diverse disciplines (McCullough 2004). Urban research provides appropriate graphic representations of a city. Architectural design supports the physical part (form) of the installation. Computer engineering enables the implementation of the dynamic interaction between people and data and most importantly, interaction design is used to translate the static data from the book (image, text, maps) into an elegant and easy-to-use participative video installation.

In the rest of this chapter, we discuss the interaction design process and we then present the implementation of the core concepts into a coherent interactive video installation. We conclude with a discussion about the application of advanced user interface technologies in art and provide some suggestions on the issues and obstacles encountered in this interdisciplinary work effort.

Interaction Design

The main design concept involves the double projection of a slideshow on a semi-transparent screen, which portrays the conflicting image that two groups of people hold about the same physical space.

In addition, we employ real and digital shadows in order to motivate participation and awareness of the image of the other side. The role of interactivity is central in the design of the system because it invites people to influence the presentation, thus making an inference to the historical impact of human actions on the current state of things, as well as to the potential for positive change. In terms of interactivity format there are two concepts: (1) interactivity with real shadows, and (2) interactivity with digital shadows.

The aforementioned initial requirements (double projection, shadows) were mapped into a basic set of concepts that guided the rest of the interaction design. The basic interactivity concepts have many implications for the technical requirements and, at the same time, the interactivity options are defined by what is technically possible. Although this is a linear manifestation of our creative process, it is worth noting that the actual design process was rather iterative. As a matter of fact, alternative scenarios were revealed through the design process that are discussed in the subsequent sections.

Early Requirements and Concepts

An early requirement for the system was to develop an interactive video installation that allows users to navigate the information on the map about Jerusalem. The initial idea was to mix a set of existing map layers and text from the book according to the position of the viewer. By changing position, some layers would be highlighted, whereas other layers would move to the background. This design concept aimed at a technical and a metaphoric effect: (1) The viewer could change the content of the map by moving in front of the screen, and (2) by moving and changing the layers, the viewer would physically and metaphorically change the image of[1] the city (Lynch 1960).

A direct implication of this early concept was that the input device, which is capturing the position and movement of the users, needed to be placed on the ceiling. An inspection of the installation site and lab experiments with video footage proved that this requirement could not be met easily, because the final site floor was black. Despite the advances in computer vision, the majority of the artistic applications have to make some assumptions about the environmental conditions at the site of installation (O'Sullivan 2007).

Although we were very fond of the idea that the presence and position of participants could affect the presentation, the conditions at the installation were not suitable and we did not want to employ a white carpet, as suggested by colleagues (Weber et al. 2007). Therefore, we had to think of alternative concepts that fulfilled the basic requirement of map navigation in a simple, engaging, and intuitive way. Moreover, the design concept should work, regardless of environmental conditions. In general, the positioning of the camera on the ceiling would have been a very flexible solution and it would have provided a straightforward two-dimensional navigation.

---

[1] http://www.v3ga.net/processing/BlobDetection/

Nevertheless, we found that this unforeseen obstacle allowed the effort of the design thinking to become the focus at the core of the requirements for this installation.

Double Projection

'As long as I have remembered myself, I have moved within two strata of consciousness, wandering in a landscape that, instead of having three spatial dimensions, had six: a three-dimensional Jewish space underlain by an equally three-dimensional Arab space.' Meron Benvenisti from the Book "City of Collision" (Misselwitz and Rieniets 2006)

The main concept for this video installation originates from the content itself: Two groups – Israelis and Palestinians – are claiming the same space, politically as well as through their different perceptions, narratives and memories. In fact, a shared screen becomes a representation of a shared physical space, which is claimed by two opposing groups (Fig. 5.2).

While two-dimensional printed maps can hardly depict this multilayered urban reality of Jerusalem, a double interactive projection opens up entirely new possibilities. In particular, a floating, semitransparent screen allowed for video projections from two sides, each side presenting a particular view of Jerusalem – an Israeli view in blue hues, and a Palestinian perspective in green hues. As the screen consists of semitransparent material, both projections are mixed on the surface and are unified to one coherent representation of the otherwise divided city of Jerusalem.

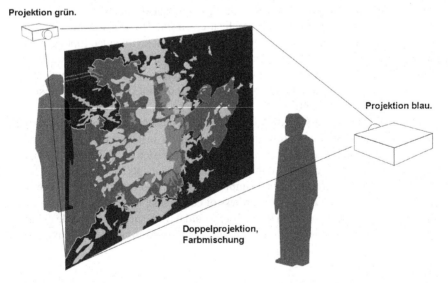

Fig. 5.2 Each of the two sides in the video installation corresponds to the respective (Israeli, Palestinian) image of the city

Additive Color Mix

By projecting from two sides onto the translucent screen, colors are mixed according to the principles of additive color mixing: the more colors that are mixed, the lighter they become (Fig. 5.3). This effect supports the concept of the double-projection of the cartographic essay. When the video installation shows a map of Jerusalem, the map consists of both views, the Israeli view (blue projection) and the Palestinian view (green projection).

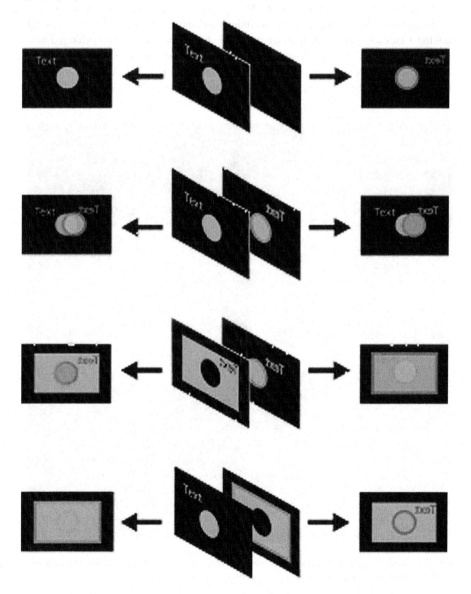

Fig. 5.3 Examples of different types of color mixing on a double projection system

Real vs. Artificial Shading

In addition to the requirement for digital interaction, we emphasized a parallel requirement for physical embodied interaction. When the viewer moves in front of the screen there are two effects: (1) the light from the projector is blocked by the body of a person, which creates an analogue (real) shadow on the respective side, and (2) at the same time digital cameras are capturing the presence of people and perform dynamic effects that combine the digital (artificial) shadow with the slide show.

We realized that although a real shadow would have been nice simply on its own, we recognized that people might misunderstand the installation and try to avoid making shadows. Thus, the need for a digital shadow was also acknowledged as a main requirement. By shading one projection, the projection of the other side suddenly appears clearly through the semitransparent fabric of screen (Fig. 5.4). This effect allows for a playful exploration of the projection on both sides, and

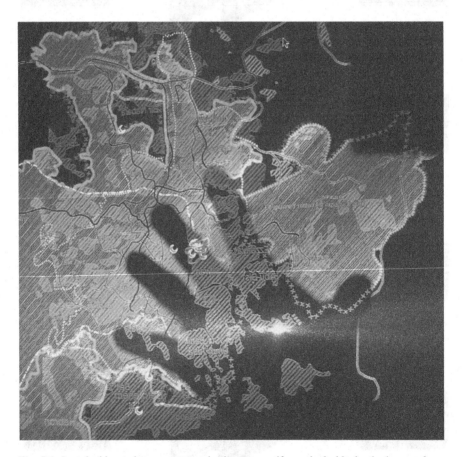

Fig. 5.4 In a double semi-transparent projection screen, if somebody blocks the image of one side, then the image of the other side is revealed

confronts the viewer with an important realization: *the more a viewer on one side is hiding (forgetting) his own "view" by shading the projection, the more he can recognize (understand) the other side.*

Final Requirements and Refined Concepts

After an analysis of the basic concepts and of the aesthetic requirements, we concluded that the interactivity had to be very subtle and the system should be technically robust and easy to both install and keep running. Moreover, we realized that the horizontal motion tracking (i.e., camera together with projector instead of the ceiling) would be the best option, because it is technically less sophisticated, less expensive (no white carpet or fancy hats are required), and it invites people to directly interact with the screen. In particular, interactivity was realized with real and artificial (digital) shadows. A "digital shadow" is an image stored inside a computer, so it could be processed in various ways. A digital shadow can be changed and transformed to create various effects (Levin 2006). First, shadows can be frozen for some seconds, or the motion of shadows can be delayed. This effect would enable people to "wipe out" their map. Moreover, digital shadows can be dynamically outlined, blurred, or they can display text and photos.

We were also aware that the shadow, however appealing, might evoke the same misunderstandings (i.e., "I am disrupting the projection"). Therefore, we had to evaluate several concepts for inviting and facilitating the involvement of the attendees. Some of these ideas included digitally transformed shadows, so that the shadow would look artificial and not be confused with the real one, or the use of the digital shadow to temporally wipe out parts of the map. Moreover, we decided to pause the slideshow when a person was close to the map. A technical implication of the latter effect was that if we employed pausing, then the two computers had to be synchronized through networking. Otherwise, the whole storyboard would be out of sync after participants have walked-in and out of the installation space.

In summary, the refined concepts mentioned here were mapped into a number of requirements which bring the interaction design closer to the final architectural and multimedia design. The detailed requirements are analyzed in the following subsections.

Maps and Narrative

The employment of maps into the video installation served two purposes: First, the maps are the graphic basis for the double projection. Early exploratory experiments revealed that the more graphic information that is projected on the screen, the better the effect of the double projection works (Fig. 5.4). Second, the maps portray all the information needed to understand the city and the urban conflict. However, the maps are rather abstract. Therefore, it became apparent that maps should be augmented with additional information in order to be legible without the full text of the book being at hand. Ideally, the maps would become most legible if a narrative was provided. The narrative was envisioned to run as a slideshow that embedded text and symbols that would refer to the current map, such as a map legend. Moreover, the slideshow between the two sides needed to be synchronized, in order to allow for comparison of the two conflicting "images of the city" through the semitransparent double projection. The slideshow consists of single layers projected one after another. Each layer contained brief text legends (e.g., "Wall; 700 km long; 8 m high; expropriating 11% of West Bank area").

Although the initial installation was planned to take place at an architecture faculty, future installation could not make such a specific assumption about the scientific background of the users. The information should also assume an audience who are not able to understand the urban scale.

Outline Effect

One favorite concept involved the drawing of an outline around the digital shadow. The outline of the digital shadow serves multiple purposes:

- It makes the "holes" (digital and real shadows) in the map more visible.
- If a person moves close to the projector, then the outline becomes a metaphorical visualization of the urban causalities like an outline on the asphalt. This concept is based on the idea of the white-chalk outline that police paint around a victim at a crime-scene. Participants could perform in front of the screen in a way that they create similar outlines on the map.
- The outline could have a conflicting color: On the Israeli side (blue) it could be green, and on the Palestinian side (green) it could be blue.
- The outlines could have the same color corresponding with the respective map borderlines so that the map-lines dynamically mix with the shadow-outlines and create "new maps" of Jerusalem.

Wipeout Effect

In addition to the shadow effect, there was also a transient wipeout effect. The shadows of the moving people delete the map, but the map rebuilds itself after the person moves out of the camera view. The objective was to create playfulness and involvement with the map views. We called this effect "person as a brush," where the size of the brush depends on the relative position of the person/camera and of the object-detection threshold.

Pause Effect

It was decided that the slideshow at both sides should stop when there was somebody in the view of the camera. If there was nobody in front of the camera, there was a delay between each slide. Of course, the software had no idea if someone was actually in front of the camera. The only thing that the software understands is that something "big enough" to be detected by the object tracking sub-system is covering a "big enough" part of the screen. The former "big enough" depends on the relative position of person/camera and the object- detection threshold, while the latter "big enough" depends on the person-detection threshold. These options were defined as calibration parameters that depend on the desired qualities, and most significantly on the characteristics of the installation location. One side-effect of the combination of the two requirements for (1) pausing in order to engage passers-by and to motivate exploration, and (2) combined narrative between back and front, which facilitates comparison and reflection is that the two parts of the projection needed be synchronized, in a way that when one of the slideshow paused (due to a person) the other one paused too.

Architectural and Multimedia Design

The physical installation of a combined architectural and multimedia system creates many challenges. Each challenge could be broadly categorized in either architectural and multimedia categories, or a combination of the two. In particular, we had to address design problems such as: an indoor installation at a public everyday place, double screen projection, corresponding narrative with maps, combining real and digital shadows, and calibration of the camera subsystem. In the rest of this section we present the design solutions devised to address the actual installation of the system in physical space.

Architectural Container

The interactive video installation was prepared for an exhibition at the hall of the faculty of architecture at ETH Zurich. The entrance hall of the building is an open public space with high ceiling and at the time of the installation it would host additional exhibitions as well as the normal daily activity of the faculty. Therefore, there was a need to explicitly define a space which would provide a context and focus for the particular video installation (Fig. 5.5).

Semitransparent Double Projection Screen

The projection screen consisted of a double layer of semitransparent satin textile material. The doubling helped to distinguish front- and back-side projection, as through the space between the layers of textile, the colors of one side appear bright, while that of the other side appear slightly dimmed.

Fig. 5.5 A model overview of the interactive video installation

The double projection provided visual comparison of the colliding image of the city between the two groups. After several experiments in the lab with video projectors displaying a simple static image of maps (Fig. 5.4), it was found that a small distance (approximately 8 mm) between the textile layers controls this effect (Fig. 5.6).

The video projectors were positioned at a height of 2.20 m. This position allowed the viewers to use the installation in two ways. First, if they looked at the screen from a longer distance, they were able to watch the installation loops without disturbing it with shadows. Second, if they moved closer to the screen they created shadows on the screen and could play with the interactivity of the system as described earlier.

Map Layers and Narrative

The original maps were rather abstract and for most people who are not directly involved with the issues in Jerusalem and who are not familiar with cartographic principles, these maps are difficult to understand. There were several cartographic layers that were produced for the book, and consequently we had to devise a coherent way to manipulate them dynamically at the software-level. We decided that the maps should be presented in a loop. The loop showed one layer after another and

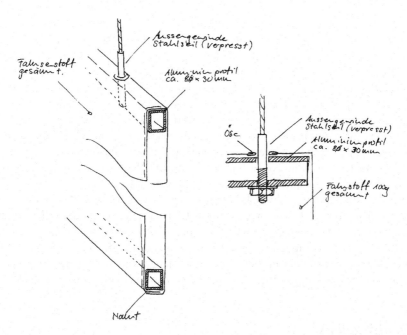

Fig. 5.6 The double projection screen consists of two sides of semi-transparent white tectile material arranged in parallel to each other and organized in the same frame, which is lightweight enough to hang from two metallic threads; thus it looks like it is hovering

provided some additional text- and symbol-based data. In this way, participants gained a gradual familiarity with the projected map space, starting with satellite images and ending up with religious meanings and historical facts. Another factor is that as a result of the double projection, one side of the installation was always mirrored. To avoid an imbalanced representation of the Israeli and Palestinian view of Jerusalem, the projections changed sides after each loop. This effect was achieved by composing the loops as Möbius strips; the end of the Israeli narrative smoothly ties in with the beginning of the Palestinian narrative, and vice versa.

According to good programming practice, the most obvious way to go forward would have been to load the layers in the software and then manipulate them dynamically and mix them with text according to a given narrative and script notation. However, at the time of coding the Processing environment, the software was still in beta version and after experimentation with a large set of images (map-layers) it was found that the Processing interpreter was rather inefficient with loading large numbers (i.e., more than a hundred) of images and manipulating them in real-time.

Computer Hardware Specification

We had to consider the performance of the available computer hardware which consisted of PowerMacs with dual G4 500 MHz processors and 1 Gbyte of RAM.

In comparison, the most contemporary interactive video installations with similar requirements employed one or more dual core computers at 2 GHz. Although in terms of software there are always many possibilities (which we discussed in the design section), in practice the performance of the available hardware turned out to be a very important factor in the selection of the concepts that could feasibly be implemented. In total, we employed two separate systems (i.e., two computers, two cameras, and two video-projectors), one for each side of the projection. Ideally the system design would also have required a separate computer to control each of the cameras, giving a total of four computers. Although a dedicated motion tracking computer would have greatly improved the responsiveness of such a system, it would have introduced the trade-off of extra networking complexity and protocol programming.

The maps were drawn in Adobe Illustrator and had to be reworked in order to make them appropriate for video projection. This meant change of colors, line width, sizes of symbols etc. Next, the map layers were imported into Adobe Flash and were edited into a narrative together with the respective text and symbols. Finally, the Flash movie was exported into a sequence of image files, which were loaded in custom-made Processing software and mixed in real-time with the digital shadow.

Digital Shadows

The system was implemented in the Processing environment, which employs the java programming language and provides simple interfacing with the functionality commonly needed in video installations, such as video tracking. The computer vision functionality was built upon the "BlobDetection" Library by v3ga1. These tools and libraries are an open source and run on a variety of platforms that support Java, thus making the application portable. Moreover, further development by the authors or other groups is feasible to be sustained in the future. The BlobDetection library is based on a threshold between light and dark. Dark and light are measured as relative terms and they therefore depend on the particular installation environment. Also, each camera has different responses. Therefore, there is no recipe for "correct" design of the system besides allowing for calibration of some parameters in the field.

Position of the Camera and Image Transformation

There are a number of possible options for the position and the viewing angle of the camera. For example, the camera may be located at the screen or it can be positioned together with the projector. The latter option was selected due to simplicity of the installation. In this case, there were also options in terms of the camera viewing angle and zoom factor. We decided to have a wide viewing angle, but we only used (achieved through the zoom facility) the central part of the image, since the rest of the projection contained text (see Fig. 5.7).

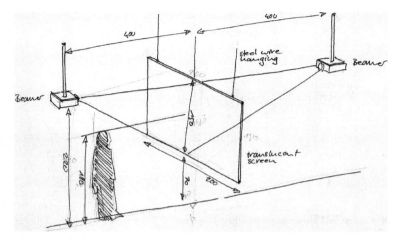

Fig. 5.7 Overview plan with scale and dimensions of the elements in the video installation

In the installation, the real shadow and the digital shadow had to be as close to each other as possible. For as long as a person remains stationary, the real and digital shadows had to be identical. For this reason, the camera was situated close to the projector. This was the only way to capture people in a position which is identical with the shadow produced by the projector. If the camera had been positioned at the screen pointing to the projector, the digital shadow would have been completely different from the real shadow.

Moreover, there were several technical advantages in overlaying real and digital shadows:

- Interactivity worked intuitively, because the digital shadows were a transformed mapping of the analogue ones.
- If the digital shadows were inaccurate (because of light cloth or other conditions), it would not have a disturbing effect. In this scenario, even if there was no digital shadow the real shadow would still remain.
- The installation can be simple: The camera can simply be attached to the projector (Fig. 5.8).

Ideally, we would have liked to have used multiple cameras (Sparacino 2002). However, in this work, there are already at least two systems involved so we chose not to add more dimensions to the input devices.

Installation and System Calibration in the Field

Before calibrating the motion tracking software there was a need to ensure the robustness of the integrated software (slideshow and motion tracking). Although

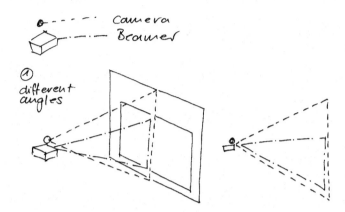

Fig. 5.8 Camera and projector are positioned together

ubiquitous computing systems are assumed to be seamlessly integrated with the environment and to work in a robust way, there is always a possibility of arbitrary input streams that could not be modeled and tested in the lab during development time. In contrast to desktop or web applications, ubiquitous computing systems are supposed to run without a pause for the duration of the day or even overnight. It is for this reason that the robustness of the system becomes a crucial requirement.

The main software (Processing) was in beta, at the time of writing, so we were aware that there might have been issues with bugs, such as inefficient memory allocation, which would have caused an application crash after a while, especially if lots of media was loaded and processed in real-time. These type of bugs are as unpredictable as the input coming from a camera installed in the field and only testing in the field can validate the system. Another remedy would have been parsing of the open-source Processing code base, but this is not within the skill-set of most artists. In engineering terminology, there is no analytic way to check that the system works prior to installation on site, so the system has to be installed and left running for many hours in order to validate robustness.

The methodology for calibrating and testing the system in the lab involved setting up one computer with the software, a camera, and a projector/screen. In this way we monitored how the system performed over a long period of time (i.e., more than a day). Simultaneously, a portable computer with a camera was taken to the field (the site of the actual installation) in order to test the system response against the (changing) ambient light and the particular reflection of the background materials (e.g., ceiling, floors, walls, etc.).

Discussion

The most important contribution of this chapter is the interdisciplinary design process that maps the initial requirements to interaction design concepts, and finally to a particular architectural and multimedia design which was feasible to implement. In the following text we present a reflection on the creative process and on the empirical findings of the design and implementation phase.

The combination of new and traditional media art can be regarded by someone as a dilemma, or even as a conflict between traditional and digital mediums, but in our view, it doesn't have to be the case. This video installation employed a "traditional" double projection semitransparent screen, instead of the approach of mixing the two maps in software over an opaque two-sided screen. Moreover, the use of a double screen allows shadows on one side to become windows that create views over the "image of the city" on the other side; which is an analogue approach. The shadows can be analogue due to the light source of the projector, or they can be digital shadows that are captured by the camera and created at the software level, which allows an infinite number of further manipulations and artistic expressions; this is the digital component. In this way, instead of competing, traditional and digital cooperate to produce a result that is more than the sum of the parts.

Ubiquitous and cooperative computer systems can contribute to the *convergence between different art forms and new media*. These systems employ multimodal sensors as input devices instead of assuming the input from a keyboard and mouse. In our work the use of a camera as an input device for a computer system responds to the objective of alternative human-computer interfaces, which seek to have minimise requirements in terms of both the skill and the effort required to use the system. In this way, the interaction between people and artworks becomes more immediate and natural.

In contrast to the narrow interaction modalities of traditional office computers, the interfaces available in ubiquitous computing provide extended opportunities for seamless integration with cultural and artistic forms. Ubiquitous computer tools include powerful, small, and portable computers, projectors, efficient computer vision, and easy-to-use programming environments. They also offer novel opportunities for artistic expression. Moreover, the relationship between tools and artists is mutual. As artists employ new tools in new projects, and the tool creators get feedback about the new uses and improve their tools. Indeed, the processing-programming environment is supported by a very active design and arts community.

In addition to the technological and design process aspects, the most interesting part of this project is undoubtedly *the potential for social impact*. The book behind this project contained much more information and visual images than could feasibly be displayed in a video installation. Yet, a book offers only restricted possibilities for engaging and creating initial awareness about the impact of political issues. Consequently, the video installation allows for an entirely new interaction with the content and becomes a portal to an appreciation of an important social issue that affects the lives of thousands of people everyday.

The motivation behind the basic concept was that the installation should be a metaphor for the situation in Jerusalem: two groups (Israelis and Palestinians) are claiming the same urban space and fighting for territorial dominance. Both groups have a completely different view of the same city (Lynch 1960). The image of the city changes very rapidly and depends upon political decisions, activism, and other events. In this way, the video installation adopts the role of a memory aid, and of a tool for understanding the current situation. In addition, the integration of computing and networking into this project provides the opportunity to display new map layers, photos, and text about new events that alter the image of the city in Jerusalem. Thus, the video installation, in addition to the artistic qualities of abstracting a geopolitical conflict, provides further opportunities as a live artwork and most importantly, as a placeholder for social encounters, interaction, and hopefully, mutual understanding.

The public installation of the system was initially regarded as an opportunity to evaluate the system in a realistic environment and collect feedback about engineering and design aspects that could inform further video installations. In addition, we would have liked to test alternative design features of the system. For instance, do people actually like the interactive options at all, or would they have preferred a simple slide transition? What is the difference in average attendance between the interactive and the simple version? Which kind of visual interactivity is the most appealing? In order to address these research questions, we have subsequently implemented some simple counters and image logging inside the motion tracking system and we also considered performing observation and note-taking during the exhibition. Unfortunately, university regulations and the scope of that particular exhibition (artistic) did not allow for such an elaborate data collection and analysis approach. Therefore, although a formal evaluation of an interactive system is technically feasible, it might not be appropriate for the particular context (artwork).

The collaboration between different disciplines was very beneficial both for the creators and for the artwork itself. In fact it would have been impossible to reach the same outcome in the realization of this project without the many roles assumed during the different phases. For example, cartographic skills were necessary to create and then to transform the vectors maps into a combined slideshow narrative. Architectural design and engineering expertise were employed to design and implement the physical aspects of the installation. Computer engineering was employed to develop a combined hardware and software system that brought together the maps and the presence of people in the exhibition. Finally, collectively all these skills were orchestrated in the process of considering the interaction design aspects of the video installation. In the following section, we summarize the main outcomes of the project and draw conclusions.

Conclusions and Ongoing Work

Three basic concepts have been crucial for this interactive video installation:

- *Semitransparent double-projection screen* allowing for a shared experience of back- and front-side.

  Maps narrative provided specific information about an urban space. The map layers and the information about them appeared in synchronized back-and-front (two parties in conflict) story line, which looped.

  Embodied interactivity invited the viewer to be "self responsible" for his/her view on the city. The presence of the viewer was sensed by means of a shadow (real or digital), which distorted the map and the flow of the slideshow.

These concepts have been progressively implemented into several installations at national and international exhibitions and into several software versions. The first version of the software part of the system was developed and tested in the lab. Then the system was installed and tested at the exhibition site in conditions that corresponded to the final installation at least in terms of scale and lighting conditions. The first public presentation of the complete installation was performed in April 2007 at the main hall of the department of Architecture at ETH Zurich in Switzerland (Fig. 5.9).

We have a number of plans to evolve the project in future. In terms of additional software features, we plan to integrate real-time photos and text from web sources. In particular we plan to employ geo-tagging of external data into the system map. Thus, we would like to enrich the linear and fixed map narrative of the video installation with live information from the field. In this way, there would be many evolving (and real-time) stories told and users would be able to compare the multiple overlaying images of the city, which would be updated in real time. With regard to the physical aspects of the system, we would also like to implement a remote version of the system, which would have screens installed remotely.

Finally, we are going to consider the application of this interactive video installation for cities that face similar issues of urban conflict, such as Nicosia (Cyprus). It is expected that there are a number of additional case studies for this system, because in most big urban places, even the most peaceful ones, there are conflicts and colliding views about the image of the city.

Fig.5.9 Installation site faces the entrance at the faculty of architecture (ETH Zurich)

Acknowledgments The work of Konstantinos Chorianopoulos was supported by the MEDIACITY project (http://www.mediacity-project.org), which is sponsored by the European Commission Marie Curie Host Fellowships for Transfer of Knowledge (MTKD-CT-2004-517121). The work of Tim Rieniets was funded by a grant form the ETH Swiss Federal Institute of Technology in Zurich and the Institute for Urban Design.

References

Levin G (2006) Computer vision for artists and designers: pedagogic tools and techniques for novice programmers. AI Soc. 20(4), 462-482. DOI= http://dx.doi.org/10.1007/s00146-006-0049-2

Lynch K (1960) The image of the city. MIT Press, Massachusetts

McCullough M (2004) Digital Ground: Architecture, Pervasive Computing, and Environmental Knowing. MIT Press, Massachusetts

Misselwitz P, Rieniets T (2006) City of Collision: Jerusalem and the Principles of Conflict Urbanism Birkhäuser, Basel

O'Sullivan D (2007) Video By The Pixel, http://tinyurl.com/2qa5gt Accessed 8 March 2008

Reas C & Fry B (2006) Processing: programming for the media arts. AI Society 20(4) 526-538. DOI= http://dx.doi.org/10.1007/s00146-006-0050-9

Sparacino F (2002) Narrative Spaces: bridging architecture and entertainment via interactive technology. 6th International Conference on Generative Art, Milan, Italy

Weber J, Stephens LD, Baumann A & Wolter A (2007) Project ION, http://mediaarchitecture.de/projekte/ion/ Accessed on March 8, 2008. Accessed 2 March 2008

Section 2
Playful Encounters

Introduction: Playful Encounters

George Roussos

Pervasive computing has emerged as an attractive new paradigm for information and communication technology. One feature that sets it apart from previous technologies is that it is inherently social, in the sense that it affects the nature of the everyday more than any other ICT to this day. As such, it is more urgent now than ever before to explore the changes technology brings to everyday life, at the same time as it is being developed. Indeed, a core ingredient for the wider success and adoption of pervasive computing is to find attractive applications that also reflect the priorities and the values of everyday users. Understanding technology in-use may, of course, not be a new requirement, but pervasive computing demands that this is considered with priority.

Yet, the need to identify and tailor desirable pervasive computing situations presents a considerable challenge. Unlike the case of well-established information technologies, where social science-inspired approaches offer effective ways to study their implications after they are in place, the current state of pervasive computing requires open-ended explorations that can efficiently reveal the costs and benefits associated with particular systems and applications. Traditional social science provides only limited tools for probing the potential of a technology before it becomes enacted. While this is clearly of some value, these methods and techniques are not always suitable for such quickly evolving and exploratory work, where the question is not well-defined, and the design space is exceptionally large. Such investigations are often more amenable to research methods and methodologies developed by design, and creative researchers and practitioners, ones that favor idiosyncratic behaviors and playfulness.

To this end, one methodology that has been used to good effect in design, health, creative arts, and education and has also been successful in this context is the so-called practice-based research. This approach produces new knowledge through investigations based on practice and the outcomes of that practice. Due to its diver-

G. Roussos (✉)
School of Computer Science and Information Systems, Birkbeck College,
University of London, Malet Street, London, WC1E 7HX, UK
e-mail: g.roussos@bbk.ac.uk

sity of application, opinions about what constitutes practice-based research vary widely, with some taking the view that the act of making or designing is research on its own merit. Others take the view that research is fundamentally an analytical activity and as such, it is completely at odds with design, which is understood as being synthetic. For the former, new knowledge is encapsulated within the constructed artifact and does not require further interpretation. For the latter, knowledge is only understood through its dissemination and interpretation, and is distinct from the object of the practice.

A particular flavor of practice-based research focuses on playful experiments, which have been found very efficient in quickly exploring the design space. Moreover, playfulness is an effective probe of ambiguity as, unlike more formal approaches, it does not view exploration as a problem to be solved. This approach introduces novel behavioral constraints, that is, modes of interaction between people and devices, on the design process that fundamentally differ from engineering. Such playful experiments have already been successful in facilitating research on how people experience pervasive computing applications. Notably, both the well-known Urban Tapestries and Can You See Me Now? projects have explored the use of cyber-physical environments to enable shared encounters between users inhabiting either the online or the real-world through the use of playful experiences designed around an open and flexible design space. As a result, they have been successful in finding ones that are desirable and outside the constraints of security-tight and commercially sensitive situations.

To be useful for pervasive computing research, playful experiments include substantial contextualization and interpretation so that any new knowledge becomes accessible to the wider community. Moreover, critical appraisal and analysis of practice is necessary to clarify the foundation of the findings, justify the originality of the work, and provide the basis for a judgment as to whether the claims are reasonable and justified by reported practice. This part of the book reports on three playful experiments conducted at the boundary of pervasive computing and creative practice. They explore different segments of the design space, namely communities, public and learning through construction, to propose interesting situations where pervasive computing can enable shared encounters.

Licoppe and Inada revisit the concept of a location-based game through their study of Mogi in Japan. In Mogi, the location of the players is made public within their community via a mapping interface and other location-specific cues. They investigate the implications of mediated co-proximity events as a form of original social gathering, which enables shared encounters. They consider the study of such events as critical in understanding social behaviors in location-aware mediated communities. In particular, they describe how playing to get individual icons to touch on the mapping interface without actually the players being physically close becomes an end in itself. They also identify the way in which such "co-presence at a distance" can trigger potentially hazardous situations, and how such conditions can be managed collectively by groups of players to enable a sense of security through participation in a community.

Stukkoff reports on her investigation of Every Passing Moment, a public artwork developed around mobile phone technology and interactive displays. Every Passing Moment tracks and records discoverable Bluetooth device to automatically seed a digital flower in a virtual garden projected onto an urban screen. Stukkoff reports on the findings from the installation of this work at the central train station in Liverpool and discusses travelers' perceptions and their reactions.

Finally, Jennings discusses her experiences with the Constructed Narratives game. Constructed Narratives allows players to collaboratively construct a world using a tangible user interface developed through material and building blocks augmented with technology. The aim of the game is to foster collaborative and facilitate discourse, the exchange of ideas and negotiation of design intentions, and choices between collaborating participants.

Chapter 6
Shared Encounters in a Location-Aware and Proximity-Aware Mobile Community. The Mogi Case.

Christian Licoppe and Yoriko Inada

Introduction

Nowhere does the development of ubiquitous computing and mobile devices impinge more singularly on the construction of public spaces than with location-aware infrastructures, and the kind of "hybrid ecologies" they enable (Crabtree and Rodden 2008). On one hand, location-aware technologies articulate space and place in new ways (Dourish 2006), and may favor the construction of hybrid "territories" as an emergent feature of recurring practices (Licoppe and Inada 2008). On the other hand, particularly when the technology makes locations visible and available through digital mapping devices, it supports forms of interaction and encounters that weave together embodied and digital forms of presence and proximity, as has been shown in some pioneering experiments (Griswold et al. 2003; Benford et al. 2003; Barkhuus et al. 2005). However, such encounters are always highly sensitive to the social and institutional practices of users (Barkhuus and Dourish 2004). Since most of the previous studies involved experiments with specially recruited players engaging once or at most a few times in the location-aware activity, what still remains to be observed and understood is the way a "hybrid" interaction order emerges from the collective interactions of members inhabiting a location-aware environment: As this takes time, as much time as is needed for a collective culture (under-determined by game design and rules) to emerge from multiple interactions in massive multiplayer online games (Steinkuehler 2006). This is precisely the direction that this chapter wants to explore.

It looks at the forms of interaction which may be observed in a location-aware community in which members have been able to dwell and interact over a long time, long enough for a culture to stabilize and for original forms of shared encounters to develop, which are constitutive of the local order that has emerged

C. Licoppe (✉), and Y. Inada
Department of Social Science, Telecom Paristech, Institut Telecom, 46 rue Barrault, 75013, Paris, France
e-mail: christian.licoppe@telecom-paristech.fr

K.S. Willis et al. (eds.), *Shared Encounters*, Computer Supported Cooperative Work, DOI 10.1007/978-1-84882-727-1_6, © Springer-Verlag London Limited 2010

within such a community, and which as we eventually argue, bear a more general relevance to most kinds of location-aware settings. Our work is based on the Mogi game, built by French designers (Licoppe and Guillot 2006), and played intensively in Japan between 2003 and 2006 by a population of a 1,000 players on the average. This was not an experiment, but a commercial venture, and players subscribed directly on the KDDI game portal. We have had access to the anonymous corpus of text messages exchanged by the players (Licoppe and Inada 2006), and also been able to interview a dozen players, some of them several times. The kind of immersion that such a corpus of interactions covering a period of 3 years provides amounts to a form of "virtual ethnography" fieldwork (Hine 2000). The metaphor is here particularly apt for we aim toward an ethnographically-oriented analysis of the culture of encounters that has developed in this singular community, and which is ultimately founded on the ways members manage properly the location-awareness, and ubiquitous computing resources made available to them by the game infrastructure. We will use particularly significant interactions gathered from our extensive analysis of the corpus to provide evidence for some key features of the interaction order in the Mogi community: the fact that locations are public, and the ways in which locations and proximities between players are made visible, recognizable, and may be monitored by members.

We will first show how the players treat locations as public data available for scrutiny and worthy to mention when deemed remarkable. A consequence of this is the occurrence of situations in which players are close, though too distant to perceive one another "directly" (which we will call mediated proximity events), and which warrant mutual recognition, and discussion by the concerned participants as well as by a wider audience of connected players. One of us has argued that in many different cultural settings, the recognition of mutual proximity projected engaging in a face-to-face encounter as a relevant course of action to follow (Licoppe 2009). The specificity of a location-aware society and the kind of collective good on which it rests are then related to the ways members may mutually appear as "close" and manage such mediated proximity-based "encounters," as well as the cases in which they seem to go awry, such as "stalking"-related situations (Licoppe and Inada 2009). Mediated proximities are so meaningful as a part of the players' experience that an unexpected and unforeseen (to the designers) genre of activity (labeled as "cara-gattai") has been invented by them. It consists in playing at breaking the location-based relation between the avatar and the body it figures, and getting the avatars to touch on the public digital game-maps, while the players' actual bodies remain at a distance from one another. We show eventually how some face-to-face encounters of a traditional type take on new meanings when they are accomplished in such "hybrid ecologies": a date between players becomes a collective public performance that extends over days and weeks, involves many players who monitor, comment on and gossip about the encounter and its progress.

The Location-Aware Multiplayer Game Mogi and its Users

The Game

The game Mogi was developed by a team led by Mathieu Castelli at a French start-up (Newtgames), and was commercialized in 2003 in Japan by the operator KDDI. The gameplay consists of collecting virtual objects with a mobile phone. These are "localized" (in the sense that users can act on them only when they are close to their virtual position), and are continuously created and renewed by the game designers. The player has an interface, the "radar," that features a map with a radius of 1 km. This map represents the player's environment with his or her pictogram in the centre of the mobile screen surrounded by those of the other players, and virtual objects situated within the 1 km radius. These data are updated with each server request.[1] When players are less than about 300 m^2 from an object, they can capture it with their terminal. Each object belongs to a collection. Completing a collection earns points, players are classified according to the points accumulated. The basic idea is to create a community of high-tech hunter-gatherers whose activity is set in an economy based on the bartering of virtual objects and a sociability based on text messaging.

The main functionalities of the game are accessible from the main menu. The five most important are as follows:

- The "radar" interface, the map of the player's immediate environment. By clicking on a sufficiently close object on the map, the player can pick it up by launching a collection module. Clicking on a player's icon on the screen opens a window for text messaging (see Fig 6.1).
- The module dedicated to text messaging. The addresses and messages exchanged are accessible only within the game server. Players can create buddy lists of favorite correspondents (Mogi friends or the members of teams to which they belong[3]).
- The exchange and transaction module (for exchanging objects missing from one's collection).

---

[1] The rapidity of these connections with the game server is critical as regards the acceptability of the game. At certain times the connection time ranged from 30 sec to 1 min, which was experienced as a real problem by players.

[2] Experience of the game is richer with a GPS terminal (the precision of geo-localization is then a matter of a few meters) but the game also offers the possibility of localization from cells. Experienced players have become accustomed to constantly switching from one to the other in their quest for objects since the map in cell mode is slightly different to the GPS map, due to the position of the antennae. It is therefore likely to reveal new objects in one or two clicks, without the player moving at all.

[3] This possibility of creating teams and getting together, introduced shortly before my study, has been highly successful.

Fig. 6.1 The radar interface that represents the local map of the game around the player (whose icon always appears in the centre of the screen) in an area of 4 km^2. The other players and geo-localized virtual objects appear on the map. The "closest Mogi-friend" is indicated at the bottom of the screen, with the distance even if it is more than 2 km. This functionality was added by the designers to facilitate the "onscreen encounters" discussed later

- The user profile: those who can choose to make all or part of the inventory of objects that they possess, as well as the type of object they want, visible.
- Public classification of players according to the number of accumulated points. This classification is frequently consulted by players and introduces competition between them.

The game objects are designed by the design team. Certain collections are very simple, for instance, precious stones spread across Japan. Others play on the players' situation and context. Certain objects are available only in some parts of the country, other collections are visible and accessible only at certain times of the day. The design was recently oriented toward more advanced objects, virtual "creatures" (that create, move or destroy nearby objects), chests (players close to them can aim for an object and thus obtain the right to open the chest, with the hope of winning a highly valuable object), or quests (additional points can be earned by moving an object close to a given place). This diversity illustrates an important property of context-aware services. Context-awareness concerns not only people or terminals, but also informational objects that can be "placed" in the mobile user's environment. As the Mogi example shows, it is possible to enhance a mobile users' environment almost infinitely, and to create rich and complex ecologies that could be called "augmented" towns.

It is also possible to log onto Mogi on a PC, through a website. In this case the interfaces and functionalities are different. The Web interface includes a chat function not accessible on mobile terminals, but its key feature is that it allows PC-based players to visualize maps showing other players and bigger geo-located objects, throughout Japan. Since they are stationary, they can pinpoint the position of highly coveted objects, or unusual movements of known players. This is well known among players, and has the very important consequence of turning the Mogi players into a location-aware community in which one's location (as presented in the interface), and by way of consequence, one's displacements become public data, always potentially accessible to other known and unknown players.

The Players

The game was played between 2003 and 2008, and on average it had about 1,000 active users, all of whom were subscribers to a service offering an unlimited mobile data transfer for a flat rate (the WIN rate of 4,200 yen offered by KDDI). Players considered that this type of rate freed them from any worry as to the intensity of their use, and that its existence had a liberating effect relative to the development of their game practices. The subscription to the game as such was 210 yens per month, which the players considered negligible. KDDI ran no adverts on the game. As part of promotion campaigns, it nevertheless offered a 1-month free trial period twice a year for Mogi and many other games on its portal. Most Mogi players who had previously had a WIN subscription had taken advantage of these promotions to try the game, after being attracted by the context-aware concept applied in Mogi.

The Mogi gameplay differs from games available on Internet because it is a multi-player game based on a very straightforward scenario. Although no precise statistics are available, user profiles are clearly very different to those observed on the Internet. There are almost as many female as male users. A large proportion of users are in the 25–40 age-group. Our study focused on five men and five women in that age-group with widely diverse social origins, from a bank manager to a packer, a sophisticated young mother to a saleslady in a department store. Two of them had a slight handicap, and found that the sociability of the game allowed them a degree of social integration[4].

Basically, with respect to playing behavior, two very different ideal types can be observed:

Accumulation-oriented collectors: they collect as many objects as they can (sometimes ten times the same collection) and interact with other players mostly to obtain the objects they still do not have.

"Social" players are less concerned about collecting virtual objects than with the game as a way to meet, to communicate, and maintain enduring social relationships with other players within the game. Those players are particularly attentive to the forms of politeness that develop in the location-aware community of players and to the proprieties of the various forms of encounters that are occasioned within the game.

Regarding such encounters, most players avoid meeting face-to-face and often elude invitations to do so. Similarly they rarely exchange their mobile email

---

[4]For cultural and religious reasons, it seems that people with handicaps find it very difficult to be socially integrated in Japan.

addresses, so that most of their text messages are sent and received on the game dedicated text messaging system. Therefore, the social interactions that are elicited in the course of playing Mogi are mostly kept within the game technical infrastructure. This apparent shyness may be a feature of inhabiting a location-aware world with unknown others (outside the scope of the game).

Location as Public Data

One's location can be seen by other players in two different ways. Either by another connected player on his or her mobile phone if and when he or she is close enough (less than 2 km away), or by any player visualizing the game maps on his or her PC. Those players can visualize the location of connected players at any time, and wherever they are.

Most experienced players are aware of this, so they treat their location has something that may be seen and noticed by other players at any time. Locations are therefore treated as public data, and as such not only are they treated as visible and noticeable, but players expect others will indeed notice. In the excerpt below, one player (T.) discusses a long and unusual trip she plans to make, and indicates how she expects others to notice, when they see the location of her icon in the maps of the game.

Extract no. 1

1. T to H (07:59:32): Tが広島行くコト TとHとAしか知らない (*^m^*)ムフフ

   れーだ見

   たヤツびっくりだなこりゃ(大爆

   Only you and A. know that I'm going as far as Hiroshima. The others

   will be surprised when they look at the radar.

   (*^m^*)

2. H to T (08:03:18) : おう、アチコチのヤツがぱにくるかもな（大 それか誰も気が付

   かない。。。それも寂しいなw

   Yes. Everywhere people will panic. Or maybe nobody will even notice.

   Which would be a bit sad. (Laugh)

3. T to H (08:07:20) : AさんとSとYヮ気づくだろう... ヾ(≧▽≦)ノ ″

   But at least A., S .and Y. will notice. ヾ(≧▽≦)ノ ″

Her correspondent responds by joking about it, even suggesting that it would be a pity if no-one noticed. This shows how players orient toward being accountable for their locations on a routine basis, and how they openly acknowledge and discuss the fact that their displacements are public and may even become a matter of open discussion between players. Locations are noticeable and warrant being mentioned, as shown in extract no. 2. One player, N., probably connected through his PC (for he gives no indication that he is anywhere around Haneda Airport), remarks on the location of another player G.

The sequential organization of the "noticing" turn is interesting. It starts with an exclamation that works as a "change of state token" (Heritage 1984), which marks that something noticeable and mentionable has occurred and invites further elaboration. This comes in the next turn construction unit, which appears as a query about the location of the recipient which embeds a candidate answer. This indicates that player N was probably playing the game as a connected PC-based player (if he had been a mobile player and sufficiently close to notice G, then the issue of co-proximity would have arisen) and familiar enough with G's mobility for the

Extract no. 2

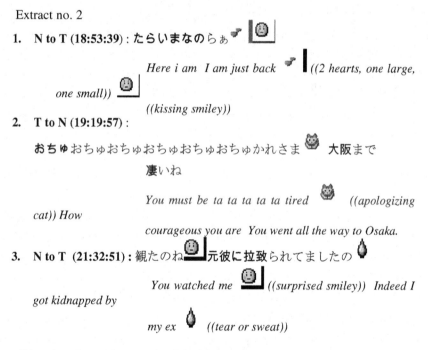

1. **N to T (18:53:39)** : たらいまなのらぁ

   Here i am   I am just back ((2 hearts, one large, one small))

   ((kissing smiley))

2. **T to N (19:19:57)** :

   おちゅおちゅおちゅおちゅおちゅおちゅかれさま　大阪まで

   凄いね

   You must be ta ta ta ta ta tired ((apologizing cat)) *How*

   courageous you are   You went all the way to Osaka.

3. **N to T (21:32:51)** : 観たのね　元彼に拉致られてましたの

   You watched me ((surprised smiley)) *Indeed I got kidnapped by*

   my ex ((tear or sweat))

candidate location to be meaningful with background knowledge of where G usually is or what he does. The familiarity is reinforced by the lack of preliminary greetings. The "query-ness" of the utterance is moreover emphasized with a "question mark" emoticon, putting some stress on the provision of an answer; this shows that in such a community of experienced location-aware players unusual location and displacements may be treated as "mentionables", and used as a legitimate pretext for initiating interaction. Discussion of the qualities of a particular location relevant to the other participant may be introduced and treated as a "safe topic" for text messaging. Discussing location within the Mogi location-aware community of players is on a par with discussing the weather in a village during a face-to-face encounter (Goffman 1971).

Treating location as noticeable and mentionable, noticing and mentioning it to invite to, and initiate a text message encounter is a routinized practice in the Mogi location-aware community. In the next extract, two players initiate an exchange by commenting almost simultaneously on the location of another.

What is interesting is that T. responds by sending the same confirmatory text message to both of them at the same time. These joint messages were rare in the Mogi text message corpus, and usually concerned with conventional, formulaic messages such as conventional greetings. So the previous excerpt provides evidence for the ritualized and routinized character of "location noticing," and messages as an invitation to engage in a text message encounter between acquainted players.

In a community where locations are public, members are vulnerable to the strategic exploitation of such knowledge, hence the worries about the possibility of "stalking" by another player (Licoppe and Inada 2009). In a less extreme form, any noticing and mentioning of a player's location by another, however routine it may appear, potentially entails a mild form of horizontal social control, and invites the

Extract no. 3

1. **S. to T.(14:28:19)**: あれ　　意外な場所にいるのね

            ah!? *((lol)) you are in an expected place*

   ((lol))

2. **Y.   to   T.   (15:00:25)**:

   今日はとんでもないとこにいらっしゃいますな

            today you (polite form) are in an incredible place
   ((lol))

3. **T. to S. & Y. (15:35:43)**: なんだよ　　岡山まで遠征だよ
   高速ヮモギりのみで

            精一杯だす

            what then? *((lol)) I am travelling to*

   Okayama. *((lol))*

            on the highway I can do nothing but play at

   Mogi *((lol))*

production of accounts related to the aforementioned location, or if questioned, call for some form of "remedial exchange" (Goffman 1971).

In this exchange, it is the mobile player who first proposes an unsolicited assessment of her mobility and current location. Since the assessment regards her own experience, it is part of her "information preserve," and she has first rights about such claims. However, the other player responds by providing in her second turn another assessment of the first player's current experiential state (you must be tired), and then further elaborates about her past mobility by stating the city she has just been to. Considering the sequential organization of assessment pairs, T. is strongly competing for epistemic rights with respect to the assessment of the matter at hand (Heritage 2005). Since that particular matter directly concerns N.'s experience, it may be seen as a potential infringement of N.'s informational preserve. N. deals with this in the third turn. She starts by exclaiming about being watched by T. Qualifying location noticing as "watching" is one way to highlight the dimension of social control which the public character of location may entail. However she goes on by providing an account for her trip to Osaka which shows she does not wish to pursue the matter any further. Such offhandedness shows how deep the expectation runs that one's location may be noticed by other players, and one may be held accountable for it.

Extract no. 4

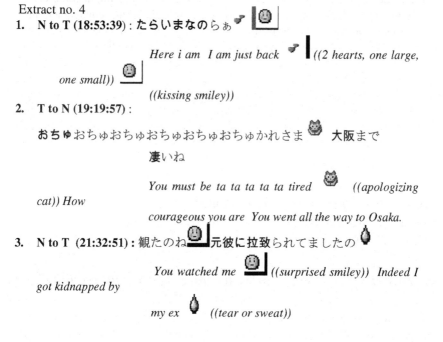

1. **N to T (18:53:39)** : たらいまなのらぁ

  Here i am   I am just back   ((2 hearts, one large, one small))

  ((kissing smiley))

2. **T to N (19:19:57)** :

  おちゅおちゅおちゅおちゅおちゅおちゅかれさま　大阪まで

  凄いね

  You must be ta ta ta ta ta tired   ((apologizing cat)) How

  courageous you are   You went all the way to Osaka.

3. **N to T (21:32:51)** : 観たのね　元彼に拉致られてましたの

  You watched me   ((surprised smiley))   Indeed I got kidnapped by

  my ex   ((tear or sweat))

In summary, the Mogi case shows that a key characteristic of a fully location-aware community is that members' locations are actually or potentially mutual and public knowledge. The categorization of players as localized and mobile entities is always relevant within the collective game activity, and pointing toward another player's location is a routine practice that displays one as a member. An immediate consequence of all this is that the current location of a given player may be treated as a "safe" mentionable topic that is always available (in principle) and warrants the initiation of a text message interchange. Location is there to be seen and noticed, but mentioning it may sometimes infringe on one's "informational preserve" and require some specific forms of remedial interchange, while it is also a way to produce affiliation markers and "doing being familiar," We believe that the "visibility" of other member's location and the kind of interactional consequences we have observed here characterize more generally some of the particular ways in which "relations in public" are managed in any kind of location-aware community (Goffman 1971), and the kind of public order that is bound to emerge from it.

It therefore comes as no surprise that the way location and displacements are made visible and accessible is a highly sensitive moral issue. Two years ago, the designers introduced a feature which provided the name of the neighborhood the player was located, which became visible when one clicked on his icon. This feature immediately aroused indignant reactions from the players, who did not want such information to be publicly divulged. Even information as apparently trite as the name of the neighborhood district in which they were located (in a world in which "geometric" locations and maps were already publicly available) was seen as problematic. For, if you know the person well enough, you might more easily infer rightly or wrongly from her/his location thus labeled her/his engagement into some forms of activity. This proved to be too great an infringement of personal territories. Players therefore seem to consider that keeping location data "geometric" and therefore as "neutral" and impersonal as possible gives more leeway and legitimacy to the ways they may notice each others' location, mention it and collaboratively accomplish various forms of consequent encounters. As we will now show, the fact that locations are (actually or potentially) public knowledge made available through location-based networked technologies, and mobile devices "afford" original forms of encounters between members.

"Mediated Co-Proximity" Events and "Encounters-at-a-Distance" as Constitutive Features of the Social Order in Location-Aware Communities

Co-Proximity Events and "Infrastructures of Encounterability"

A particular form of invitation to further forms of encounters is occasioned by co-proximity events. While a lot of attention has been paid to co-present interaction in the work of Goffman and related texts, much less attention has been given to "co-proximity events" (Licoppe 2009). A co-proximity event is a situation in which two persons are made aware that though they are not co-present, they are close to one another, close enough that getting into a face-to-face interaction may become an issue, usually to be resolved through communication at a distance. In a recent study of mobile phone call recordings[5] instances of the construction of co-proximity events involved a couple calling one another to update their mutual knowledge about their respective locations, particularly as they got closer and one passed a shared meaningful landmark, or perhaps more typically, a woman calling the home of her best friend from her mobile and leaving a message stating that she happened to be in the vicinity and checking whether her friend was at home and potentially available for a visit and a chat. In all these examples, one participant is (1) aware of a particular form of proximity to the other, (2) calls the other to turn this into a shared knowledge, thus "grounding" (Clark 1996) the co-proximity event, (3) presents it as a serendipitous happenstance that projects somehow a face-to-face encounter as a relevant segue to the recognition of the co-proximity event. One could think easily of similar examples in professional contexts. Such situations occur mostly between people who are familiar with one another, because the one who notices the proximity event does it on the basis of previous interactions and extensive knowledge about the habits and mobility patterns of the other person.

There is therefore a spatio-temporal "infrastructure of encounterability" that extends much beyond the times and scenes for co-present interaction. Space and time are deeply interwoven with relational knowledge and shared histories, so that for a given pair of acquainted subjects, it is textured so as to afford a sense of closeness (in absence), that warrants getting in touch and whose experience may be turned into a serendipitous opportunity for various forms of encounters and affiliation-building. Technological systems providing subjects with mutual location-awareness provide new occasions and new formats for constituting co-proximity events, or what could be more aptly described as "mediated" co-proximity events to account for the particular technological mediations through which co-proximity may be mutually recognized. In location-aware communities, the experience of the places members dwell in are augmented with a new "infrastructure for encounterability." Conversely, the particular "co-proximity" events and related social encounter that may occur are characteristic of a given location-aware community and of its emergent culture. In what follows we will show some of the more particular forms of co-proximity events supported by the Mogi infrastructure and the kind of often unusual social encounters that have developed around it.

The Interactional Consequences of Seeing One Another on the Same Mobile Screen Map

A typical Mogi-supported co-proximity event occurs when two players connect to the game and see one another on their mobile device, through the "radar" map interface. Such mediated co-proximities events are specific to location-aware technologies.

---

[5]Julien Morel, 2006, private conversation

The greater the density of players the more frequent co-proximity events may become (Licoppe and Inada 2006). One of their key properties is that players expect such events to be mutually perceived and noticed by both participants, supposedly connected and playing at the same time. Participants treat such mediated co-proximity events as projecting a possible face-to-face encounter. It is conventionally expected that acquainted players who mutually realize they are close might meet, and if they do not they will somehow have to account of it in their text message exchanges. In cases in which another player is close and remains silent (he does not remark on such proximity nor responds to text messages), the other player has grounds to suspect such a proximity to be "ill intended" that is a case of "stalking" (Licoppe and Inada 2009). Some culturally significant ways of noticing such mediated proximities have been evolved in the community of players, such as an expectation that expert players should take the initiative when they appear to be close in this way to novice players and make them the small gift of a low value item as a token of goodwill (Licoppe and Inada 2006). Players have even given situations in which they are close and fail to notice it the name of "near miss," which also reflects the notion that (contrary to the air traffic control contexts in which this expression was initially coined) an actual encounter would be a positive and expected outcome of a mediated co-proximity event.

Such mediated co-proximity events always make salient some degree of spatial closeness, which is shaped by the interfaces of the technological system. Seeing one another on screen and therefore mutually realizing we are less than a few 100 m apart is treated as a decree of closeness that projects a face-to-face encounter as a relevant segue. How is this practically accomplished? The kind of conventionally expected beginning that such a situation occasions takes the form of an adjacent pair of the type A: "We're close, aren't we?". B: "Yes we are close." This opening makes explicit the mutual recognition of proximity and puts the co-proximity event on common ground for both participants. Such a conventional beginning can be said: (a) to occur near a situational threshold or boundary (marked by the recognition of the co-proximity event which such a beginning makes common knowledge between the participants), (b) to establish a shared perceptual field of interaction (the mobile radar interfaces), (c) to constitute a form of "adjacent pair," (d) to have relatively predictable form and content, (e) to establish implicitly a spatio-temporal unit of interaction, and (f) to mark the addressee as being worthy of cognitive and social recognition. Such mediated co-proximity recognition-oriented beginnings share all the criteria that define greetings for linguistic anthropology (Duranti 1997). They can be considered as constitutive of a particular form of encounter, whether or not a face-to-face meeting actually occurs, and which we think is characteristic of location-aware communities connected through text messaging, in which locations are public and rendered through map-like representations that make the proximity between members recognizable.

The next extract provides an example of such openings and the kind of moral expectations that accompany their accomplishment:

The reference to S's proximity in turn 1 is characteristically modulated by a marker which tones it down in a kind of hypothetical question ("It seems that...,"

Extract no. 5

1. **N to S (20:19:38)** : 今晩、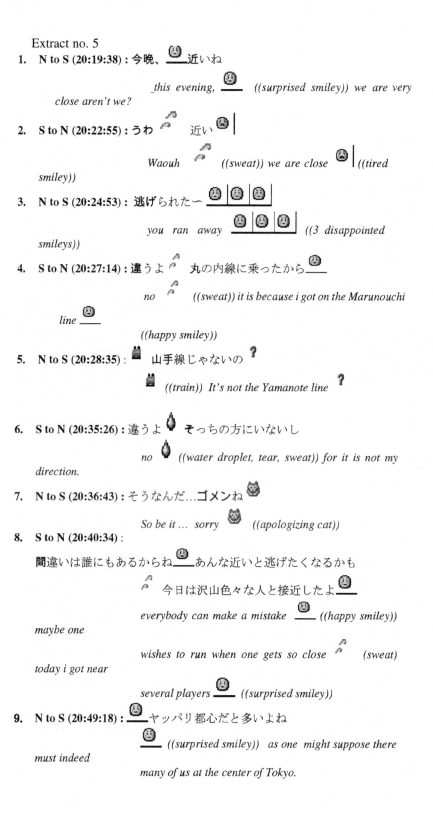近いね

   _this evening, ((surprised smiley)) we are very close aren't we?

2. **S to N (20:22:55)** : うわ♪　近い｜

   Waouh ((sweat)) we are close ｜((tired smiley))

3. **N to S (20:24:53)** : 逃げられた〜

   you ran away ((3 disappointed smileys))

4. **S to N (20:27:14)** : 違うよ♪　丸の内線に乗ったから

   no ♪ ((sweat)) it is because i got on the Marunouchi line ((happy smiley))

5. **N to S (20:28:35)** : 山手線じゃないの？

   ((train)) It's not the Yamanote line ？

6. **S to N (20:35:26)** : 違うよ　そっちの方にいないし

   no ((water droplet, tear, sweat)) for it is not my direction.

7. **N to S (20:36:43)** : そうなんだ...ゴメンね

   So be it ... sorry ((apologizing cat))

8. **S to N (20:40:34)** :

   間違いは誰にもあるからねあんな近いと逃げたくなるかも

   ♪　今日は沢山色々な人と接近したよ

   everybody can make a mistake ((happy smiley)) maybe one

   wishes to run when one gets so close ♪ (sweat) today i got near

   several players ((surprised smiley))

9. **N to S (20:49:18)** : ヤッパリ都心だと多いよね

   ((surprised smiley)) as one might suppose there must indeed

   many of us at the center of Tokyo.

"It appears that…," "not so?"). In each case observed, the respondent did indeed treat the first turn as a request to confirm this mutual proximity, after which the interaction continued. The opening of the interaction by an adjacent pair oriented toward enunciation and confirmation of the participants' mutual proximity is a conventional device for initiating text message-based interactions, which relies on location-awareness. Such a convention was shaped by use, and is part of the emergent culture of Mogi. Treating the recognition of mediated co-proximity as a form of social encounter is part of the experience of inhabiting a location-aware world.

N then regrets her having moved away, therefore making a face-to-face encounter a possible and expected outcome of their mediated co-proximity. Interestingly, she first offers an account to counter the potential inference that she might have tried to elude that expected outcome (turn 4) and later provides (turn 8) a kind of rule-based justification for being entitled to evade the face-to-face encounters that might ensue from the serendipitous mediated recognition of mutual proximity. She experienced too many mediated co-proximity events on that day, and she cannot be expected to turn all of them into fully blown face-to-face encounters. The implicit inference here is that one cannot treat "properly" all co-proximity events, and N. takes up that inference in his admission that indeed there are many players, which closes the issue (turn 9). Players orient themselves toward treating the onscreen co-proximity as a legitimate occasion for a text message encounter, and possibly, a face-to-face encounter (even if they almost always avoid such an unplanned meeting).

Getting Avatars to "Meet": The Playful "Fabrication" of Mediated Co-Proximity Events

Any activity can be accomplished in different "keyings" (such as play), and is vulnerable to fabrication (Goffman 1974). Players have developed on their own an original kind of collective activity, which was not part of the "official" gameplay, in which they play at "fabricating" co-proximity events. This shows how significant the latter are with respect to the interaction order, and we will now describe that singular practice known as "cara-gattai" (literally, the "meeting of avatars," cara standing as an abbreviation for character or icon and "gattai" referring to the concept of joining, or rejoining). Unforeseen by the designers, "cara-gattai" also testifies to the way the Mogi users engage in an active and innovative appropriation of the game: they are "active users," a theme of growing concern for Science and Technology Studies (Oodshorn and Pinch 2003), and particular relevant to online game communities.

Without intending it, the designers of Mogi have left open the possibility for players to "freeze" their positions in a given place, by getting there, connecting to the game, and not refreshing their radar screen after they have left the place. Players have been quick to discover and exploit this loophole in the game software. They

Extract no. 6

1. D to F (16:07:41) : 合体おめでとうございます

Congratulations for the gattai _____ *((lol))*

2. F to D (16:09:22) : バレた

Did you see it

3. D to F (16:12:55) : すぐわかるから Gさんゎ昨日から頑張ってたみたいだけど

I found it immediately _____ It seems thar Mr G was trying hard since

yesterday

have used it to invent a new form of playful encounter based on the disjunction of their actual embodied location, and the apparent onscreen location of their icon that such a "freezing" of the icon's position on the game map allows. The goal is for a player to position his icon at a given place so that later another player will move so that his own icon will appear onscreen close to the first one, or better still, will touch it, creating the appearance of an extreme case of co-proximity event. The whole point of the performance is that the subject of the "cara-gattai," and other players will appreciate it as a feat. It is a performance meant to be public, which therefore relies on the fact that locations are public data.

Extract no. 6 provides a typical "cara-gattai"-related exchange.

D initiates the exchange by commenting on a gattai performance. She constitutes herself as a witness of it in her PC (and therefore as a member of the gameplay as a public space), and treats its recognition as something noticeable, even standing out (she could see it "immediately," turn 3), worthy of a casual appreciative comment. F collaborates to that treatment of the Gattai as an interactionally relevant topic by returning a question calling for some elaboration n D's part, i.e., "fishing" for more positive appreciations of the performance.

We have observed several instances in which either a player initiated an attempt to do "cara-gattai" with another, and discussed this accomplishment with others. In some cases, a distant player suggested that possibility to a moving player. "Cara-gattai" is a fundamentally a public performance whose accomplishment by two players (one acting deliberately and the other collaborating deliberately or participating unwittingly

Extract no. 7

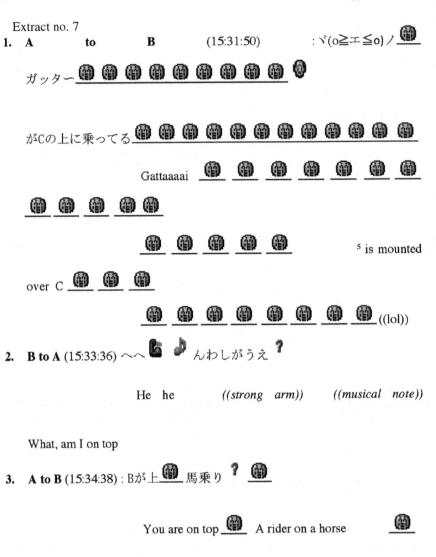

1. A   to   B   (15:31:50)   : v(o≧ｴ≦o)ノ

ガッター

がCの上に乗ってる

Gattaaaai

⁵ is mounted

over C

((lol))

2. B to A (15:33:36) へへ 　 んわしがうえ

He he   ((strong arm))   ((musical note))

What, am I on top

3. A to B (15:34:38) : Bが上　馬乗り

You are on top　 A rider on a horse

through his current displacements) rely on the noticing and the appreciation of an audience of skilled connected players, liable to make inferences from positions and movements of icons on the screen to potential or actual co-proximity events.

Sexual undertones that play on the embodied intimacies of (public) mediated co-proximity events are often alluded to displaying a particular mode of appreciation of "cara-gattai" as a paradoxically embodied (since the whole point is that players' bodies are not actually close) form of public performance. In the following extract, one female player spontaneously "exclaims" on the "cara-gattai" performed by the other player, he asks her about their exact gattai configuration which he has not seen itself (displaying his interest in the actual iconic consequences of that achievement), and she answers by developing the sexual implications of the configuration she has noticed.

The development of "cara-gattai" as a shared playful practice among the community of players stems from the ability to assess and monitor the distance of icons on game maps with respect to the possible production of a co-proximity event), and on the way the design of the game supports the noticing of screen-mediated co-proximity events. Moreover the practice of doing "cara-gattai" ostensibly relies on the disjunction between what happens in the screens and in the space of ordinary perception: "cara-gattai" is meaningful in the way it actually disjoins co-proximity and co-presence, while preserving co-presence a salient feature of the situation, as a potential relevant development that may be mentioned, discussed, and joked upon. It shows how players orient toward a dual accountability regime, in which they work to make their location and mutual positioning accountable both in the "physical" space of "ordinary" embodied experience, and in the mediated spaces constituted by Mogi players' screens. "Doing cara-gattai" also makes visible how much the collective ethos of the game is grounded in normative expectations about the public character of location. As one player puts it, "one wants to show others that we are in the same place and having fun." The practice of "cara-gattai" testifies to one's commitment to that collective ethos, through a normatively expected contribution to the kind of public good on which such a location-aware, leisure-oriented community is founded: creating collective fun by playing in a meaningful way with publicly noticeable mediated co-proximities.

With respect to actual face-to-face encounters, doing "cara-gattai" is a way to play with the meanings of co-present situations while keeping actual co-presence at bay. This displays co-presence in the location-aware community as something which is fraught with potential dangers, and that is to be avoided most of the time. Through the collective practice of "cara-gattai," face-to-face encounters within the location-aware community are constructed as highly consequential situations, and that as such, are to remain exceptional. When they do occur, however, they may take the unusual form of a public and collective performance.

When Face-to-Face Encounters Become a Collective Public Performance

Players rarely get to meet face-to-face. When they do so, such a face-to-face encounter, if it occurs while they are connected, will be a public occurrence and a highly noticeable and noticed event, for it will lead to a superposition of their icons on the gameplay maps. If the encounter involves a male and a female player, they also would be open to all sorts of lewd inferences and comments. Players therefore often react to the very singular mediated public character of face-to-face encounters in the game community by logging out during the encounter. But then they stop sharing their location with other players, a sharing in which the social order of the Mogi community is grounded. A player we have interviewed summarizes this particular tension thus:

> If a man meets a woman face-to-face, other players will notice the two superposed icons, and rumors will start to propagate. It will become difficult for them to go on playing Mogi. (Question: but they can always log out when they meet?) In that case only they will have fun. It is a dilemma. One wants to show others that we are in the same place and having fun. Then there is a struggle between the desire to show oneself to others and the embarrassment to be seen by others

There are some instances that vividly show the way the meaning of face-to-face encounters may be reshaped in a location-aware community. In the example we want to discuss here, one (female) player travels with her sister and her children to another region for a short vacation. It happens that a player in the same team with whom she is well acquainted and has been flirting lives in the same region, and she has told him about her trip. He then decides to move toward her destination.

In line with the behavior discussed in the previous section, their trip becomes a public performance. Other players from their own team, or players they are acquainted with from other teams keep noticing they are on the move and judge they might be getting into one form or another of co-proximity later on. They send them text-messages that make explicit such noticing and invite the mobile players to elaborate, which leads to the type of exchange shown in sect. 6.3. As they get closer, some players (those with whom they text messages on a regular basis) suggest to the moving players that since they are getting closer and this is an unusual occasion, they might seize it to accomplish a "cara gattai" encounter. The male player responds enthusiastically to this suggestion, which leads to many text messages discussing his successive attempts to accomplish "cara-gattai" with the travelling female player.

Meanwhile, he has been continuously flirting with her, and the possibility of an actual romantic encounter has emerged as a salient possibility. Again the potential face-to-face encounter is discussed by text messages with some other players who appear to be aware of (if not monitoring) their growing mutual attachment. The romantic encounter will eventually occur, but out of the "public" eye, for during a few hours during that particular night, the two involved players will log out the game altogether. This was the only moment in those few days before and after, during which they could be considered "off line" from the location-aware community of players (with whom they usually exchange many dozens of text messages per day). The next day, the usual intense text message activity was resumed with both players discussing and commenting what happened, with different degrees of explicitness according to the correspondents.

What has occurred here? A face-to-face encounter, but a very singular one, whose occurrence not only involved the coordinated displacements and mutual agreement of both parties, but also a dozen of other players and hundreds of text messages discussing and commenting the event over 2 weeks. Such a face-to-face encounter, "real gattai," must be considered as a public performance and a collective accomplishment. By being produced and displayed as a rare event, it contributes to build and reassert the ethos of the location-aware community as one in which one's displacements and positioning with respect to other members is something which is always noticeable and liable to be noticed and legitimately so (except during the face-to-face encounter itself), and for which by way of consequence co-proximity and face-to-face encounters are especially meaningful.

Conclusion: Toward an Anthropology of Encounters and Social Life in Location-Aware Cultures

By analyzing in detail a corpus of text messages exchanged by the Mogi players, who compose one of the first instances of a non-experimental location-aware community, we have been able to identify some crucial features of the kind of interaction order it supports. Much revolves around two characteristic features. First, players' locations are treated by them as public data which may be monitored and noticed by other known and unknown (mostly PC-based) players at any time, on a mundane basis. Such noticing is usually performed so as to turn the current location of a given player into a meaningful event (presenting such location as unusual, or remarking on a chance co-proximity) that is worthy of notice. Location becomes a "mentionable" item that can be discussed between acquainted players. It is a "safe topic" to initiate or fill a text-message exchange, much as the weather in co-present encounters in a rural "British" village.

Second, because the game offers different maps figuring geolocalized players, such as the mobile "radar" interface, the degrees of spatial proximity between players become visible. This gives rise to "mediated" co-proximity events where two participants may mutually recognize they appear simultaneously on their mobile screen's maps. This is treated as being close and gives rise to a particular, conventional form of greeting (and therefore of encounter) which topicalizes such closeness (of the type "We are close? Yes we are close"). We have shown how such a mutual recognition of proximity entailed an expectation that a face-to-face encounter would be relevant next, and how such an expectation was treated in this location-aware culture, i.e., by avoiding such an encounter most of the time, but accounting for not having been able to do so. We have also shown how such co-proximity events were so central to the form-of-life which dwells in such a location-aware setting that such events were playfully fabricated by the players, in the frame of an unintended and unforeseen (by the designers) gameplay to which they have even given a name, that is "cara gattai": playing to get one's icon to touch that of another player (who may be aware or not of the game), and expecting such a performance to be noticed and appreciated by an audience of players within the location-aware community.

With respect to encounters, players in a location-aware world are oriented and engaged simultaneously in two different interaction orders, one based on "ordinary" embodied presence and proximity, leading to co-present encounters. The other relies on the mediated visibility of location and recognition of proximity of avatars on electronic map-like representations. So wherever they may be, they are always in a sense "beyond being there" (Hollan and Stornetta 1992). This is striking in some of the forms that some co-present encounters, such as dating, may take in Mogi: such face-to-face encounters may become shared performances and large-scale collective public events, with many players monitoring, commenting, and gossiping about the progress of the main participants. They constitute a kind of collective ritual which displays prominently the resources from which a location-aware "society" is built.

More generally, the accomplishment of the original forms of encounter we have described ties some game-specific resources (the public availability of location, the possibility of jointly recognizing and monitoring on screen spatial proximities) to core cultural meanings of social life in the Mogi location-aware world. This goes beyond Mogi. The Mogi players may look like a strange kind of tribe in the anthropological sense (and they are indeed), but their social behavior has a wider relevance. It is bound to be a feature of any location-aware group that it will have to develop collective ways to deal with the social consequences of the public availability, recognizability, and sharing of locations and proximities: the interaction order and the culture of location-aware communities will be for a great part founded on the meanings, and expectations that have been elaborated to deal collectively with the social consequences of proximity-at-a-distance and of the unusual forms of shared encounters they entail. And emerging location-aware cultures will always involve the interplay of design practices (which shape the artefactual mediations through which members become aware of locations and proximities), and of the inhabitants' repeated copings with augmented social gatherings over extended periods, neither of which suffices by itself to determine the outcome. Because players have enduringly inhabited the Mogi world and learned to make sense of it together, it is highly significant as a kind of laboratory in the wild, from the standpoint of which we may start to understand how collective experiences of location-awareness and shared encounters are shaped and coalesce into original cultures.

References

Barkhuus L & Dourish P (2004) Everyday encounters with context-aware computing in a campus environment. In: Proceedings of Ubicomp '04, 232-249. Springer, Berlin

Barkhuus L, Chalmers M, Tennent P, Hall M, Bell M, Sherwood R & Brown B (2005) Picking pockets on the lawn; the development of tactics and strategies in a mobile game. In: Proceedings of Ubicomp 2005, 358-374. Springer, Berlin

Benford S, Anastasi R, Flintham M, Drozd A Crabtree A, Greenhalgh C, Tandavanitj N, Adams, M & Row-Farr J (2003) Coping with uncertainty in a location-based game. IEEE Pervasive Computing 2 (3), 34-41. DOI= http://dx.doi.org/10.1109/MPRV.2003.1228525

Clark H (1996) Using language. Cambridge University Press, Cambridge

Crabtree A & Rodden T (2008) Hybrid ecologies: understanding cooperative interaction in emerging physical-digital environments. Personal Ubiquitous Comput. 12 (7), 481-493. DOI= http://dx.doi.org/10.1007/s00779-007-0142-7

Dourish P (2006) Re-space-ing place :"place" and "space" Ten years on. In: Proceedings of CSCW 2006, 299-308. ACM Press, New York

Duranti A (1997) Universal and culture-specific properties of greetings. Journal of Linguistic Anthropology 7(1), 63-97

Goffman E (1971) Relations in public. microstructure of the public order. Harper & Row, New York

Goffman E (1974) Frame Analysis. An essay on the Organization of experience. New York: Harper and Row

Griswold W, Shanahan G, Brown S, Boyer R, Ratto M, Shapiro R & Truong T (2003). ActiveCampus. experiments in community-oriented ubiquitous computing. Computer 37 (10), 73-81. DOI= http://dx.doi.org/10.1109/MC.2004.149

Heritage J (1984) A change-of-state token and aspects of its sequential placement. In: Atkinson JM & Heritage J (eds) structures of social action, 299-345. Cambridge University Press, Cambridge

Heritage J (2005) The terms of agreement: indexing epistemic authority and subordination in talk-in-interaction. Social Psychological Quarterly 68(1), 15-38

Hine C (2000) Virtual ethnography. Sage, London

Hollan J & Stornetta S (1992). Beyond being there. In: Proceedings of CHI'92, 119-125. ACM Press, New York

Licoppe C (2009 in press) Recognizing mitual 'proximity' at a distance. Weaving together mobility, sociality and technology. Journal of Pragmatics 41

Licoppe C & Guillot R (2006) ICTs and the engineering of encounters. A case study of the development of a mobile game based on the geolocation of terminals. In: Urry J & Sheller, M (eds) mobile technologies of the city, 152-176. Taylor and Francis, London

Licoppe C & Inada Y (2006) Emergent uses of a location aware multiplayer game. Mobilities 1 (1), 39-61

Licoppe C & Inada Y (2008) Geolocalized technologies, location-aware communities and personal territories: The mogi case. Journal of Urban Technology 15(3), 5-24

Licoppe C & Inada Y (2009 in press) Mediated proximity and its dangers in a location aware community: a case of 'stalking'. In: De Souza Silva A & Sutko DM (eds) digital cityscapes: merging digital and urban playspaces. Peter Lang, New York

Oodshorn N & Pinch T (2003) How users and non users matter. In: Oodshorn N & T (eds), How users matter. The co-construction of users and technology, 1-25. M.I.T. Press, Massachusetts

Steinkuehler C (2006) The mangle of play. Games and Culture 1 (3), 199-213

Chapter 7
Bluetooth as a Playful Public Art Interface

Maria N. Stukoff

Introduction

Recent innovations in the use of emergent communication technologies are projects that take playful encounters to the next level. Big games (Lantz 2006), location-based games (Hemment 2004) or pervasive games (Benford et al. 2003) are the latest HCI paradigms that combine the complexities of real-time, physical/virtual space and multiuser interaction into newly-negotiated urban playgrounds. Projects such as Pac-Lan (2006) designed by Mobile Radicals[1] present a mixed reality environment played out via mobile phone and RIDF tags. Hamilton and Southern (2007)landlines technology turns complex GPS data into multiple line drawings to interpret and record peoples' movement through physical spaces. Blast Theory's Day of the Figurines (2007), was a multiuser play environment where the progress or context of a virtual city and its miniature inhabitants were kept up-to-date by tracking people's activities via text messaging. Building on earlier communication-based projects including Hole-In-Space by Galloway and Rabinowitz (1980), as well as the telematic networking installations such as Telematic Dreaming created by Sermon and Zapp (1992), blu_box enabled shared experiences between participants that took hold of the "virtual and actual, here and now" (Hjorth 2007). The blu_box system enabled the public to interconnect with both the virtual and physical performance space in the same manner that new social encounters were made possible by the afore-mentioned applications of integrated telecommunication tools and live satellite links. The concept of public art was explored in terms of how mobile and wireless networks can inspire members of the public to consciously collaborate (Lacy 1995) with each other in a socially dynamic (Kluitenberg 2000) urban playground.

M. Stukoff (✉)
The Manchester Digital Development Agency (MDDA) and the Manchester Institute for Research and Innovation in Art and Design (MIRAD), Manchester Metropolitan University (UK), Righton Building, Cavendish Street, Manchester, M15 6BG, UK
e-mail: mstukoff@yahoo.co.uk

[1] http://www.mobileradicals.com/i

K.S. Willis et al. (eds.), *Shared Encounters*, Computer Supported Cooperative Work,
DOI 10.1007/978-1-84882-727-1_7, © Springer-Verlag London Limited 2010

These examples suggest that physical co-presence of the public and the importance of face-to-face communication have been critical in establishing meaningful shared experiences in mixed-reality environments. The HCI design tools and applications alone would achieve little, "without real-world interactions" (Büscher 2008) to enable trust between users as they explore the technical interface and the purpose for which to use the technology. It is this socially shared common goal and the exploration of a hybrid environment between real and virtual places, where play (Huizinga, 1936) can take place. Thus, in considering public art as a playful social encounter, I refer to Susanne Lacy's (Lacy 1995) description of new genre public art (NGPA) practices, which she describes as follows:

> …not built on material, spaces and artistic media but rather on concepts of audiences relationship to communication and the ability to create social meaning

This was the starting point of the research project to interlink public art, process-based design approaches, and emergent communication technologies.

Every Passing Moment

EPM was a 2D-animated graphic landscape coaxed into existence by incoming MAC ID data recorded by the blu_box system (see Fig. 7.1). As people walked across the Clayton Square in front of the Liverpool BBC big screen in United Kingdom, anyone with an active Bluetooth device automatically seeded a flower in the virtual landscape.

Fig. 7.1 Every passing moment a new flower appears! One of 12 EPM landscape scenes

Depending on the public's path, a small red, blue, and yellow flower pod was generated in an allocated garden patch. The color of a flower depended on the public's proximity to an urban gardener (i.e., three project guides dressed as gardeners) wearing colored T-shirts that corresponded to the flower types they activated. Each guide was equipped with a mobile phone installed with the blu_box system that referenced the colored tag of the performer with the colored tag of the digital flower. If a MAC ID number was only recorded once, the initially planted flower slowly began to fade away, denoting that the person was no longer present in the playground. Larger and taller flowers only became activated as the public became willing team members, and their MAC ID was repeatedly registered by blu_box. At a growth rate of 50% of the fully-grown flower, the bud began to spin, and released a short chime sound (see Figs. 7.2 and 7.3). This indicated that a person had stood in the garden nurturing their flower long enough to be considered an active player. Each garden was given its own unique chime sound harmonized to complement twelve atmospheric sound tracks arranged for each of the landscape levels. Additional sounds of bird songs, rain and wind, kids laughing, and animal sounds such as sheep baa-ing or dogs barking were randomly triggered to catch the attention of passersby. The aim was to break the usual cacophony of urban sounds surrounding the urban screen, such as music coming from a shop, the hum of people, and the familiar noise of BBC news broadcasts.

The role of the gardeners was threefold. First, they invited the passing public to join their urban garden and to nurture a seeded flower to maturity. Second, they encouraged a competitive element by recruiting players to their own team. Teams competed against each other in growing the largest flower display to cover the urban screen. Third, the gardeners acted as project guides, providing information

Fig. 7.2 Typical landscape level with a variety of flowers growing on the BBC big screen

Fig. 7.3 Left area of screen: flowers nurtered by red team players, center: flowers from blue team, right: yellow team flowers

Fig. 7.4 An explanation of how to take part and play EPM was screened every six landscapes

about Bluetooth and mobile technology (see Fig. 7.4). When a player chose a gardener, their small flower pod started to flourish. The temperament of each plant, for example, height and bud growth, was solely determined by the duration that a player stayed in the Bluetooth zone. Once a team had won the screen (see Fig. 7.5), a new garden landscape and flower types were launched.

Fig. 7.5   The winning flower garden covered the entire screen

No flower or growth characteristic was ever the same. The character of each flower was uniquely based on the recorded MAC ID number, and each garden level offered a new visual play experience. Each of the twelve landscapes lasted four minutes in duration covering an hour of screening time, with its own unique flower types and generative actions. Anyone with a Bluetooth–enabled mobile phone instantly contributed to the garden and could play along. No prior downloading of an application or registration to a website, or login was necessary.

Research Investigation

The opportunity to develop the blu_box system arose during the Oxford Road Cultural Corridor development scheme (established in 2004). Oxford Road is a major traffic route running into the city of Manchester, United Kingdom and is to become a site to be made into destination places by a challenging and integrated Public Arts initiative. This offered artists a blank canvas for testing new public art experiences that were to network audiences, architecture, cafes, and bars using mobile and wireless technologies. This research into play in the public realm was derived from this initial urban development scheme, and combines aspects of interactivity, performance, and installation explored in my art practice.

One can suggest that the sprawl of urbanization, alongside the growth of hard-wired gaming devices, such as the home PC and video consoles, has contributed to the decline of physical games being played in the streets. Here I draw an important distinction between sport-orientated game activity, for example skateboarding or kicking the football, as opposed to games of "Chase" or "Cowboys and Indians." The advancement of mobile and wireless communication technologies have made it possible to revive social play in "real world" (Benford et al. 2003), and provide alternative outdoor game experiences. Public squares and urban screens have been converted into interactive and responsive playgrounds. Blu_box aimed to establish just such a real-world playground using Bluetooth protocol, to encourage collective and social action (Galloway 2005) as the art experience.

Development of Blu_Box

Blu_box was developed in partnership with ONTECA, a Liverpool-based game and media lab lead by creative director Jon Wetherall.[2] As a team, we developed and tested blu_box in three project prototypes: foto_box, eco_box, and EMP between 2004 and 2008. From the outset we made a conscious decision to work with commercially available mobile phones in order to reach the widest possible audience for delivering the artwork. During the first twelve months, we focused on the technical interaction between the Bluetooth system and end-user to test potential play interfaces. This prototyping was integral to the design of a Bluetooth-enabled system that connected large numbers of discoverable Bluetooth devices in close proximity of each other. We examined and evaluated commercial Bluetooth solutions that supported Java applications for routing data to and from mobile phones. After testing the Possion PX30,[3] a hackable Linux-based wireless router featuring WLAN, we decided on the Blip System due to its high bandwidth connectivity solution.[4] Blip was tested during the first two trials: foto_box and eco_box, then abandoned. Blip's hardwired node required a local power source, and with the consideration to design battery-operated nodes, there were few available installation sites inside the outdoor performance zone. This initially limited our design trajectory for using the Blip system. The potential for unstable connections between Blip nodes and players for which Bluetooth networking is renowned; and in this case the fluctuating and ebbing (Locke 2005) signal between devices may have affected the playful encounter between the player and the artwork. To provide the best possible interactive user-experience, we had to create an interface that did not rely on Bluetooth connection permissions to allow the up-load of data to and from a player's device.

The completed blu_box system overcame this problem by searching only for MAC ID numbers as its interaction trigger. As a preloaded JAVA application, blu_box was running on three mobile phones carried by the three project guides in the physical playground. The collected data was automatically sent via GPRS to a server running MySql (a multiuser SQL database management system). From here,

---

[2] http://www.onteca.com

[3] http://www.linuxdevices.com/articles/AT7459336271.html

[4] http://www.blipsystems.com

the twelve numbers were interpreted via a PHP scripting language into our Adobe Flash-based game engine to activate generative growth factors. These in turn animated the flower objects on the urban screen.

Prototype 1

The first blu_box interface was tested during the opening night of the third Salford Film Festival 2005. Working with the host venue LIME Bar, the blu_box system was connected to an LED screen behind the bar creating a photo-slide situation: foto_box. At 20-minute intervals, blu_box projected a custom-made image inviting festival-goers to search for the discoverable foto_box nodes and to send their images or movies to the LED screen for public broadcast. To cope with the eventuality of potential connection failures and to explain the work to those unfamiliar with Bluetooth networking, two team members were placed amongst the audience. They also assumed an observatory role to watch how people engaged with the Bluetooth network. Foto_box was to be a user-friendly application for building shared experiences in public place.

During the initial prototyping, we realized that multiple signals got jammed or devices disconnected when multiple users simultaneously connected to one of the Bluetooth nodes. This made it a very cumbersome interface. To overcome this dilemma, the Java-enabled blu_box system automatically alternated between the two Blip nodes by buffering and processing multiple data streams. This allowed a stream of images to be projected onto the LED screen.

Prototype 1 Outcomes

Over 500 personalized images and several movies were sent to foto_box for public viewing. The most popular projections were images of cats and dogs, family poses, people in funny positions, and landscape shots. Some unsuitable images (i.e., nudes) had to be swiftly replaced on-the-fly by the project team members. Being an over-eighteen's venue, such imagery did not seem to cause any complaints or to disturb the viewing crowd, especially as the next image was already cued by blu_ box. During our observations we noticed that other playful connections were being established via foto_box that we had not anticipated. A game broke out between players and one team member over how many of their photos were shown on the screen, and for a great length of time images of family, friends, pets, and funny-faces were displayed. As in a game of cards that matches like-for-like, image content followed a theme whereby a series of animals or funny faces would follow on from each other. Several images appeared again and again, competing for the longest duration on screen. We observed several guests looking about the bar with mobile phone poised in hand, standing up from their seats to look for opponents. In the questionnaire, we asked players about their knowledge of Bluetooth, ways they use and would like to use Bluetooth, and the overall experience of broadcasting to foto_box. We received very positive feedback, stating it was fun to interact with the screen and see their images displayed. Out of the 28 returned feedback forms, only 4 players had initial difficulty connecting to foto_box throughout the 5-hour screening. Thirty-five percent of participant feedback said they never had used Bluetooth before, and foto_box was their first experience of sending files via Bluetooth.

Further discussion with participants revealed that many of the mobile phones used that evening were newly purchased and that the owners were unaware of how to turn Bluetooth on, or knew that their phone has already been set to discovery mode. This was backed up by the data we found on the blu_box server with a large number of mobile phone factory model names amongst the personalized nicknames frequent Bluetooth users choose to give their phones. The fact that many of the newly purchased mobile phones were automatically set to Bluetooth-On was a huge discovery for us. We also learned that having team members in the audience was a beneficial decision. Team members were able to put first-time Bluetooth users at ease and allowed them time to get familiar with the technology so that they could participate. We observed that this confidence helped open up conversation between strangers as they helped each other to connect to foto_box.

Development of Prototype 1

Beyond the simple user-generated content sharing of the foto_box project, the potential for Bluetooth to create highly social encounters between players and/or strangers emerged. The potential for playful interaction with many individual mobile phones at any given moment set us thinking about proximity between players and the Blip nodes, and ways to employ signal strength between Bluetooth devices as a visible and playful interface. Outcomes for prototype development included:

1. Use of multiple nodes streamlining simultaneous Bluetooth connections
2. Potential for multiplayer activity between public and a public screen
3. Networking players in close proximity of each other via Bluetooth
4. Support users unfamiliar with the interface via face-to-face communication

Prototype 2

The second version of blu_box built on the potential for Bluetooth proximity as a multiuser gaming interface. As part of our research, we investigated other proximity software including Nokia's SENOR technology[5] and Microsoft's Zune MP3 player.[6] SENOR allowed users to discover other SENOR users in their immediate

---

[5]http://press.nokia.com/PR/200506/997857_5.html

[6]http://www.zune.net/en-US/

proximity and to read each others' profiles. Zune's capabilities as an always on device, searched to establish connections with other Zune devices to temporally link music libraries. The growing number of commercially available Bluetooth applications utilizing close-range networking energized our research. To test the close-proximity networking, we proposed the eco_box garden environment, which could be populated with a variety of digital plants brought to life by proximity readings and repeat visits to the blu_box nodes. The garden concept was considered a communal space where people would automatically understand the goal and could nurture a series of generative plants to populate a public garden. The concept was initially developed as a downloadable Java application to be installed onto a mobile phone prior to the game experience.

Once downloaded, the player had the necessary game functionality to monitor flower growth via signal strength to the various blu_box nodes placed along Oxford Rd (see Fig. 7.6). The proximity readings acted as a feeding sensor for the plant life displayed on the user's phone (see Fig. 7.7). The closer a player came to a node, the higher the signal strength, causing the plant to grow faster and taller until it reached maturity.

On completion, the plant data would be uploaded back to the blu_box system and then automatically inserted into a communal garden projected on an urban screen. The creation and the design of the garden was solely the responsibility of the players. This was dependent on the time players devoted to nurturing the organic structure in

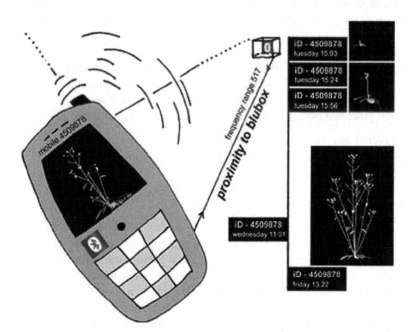

Fig. 7.6 Artist impression of eco_box running on a mobile phone showing the time and date when a MAC ID number is registered by blu_box to continue nurturing the plant

Fig. 7.7 Testing the proximity levels as a generative action to feed the plant on the mobile phone screen

the blu_box zone as they went about their everyday activities along Oxford Rd. However, with the pregame installation process, we lost the intended immediacy of play, the here and now, and the accessibility for everyone with a mobile phone to contribute to the garden. We reconsidered ways in which blu_box could register any active Bluetooth signal and allow passersby to contribute to the garden without downloading the eco_box application. The design concept also tested ways of incorporating any visible Bluetooth active device passing through the blu_box zone without prior download. This transit data was to become aggregators for creating "anomalies" in the garden such as the appearance of butterflies. This new design approach generated two new levels of participatory engagement.

- Registered and dynamic play to consciously contributing to the garden.
- Unregistered and unconscious play, unknowingly activating anomalies.

Outcomes of Prototype 2

The eco_box prototype was never realized as a final artwork. The functionality however, was tested successfully creating the desired plant levels generated by proximity readings and time measurements. Eco_box, we realized, was only a single player application that enabled individuals to contribute to a group environment rather than fostering social encounters between players in a shared experience. However, what we wanted to design was an interface that could support multiple users interacting simultaneously. Download and installation procedures as well as the expected level of Bluetooth networking were too unfriendly – especially to those users still unsure of Bluetooth networking protocol. To maximize participation, blu_box had to be free of any of the registration processes that we had ourselves experienced as being awkward in other Big Game projects, including our own eco_box prototype.

Prototype 3

Bringing together lessons learnt from the previous blu_box trials, the final interface for EPM had to be user-friendly and facilitate multiuser interaction. Technically, the playful encounter had to be easy to follow to ensure open accessibility to the artwork. The physical co-presence of project team members was reintroduced as an essential component for establishing contact with the passing public, explaining the work and helping inexperienced Bluetooth users. Earlier observations confirmed that face-to-face support of participants resulted in confident play activity, and thus in a more meaningful encounter between players. Furthermore, blu_box had to be a seamless interaction tool and avoid unstable and inconsistent Bluetooth connections (mentioned earlier in the chapter) to avoid disenchantment with the interaction experience. This was overcome by designing an interface that only searched for Bluetooth active devices without having to establish a connection.

By recording only MAC ID numbers, blu_box bypassed connection permissions to send/receive data, thus enabling people with all levels of technical ability to play. Blu_box thus allowed for a truly ubiquitous interaction experience (see Fig. 7.8). The new blu_box system also reassured potential privacy issues that had been

Fig. 7.8 Project guide watching his yellow garden prosper with two players

raised by the BBC screen management concerned that blu_box could establish unauthorized connections to the public. Having to adhere to the BBC's public broadcasting guidelines, EPM could not record any personal data (including the personalized names of a mobile phone) without copyright releases from those individuals. The MAC ID number collected by blu_box was considered as identifying an openly accessible device, not a person with whom one could associate a personalized nametag given to a mobile phone.

Because no external buttons or controls had to be navigated, the playful exploration of EPM was not hindered by a technical device. The Bluetooth-On mobile phone could be left in a handbag or jacket pocket, allowing players to freely engage with the space around them and to safely interact with team members and strangers around them. The focus was on play, having fun, and competing with other garden teams without the technology as a focus. Through prototyping we developed a technical interface truly omnipresent in the encounter between the players, our live performers, the art experience, and the city screen. The EPM emerged as an example of public art driven by collective action and playful encounters.

Every Passing Moment: Review

The EPM was shown in four one-hour sessions on the Liverpool BBC big screen over two consecutive days in June 2008. In each hour, the full 12 EPM landscape levels were broadcast in conjunction with their atmospheric sound track, and the randomly triggered environmental noises. To study how the public engaged with EPM, and to evaluate mobile and wireless networks as a new paradigm for contemporary public art practices, we conducted a series of project observations. The project guides collected first-hand the reactions of participants as they progressed from unconscious, to conscious through to dynamic player, and noted the shift in their participation as the artwork was it was explained to them. Further observations were conducted by myself and team members standing outside the blu_box playground, watching and witnessing the unfolding interaction between players, the gardeners, and the urban screen. To survey the impact that the performance space and the urban gardeners had upon passersby in more detail, we documented one event on video. In addition, players were asked to fill in a basic tick-box questionnaire to describe their encounter with EPM. From the blu_box server we collected data regarding the number of Bluetooth devices recorded that actively grew flowers and the volume of devices overall seen that contributed to the content of EPM. Through these methods we were able to evaluate whether Bluetooth networking could provide socially dynamic and playful environments for emergent art practices to augment the built environment.

Public Participation

During the 2-day observation period we recognized three distinct levels of public activity with the artwork. These levels we defined as unconscious (unaware contribution), conscious participation (understanding their role of growing flowers), and dynamic play (actively involved in winning the flower competition).

Unconscious Contribution

This refers to individuals unknowingly planting a small flower in the garden as blu_box registered their Bluetooth active device. Every MAC ID was able to plant up to three small flowers, depending on their trajectory through the BBC big screen area, and proximity to each of the color-coded gardeners. In each case, one small flower would appear in the red, yellow, or blue garden patch as they moved through the blu_box network. This unaware connection to blu_box was an important process in building the information architecture on the urban screen. It gave the visual clue to passersby that something was taking place on the screen other than the usual BBC programming. It was also the first step to set in motion the Bluetooth network, assisting the project guides in explaining the evolving artwork, the interface, and the pending game-play. This shifted the otherwise transient public into conscious garden contributors.

Conscious Participation

We observed two different ways in which conscious participation evolved. In the first instance people became aware of the 2D visuals of the animated flower pods on the screen and/or noticed the sound track. People usually slowed down, then stopped to take a longer look at what was happening on the screen or looked around to locate where the sound was emanating from. On the other hand, certain people seemed more intrigued by the activity of the urban gardeners dressed up in green aprons and asked them directly what they were doing or what was happening. In both cases it provided the project guides with the opportunity to approach the public (by inviting them to play), or they were immediately engaged in a conversation about the artwork. At this juncture, unconscious contributors became aware of their personal interaction with the screen and conscious of their involvement in growing flowers. Through this face-to-face dialogue, enough time had passed for blu_box to register the person's MAC ID number repeatedly to spur on the small flower pod. As the flower reached the 50% growth level, the flower bud began spinning and released the attached chime sound to indicate a registered player.

At this point we noticed two behavioral patterns emerge in conscious participants (see Fig. 7.9). The first group stayed to watch their flower grow in the landscape until one of the three gardens won the screen, then moved on without further engagement. Their initial curiosity had been satisfied, as explained in their verbal feedback. The second group became more curious about the idea of a competition and motivated to win the screen for their chosen garden. We witnessed that this allegiance usually occurred on the release of the flower's chime sound. Players began pointing vividly at the screen, identifying themselves with the taller animated flower on the screen. The chime sound seemed to evoke the sense of real-time

Fig. 7.9 Yellow gardener explaining the Bluetooth interface and how to grow a flower

participation in the artwork and we noticed a shift in the way people started to feel responsible for the garden. The invisible link between the physical world and the virtual space of the digital garden was now visible to the players. It appeared that the sound was able to intensify the emotional response of the players to their flower. As different chime sounds were heard in succession, players become aware of other players growing flowers with the other gardeners at the same time. The notion of a competition and playing a game became accelerated as players and the gardeners started to point at the other teams across the playground, counting how many players were gathering about the competing teams. Thus, the physical playground between the three urban gardeners and their team members became visible in front of the BBC big screen.

Dynamic Play

The EPM's competitive element propelled conscious participants to gear up into a dynamic player mode. Dynamic players took ownership of the competitive situation without assistance or incentive from the project guides. Some players took it upon themselves to recruit new players by inviting the passing public to join their team to help win the flower display. Dynamic play also involved players trying to recruit other gardener's players trying to convince them to join their team instead. Through this dynamic participation, the player's encounter between strangers became more social with a common goal of winning as many flower gardens as possible. At the height of one game scenario, jubilant hand gestures were directed toward a losing team in a celebratory manner.

Playful Encounters

Review of the feedback forms and the observational study suggested that conscious participants and dynamic players experienced a playful encounter with the artwork. Furthermore, we witnessed social encounters taking place between strangers as individual players took a lead in recruiting passersby to their teams and began interacting with other players. It became evident that this type of behavior took hold when participants felt confident with the performance environment, understood their role, and that they could interact with the urban screen without the hindrance of any specialized technical know-how (see Fig. 7.10). We deduced that play and the experience of making the artwork come alive was further encouraged by team spirit and the common goal to win. When asked to describe how they felt about interacting with the screen without a visual interaction tool, written responses included:

Fig. 7.10   A project guide is explaining the work to three players

I never seen this done before, really like it

Seeing the garden grow without knowing how was interesting

Kinda strange but was great to take part

Really unusual – wouldn't have thought it possible.

Very different, new and interesting

Was confused at first, then interesting. What I liked best was the active participation

What I liked best was seeing the flowers grow

Winning was great and talking to people

Wanted to find new ways to boost my gardener's flower!

Throughout our observations, we noticed how some people drifted between all three gardeners to test how their presence impacted on the flower garden, and if they could grow more than one flower to contribute to the garden. This was a critical discovery as players involved themselves in all aspects of the art-making process by testing and pushing the boundaries of the experience the artwork could deliver.

Observers and Unwilling Audience

On several occasions we noticed that another audience group emerged on the periphery of the playground. These were members of the public who seemed aware of a performance taking place, watched how people gathered around the three performers, and listened to the project guides explaining what was happening on the urban screen. This group never actually ventured into the heart of the playground but stood outside looking inward, apparently careful not to get involved. On two occasions, I witnessed an outside viewer (in both cases an older lady) approach a recent player (a female player) to find out information about the work instead of asking a project guide.

I was able to approach one of the ladies myself and asked her if she would like to join in and why she did not approach one of the gardeners. The women said that she had noticed people looking at their mobile phones and because she did not have her mobile with her, she deduced she could not take part and did not want to interfere. However, she was interested to know what was happening because she liked the bird song (one of the environmental sound effects). In contrast, we expected to meet with passersby who were reluctant to take part when gardeners approached them. When asked if they wanted to participate and to grow a flower on the screen, the gardeners received comments such as:

Ah sorry got to get my shopping done

No thanks

Not today, maybe next time

Table 7.1 Participation data by time

	Day1: Hour1	Day1: Hour2	Day2: Hour1	Day2: Hour2
Individual Bluetooth active devices seen	1,691	1,600	1,032	2,350
Devices recorded more than 3 times. Activated a fully grown flower	1,444	1,420	852	1,990
Devices seen less than three times: Transitory creating the smaller flower pods	247	418	180	360
Overall detections made to Bluetooth devices	26,730	18,732	13,128	27,099

Participation Data

From the four events, blu_box provided us with data to review how many devices contributed to the EPM garden and how many devices grew mature flowers (Table 7.1). Although this data displays a very high number of active flowers growers, we cannot be certain that all these numbers recorded higher than three times are conscious players.

With commercial shops surrounding the play area, any shoppers with Bluetooth active devices waiting in a queue, for example, could have been picked up by blu_box and added to the flower display. It became apparent to us that many new handsets equipped with Bluetooth 2.0 have a wider signal strength that goes beyond the standard short range of 10 m – exactly the radius we marked out for each performer's space and the blu_box nodes. The data provided us with verification that Bluetooth networking could be a very accessible public infrastructure and used for the exploration of public art or other cultural events. On an average 1,426 flowers were generated in the hour-long screening, far more than we had ever anticipated from the first public trials. In terms of evaluating playful encounters with mobile and wireless networks as a public art experience, we feel that we achieved our goal.

Every Passing Moment: Design Review

The research provided us with an in-depth understanding of how mobile and wireless networks have the potential to create playful public art experiences. Through the diligence of team observation and collected participant feedback, we would be able to review the design of the blu_box interface and to build a better understanding of the relationship that occurred between the public, the performers, the screen, and the artwork. We are particularly interested in how to improve the visualization of the transient Bluetooth data in an interactive playground. We are keen to experiment further with how blu_box could render the digital urban environment more legible (Ingram and Benford 1995) for networked play. The EPM contributed to the imaginative development of art in the public realm and to what constitutes contemporary "placemaking" through emergent communication technologies. Three major design considerations for further improving the blu_box interface emerged from our evaluation.

Tagging Flowers with Mobile Name

To help provide better clues for players to identify their flower, we first considered options to tag each flower with the personal device name often given to mobile phones. However, due to BBC broadcasting guidelines that prohibit the display of personal data without consent (as mentioned earlier in the chapter), this option was not applicable for EPM. By tagging flowers and players, we did not want players to become solely concerned with growing their individual flower - as EPM was about inspiring teamwork. The play mechanics required players to work in collaboration with as many people as possible in order to win the game. We still wanted some type of signal for players to identify their presence in the artwork, and for them to recognize how their contribution (measured in terms of time spent with the gardener), effected the flower's development. This has led us to concentrate more on sound tags to record the growing numbers of players on each team. To differentiate between temporarily seeded flower pods (those created by unconscious passersby) and flowers that were starting to develop their full characteristics, (activated by conscious participants) a chime sound was attached to flowers to indicate when a 50% growth rate had been achieved. Furthermore, the flower bud started to spin for the duration of the sound clip before bursting out with larger flower petals. Each garden was assigned a differently pitched chime effect to announce which garden had registered players and was growing fully fledged flowers. With the sounding of each chime, we observed how participants took more notice of the screen and the number of growing flowers within the color garden they had chosen to play in. On several occasions, as more chime sounds were heard, players counted the larger flowers to match up with the number of players in the team. The sound effect became the key ingredient that cemented a players understanding of being "in-game." This understanding of sound in public place became a crucial HCI component, which will be continued in the next blu_box prototype.

During the event we received a variety of suggestions on how to build on EPM's audio-visual language to reinforce the connection between real place and virtual space. This included the tagging flowers by the display of the mobile phone manufacturer. Each handset has its own Bluetooth prefix; thus players could identify their flower by their handset name (Nokia, Sony, Samsung etc.). This could be a simple and playful visualization technique to make legible the Bluetooth interface between the player and their flower.

We also talked to three participants who suggested that they wanted to receive the image of their flower back onto their handsets when they were winning. We are considering a blu_box design option whereby the winning MAC ID numbers would be sent a flower from the garden via Bluetooth. The participant would therefore have to agree to receive and accept the data sent to their handsets.

Bluetooth Proximity

On the last performance day, the physical space in front of the BBC screen had changed due to the arrival of an ice-cream van. The van occupied almost a quarter of the space in-between project guides, which was necessary in maintaining the 10 m circumferences around the blu_box nodes. The foreshortening of the performance area meant that two performers stood closer together and were in direct competition with each other in recording MAC ID data. We were aware that this may have resulted in players nurturing more than one flower and contributed to the winning of either one of two teams. This is reflected in the blu_box server data from Day 2: Hour 2 (see Table 7.1), where a significant increase in the individual devices was noted from the previous three performance events. We realized that we need to build a proximity guide between gardeners and their players into the future blu_box interface. The new blu_box design would allow only one MAC ID to appear between the three nodes without compromising the transient MAC ID numbers we wish to collect as part of the garden environment.

Performative Role of Project Guides

The importance of legitimizing the role of the project guides as "public actors" in the public square was something we had underestimated. The costume of green aprons and the color-coded T-shirts signaled that each performer was "doing something" but did not effectively communicate the fact that a publicly accessible event was taking place. In our trials, Simon, one of our project guides responsible for activating yellow flowers, noted that:

> ...it would be helpful to have a stronger garden visibility in the square to show I am genuine... because as a guy approaching groups of women or passing mothers with prams felt a bit uncomfortable

We recognized that although people were initially curious about the three performers, no other signage was present in the playground to help clarify the link between the performers and the urban screen. To heighten the performer's role, a small performance stage was created for each project guide to link the animated digital space to what was happing in Clayton Square. Each project guide received a 1 m × 1 m patch of green Astroturf decorated with a selection of silk flowers corresponding to each color garden. This gave each performer a base from which to connect with the public, and a central base of operation to gather players around. It also helped in opening up conversation to strangers to join their garden patch and to help grow flowers on the screen.

The combination of performer and the performance platform made the physical playground more legible (see Figs. 7.11 and 7.12). This relationship between the real physical performance space in front of the urban screen and the projected virtual world will be developed for future EPM events.

Participant Feedback

A generic tick box questionnaire with additional open-ended questions was handed out to participants. The first question gave a selection of five options to choose from to best to describe the EPM event. From the collected forms, 60% chose public art over mobile game, screen entertainment, performance piece, or installation. Asking players to freely describe their experience of EPM the written feedback included:

- Very interesting
- Happy
- Really unusual wont thought it possible
- I liked winning

Fig. 7.11 Each Astroturf was placed within the epicentre of the 10 m radius of the *blu_box* node

Fig. 7.12   Yellow gardener with the performance base at the end of an event

- Weird but fun
- Bizarre
- Wanted to find ways to boost my flower
- Didn't know this could be done
- Felt a bit lost because our garden never won!

Note: No other negative comments were recorded except that *"losing wasn't fun"*

When asked to select the best possible way to describe the interaction with EPM, 80% of those asked wrote that the initial encounter was: "strange at first" but then "really fun." We also provided a question to ascertain how the gardener's role contributed to the art experience. The top answer, chosen by 80% of respondents was that "they explained the work" while 50% also selected "they invited me to take part" and 20% ticked "gave me a point of reference." In response to a question about how players engaged with other team members, 80% ticked; "I talked to people I didn't know before" followed by; "I started inviting strangers to help grow the garden." When asked to comment on how they discovered they were growing a flower on the urban screen, 47% ticked: "I asked the gardener," and the same number of people selected: "watching others play" (see Figs. 7.13 and 7.14).

The feedback from participants confirmed what we had seen in our observation, that by watching others "doing it first," a group of observers decided to take part and became conscious participants. This echoes the concept of social infection (Sheridan et al. 2007) where on-lookers feel more at ease with getting involved when they hear other people talk about it, or observe what is expected of them before they join in. Additional feedback from each of the project guides also

Fig. 7.13 Small crowd of conscious participants gathering around the red performance base

Fig. 7.14 A successful win for the red gardener!

alluded to the fact that players quickly understood that without them, there would be no flowers on the screen and that their collective action was, "making things happen." One player is quoted as saying: "so I am actually doing the artwork on the screen!" From these testimonies we were able to conclude that EPM successfully created a playful encounter between the public and a public artwork.

Finally, commenting on EPM being promoted as a public artwork, Bren O'Callaghan, programme manager of the BBC Big Screen Manager Liverpool stated:

> The majority of submissions I receive for interactive and pervasive media proposals throw up walls of specialist and obtuse "game-play," suited almost exclusively to gadget-addicts and bequiffed culture junkies. Instead, Every Passing Moment makes a crucial deviation. Here, the user-facing interface is a real person in the form of "urban gardeners" who must compete, entice and persuade the passing public to participate. In doing so they present both context and instructions in a form accessible to all – using speech, eye contact, laughter – instead of relying upon the limited specialism of a few without thought to the many (O'Callaghan 2008)

Conclusions

This research presented the way in which Bluetooth networking can effectively create playful encounters as a public art experience. Three distinct behavioral patterns emerged from the encounter with regard to how the public interfaced with the virtual flower garden of EPM. The way passersby took part can be described as unconscious contributors becoming conscious participants and going on to dynamic players, who engaged with the EPM experience. It also illustrated how the serendipitous nature of Bluetooth networking can successfully function as an HCI tool between people on the move and city infrastructures such as an urban screen. Furthermore, we demonstrated how the application of capturing MAC ID numbers removed the authorization protocol for players to allow connectivity between devices and create an open and accessible public art experience. This became an integral part of the interface design, giving the public room to pay attention to their role as a player instead of focusing on establishing connections or how to use the mobile phone as an interaction tool. Through the EPM process it was revealed that the face-to-face project support (i.e., three live performers) was a crucial component in the design of location-sensitive HCI in outdoor public places. Performers were instrumental in making these new interaction paradigms visible for the public. Moreover, we learnt that the planning and the design of the physical playground needed careful consideration to seamlessly connect the real performance activity with the digital activity seen on the urban screen, and also, to overcome any real-life incidences that may cause unforeseen changes in the use of the public site.

However, one of the most important issues that arose in the study of EPM was how sound transported people into the play activity of the artwork. The chime effects of the animated flowers were able to communicate a real-time interaction that alerted the public to their involvement in that instant more than the animated images on the urban screen. This was an interface design discovery we had not anticipated, and which will lead to further research into the effect of sound in artwork situated in public place. This provides an exciting opportunity for artists to develop communication-rich public art experiences that enhance and build public sites for temporary relaxation (Foucault 1967) and for playful social encounters in the everyday use of urban environments.

Description of Future Work

The next phase is to tour EPM to other screen sites around the United Kingdom and to experiment with blu_box in new context-aware situations in the public sphere. In light of the feedback, we are making several changes to the performance area and the way in which the project guides interact with the passing public.

1. The performance space in the playground needs to be reviewed to authenticate the gardener's presence and their purpose of approaching the passing public. Although the small Astroturf patch sparked conversation between the public and the performer, it was not enough to accentuate its relationship to the screen and the pending game-play.
2. Additional volunteers (i.e., garden assistants) need to be appointed to collectively approach the public and build the team environment. Feedback from the project guides suggested that more women acting as gardeners could help the team dynamics and the potential to reduce initial suspicion when male performers approached women in public.
3. On-site information explaining the art event needs to be provided. We are looking at the possibility of handing out EPM postcards or flyers for people to read in their own time. This is in response to public enquires requesting information about times and dates the next event will take place, and for passing information on to other people.

Acknowledgments EPM and the development of *blu_box* were supported by the Arts Council of England NW. The initial *blu_box* prototype was funded by the Regional Office, Manchester Metropolitan University (MMU). The Manchester City Digital Development Agency (MDDA) kindly financed the research. Many thanks are due to the Liverpool's Big Screen manager and curator, Bren O'Callaghan for all his support. We would also like to thank Jonathan Fisher for the environmental sounds and all the additional assistance of performers and friends, especially ONTECA and Jon Wetherall, who made this artwork possible!

References

Benford S, Anasasi R, Flintham M, Drozd A, Crabtress A, Greenhalgh C, Tandavaitj M, Adams M & Row-Farr J (2003) Coping with uncertainty in a location-based game. IEEE Pervasive Computing, September 2003

Blast Theory (2007) Day Of The Figurines. http://www.dayofthefigurines.co.uk/. Retrieved March 2008

Büscher, M (2008) Participatory Media. Paper presentation at Futuresonic2008, Manchester, UK.

Foucault, M (1967) Of other spaces. French journal Architecture /Mouvement/ Continuité (1984) Translated from the French by Jay Miskowiec.

Galloway, A (2005) Playful mobilities. Presentation at the Ubiquitous Computing lecture series, Emerson College, USA. http://institute.emerson.edu/floatingpoints/05/anne_galloway.php. Retrieved Jan 2006

Galloway K & Rabinowitz S (1980) Hole-In-Space. http://www.ecafe.com/getty/HIS/. Retrieved 3 February 2009

Hamilton J & Southern J (2007) Landlines. http://www.landlines.org/. Retrieved 3 February 2009

Hemment, D (2004) Locative Art. http://www.drewhemment.com/2004/locative_arts.html Retrieved 4 October 2004

Hjorth, L (2007) Domesticating new media: A discussion on locating mobile media. Mobile Media conference proceedings. 2-4th July, University of Sydney, Australia, 179

Huizinga, J (1936) Homo ludens: a study of the play-element in culture. Temple Smith, London

Ingram, R. and S. Benford (1995). Improving the Legibility of Virtual Environments. In Proceedings of 2nd Eurographics Workshop on Virtual Environments, Monte Carlo. Available at: http://www.crg.cs.nott.ac.uk/research/publications/papers/VE95.pdf.

Kluitenberg, E (2000) Media without an audience. http://www.nettime.org/Lists-Archives/nettime-l-0010/msg00204.html. Retrieved June 2005

Lacy, S (ed) (1995) Mapping the terrain. New Genre Public Art. BayPress. Seattle, USA.

Locke M (2005) Being here – some moving stories about mobile technology. Published on receiver #5. Vodafone Group 2006. http://www.receiver.vodafone.com/05/index.html Retrieved Dec 2005

Lantz, F (2006) Big Games and the porous border between the real and the mediated. Published on receiver #16. Vodafone Group 2006. www.receiver.vodafone.com.

O'Callaghan, Bren (2008) Review of 'Every Passing Moment' after the first public art event at the BBC big screen, Liverpool UK.

Pac-Lan (2006) Available at: http://www.pac-lan.com/

Sermon, Paul and Zapp, Andrea (1992) Telematic Dreaming. Available at: http://www.hgb-leipzig.de/~sermon/dream/

Sheridan JG, Bryan-Kinns N & Baylss A (2007). Encouraging witting participation and performance in digital live art. 21st British HCI Group Annual Conference Proceedings, 3-7 September, Lancaster, UK

Chapter 8
A Theoretical Construct of Serious Play and the Design of a Tangible Social Interface

Pamela L. Jennings

Introduction

With the advent of the "serious game" movement, researchers, educators, gamers, digital media artists, and other technology enthusiasts have jumped on the bandwagon of introducing, incorporating, and exploiting social and cultural issues into platforms designed for zero-sum realities. This work is important in an age when computer games have risen in global popularity and the content of many of the most popular games is suspect to violence, stereotypes, and dulling of problem-solving capacities beyond survivalists' notions of weapons and force. With the advent of the "serious" in creative information technologies, it is important to consider the knowledge and wisdom gained from contemporary critical theories on the relationship between us (humans), the tools we make, and their implications on culture and society.

This chapter introduces a theory of creative information technology research and practice called *critical creative technology* (CCT). The theory examines methods to design new interfaces and technologies for facilitating discourse and learning. The theory of CCT is influenced by the premises arising from design theory, theory of communicative acts and the public sphere, and critical theories of technology. Notions about collaboration and conflict resolution through play become a core value from which these new technologies, applications, and interactive experiences are developed. This chapter introduces theories of design thinking and social constructs of play, both key components of the theory of CCT.

The *constructed narratives electronic construction kit* is introduced as an experiment in developing collaborative technologies that are strongly influenced by the confluence of theoretical concepts derived from the theory of CCT. The constructed narrative game is a tangible social interface. Designed for experiments in social networking and learning in co-located environments, the tangible social interface is based on the premises of the tangible user interface (TUI) – physical objects embedded

P.L. Jennings (✉)
Computer & Information Science & Engineering Directorate, Information and Intelligent Systems Division, National Science Foundation, 2100 Wilson Blvd., Arlington, VA, U.S.A.
e-mail: pljenn@gmail.com

with hardware sensors that serve as an interface between embodied gestures and a responsive computer application (Ishii and Ullmer 1997). The "S" for social replaces the "U" for user in the commonly descriptive term TUI. This transforms the applied nature of tangibles into a tool, whose primary goal is to facilitate communication, learning, and discovery between its users. Key to the function of the tangible social interface is the feedback that is simultaneously personalized and yet affected by the collective actions of people collaborating with and through the system. This is a gestalt interaction paradigm where the "whole is greater than the sum of the parts." In the case of the *constructed narratives electronic construction kit* the "whole" is formed as each individual builder contributes to the emerging construction by adding and removing blocks that in turn trigger word shifts in the textual landscape that is mapped to a three-dimensional visualization of the physical construction, and projected into the shared play space.

Critical Creative Technology and Design Thinking

The CCT framework is a foundation for understanding how creative information technologies can facilitate critical discourse between people. The social cartography, a map of confounding social and theoretical ideas and theories, for CCT is founded on a confluence of critical ideas and practices that emphasize social engagement and discourse as agents of negotiation and change (Paulston and Liebman 1995). A web of synergies is metaphorically drawn to connect the following key philosophical influences on the development of social technologies (Jennings 2006):

(a) Embodied interaction – the development of tools and systems that "support an engaged interaction that highlights, celebrates, and augments the social, cultural, and historical importance of how people construct meaning" (Dourish 2001).
(b) Constructivism – the idea that an individual's social, cultural, and historical situation, or "social matrix," impacts the individual's ability to learn and live in the culture in which he/she resides (Spivey 1996; Penuel and Wertsch 1995).
(c) Communicative action and the Bourgeois Public Sphere and its critics – an analysis of the normative rules used to validate speech acts between a speaker and hearer to arrive at a rational consensus about a given topic, and the historical and cultural implications on the development of a theory of the public sphere (Habermas 1962, 2001).
(d) Critical theories of technology – an examination of instrumental and substantive theories of technology as a means to inform a dialectics of technology based on four principles, concretization, vocation, aesthetics, and collegiality (Feenberg 1991).

The New London Group's theory of multiliteracies has strongly influenced the framework and design practices of CCT and *tangible social interfaces*. Multiliteracies center on the concept of design thinking as a critical metaphor, as well as practice, for contemporary pedagogy. The theory supports the juxtaposition of different languages, discourses, styles, and approaches by incorporating design thinking as an integral process in the development of meta-cognitive and meta-linguistic abilities (New London Group 1996). This concept is supported by several influential theories of design thinking including wicked problems in design, convivial tools, the reflective practitioner, and metadesign (Rittel 1984; Buchanan 1995; Schön 1983; Fischer 1999; Fischer and Scharff 2000). The emphasis in these theories of design is the importance of open systems that enable "users to invest the world with their meaning, to enrich the environment with the fruits of their vision and to use them for the accomplishment of a purpose they have chosen" (Illich 1973). "Re-design," as defined by the theory of multiliteracies, is the most transformative design process. "Re-design" involves the making of new meaning, knowledge, and understanding from current discourse. To transform meaning is to transform relationships among people and to transform the individual through the process of examining, deconstructing, and negotiating common ground for discourse and learning. To re-design is to not only think outside of the box, but to get outside of the box, disregard the box, change its form, or build a new larger, more encompassing shell around the box to expand one's potential and possibilities. The act of re-design is the act of empowerment through the transformation of ideas, values, and actions. Information computer technology applications that support the concept of "re-design" bring to question the human computer interaction subject as user. The "user" is transformed into the "constructor." He is the one who is empowered to transform meaning and effect change in the relationship between themselves and others with tools designed to support self-reflection, creative problem solving, negotiation, and learning through the deconstruction and reconstruction of multimodal forms of expression.

Design Principles for Critical Creative Technology

The CCT framework yields three principles that inform the design of tangible social interfaces and creative information technologies (Jennings 2006). The third principle, "serious play," is discussed in the next section.

1. *Connected space* is supported by theories that define space as a logistical construct and place as a contextual construct (Harrison and Dourish 1996). Edward Hall notes that "space perception is not only a matter of what can be perceived but what can be screened out." As children we are taught what to focus on and what to screen out in our environments. These "perceptual patterns" remain consistent throughout life unless challenged by a profound experience that overpowers the culturally reinforced pattern (Hall 1968, 1969).
2. *Intersubjective intentionality* takes its lead from the Thompson's (2001) theory of enactive cognition and Dourish's embodied interaction as a means to merge popular contemporary critical theory and practice in embodied interaction, situated practice, and technologies that support empathic experiences. In particular, the

principle encourages the incorporation of Thompson's four categories of empathy; passive association, imaginative transposition, understanding oneself as an interpretation of the other, and ethical responsibilities that result from the previous category into the structural design of collaborative systems and interfaces (Spariosu 1989).

3. *Serious play* supports the concept of discourse facilitated through play by examining western historical and philosophical theories in which play has been relegated as an important element of society or treated as an unnecessary distraction to rational discourse (Kant 1781). Play as a global phenomenon exists in all cultures past and present, even though method, technique, and values equated with play have differed. Whereas Kant equated play and art as frivolous distractions from the good work of rational thought; Schiller insisted that Spieltrieb (play drive) is a powerful catalyst for facilitating dialogue and reconciliation (Schiller 1793; Spariosu 1989).

On Serious Play

Play is a global phenomenon that exists in all historical and contemporary cultures. Play, as a concept, has nurtured the global imagination even though the method, technique, and value proposition may differ. A continuum from zero-sum games to open exploration represents the breadth of activities that are identified as play. The pervasive presence of play defies the formation of general methods and rules. With the advent of the "serious games" movement, it is evident that play continues to be a vital component for civil engagement and learning.

Play, or agon, can be divided into two sociological categories. That being prerational agon and rational agon (Kant 1781). Historical placement may not be appropriate as contemporary cultures tend to waver back and forth between beliefs and actions that embody attributes of prerationality and rationality. As both prerational and rational play are driven by strategies of chance, necessity, and power. Prerational tend to credit superhuman entities, such as nature, gods, and spirits, as primary forces in the development and determination of world order. It is defined as an unrestrained form of play with attributes of arbitrariness, violence, and conflict-ridden strategies. Whereas, strategies of rational play are mediated by rule-based structures that reflect the sociocultural and historical precedence of the society in which the form of play resides. The superhuman forces that determine the destiny of *pre-rational* play are trumped by abstract philosophical and scientific reasoning of a *rational* society.

Kant Can't Play Today

In the *critique of pure reason*, Kant situates play as an elusive concept in need of discipline. Kant's philosophical perspective can perhaps be seen as an epicenter from which many contemporary western critical thinkers develop alternative principles and concepts regarding the role of play in society that emphasize positive effects of play – rejuvenation, self-reflection, teaching, and rewarding adherence to societal norms and engagement with others. Kant proclaims that competitive play (*sensus omnium*) has interfered with the serious business of philosophy (pursuit of scientific knowledge), in the *critique of pure reason.* An "orderly establishment of principles, clear determination of concepts, and insistence upon strict proof and avoidance of venturesome, nonconsecutive steps in our inferences" is preferred. To defy the natural order of those procedures is to have "no aim than to shake off the fetters of science altogether and thus to change work into play, certainty into opinion and philosophy into philodoxy" (Spariosu 1989). Play, for Kant, is the antithesis of reason. Kant maintains a hierarchical status of reason over imagination, philosophy and science over art, and morality and seriousness over play. Despite his acceptance of the validity of aesthetic judgments in the *third critique,* aesthetics and play maintained a status of "purposiveness without purpose" (*Zweckmässigkeit ohne Zweck*) (Kant 1787). Kant presents a hierarchy of three categories of art that correlate with three epistemological divisions: (a) arts of speech (thought); (b) formative arts (intuition); and (c) arts of play using the as if (german: als ob) approach. Poetry is the highest form of art. It is "the art of conducting a free play of the imagination as if it were a serious business of the understanding" (Spariosu 1989). Poetry understands its subordinate role in understanding and merely acts as a mediator for reason, sin, and judgment between abstract ideas and the senses (Kant 1798). Play is a frivolous enterprise devoid of cognitive value and conducive to error. Kant writes that, "to surrender oneself" to the "play of the unpremeditatedly creative imagination" is to "reverse the natural order of the cognitive powers, since then the rational elements do not take the lead (as they should) but instead follow behind" (Spariosu 1989, p. 51; Kant 1798, p. 33). Play, in contrast to work, is more harmful than beneficial. Overindulgence in play leads to "bad habits, causing the weakening of the mental powers." It encourages laziness (Kant 1798, p. 86) Games of chance foster the illusion of control when in reality the players are "mere toys in the hands of nature" (Kant 1798, p. 88). The social factor of play runs the risk of becoming a means for passion and obsession, whereas, music, dance, and play in general "are conducive to company without conversation" that does not encourage "mutual exchange of thought," denying the union of social living with virtue (Schiller 1793).

Schiller's Spieltrieb (Play-Drive)

> For to mince matters no longer, man only plays when he is in the fullest sense of the word a human being and he is only fully a human being when he play (Spariosu 1989)

Frederick Schiller was influenced by Kant's enlightenment and acceptance of the validity of aesthetic judgments toward defining desire, beauty, and the artist as genius. Schiller calls for an "aesthetic state" to replace the traditional European State that was born from the destructive violence of the French revolution.

Schiller challenges Kant's stance on the frivolity of play by viewing it to be a primary enabler of reason and as an integral component in the structure of society. Play, for Schiller, is an important motivating factor in philosophical discourse. His seminal 1795 work Über die Asthetische Erziehung des Menschen in Einer Reihevon Briefen (Aesthetical and Philosophical Essay) places art as an arbitrator between play and seriousness, sensuousness and rationality, utility and superfluity. The emphasis on play as serious work and mediator for cultural, social, and moral existence sets the stage for all subsequent contemporary theoretical discussions about play (Schiller 1793). As a philosopher and artist, Schiller positions the fine arts in the role of mediator between philosophical–scientific discourse and the unknowable reality and the chaotic physical world made complex by human morality and action. He noted that, "both rejoice in absolute immunity from human arbitrariness," where "truth and beauty will always struggle to the surface" (Schiller 1793). Art dares to unearth and poke at questions that do not have answers that can be derived from rational methodologies, but are imperative in the development and survival of humanity. Schiller elevates the notion of play to that of the "noblest" activity of reason. Schiller's theory of society is based on three essential human drives: (a) sense-drive (Stofftrieb, Sinnlicher Trieb); (b) form-drive (Formtrieb, Vernünftiger Trieb); and (c) play-drive (Spieltrieb). Sense-drive and form-drive are aligned in an agonistic relationship to each other. For example, law is generated by form-drive and individuality by sense-drive. Sense-drive develops from the physical essence of humans. This drive is malleable and evolves over time. Form-drive develops from the rational relationship between humans, nature, and objects. Form-drive is "intent on giving him [a person] freedom to bring harmony into the diversity of his manifestations and to affirm his person among all his changes of condition" (Schiller 1793).

> The seriousness of your principles will frighten them [the artists' contemporaries] away, but in the play of your semblance they will be prepared to tolerate them… In vain will you assail their precepts, in vain condemn their practice; but on their leisure hours you can try your shaping hand. Banish from their pleasures, caprice, frivolity and coarseness and imperceptibly you will banish these from their actions and, eventually, from their inclinations, too (Spariosu 1989, p. 58; Gadamer 1990)

Play-drive is the discourse wrangler between the sense-drive and the form-drive. With its myriad of techniques and methods, it mediates between differences and similarities of rational thought, desire, and action. Spieltribe (play-drive) establishes play as a rational fiction that has great influence on moral imperatives and is an essential element of humanity.

Transformative Play

> Nur dann erfülit ja Spiel den Zweck, den es hat; wenn der Spielende im Spielen aufgeht. Alles Spielen ist ein Gespieltwerden. Das Spiel ist es, was den Spieler in seinen Bann scwägt, was ihn ins Spiel verstrickt, im Spiel halt. Der Spielende erfahrt das Spiel als eine ihn übertreffende Wirklichkeit

> Play fulfills its purpose only when the player is wholly involved in play. All playing is being played. The play's the thing that captures the player, enraptures him and holds him in play. The player experiences play as a reality that surpasses him (Gadamer 1990)

Hans-Georg Gadamer and Jacques Derrida's work addresses the transformative and elusive nature of play and language. Gadamer's belief that art and play are transformative experiences aligns with Dewey's premise, in *Art as Experience*, that art is a transformative process. Gadamer claims that "human play finds its true perfection" in art that is an "independent and superior mode of being" (Spariosu 1989; Dewey 1934; Rokeby 1995). Art and play do not occur outside of the participants' experience. Rather it is made manifest through the participants' engagement with each other and/or objects designed to facilitate a physical or contemplative act. Games and art are simply different forms of play. Games, as a form of rational play, are based on rule structures that integrate components of play as stated earlier, chance, necessity, and power. The art experience is born from interplay between audience and subject. The audience, participant, interactor, builder... is the interpreter and the interpreted, the player and the played, the designer and the redesigned. Gadamer sets forth the premise that the mirroring process of language, art, and play is the means of connecting processes of "being" and "becoming." This notion of interplay is aligned with Rokeby's metaphor of the transforming mirror as a motivating factor in the design of interactive technologies (Gadamer 1989). Interface as a transforming mirror creates a means by which the participant, interactor, constructor, builder can challenge their everyday assumptions by, re-aligning, re-thinking, and re-designing. The terms participant, user, interactor, constructor, builder are lumped together to illustrate the inability of language to define the human component of an interactive system.

Gadamer views language to be a fundamental binding property in our relationship to the world. Language is the "advent-event of being," and provides the structure by which presence is manifest (Spariosu 1989). Literature, with its fictional stance, allows other linguistic inventions (scientific, philosophical, historical, ethical, political, juridical, and religious) "to be invested with the authority of knowledge and truth" (Gadamer 1989). Language does not have a "being-in-itself which is different from its reproduction or the contingency of its appearance" (Wittgenstein 1958). As Wittgenstein proclaimed, language is a game dependent on the context in which it is used. As Laurie Anderson proclaimed, it "is a virus" (Anderson 1986; Derrida 1983).

Derrida's Language Play

Derrida's critique of the elusiveness of language plays on methods of delivery, reception, and interpretation. His well-known theories of deconstruction, différance, play (jeu libre), and history (trace) create a language game of theatrical magnitude that exposes the impact of delivery, reception, and interpretation on meaning. In essence, his critique on language and meaning forms a serpentine chain, where the elusiveness of language is deceived by its platform of delivery.

A 1983 response to a colleague's inquiry regarding the definition of *deconstruction* Derrida responded.

> To be very schematic I would say that the difficulty of defining and therefore also of translating the word "deconstruction" stems from the fact that all the predicates, all the defining concepts, all the lexical significations and even the syntactic articulations, which seem at one moment to lend themselves to this definition or to that translation, are also deconstructed or deconstructible, directly or otherwise, etc. and that goes for the word deconstruction, as for every word (Derrida 1982)

The concept of *deconstruction* is ephemeral. Its elusive qualities can only be anchored by secondary concepts and words that align the thing being deconstructed to a cultural context. As the cultural constructs shift, a perpetual and indeterminate condition of substitution is set in motion.

A case in point is Derrida's exegesis on the word *différance*. *Différance* is an imaginary word formed from Derrida's language game with the Latin verb *differer* which has two distinct meanings. The first meaning is the "action of putting off until later, of taking into account, or taking account of time of the forces of an operation that implies an economical calculation, a detour, a delay, a relay, a reserve, a representation." This definition of the word *differ* aligns with the concept of temporization, "to take recourse consciously or unconsciously, in the temporal and temporizing mediation of a detour that suspends the accomplishment nor fulfillment of 'desire' or 'will' and equally effects this suspension in a mode that annuls or tempers its own effect." Time is inserted between the subject and its contemplation and presence. The present, is constantly shifted, renegotiated by readjusting spaces between the past (history), the present, and the future. The second meaning of the Latin verb *differer* describes the relationship of being other and not identical. Space is inserted between the subject and its comparison (Derrida 1982). The pun at the end of the exercise is that the word différance can only be discerned by its contextual and strategic placement within the text. The "a" in différance is silent and "cannot be exposed," in spoken language – it cannot become present. The difference between difference and différance is discerned visually in a "purely graphic" form (Derrida 1978).

Derrida's dance with différance is a generative process mediated by free play (*jeu libre*) of differences, oppositions, joining, colliding, negotiating, consuming, and being consumed. Différance is "the movement according to which language, or any code or system of referral is constituted 'historically' as a weave of differences." Différance brings to light that sign systems are a process complicit with history, production, and constitution of its subjects. It defies points of origin, a center, or transcendental inception. "The center could not be thought in the form of a present-being, that the center had no natural site, that it was not a fixed locus, but a function, a sort of non-locus in which an infinite number of sign substations came into play" (Derrida 1978). Derrida supported the concept that the structural center is a space of refraction that hosts "an infinite number of sign-substitutions... ." The transgression of domains by which signifiers reside is the *jeu libre* (free play) of infinite substitutions in a finite field of possibilities. "The central signified, the original or transcendental signified (e.g., god, nature, divinities, chance, etc.), is never absolutely present outside a system of differences." (Derrida 1978). In other words, there is no absolute transcendental figure that exists outside of discourse.

Play is the act of substitution where the sign that temporarily makes the core of the structure is a *temporary authoritative occupant* (Jennings 2006). Play is an act of disruption that provokes a tension between play and history and play and presence. The constructed narratives' electronic construction kit has been designed for making the concepts of différance tangible, if only for a fleeting moment before a construction is altered and shifted by the design intentions of the self or the collaborating other.

The Constructed Narratives' Electronic Construction Kit

Constructed narratives is a collaborative game where players construct a world in which they provide the dynamic contextual materials that give form to the world that they are constructing. It has been designed as a collaborative game to facilitate discourse, exchange of ideas and negotiation of design intentions, and choices between collaborating participants. Designed for adults and older teenagers, the game presents an open-ended construction metaphor to elicit childlike curiosity to explore through collaboration and negotiation. Constructed narratives have been likened to a combination between Scrabble™ and the Rubik Cube™, a physical magnetic poetry or Exquisite Corpse. As both a mechanical puzzle and a language game, constructed narratives support collaboration and social networking with other players as a strategic method of play. As a matter of fact, several components of the construction kit support the exploration of différance, deconstruction, and re-design. The first is the building process with the pentomino shaped blocks that support a seemingly infinite number of abstract designs that can be stacked, packed, expanded, bridged, and cantilevered. The block shapes support open-ended, imaginatively built systems that reference minimalist architectural styles. The second component and perhaps the most important, is the textual landscape of words that appear embedded inside each block in the three-dimensional visualization of the physical construction. This is supported in part by a game engine that generates several interlinked representations of the players' actions and interactions from the built physical structure to a mixed-reality three-dimensional visualization feedback.

Constructed narratives are a tangible electronic construction kit of pentomino shaped blocks (complex shapes assembled from five cubes) (Fig. 8.1). This virtual replication is projected into the game play area. The visualization application has also been developed for interactive dissemination on the Internet. The virtual replication of the physical construction includes a textual landscape of words that are printed on the virtual blocks (Fig. 8.2).

The textual landscape is generated by a component of the visualization application called the semantic engine. Key is the fact that words are not hard-coded to specific block combinations. The function of the semantic engine combines an

Fig. 8.1 Constructed narratives electronic construction
kit prototype set

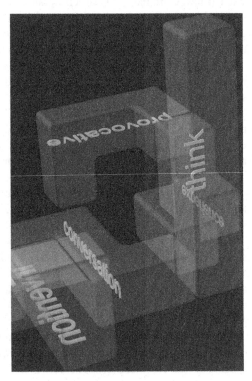

Fig. 8.2 Three-dimension visualization
application

iterative pattern search and optimization algorithm. The results are used to trigger word searches using the WordNet API.[1] The textual landscape updates dynamically as players claim and/or lose block ownership and the construction patterns. Block ownership is determined by enacted gestures with the tangible blocks. Gestures are sensed by embedded sensors. By doing this the player indicates to the system his/her intention to own or annotate that block with metadata that is stored in the system database. The constructed narratives' electronic construction kit has been designed with the following goals.

1. Develop a tangible game that encourages discourse, negotiation, and collaboration between players.
2. Develop an intuitive physical interface that encourages learning through discovery and exploration.
3. Develop a component tracking system that requires a minimum of external devices beyond core interface devices.
4. Develop a tangible system for building and annotating physical models.

Constructed Narratives Game Scenarios

The Airport

Seated at the game table, in the frequent flyers lounge at the Auckland International Airport, is a Sara, a 25 year-old college student and Thomas, a 40 year-old banker. They have a 2-h layover for their flight to Los Angeles. Sara arrived from Sydney, Australia. Her final destination is San Francisco, where she is about to start a new job at a Napa valley winery.

Sara was born outside of Sydney, Australia in a small fishing village. Her father is an aboriginal and her mother immigrated to Australia from England. Thomas is from Christchurch, New Zealand. He grew up on a sheep farm and is the first member of his Anglican farming family to work as an executive for a major corporation. He commutes to Auckland, a 1-h flight, 3 times a week for meetings. However, he spends on average 6 h a week waiting in the airport for his flight. Occasionally, he travels to executive meetings at the bank headquarters in Los Angeles. Generally, the flight layover is not long enough to do work on his laptop, so he spends the time reading the newspaper, talking to his children on the mobile phone, and watching people.

Placed on top of the game table is a set of pentomino-shaped building blocks. The game begins when Thomas selects one of the blocks, turns it around in his hand to examine its shape and attaches it to one of the other blocks on the table.

---

[1] www.agentkernel.com

Sara follows suit with a differently shaped pentomino block. As the blocks connect, a low volume "click" is heard from inside the connected blocks and a virtual rendition of the physical construction appears in the virtual build application. Thomas and Sara can view the visualization on an LCD monitor embedded in the game play surface.

The blocks in the virtual rendition of the physical construction are unique colors and opacities that identify patterns of player ownership in the construction. Each player can claim "ownership" on a block or group of blocks by making simple gestures with the blocks. With ownership declared, the underlying software system outputs a dynamic textual landscape of words that are embedded and animated inside each virtual block in the three-dimensional visualization application. The semantic engine, a component of the underlying software system, selects the words based upon recognized patterns in the connected tangible blocks, the person responsible for placing the block, and a few general questions about the interests, hobbies, and social concerns of each player completed on the online builder's profile application prior to game play.

Sara and Thomas are amazed that the words, though poetically juxtaposed, refer to topics and events that relate to their lives and interests. Each action made by the builders alters the block words and their relational meanings. Working together, they quickly realize that they have similar ideas about the environment that stem from different perspectives and activities. Sara is an activist who participates in tactical media events and street protests with friends on her college campus. Thomas supports the New Zealand environmental protection agency. He is an avid recycler. Of course, the words on the blocks didn't spell this out in detail. Rather, the act of construction and using language as a fundamental building block provided a common ground where an unlikely conversation between two people occupying the same physical location commenced. Sara and Thomas have collaboratively constructed a world in which their ideas, beliefs, interests, concerns, and pleasures are the very material from which this constructed world is made.

A boarding announcement from the crackling public address system is heard over the loudspeaker. Sara and Thomas place their blocks in the charging station next to the builder's profile screen; gather their bags and head to the gate. Thomas bids a fond farewell as he proceeds to the front of the crowd to board in the first class section and Sara patiently waits among the gathering crowd of travelers for her coach row to be announced. As Sara and Thomas board their flight, Alessandria a young backpacker from Brazil and Yuchang, a school teacher from China complete the builder's profile application and begin to play.

The Hospital Waiting Room

Sitting in the UPMC surgery waiting room, Paula is watching other people who are also waiting. Some are waiting for out-patient surgery; others are waiting for friends and family members to complete surgery. The room is long and narrow and designed like an architectural afterthought. Its purely utilitarian nature shows that it is just a space to store people. There is a poorly executed attempt to make the space "homey" with a large plasma screen playing daytime television programs. The space is crowded with oversize wood rocking chairs that are placed inches away from each other and all facing in attention to the plasma screen. There is one very large oak table in the back section of the room. Two women are sitting at the table, talking. Most other people in this rather inhospitable space are facing the television monitor – awkwardly negotiating its discomfort. Paula rocks as she observes and realizes the untapped potential for making this space more comfortable through simple things like proper furniture and its arrangement and the enculturation of collaborative activities that promote social engagement. She remarks to herself, "This is a perfect space for the *constructed narratives* game."

Senior Activity Center

Mary Ethel and Elaine have been best friends since their early twenties when they met through their husbands who where both Korean War veterans. Their husbands are no longer alive, but they have remained connected like blood sisters. Through the years, they have been very active in local civic groups, reading clubs, knitting circles, and chaperoning their now grown children at school activities. Both are concerned about aging and losing their cognitive capacities. They meet regularly at the local senior citizens activity center to work on crossword puzzles and play scrabble. Coming together to play these games serves a greater purpose. For they live alone and spend a lot of time in solitude. Trips to the center are an opportunity for them to break free from this life of silence. Even on days when simply being in each other's presence is enough. Mary Ethel is concerned that she is losing her motor coordination. Her eye/hand coordination is not what it used to be. She longs for an activity, that will not be too taxing, that will allow her to exercise her mind and her body. Physical puzzles that will encourage her to reach, grasp, and lift with a degree of accuracy would be a perfect solution for entertainment, cognitive, and physical therapy. One saturday afternoon, Mary Ethel and Elaine were pleasantly surprised to see the addition of a new social game, *constructed narratives*. This was a game that broke away from the individual monotony of crossword, word search, and Sudoku puzzles and maintained the important social attributes of scrabble. Lifting and connecting the blocks spoke to their physical motor skill needs, love for making things, language and conversation.

Conclusions and Future Goals

Play has become a popular mantra of digital media producers seeking to integrate value-laden content with popular entertainment media. This phenomenon is often practiced under the umbrella of "serious games." As this next media phenomenon matures, we are behooved to understand the impact of play beyond the affordance of making learning palpable by interjecting fun. One method for doing this is by understanding the impact of philosophical and critical ideas that examine premises about empathy, inter-subjectivity, and discourse. Philosophers and critical schools of thought introduced in this chapter provide such a possible foundation. This chapter introduces the tip of a theory of engagement with information and creative technologies that supports social networking (particularly face-to-face) and community building that I call the theory of CCT. The *constructed narratives electronic construction kit* is a first experiment in the research and development of social tangible interfaces. Technology developed for this project will serve as a platform for continued research and design of interactive applications that take advantage of advanced wireless networks in support of social engagement through discourse, discovery, and learning.

There is an added challenge developing technology under the umbrella of the arts and design, as institutional structures are rarely equipped to support contiguous research efforts – both financially and operationally. With this noted, components of the constructed narratives electronic construction kit, have been demonstrated and/or exhibited at 2003 Interact, Zurich, Switzerland; 2004 International Society of Electronic Arts Conference, Helsinki, Finland; 2008 ACM Computer Human Interaction Conference, Florence, Italy; 2008 ACM Multimedia conference in Vancouver, Canada; and the 2009 Future of Media Arts, Science and Technology NSF Workshop, Santa Barbara, California. Each demonstration has presented opportunities for informal observations of the system in the hands of people beyond the development team. Although this information was gathered informally, it was revealed that people approach building with the blocks based upon models of building from previous experience with construction toys (e.g., children's blocks and LEGO). Several methods of building where observed:

1. *Collaboration*: Synchronous and asynchronous (Fig. 8.3).
2. *Lift*: Attempts to lift a construction up from the table.
3. *Indexing*: Aligning the blocks in a row to understand the shape system (Fig. 8.4).
4. *Packing*: Constructing the blocks into a compact, tight structure (Fig. 8.5).
5. *Stacking*: Constructing vertically, until the structure collapses (Fig. 8.6).
6. *Bridging*: Exploiting the cantilever features of the blocks to build constructions with extruding features (Fig. 8.7).
7. *Leaning*: Using the block to support full body weight while leaning in close to talk with another person on the other side of the table (Fig. 8.8).
8. *Fluidity*: Design re-construction resulting in multiple design solutions (Fig. 8.9).
9. *Options*: Placing a block in several locations before selecting a final position.

Development of components of the system, both technical and theoretical will continue, as research on methods and development techniques and application evaluation yield fresh insights to the design of tangible social interfaces. With the

Fig. 8.3 Collaboration. Documentation from the interactive showcase at the 2008 ACM computer human interaction conference, Florence, Italy

Fig. 8.4 Indexing. Documentation from the interactive showcase at the 2008 ACM computer human interaction conference, Florence, Italy

pending implementation of stabilizing components for the mechanical attributes of the system, we will pursue more formalized evaluations of the collaboration, play and discourse supporting qualities of the system and the contributions of the mixed reality visualization component to these ends.

Fig. 8.5 Packing. Documentation from the interactive showcase at the 2008 ACM computer human interaction conference, Florence, Italy

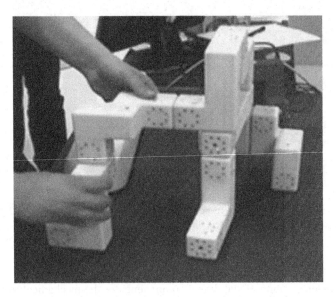

Fig. 8.6 Stacking. Documentation from the interactive showcase at the 2008 ACM computer human interaction conference, Florence, Italy

Fig. 8.7 Bridging. Documentation from the interactive showcase at the 2008 ACM computer human interaction conference, Florence, Italy

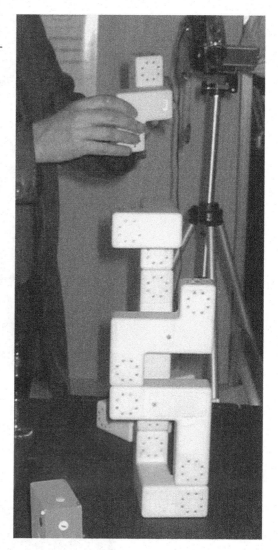

Fig. 8.8 Leaning. Documentation from the interactive showcase at the 2008 ACM computer human interaction conference, Florence, Italy

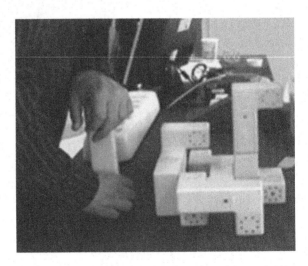

Fig. 8.9 Fluidity. Documentation from the interactive showcase at the 2008 ACM computer human interaction conference, Florence, Italy

Acknowledgments Special thanks to National Science Foundation Creative IT Program Award #0715304: "Designing Critical Creative Technologies" to Support Collaboration in Public Spaces, without which the Constructed Narratives prototype could not have been made. Thanks also to Matt Beale and team from Daedalus-Excel, Inc. and Paul Cunningham from Comet Way, Inc. Additional funding for earlier research prototypes was received from the Rockefeller Foundation, the Pennsylvania Council for the Arts and the Carnegie Mellon University Dean of the School of Computer Science.

References

Anderson L (1986) Language is a virus from film "Home of the Brave" http://www.amazon.com/Home-Brave-Film-Laurie-Anderson/dp/B000002L9F

Buchanan R (1995) Wicked problems in design thinking. In: Margolin V & Buchanan R (eds) The idea of design: a design issues reader. MIT Press, Massachusetts

Derrida J (1978) Structure and play in discourse of human sciences. In: Derrida, J writing and difference, 278–294. Routledge, London

Derrida J (1982) Différance. In: Bass A (Trans.) Margins of philosophy. University of Chicago Press, Chicago

Derrida J (1983) Letter to a Japanese friend. In: Wood & Bernsconi (eds) Derrida and difference. Parousia Press, Coventry

Dewey J. (1934) Art as experience. Perigee Books, New York

Dourish P (2001) Where the action is: The foundations of embodied interaction. MIT Press, Massachusetts

Feenberg A (1991) Critical theory of technology. Oxford University Press, Oxford

Fischer G (1999) Symmetry of ignorance, social creativity and meta-design. Knowledge Based Systems 13 (7–8): 527–537

Fischer, G. and Scharff, E. 2000. Meta-design: design for designers. In: Boyarski D and Kellogg W, (Eds.) DIS '00. 396–405. ACM, New York. DOI= http://doi.acm.org/10.1145/347642.347798

Gadamer H (1989) Truth and method. Crossroad, New York

Gadamer H (1990) Play as a guideline to ontological explanation. In: Mohr JCB (ed) Hermeneutik I, truth and method. Tübingen, 107–139

Habermas, Jürgen (1962) The structural transformation of the public sphere: an inquiry into a category of bourgeois society, Polity, Cambridge

Habermas J (2001) On the pragmatics of social interaction: preliminary studies in the theory of communicative action. MIT Press, Massachusetts

Hall ET (1968) Proxemics. Current Anthropologist 9 (2–3): 83–100

Hall ET (1969) The hidden dimension. Doubleday, New York

Harrison S & Dourish P (1996) Re-place-ing space: the roles of place and space in collaborative systems. In: Ackerman, AS (ed) Proceedings of the CSCW '96, 67–76. ACM, New York, NY. DOI= http://doi.acm.org/10.1145/240080.240193

Illich I (1973) Tools for conviviality. Harper & Row, New York

Ishii H & Ullmer B (1997) Tangible bits: towards seamless interfaces between people, bits and atoms. In: Proceedings HCI 1997, 234–24. Doi: 10.1145/258549.258715

Jennings, P. (2006). Interactive technologies for the public sphere: toward a theory of critical creative technology. Ph.D. thesis, University of Plymouth, United Kingdom.

Kant I (1781) Critique of pure reason. Macmillan, London. London http://gutenberg.spiegel.de/?id=5&xid=1368&kapitel=125&cHash=3a05522a12krva118#gb_found. Retrieved 7 October 2006

Kant I (1798) Anthropology from a pragmatic point of view. Trans. V.L. Dowdell, Ed., and Rev. H.H. Rudnick (Carbondale, Ill, 1978). Cambridge University Press, Cambridge

New London Group (1996) Pedagogy of multiliteracies: designing social futures. Harvard Education Review 66(1), 60–92

Paulston RG & Liebman M (1995) The promise of critical social cartography. Inter American Review of Educational Development (OAS) 119

Penuel WR & Wertsch J (1995) Vygotsky identity formation: A socio-cultural approach. Educational Psychologist 30(2), 83–92

Rittel H (1984) Second-generation design methods. In: Cross N (ed) Developments in design methodology, 317–327. Wiley, New York

Rokeby D (1995) Transforming mirrors: subjectivity and control in interactive media. In: Penny S (ed) Critical Issues in Electronic Media. State University of NY Press, Albany

Schiller F (1793) On the aesthetic education of man, in a Series of Letters. E. M. Wilkinson & L.S. Willoughby (Trans.). (Oxford, 1967) Gutenberg Press http://www.gutenberg.org/files/6798/6798-h/6798-h.htm.

Schön DA (1983) The reflective practitioner: how professionals think in action. Basic Books, New York

Spariosu M (1989) Dionysus reborn: play and the aesthetic dimension in modern philosophical and scientific discourse. Cornell University Press, New York

Spivey N (1996) The constructivist metaphor: reading, writing and the making of meaning. Academic Press, Massachusetts

Thompson E (2001) Empathy and consciousness. Journal of Consciousness Studies 8 (5–7): 1–32

Wittgenstein L (1958) Philosophical investigations. Blackwell Publishing, Oxford

Section 3
Spatial Settings

Introduction: Spatial Settings

Malcolm McCullough

To a world that is interlinked and on the move, spatial settings cannot determine the course of life the way blood soil once did. Even the most intentional architectures cannot make a city as legible as the uncontested power of church or king who once had it. Dictates of conduct and dress now vary much less from setting to setting. Your address tells less about you than it once might have done. And in all of this there is some liberation up to a point. The opposite extremes of placeless anomie, faceless casual drift, and anytime-anyplace one-size-fits all sameness leave humanity less human. A relentless flood of media assumes that people require constant entertainment, as if they no longer know how to have a conversation.

Except against this is a new flood of conversations, displaced in space or time by mobile personal information media. As you stand on a street corner wondering whether all these people yakking into their cellphones are less-tapped into the city for all their distractions, or more so for all their connections, it is worth-noting two rising aspects of ambient information.

The first of these is that instead of belonging to one place or community, which if not "blood soil" might be "nostalgie de la boue," instead more people belong to more multiple places and communities partially, by degrees. Of course, they use information technology to mediate that belonging, especially wherever expressions of belonging may stream. Thus, the second noteworthy rise is in sharing, which in its many forms has become the central focus of many digital design theorists and enterprises. Networked social production now almost goes without saying. Or at least, here, we may focus on one very particular aspect of that.

This section of Shared Encounters turns the focus to the role of spatial settings. It does so with particular regard to how physical settings might cue social constructions of ambient information. And to focus that into a single word, you might ask, as you read, how much the success of that process depends on "underspecification." The word comes from cybernetics pioneer Gordon Pask. Omar Khan's paper unpacks the principle here.

M. McCullough (✉)
Taubman College of Architecture and Urban Planning, University of Michigan,
2000 Bonisteel Boulevard, Ann Arbor, MI, 48103, USA
e-mail: mmmc@umich.edu

It begins from letting go of rules. The chapters in this section explore the spatial settings of shared encounters with clear attention to this relationship of structure and improvisation. This is familiar in the literature of human–computer interaction. Beginners and machines follow rules, but experts may not, especially in the presence of other experts. Instead, they pick up cues from physical, organization, and especially interpersonal patterns. In other words, people play situations, even at work. This situational play resembles the inflection of language more than a game. Life (and expertise) would be dull without it. Whether in domesticity, conviviality, travel, or work, shared encounters make use of context in ways that bring more particularity, but less determinacy to them. Expertise in physical context may first seem like street smarts, but also turns out to involve studio practices, organizational memory, and more. In another chapter in this set, Schieck Kostakos and Penn have introduced a novel element that induces spontaneity. They refer to it as a stage, and one that reveals remarkably playful expertise among pedestrians at street level.

In the third chapter here, Garcia, Foth, and Hearn caution about overspecification, in this case the prevalence of engineered identity in master planned inventions of neotraditional villages. An overspecified spatial setting declares its identity, often by branding, and pushes that at us. Its owners often regard unplanned activities with suspicion. By contrast, an underspecificied space invites unplanned activities, and evolves socially toward those activities that are considered appropriate. Over time, its denizens come to identify with the space for all that has happened there. This is how space becomes place—not by branding.

Ubiquitous telecommunications complicate all this, of course. According to the classic critique by Meyrowitz, electronic feeds undermine perceptions of whether one is "onstage" or "backstage" in the a given situation. This leads to a uniform tyranny of the casual. What Goffman called "presentation of self" gets devalued. What arises instead is an obsession with messages. To send and receive as many of messages as possible, amid as many physical settings as conceivable, becomes the new mark of standing. Even this ubiquitous chattering bodes better for physical space than what was expected of telecommunications a decade ago, however, namely some disembodied cyberspace. Even the most technocentric of futurists have moved away from that worldview.

Ambient information also transforms the play of situations. This, rather parking your atoms before the looking glass of the desktop screen, has become the normative future. Ambient information makes noise and pollutes cities. But it also annotates and explains spatial settings. It may even give rise (for example, in response to new forms of pollution) to new notions of cultural commons. And sometimes, according to legend, it can stay out of the way, and even serve to calm.

Several of the projects explored in this section demonstrate new prospects in ambient information. The LED Urban Carpet may be the most vivid among these, for it "has provided a platform for an unintentional-conscious encounter," where "Unpredicted social behaviors may emerge." *HistoryLines*, a web project, lets people annotate their neighborhood. The tacit boundaries of a neighborhood's social geography are intrinsically displayed through. Bluetooth data projection. Part of what emerges may be unintentional, however. Rumor Ring, which uses a specific spatial setting of electronic messages, the telephone booth (which is still not obsolete for these without a mobile phone), to show how underspecification can lead to infills of disinformation, what Khan calls "an ambient babble." Screen Enabling Employed Narratives—Fruits of our Labor may be the most public of the projects here, or at least the largest. Here, the mediation necessary to view the spectrum of an infrared LED screen "personalizes the information and the consequent capture and sharing moves the work from the public realm into more private communication channels." The underspecification leads to casual philosophical conversations, which seem distinctly absent from overspecified environments such as chain restaurants. (You might recall the Monty Python skit where the waiter brings a menu of conversation topics.)

All told, this small sample suggests how far the study of environment and behavior has come from the days of the positivists, the Skinnerians, or those who would strive for predictable command and control.

Chapter 9
Exploring Digital Encounters in the Public Arena

Ava Fatah gen. Schieck, Vassilis Kostakos, and Alan Penn

Introduction

The urban physical environment plays a critical role in the construction and reflection of social behaviors. This can be seen in the way it acts to structure space (Hillier and Hanson 1984). In this respect, it does not only reflect social patterns, but can also play a vital role in generating these patterns, providing a platform for rich and diverse social encounters. For instance, public spaces such as the bus stop or the cafe can act as "encounter stages" on which people negotiate boundaries of a social and cultural nature. From time to time, events alter the status of these interactions – the bus being late may stimulate conversations between strangers – but on the whole, these interactions seem strongly bound to social conventions.

Encounters are unexpected or casual meetings with people we know or with completely unknown strangers, we encounter once and never see again. The encounter can consist of briefly saying "Hello," or having coffee and lunch. More importantly, a shared encounter between two participants contributes to the development of common context, both personal and communal (Kostakos et al. 2006). Conversation, as well as other common activities like dancing, shopping, or dining can contribute to common context. This, in turn, frames peoples' communications with each other, helps identify group memberships, contributes to the understanding of social beliefs, and ultimately provides a process by which society evolves.

The use of technology to enhance, rather than replace, human encounter raises certain issues that need to be addressed. In cases where technology replaces human capabilities, without the technology, an encounter is simply impossible. A good

A.F. gen. Schieck (✉) and A. Penn
The Bartlett School of Graduate Studies, University College London, 1-19 Torrington Place,
London WC1E 6BT, UK
e-mail: ava.fatah@ucl.ac.uk

V. Kostakos
Department of Mathematics & Engineering, University of Madeira,
Funchal 9000-319, Portugal
e-mail: vassilis@cmu.edu

K.S. Willis et al. (eds.), *Shared Encounters*, Computer Supported Cooperative Work,   179
DOI 10.1007/978-1-84882-727-1_9, © Springer-Verlag London Limited 2010

example of this is the telephone, without which communication across the Atlantic is not possible. However, we question in a city context, where an encounter is possible even without the use of technology, what constitutes a digital encounter? If the users' devices communicate automatically and without any user input, does that constitute a digital encounter? Does the encounter need to be two-way, or can it be one-way?

The above issues need to be addressed in a consistent manner before we proceed any further. In the following section, we describe the concepts underlying a digital encounter, and provide a discussion of what constitutes a digital encounter. We then proceed to describe two prototypes that explore different types of digital encounters in the city. The first prototype is a digital portable installation with a grid of LEDs that can be embedded as a horizontal responsive surface in the urban environment and the second is a vertical public display "sensing and projecting" the digital identity "represented by Bluetooth names" in the public arena.

What is a Digital Encounter?

Our definition of a digital encounter is an ephemeral form of communication and interaction augmented by technology. Note that the use of technology to augment, rather than replace human communication and interaction means that now each person has a digital agent that can take part in the encounter (e.g., the mobile device), as shown in Fig. 9.1. Additionally, artifacts in the environment, such as shared displays, can act as agents. Each person or agent can communicate with the other agents or persons (e.g., a person can use a shared screen, or a device can detect a person).

Which type of communication constitutes a digital encounter? Walking down the street, a mobile device or laptop is likely to communicate with other nearbyw devices. Is this an encounter? Similarly, in a shop, I am confronted with a screen that feeds me with personalized adverts. Is this a digital encounter? Or consider the automated ticket machine at the train station. Should its use be considered as a digital encounter? What about mobile devices that advertise their owner's profiles and identity, much like people's t-shirts? What if a public screen draws my attention to people around me who are within the Bluetooth range of my device? Have I just encountered those people?

In exploring different scenarios of encounters in the city, it becomes apparent that a large number of humans and agents can interact and communicate at any given instant. Our way of describing these interactions is by focusing on humans. Specifically, our scenarios rely on two key human capacities: *consciousness* of communication and *intention* of interaction. Furthermore, technology allows for digital, in addition to physical "encounter stages." For example, a plaza acts as a physical encounter stage, while Bluetooth devices that can talk through walls could create a digital encounter platform.

In our analysis, rather than drawing boundaries that specify what is, or is not a digital encounter, we chose to provide a mapping that explores human consciousness and intention orthogonally. These are considered in instances where one party communicates/interacts with another party. This can involve any combination of human or device as shown at the bottom of Fig. 9.1c. Our mapping takes the very

Fig. 9.1 Human communication (**1**), communication replaced by technology (**2**), or augmented by technology (**3**)

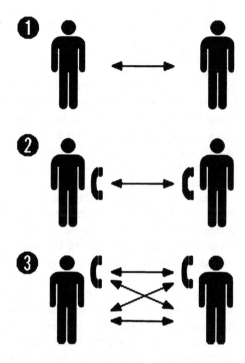

Table 9.1 A digital encounter consists of communication and interaction; users may be conscious or unconscious of the communication, while interactions can be intentional or non-intentional

Awareness of communication		Intention of interaction	
		Intentional	Non-intentional
	Conscious	Goal orientated: (particular) talk to a friend	Circumstantial: (non-particular) friend talks to me
	Unconscious	(Particular) Broadcast	Ambient: (non-particular) co-presence

simplistic form in Table 9.1, where at any given instant a human can be conscious or unconscious of the communications taking place, and can carry out interactions intentionally or unintentionally.

It is useful to keep in mind that during an encounter, the experience and state of each of the two parties may be different. Conscious–intentional encounters are the ones that a person initiates, for example, seeing a friend on the street and shouting to get their attention. Similarly, humans using their mobile device, such as calling a friend or sending a photograph to a nearby person using Bluetooth can initiate such encounters. Conscious–nonintentional encounters are situations where a person is aware of the communication that is taking place, but does not intentionally interact.

Examples of this are when a person is talked to on the street, or is the recipient of a Bluetooth message in a café.

By using technology, communication can be unconscious (on the part of the human). Examples are applications running on mobile phones that broadcast their owners' identity or preferences. This broadcasting is done intentionally by the user, however, the user is unconscious of when it actually happens, how often it happens, or who responds to it. Similar examples of unconscious intentional encounters are applications such as Nokia Sensor and Mobiluck, which broadcast user profiles and negotiate with other devices the similarity of their profiles. Users are notified of a nearby device with a similar profile (Nokia & Nokia sensor 2009; Mobiluck 2009).

Finally, in addition to being unconscious about the communication, users can also be nonintentional about the interaction. This is typically the case in device-to-device encounters. For example, many Bluetooth devices interact with nearby devices by default and due to the Bluetooth protocol and the manufacturers' setup. Of course, there are other aspects that one could consider. For example, synchronicity and duration are certainly aspects of encounter that one could explore. However, we suggest that the combination of consciousness and intention, which we present here, becomes particularly interesting with the introduction of technology to enhance, rather than replace, encounters.

In our work, we are interested in understanding different types of interactions, enabled through pervasive and mobile-computing systems. In order to achieve this, we apply a series of different methods (Schieck et al. 2006, 2008a, b). As part of our methods, we are projecting Bluetooth names in public and capturing the way that people react toward the projection. In the United Kingdom, there is a thriving culture of giving Bluetooth names to mobile phones. Users appropriate the way in which Bluetooth operates, as a partially embedded medium, to project their digital identity, making it a unique paradigm of socially and physically embedded communication. Through the selection of Bluetooth name, the user defines the "feel" of that interaction space (Kindberg and Jones 2007).

According to the Bluetooth protocol, each device can have a "name" which can help users communicate using the device. A device will broadcast information about this "digital identity," as long as its Bluetooth is switched on and set to discoverable. When a person moves into the range of Bluetooth sensors, his/her digital presence can be sensed and information about his/her digital identity can be communicated. By default, the Bluetooth names on mobile phones are set to the phone model, for example, *"Nokia N70";* however, users may customize their name and select their own digital identity. What happens when people are made aware of their digital identity in the public space? How does this affect or re-inform people's perception of the space itself? Would this encourage different types of interactions?

In order to understand various facets of sociotechnical behaviors, we have deployed various prototypes. In the next sections, we describe two systems that explore technology-enabled encounters and address different perspectives related to the physical and social aspects within the urban context.

Prototype 1: The Digital Carpet

The LEDs urban carpet is a digital portable urban installation with a grid of LEDs that can be embedded in the form of a responsive surface in the urban environment (Briones et al. 2007). When pedestrians walk over the surface, a pattern of lights is generated dynamically following the pedestrians' movement over it (Fig. 9.2).

Our aim was to generate a rich urban experience that can be introduced in various locations in the city, and to enrich the social awareness and engagement created by the casual encounter of people interacting with the carpet.

The installation was tested in various locations in the city; we selected locations with low, medium, and high pedestrian flows. A range of empirical observation methods were implemented including observing and recording the movements in

Fig. 9.2 Friends using the prototype as a dance stage

and out of the interaction space, as well as the type of activity taking place in the surrounding space. The form of peoples' interactions with the prototype, and with the other people in the area, was captured and video-taped by two researchers. In addition, peoples' movement on the surface was tracked. Following the observation sessions, a selected number of participants were interviewed using a structured discussion and a questionnaire.

The LED surface acted as a physical encounter stage, and during the sessions, we observed various emergent patterns of behavior. The installation set-up process, for instance, created the feel of an urban performance as it unfolds in real-time. Over time, people started gathering around the set-up location waiting for the "event" to start.

Different levels of awareness were observed among people walking around the area, from those simply glancing at the interactive prototype, to people stopping around the prototype and asking about it, trying to understand how it works – from peripheral awareness, focal awareness to direct interaction (Fig. 9.3 left). In some cases, this was anticipated as people used relevant prior experience and expectations of a new experience, for example, often people recognized the prototype as a "dance floor" before they interacted with it.

After trying the installation, some people started to comment on the experience and engage with people nearby by explaining rules of interaction, and this generated a kind of nonintentional conscious shared social encounter. Furthermore, people behaved differently in different situations and the experiences varied depending on whether the interaction took place among friends or strangers (Fig. 9.3 middle and right). During the test sessions, most people shared the experiences with friends. In this case, the digital surface generated a conscious intentional encounter; however a few of the participants shared the experience with a stranger. The most common pattern observed when strangers were interacting was that they were waiting for their turn. In this case, the digital surface provided a platform for a nonintentional conscious encounter.

Finally, our investigation suggests that the success of implementing a large digital surface in the urban environment depends on internal factors such as the properties of the digital platform and on the external factors relating to the social, temporal, and the physical settings of the surroundings. Our observations suggest that public interactive installations, like the one presented here, provide a platform for rich social interactions and awareness among the various people involved. However, by situating it in different locations and social environments, diverse and unpredicted social behaviors may emerge. Our evaluation demonstrated that the physical setting of the built environment had a direct influence on the movement flow of passersby, and the activities taking place near the locations, which in turn had a direct impact on the characteristics of the social encounter and the shared experience. Different types of behavior were observed in relation to the spatial properties, for instance, in a wide and highly integrated street, which is characterized by a fast walking pace, people tended to simply glance at the prototype and continue walking with the same pace toward their destination. In contrast, in a highly integrated area with a lower pace, characterized as being an intersection of more than one pedestrian route, people tended to stop around the prototype and

Fig. 9.3 Awareness varied from peripheral awareness to direct interaction. The most common pattern observed when strangers were interacting was that they were waiting for their turn (*middle*). Unlike the case with friends, strangers tended to define their territory and stay on one side, not crossing the interaction area of the other user, leaving a kind of mutual acceptance distance between users (*right*)

share the experience with other people. This varied during different times of the day, which seems to be supported by the temporal and the spatial properties of the physical space (Schieck et al. 2008a, b).

Prototype 2: Bluetooth Encounters

Our second prototype was a public display installation. First, we carried out a trial on the Bath University campus. A screen was augmented with software and hardware that carried out constant scanning for Bluetooth devices. When a Bluetooth device was detected nearby, its name was shown on the screen. Our intention for this system was to present what it can sense about people, and to give a representation of people's visiting patterns. For a device to be detected it must have Bluetooth switched on and set to discoverable. When a device is out of range of our scanner, the name disappeared.

This prototype was installed for a period of two months. During this period, the installation was operational throughout the day. The screen was installed on the university campus, behind an office window (Fig. 9.4). We evaluated this prototype by informally interviewing some of our colleagues who appeared to be intrigued by the system.

In terms of encounter, this system typically provides a nonconscious intentional encounter, with users gradually becoming more aware of the encounter as they notice the screen and realize that their name is displayed on it. In other words, users consciously enable Bluetooth on their devices, but the interaction with the display is in most cases nonintentional. Of course, the interaction can be *unconscious nonintentional*, which was the case with some users who simply did not know that their phone actually had Bluetooth. For instance, one person was baffled by the fact that her phone was picked up by our Bluetooth scanner when the phone "does not have strong signal on campus."

Our findings, albeit rather informal, indicate that the Bluetooth encounter prototype was quite well-received, and very few negative comments were made about it. The screen, in addition to showing who is standing also reflected who was scanned recently (up to two minutes in the past). Our prototype in many cases acted as an object of discussion, and prompted people to talk to each other about it. Most of the user comments focused on the interactivity and responsiveness of the display. A common reaction to the system was for users, especially children, to change the name of their phone in order to observe the change on the displayed names. This is an instantiation of the *conscious intentional* encounter, where the users, having been made aware of the screen, intentionally initiate an interaction (change of name) in order to perceive the effect on the screen. This prototype is an example of a system that can be different things to different people. Users of this system may or may not be aware of the display's existence, of Bluetooth and its properties, and additionally may or may not intentionally interact with this display.

In the next stage in our study and as an attempt to trigger people's attention to what was projected on the screen, we applied an experimental approach based on

Fig. 9.4 Screenshots of our installation with the Bluetooth encounter prototype. The location was on the university campus, and the screen was installed behind an office window

intervention through "sensing and projecting" Bluetooth names and people's digital identity in order to investigate the interrelation between the Bluetooth names, digital identity, and active participation within the public arena. This was complemented by an attempt to provoke people's awareness by "tagging" the digital identity in public with an additional phrase.

In the following section we describe our method; we then describe early responses before we outline some factors that may influence this approach.

The Experiment

We ran an experiment at two sites in the city of Bath: in a café during day time and inside a night club during the evening. The aim was to identify people's interaction forms and possible changes in the Bluetooth names triggered by our intervention.

Bluetooth names were scanned and projected on a projection surface in real-time. This was complemented by "snapshot" observation techniques, where an observer takes a mental snapshot of the activities at the moment of observation. The snapshot is then recorded on a plan, with coding according to activities (Vaughan 2001). During the sessions, a human observer recorded people's positions, behaviors, and movements through space, as well as the time of these activities. The form of interactions with the projection surface and the projected information was captured. In addition, the type of interactions with the other people in the area was observed and recorded with a digital camera. Various interactions were video-taped by two researchers using a digital video camera. Finally, changes in the Bluetooth names (projected on the surface) were tracked over time and analyzed. These observations were subsequently compared with the data recorded by our Bluetooth scanners. Following the scan sessions, a selected number of participants were asked to fill in questionnaires. Twenty-five questionnaires were collected, 10 at the club and 15 at the café.

Methodology and Data Collection

The Bluetooth discoverable devices were detected using a computer that was constantly recording Bluetooth devices and their Bluetooth names within a ten-meter range. The scanned Bluetooth names were visualized in real-time using a program written in the Processing language and results were projected on a surface in a noticeable location.

Data Visualization

Whenever a device was detected, its Bluetooth name was displayed on the projection surface. At the same time, a tentacle appeared around the name (Fig. 9.5). As an attempt to trigger people's attention to what was projected on the screen, and in order to encourage the emergence of novel social interactions, a "tag" was attached on each name (e.g., an expression or a social description such as *hey!* or *Is looking good!*). Every Bluetooth name was linked to a randomly selected "tag." This meant that the visual representation was not limited to the presentation of the "name" of the Bluetooth device assigned by its user, but it was rather an attempt to provoke reactions by creating a kind of dialogue between the people and the screen content.

With several names appearing along with several tags, the visualization became a dynamic representation of an evolving social network. Once the Bluetooth device was not detected, the tag faded away and disappeared from the projection screen. This meant that the projection represented all devices that were present at the same time at the same place.

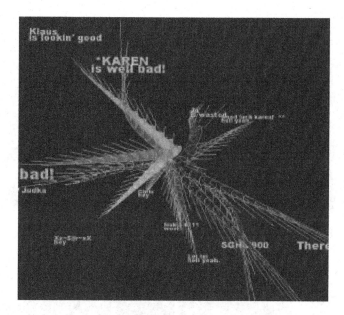

Fig. 9.5 Scanned Bluetooth name is linked to a randomly selected "tag"

The Projection Surface

At the club, the projection surface was sufficiently large, it was placed in the centre of the main wall in front of the main entrance to the space, so it could be seen directly when people entered the space (Fig. 9.6 left). In the café, unlike the club, there was no dedicated projection space. The projection was on the wall next to the entrance, but in a less obvious location. Its size was smaller, and the ambient lighting made it less clear (Fig. 9.6 right). People were therefore not as immediately aware of it as they entered the room as they were at the club.

Sensing Bluetooth Names and Observers' Reactions

Our approach in the real setting, unlike in a "lab" setting, involved applying a range of methods from interpretative–ethnographic to experimental. The approach we adopted was engaging. Assigning the "tag" to the Bluetooth names triggered mixed reactions by the observers. Questionnaires showed that people varied in how comfortable they were with the projection. The casual atmosphere at the club made people somewhat more receptive to the projection, whereas in the café, people's reactions were more reserved and the social interaction was very limited and it seemed that having the projection of Bluetooth names in such a space was unexpected and to a certain extent, rather intrusive.

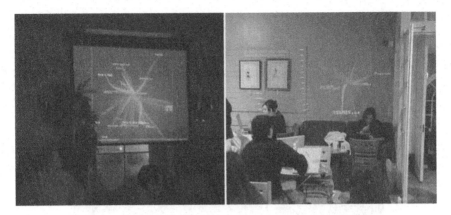

Fig. 9.6 Projecting the digital identity in two places; a club (*left*) and a café (*right*)

Fig. 9.7 People found the approach playful and entertaining. Some people started changing their Bluetooth name, using the projection as an interactive message board

In the club, when people were faced with the visualization of Bluetooth names of other people present in the physical space, various social interactions were triggered. Most people found the process playful and entertaining; they kept changing their Bluetooth names and waited to see the result on the screen (Fig. 9.7). For instance, *"Davey-G"* changed his/her name twice. From *"Davey-G"* into *"Everyone wants lonsdale!"* and then changed it into *"Pete has ten inches?"*

Some people used the projection as an interactive message board with their mobile phone. For instance, from Table 9.2, we can see how *"Optimus prime"* turned her/his Bluetooth name into *"Hi camera lady"* referring to our human observer who was capturing the interactions with her camera. Altering the device's name may suggest an intention for social interaction with the observer through this new electronic medium.

Table 9.2 Interactions though the Bluetooth names at the club

Time sessions	No. of people at the club	Scanned bluetooth names		Tags
22.00-22.15	25	Hello beautiful!		Is looking good
		Davey-G		Woot!
		Jodie		Hey
		Jx		ROCKS!
		W880		Is bitchin'!
		JawaDeman		
		Scarlet x x		
		Man Mountain		
		Kuva!		
		Gorgeous		
		D*ck Willie C* x		
		Princess		
		Two unknown		
22.15-22.30	38	Pleb Nokia 6300		Smelly
		S*X Appeal but desperate plz		Is well bad
		Gem		-
		Abel		Is wasted
		Lonsdale is GAY		
		Optimus Prime		
22.30-22.45	45	Everyone wants Lonsdale!	(from Davey-G)	
			(from Optimus Prime)	
			(from Davey-G)	
			(from Gem)	
			(from D*ck Willie C* x)	
			(from Lonsdale is GAY)	
		Jodie	(from Rob N Roll)	
		Get ur spade out!		
		Rob N Roll		
		Hey camera lady.		
		Pete has 10 in.?		
		Jesson is Gay		
		Newman is a s* x pest		
		Likes To L*ck		
		BP 4232-MBPRO-4		
		Jo wants to sh*g Dom		
		Rob N F**kin Roll		
		One unknown		
22.45-23.00	42	Helphire are shite		Woot!
		Mcraith wants jesson		Hey
		I want c*ck!		Is well bad
		Tjeres only one!		-
		Two unknown		Is shaking it good-

Data collected through the questionnaires indicated that people who were broadcasting devices' names were mainly between 21 and 25 years old. Older people tended to suggest that they did not know this technology well and that they were not inclined to use it. To the question "How do you feel about your name made public and interacted with?" eight people were comfortable and only two responded negatively. These reacted in an extreme way and expressed their anger about this type of "surveillance" and the way technology was projecting hers and her friends' personal information. Interestingly, to the questions "Do you feel this kind of interaction can have an impact on the space?" and "Does it enhance your experience of that space?," only 11 out of 25 expressed positive feelings.

Our findings, although quite informal, indicated that most people liked the experiment and wanted to participate in the playful interactions. Only a few people were critical about the exposure of their personal data, and about our approach in provoking change to their digital identity.

Reflecting on this pilot study of our research, we believe that a number of factors may have influenced people's responses encouraging mixed and sometimes ambivalent reactions. These related to the individual, such as age, knowledge, and use of digital media, and perhaps socio-economic status. Other factors related to the space and activities in that space, and finally factors related to the projection itself such as the projection location and its relation to the main space, clarity, and the projection time and length.

This study demonstrated that the projection of one's "invisible" digital identity and making it part of our physical environment triggers various types of interaction, not only in a *conscious intentional* form of interaction, but also as a nonintentional projection of our self. This experiment was a pilot study and only ran for a short period of time. We believe that further research is needed in order to evaluate the degree to which this approach might provide a motivation to change the way people communicate and engage with others in various environments. We need to examine in greater detail which factors influence people's behavior and, possibly, to quantify the role of different factors relating to the participants and to their spatial context.

Discussion

The public arena offers temporal and spatial mechanisms for generating and promoting various social interactions. With the advent of mobile and pervasive systems, the environment for interaction is likely to change. The introduction of new technologies might modify existing social practices, and on occasion encourage the emergence of new social behaviors.

We apply "digitally augmented" approaches as a way of exploring various types of shared interactions that technology facilitates. As part of our ongoing effort to understand the city as a system encompassing both the built environment and pervasive digital technologies, an attempt was made to map and understand shared social encounters mediated by digital technologies and to explore the relation to the spatial properties of the surroundings.

In this chapter we presented two prototypes: a physical prototype, in the form of a digital surface, was implemented in different locations in the city. These locations differ in the way they relate to the built environment and the way they construct users' relationships to their surroundings. We described initial findings from the deployment of the digital suface. The surface was embeded in the built environment, acting as a facilitator between people and their surrounding. The aim was to generate a novel urban experience that triggers social interactions among friends, observers, or strangers.

Our initial evaluation suggests that by setting up the digital surface and introducing a change in an area within the urban space, people were made aware of other people around them. This has influenced their behavior and provided a motivation to change the way they communicate and engage with others, generating diverse shared encounters. While demonstrating differences in how users' intentions and consciousness can vary, our approach offered a digital stage that facilitated and encouraged different types of social interactions, creating the feel of an urban performance that unfolds over time, and it seems that in order for this kind of public display to be engaging, the viewer needed to be able to construct a socially meaningful relationship of which the display and the human observer form a part.

In order to understand various facets of socio-technical behaviors in the public arena, we deploy digital methods that cover different perspectives related to the physical and social context. As part of our approach, we apply Bluetooth scanning coupled with human observations in a context where people are likely to use mobile and wireless technologies. "What happens when people are made aware of their digital presence and identity in the public space?" "Would this encourage different types of interactions?" in order to answer these questions, we conducted a pilot study by projecting the scanned Bluetooth names in a café and a club on a surface as part of these spaces. We applied an experimental approach in order to trigger people's attention to what was projected on the screen. A particularly important insight comes from the effects, we observed of "tagging" the digital identity in public with an additional phrase. It seemed that this was interpreted by the viewers as giving the installation a personality, or at least suggesting that there was a human author involved in the piece. It encouraged a conversational form of interaction, including name changing or the use of the Bluetooth device name to establish a conversation. We suspect that in order for public display of these technologies to be engaging, the viewer needs to be able to construct a meaningful social relationship of which the display forms part. The engagement with the "camera girl" offers one example of this, and required that user to put together the presence and behavior of the display with the presence and activity of the human observer recording the event.

The conversation between "*Davey-G*" and, presumably, one of his friends "*Pete*" offers a different kind of socially meaningful engagement. This time by making public a socially risky innuendo, the user took advantage of the degree of personal anonymity coupled to very public display afforded by this medium. Everyone in the club could see the display, but there would have been some doubt in the minds of all those except close friends as to the identity of "*Davey-G*."

Our approach offered a digital platform that facilitated and encouraged different types of social interactions. Presenting people with a visualization of their *unconscious intentional* (or nonintentional) projection of their digital identity and sharing it with others made people aware of it and its impact, and this triggered the emergence of novel social interactions mediated through the digital platform.

While demonstrating differences in how users' intention to interact and their awareness of the various communications have influenced the type of shared interactions, our prototypes illustrate an approach to facilitate and encourage shared encounters in the city.

Conclusions and Ongoing Work

We have presented two prototypes that investigate the relation between consciousness of communication and intention of interaction in a city context. Both examples explore different roles of technology in supporting social encounters within the surrounding environment. The two prototypes differ in the way they relate to the built environment in which they are embedded, and also in the way they reconstruct the relationship of the users to their surrounding.

More specifically, Prototype I supported the spatial configuration in which it was embedded, and was similarly affected by it. Prototype II overcame limitations in encounter and communication imposed by the surrounding built environment and provided a digital encounter platform. While demonstrating differences in how users' intentions and consciousness can vary, our two prototypes also illustrate two approaches to facilitating and encouraging encounters in the city: providing either a physical or digital stage that encourages encounters.

Our initial findings suggest that by altering the relation between consciousness of communication and the intention of interaction, technology can be appropriated to support emergent social interactions. This may help throw further light on the complex relationship between the digital space and public space in general, and the way that this is mediated by, and mediates people's relationship to each other.

Changing the encounter, illustrated in Table 9.1, from one type into another creates a potential for stimulating richer experience. For instance, in the Bluetooth prototype, presenting people with a visualization of their *unconscious intentional* (or non-intentional) encounters with others makes people aware of these encounters. This can possibly influence their behavior or provide a motivation to alter the way they communicate and engage with others.

As part of our ongoing work, we are trying to address a number of issues that came up through our implementation of the two prototypes. Specifically, we are exploring how digital encounters can affect the experience in the urban space, and how a system can improve the quality of social encounters. The next steps will involve a longitudinal deployment of the Bluetooth system, which will run for a couple of weeks in selected locations in the city. Users' reactions and feedback will be captured using observations and interviews.

Acknowledgments The authors would like to thank Carolina Briones, Kaiti Papapavlou, Adi Ahmad, and Olivier Ottevaere from the MSc AAC, UCL London. We thank Tim Kindberg, Kharsim (Kaz) Al Mosawi and Eamonn O'Neill for their contribution. This research is partly funded by the UK Engineering and Physical Sciences Research Council grant EP/C547683/1 (Cityware: urban design and pervasive systems).

References

Hillier B and Hanson (1984) The social logic of the space. Cambridge University Press, London

Kostakos V, O'Neill E. and Shahi A. (2006) Building common ground for face to face interactions by sharing mobile device context. In: Proceedings of LOCA 2006, Dublin, Ireland. LNCS 3987, 222–238. Springer, Germany

Nokia Corporation, Nokia sensor, www.nokia-asia.com. Accessed 26 February 2009.

Mobiluck, http: www.mobiluck.com. Accessed 26 February 2009

Fatah gen. Schieck A, Penn A, Kostakos V, O'Neill E, Kindberg T, Stanton-Fraser D and Jones T (2006) Design tools for pervasive computing in urban environment. In: Leeuwen J & Timmerman H (eds) 9th International Conference on Design & Decision Support Systems in Architecture and Urban Planning. Eindhoven: Eindhoven University of Technology.

Fatah gen. Schieck A, Penn A and O'Neill E (2008a) Mapping, sensing and visualising the digital co-presence in the public arena. In: Timmermans H & de Vries B (eds) Design & Decision Support Systems in Architecture and Urban Planning, 38–58, Springer, Eindhoven

Fatah gen. Schieck A, Briones C and Mottram C (2008b) Exploring the role of place within the urban space: the urban Screen as a socialising platform. In Eckhardt F, Geelhaar J, Colini L, Willis K, Chorianopoulos K and Henning R (eds.) MEDIACITY; Situations Practices and Encounters, 285–305. Frank & Timme, Germany

Kindberg T and Jones T (2007) Merolyn the phone: A study of Bluetooth naming practices. In: Krumm J, Abowd GD Seneviratne A and Strang TH (eds) Proceedings of Ubicomp 2007, 318–335. Springer, Berlin

Briones C, Fatah gen. Schieck A and Mottram C (2007) A socializing interactive installation for the urban environments. In: IADIS Applied Computing International Conference 2007, 18–20 February 2007, Salamanca, Spain

Fatah gen. Schieck A, Briones C and Mottram C (2008b) Exploring the role of place within the urban space: the urban Screen as a socialising platform. In Eckhardt F, Geelhaar J, Colini L, Willis K, Chorianopoulos K and Henning R (eds.) MEDIACITY; Situations Practices and Encounters, 285–305. Frank & Timme, Germany

Vaughan L (2001) Space Syntax Observation Manual. Space Syntax Ltd, London

Chapter 10
Mis(sed)information in Public Space

Omar Khan

Introduction

Stewart Brand's ambiguous aphorism, "information wants to be free," has become a battle cry of resistance against information controls. A variety of its interpretations provide useful insights into what might constitute "freedom" in the information age. For designers of interactive and responsive systems that include interactive media and architecture projects, negotiating control and freedom in their designs remains a critical issue. How open should such systems be? What role should public participation play in their design? How should they engage the space of the "public"? Who should operationally maintain it? Who or what should control its objectives? The designer? The public? Using concepts from second-order cybernetics, this chapter looks at designing systems that can handle changing objectives without becoming *over-specified* (Pask 1969; Beer 1974). Two media architecture projects, one speculative – RRing (rumor ring) (2005) and another realized – SEEN (screen enabling employed narratives)-Fruits of our Labor (2006) examine the possibility of creating alternative channels for information exchange in public space. They present the argument that information, like public space, is a collective construction that requires public participation to establish and sustain. The act of informing is not presented as a communication problem where better channels of moving information are to be explored, but a construction problem where networked technologies can play an empowering role to encourage collective interaction. This provides a unique opportunity to examine how information, or better the act of informing can come about. In the case of RRing, the communication exchange is focused on local rumors (misinformation) while SEEN sets its sights on collecting the personal aspirations of individuals from three communities that predominantly engage one

O. Khan (✉)
Situated Technologies Research Group, Department of Architecture,
School of Architecture and Planning, University at Buffalo, 3435 Main Street,
Buffalo, NY, USA, 14214
e-mail: omarkhan@buffalo.edu

K.S. Willis et al. (eds.), *Shared Encounters*, Computer Supported Cooperative Work,
DOI 10.1007/978-1-84882-727-1_10, © Springer-Verlag London Limited 2010

another through work (missed information). In both cases, the need to create alternative channels of exchange speaks to the role such systems can play in public space as vehicles for facilitating mutual understanding and self-reflection.

Information Wants to be Free; The Public Wants to be in Control

Brand's statement at the Hacker Conference in 1984 reflected on the changing economics of producing and distributing information:

On the one hand information wants to be expensive, because it's so valuable. The right information in the right place just changes your life. On the other hand, information wants to be free, because the cost of getting it out is getting lower and lower all the time. So you have these two fighting against each other (Brand 1988).

The aphorism, information wants to be free, as other commentators have noted, has taken on a life of its own (Barlow 1994; Clarke 2000). It has developed into a meme that pervades discussions on and of the information society. However, in our attempt to appreciate what is meant by "free," we need to first clarify what we understand to be information. Three interpretations gleaned from the aphorism include: information as an exchangeable commodity, information as a shared resource, and information as a willful subject. In the case of information as a commodity, free is understood to mean costing nothing to distribute and exchange. This speaks of the digitalization of information that allows it to "lose its body" (Hayles 1999), and therefore not incur the spatial and monetary costs encumbered by materialization. As a digital commodity, it can easily be disseminated over wired and wireless channels and copied without losing fidelity. However, such economic freedoms are being tested by bootlegged and cracked software that capitalizes on the mobility of exchange made possible by dematerialization. Another interpretation of information would be as a shared resource, accessible free from political controls. Like air, information is understood to be a right of citizenry that shouldn't be hindered by political censorship. This has been the underlying vision of Municipal Wi-Fi; to provide free Wi-Fi across a city. However, for both political and economic reasons, this has not met with much success worldwide. Freedoms are being tested as political and economic entities negotiate controls on how and what people can access. Finally, information can also be understood as a subject that strives through its own means to be free. It forecasts an internet of things where animate devices become producers and exchangers of information, functioning outside of direct human supervision and control (ITU Internet Reports 2005). Here, information has its own agency that isn't dependent on human valuation. At this time, it isn't clear as to what types of freedoms may be required by such a network to properly function. In all three of these interpretations, information is understood as a "thing" that, while not material, has an identity. Michael Buckland in "information as thing" argues that while many theorists object to the tangibility of information, it is through representations of knowledge such as data, signs, texts, objects etc. that is, things that we in fact operate (Buckland 1991). In this regard, information systems, whether they are computers, archives, libraries etc. can only deal with "information-as-thing." At the same time, on the other side of Brand's aphorism is its paradox, "information wants to be expensive." Here, another quality of information – that of an effect – is introduced. Information is understood to be intangible, and must be bestowed value by someone or something. This speaks of information as a process that may be informative for one person, but not necessarily another. It is a construction that is given form by its users in the act of using it. Both these understandings of information, as a thing and an affect are necessary to be considered by designers of interactive media and architecture. For the case of information-as-thing, designers must be able to provide users with the necessary freedom of access, production, and manipulation, while in the case of information-as-affect, it is necessary to give users the adequate control so that information can become meaningful for them.

Because of the increasing reliance on information in contemporary society, personal and societal freedoms are likewise implicitly tied to information freedoms. This would suggest that by extension, our freedom to produce, distribute, access, and most significantly to act will be mirrored in the way information is controlled and exchanged. Public space is the forum wherein we perform these freedoms. As others have observed, there is a steady increase of controls by both governmental and commercial interests in such spaces (Besser 2001; Mitchell 1995). The problem that we face is how to negotiate these controls in light of our democratic ideals. The proliferation of surveillance devices in traditional public spaces (city plazas, streets, and transportation hubs) can encroach on the public's privacy, causing people to self-censor their behavior. However, such devices can also be effective for monitoring and identifying criminal behavior as well as recording abuses of authority. The camera may not lie, but depending on who controls the image, it can serve both disciplinary and libertarian ends. It is in this ambivalence of acceptable control and exercised freedom that people inevitably engage public spaces. Take for example the pseudo public spaces of malls and stadiums where seemingly innocuous activities, like handing out leaflets or making speeches can result in your expulsion (Mitchell 1995). Here, control is exercised through a variety of means; the most common being costs for admission, prescribed dress codes, and enforced rules of behavior. The general public accepts these restrictions because they guarantee the necessary ambience they expect from such spaces. Hence, it is important to understand that public spaces, like information, are constructions contested and negotiated between people. We inevitably juggle to accommodate multiple interests even as they chip away at some of our own or our fellow citizens' freedoms.

People's freedom to *produce*, *distribute*, *access*, and *act* in public space is contingent on their ability to access and exchange information. As designers of interactive systems that are contingent on the participation of the general public to make them function, we need to understand how our designs exercise controls on information while providing adequate openness to manipulation by the public that wants to use them. Beyond the technical issues for implementing such technologies, we need to understand the role that existing protocols of public space – how people use it, what they expect from it, how freedoms can be performed in it – contribute to the concept and design of an interactive architecture.

Designing Freedom

This chapter proposes a particular approach for the design of interactive systems that builds on the pioneering work of cyberneticians Gordon Pask and Stafford Beer. More specifically, it examines the idea of *underspecifying* a system, an idea that is in need of reconsideration in light of the participatory technologies that we aim to create. This section introduces the concept and strategies of *underspecification* as they are presented in both Pask's and Beer's second-order cybernetics.[1]

Gordon Pask's (1969) article "The Architectural Relevance of Cybernetics" ends with a listing of considerations for a "cybernetic design paradigm." Its key point, which is echoed throughout the rest of the list, is contained in the first clause:

Specification of the purpose or goal of the system (with respect to the human inhabitants). It should be emphasized that the goal may be and nearly always will be underspecified, i.e., the architect will no more know the purpose of the system than he really knows the purpose of a conventional house. His aim is to provide a set of constraints that allow for certain, presumably desirable, modes of evolution (Pask 1969).

The term *underspecification* is never defined by Pask as a concept in its own right. Instead, it is used descriptively, to denote incompleteness in a system's goals. This is so that participants (human and artificial) through a very engaged form of interaction (what Pask calls *conversation*) can mutually construct unique responses to their specific situation. Pask's provocation here is to steer the designer/architect away from designing the entire system and instead allowing its in situ performance to guide the design. As such, the emphasis of the design is on the "*form* (rather than the material constitution) of structures" (Pask 1969). Form is dynamic and mutable, while materials are static and fixed. However, form must be understood not as a *shape,* but a *shaping* that is open to the contingencies of the situation including its use and inhabitation. In this regard, *underspecified* systems concern themselves with how forms come about and evolve rather than with which forms should be used.

Another aspect of *underspecification* is concerned with loosely defining the purpose of a design. This is seen to be an outcome of the circularity of interactions between participant(s) and their environment. In this sense, by opening purpose up to the vagaries of interaction, one inevitably also lets in *unpredictability* and *chance.* The root of this idea as it pertains to intelligent systems was discussed at the Eighth Macy Conference (1951),[2] where Donald Mackay received a rebuke from statistician Leonard Savage for suggesting that an automaton could make inductive inferences through chance operations. Savage and the other first-order cyberneticians dismissed chance as contributing neither to mimicking human behavior nor improving efficiency in solving problems. However, at the following Ninth Macy Conference (1952) Ross Ashby's two papers, one on his homeostat and

---

[1]For further elaboration on the differences between first- and second-order cybernetics, see Scott (2004).

[2]http://www.asc-cybernetics.org/foundations/history/MacySummary.htm

the other on a chess playing automaton that used random tactics, turned the issue on its head and effectively showed that chance was as good a way as any for devising solutions and hence learning (Ashby 1960). Ashby's radical demonstration, discredited the mechanistic and deterministic formulations of purpose of the first-order cybernetics, and in its place demonstrated it as the outcome of interaction. Shannon and Weaver's *noise* in the channel (Weaver and Shannon 1949), which had been seen as a deterrent to communication could now be reinterpreted as in fact the catalyst for more meaningful exchange.

But what are the mechanisms for designing an *underspecified* system? How can it negotiate change? How can it develop the necessary responses to all the perturbations that are presented in the environment within which it is deployed? Stafford Beer, in his formulations for a "liberty machine" describes a strategy for creating a system that develops through interactions, the necessary variety for adapting to change. It does so by *attenuating* the environmental variety it is given while *amplifying* its own internal responses to it. *Attenuation* is a filtering mechanism that reduces possibilities in a system while *amplification* is a generative process that increases it. By reducing environmental variety, the system only acts on those inputs for which it has requisite responses. Meanwhile, it generates further variations on these responses based upon its experience with the type of inputs it has received. In other words, the system working as a recursive loop, through use increases its internal variety by *learning* from its past interactions with its environment. This opens the system up to change making it adaptable to its actual situation.

Beer's is an idealized model that provides a useful way to think about responsive technologies in public space. The key point being that an *underspecified* design must be open in its ability to engage and use information. While the designer designs its organizational closure, the way it looks and the way in which it behaves, she must also devise the necessary protocols of interaction and responsiveness which allow for the system to evolve under the control of the people that use it. It is in the negotiation between internal organization and external information, the designer and the user that allows the system to be malleable.

Situating Information

But can't any object or thing be informative? Buckland recognizes the potential arbitrariness of designating things-as-information, but emphasizes that it is the *situation* that makes a particular set of things informative for the people involved. What I would like to argue is that this situational aspect of information, the necessity of a context to make certain things informative or not, speaks of the fact that in *underspecified* designs, information itself can become the object of construction.

To further expound on this idea, I use two projects, *RRing* (2005) and *SEEN-Fruits of our Labor* (2006)[3] produced by media artist Osman Khan and myself to talk

---

[3] http://www.fruitsofourlabor.org/

about a constructionist approach to information production and the deployment of *underspecified* systems in public space. These interactive media architectures allow participants to engage in necessary discursive activity to not only construct information – but also the public in public space.

Rumor Ring (RRing)

RRing (2004) was a proposal for public arts project that used the payphone infrastructure of New York City to organize an ad hoc public. It is conceived as a calling service that collects and disseminates local rumors by making cold calls to 20 randomly selected public payphones in lower Manhattan (Fig. 10.1) every hour, on the hour.

It announces itself to the receiver as a community archive project called RRing, and asks them to share a rumor about their neighborhood. The system records that message and catalogues it in a database. In addition, it also records the date, time, and telephone from which the message was received. This information is then processed and re-presented back to the public in two ways. In the first, an application organizes the database so that it is accessible through a phone answering service. A toll free number (1,800-myRumor) posted on payphones in lower Manhattan allows people to call into the service and listen to the daily rumors. The service also allows people to verify, refute, and add additional rumors to the database. At the same time, another application automatically reads the database and prepares a day's worth of recordings to be played back in a continuously looped audio performance

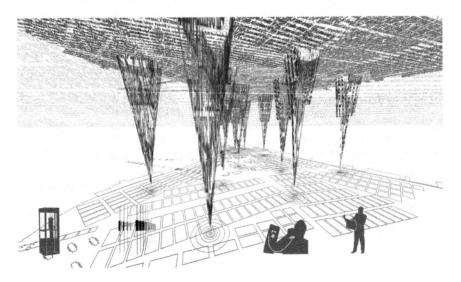

Fig. 10.1 Visualization of rumor ring service

Fig. 10.2 Visualization of pay phones in rumor ring

estimated at about an hour. Twenty-four hours are compressed into 1 h and presented back to the public through an installation of 20 payphones with their handsets facing outward (Fig. 10.2).

This installation would playback the previous day's rumors as a soundscape every hour. The rumors would no longer be legible for their content, but instead exist as noise that would reflect the ebbs and surges in the day's collection. The project purposely uses the slowly disappearing payphone infrastructure to imagine another use for it. With mobile phones replacing much of the usefulness of the payphone, it seemed opportunistic to reframe this infrastructure as a public service.

Rumors occupy a paradoxical role in human communication. They are produced as stand-ins for missing information whose void creates uncertainty, and consequently anxiety. Because they are unverifiable, their role as pseudo-information makes them particularly problematic if they begin to take hold as facts and hence misinformation. In the late 60s, rumor control centers (RCC) were set up in cities where there was a propensity for civil unrest. Their aim was to investigate rumors and disseminate facts to stop further rumors. Their mandate included, "alleviating callers' fears and anxieties and monitoring relations so as to serve as a 'barometer' for community tensions" (Pointing 1973). In spite of their potential negative effects, rumors do serve a community as a vehicle for catharsis. Rosnow (1988) defines rumor as the public's means to communicate private notions of how the world works and Shibutani (1966) suggests that they allow "men [and women] to come to terms with the exigencies of life." Because they serve as improvised news, they replace information that is not forthcoming. RRing plays a strategic role in this dynamic by creating a publicly accessible channel of communication, where people can voice their uncertainties and in process collectively come to be informed about each other.

While RRing remains unrealized, it may suffice to reflect on some of the issues it raises for *underspecifying* a design. The appropriation of existing payphones as the reception and delivery devices allows us to engage their protocols of use. There is no reason to introduce a new form of communication, but instead reshape an existing one. The situated and familiar workings of these phones allow RRing to manipulate their performance to achieve alternative effects. In the first, the ringing of phones on the hour whether answered or not provides an aural representation of this system to the public. This subversion of the everyday – who's calling every hour? Why are all the phones ringing simultaneously? – will draw notice and is predicted to encourage interaction. Second, since all interactions can occur through the familiar payphone, there is no need to train the participants on using the system. This speaks of the issue of easy and free access that more often than not is hindered by complicated or proprietary technology. Then there is the actual feedback of the rumors, its purpose-fulness, to the public. While we are not sure what the project will actually yield, this is ultimately the least important. What is important is the process that it sets into play. Both representations, whether as legible rumors saved as messages or an ambient *babble*, engage the public to inform itself by reconstructing what is considered misinformation. In the case of the recorded messages, people can participate by refuting or verifying their claims. This allows the public to construct not through consensus, but discourse information-as-thing. The *ring* and the *babble* as an alternative representation suggest the need to engage "noise" in order to make the information perceptible to people. Here, information is communicated through an ambient effect that allows the project to reach a larger audience.

SEEN-Fruits of Our Labor

SEEN-Fruits of our Labor (2006) was a commissioned work for the ZeroOne San Jose Festival that addressed the heated issue of immigration and globalization of labor through three communities, sharing San Jose's labor needs. The communities included the technology workers of Silicon Valley, many of whom are recent immi-grants, service workers (migrant workers from Mexico, Central America, Vietnam, etc.) engaged in San Jose's service industry, and the remote call center workers in India to whom customer service and technical support has been outsourced. The project sought to clarify how these economically and geographically disparate groups in fact form a community. A survey was conducted that asked everybody a single question: *What is the fruit of your labor?* Their responses were collected and during the weeklong festival displayed them back to the general public on a large *infrared (IR) LED screen* located on a prominent plaza (Fig. 10.3).

The screen's display technology is critical to the way it communicates its intent. It uses IR LEDs as opposed to visible spectrum LEDs. The unique technological possibility offered by IR is that although they are invisible to the naked human eye, they can be seen through all digital imaging devices, including still, video, and cell phone cameras. This is because all CCD sensors in addition to being sensitive to

Fig. 10.3 Fruits of our labor in San Jose 2006

the visible spectrum are also able to capture IR wavelengths. So when the screen, which measures $4' \times 8'$, is viewed without the aid of a mediating device, its black acrylic surface simply reflects the viewer. But when viewed through an imaging device, the projection's content is revealed.

SEEN-Fruits of our Labor was well-attended and viewed during the ZeroOne San Jose Festival 2006. The crowds were infectious and people pulled out their mobile phone cameras to see the content. In our original formulation, we imagined that because the access to the information required a mediating device it would create a technological haves and have-nots in front of the screen, which may provoke impromptu sharing and potentially meaningful encounters. What actually happened was more subtle. The technological divide did not break along the economic lines as we anticipated. Our service workers all had cell phones with cameras, as did most other people. It was the occasional elderly person or the rare technological Luddite that was caught needing, but other conscientious viewers quickly accommodated them. Another interesting outcome of these shared encounters was the way in which personal communication devices became open to public sharing. It is rare to share even with one's close friends and even less strangers the screen of one personal communication devices. They are small and designed for view by a single person. However, SEEN sanctioned a new engagement with this technology, allowing people to look over each other's shoulders and be in close physical proximity to view the information (Fig. 10.4).

These impromptu encounters moved to discussing the content – Do you see what I see? What did it say? What is my response? What is the fruit of your labor?

Fig. 10.4 Public sharing with SEEN

Fig. 10.5 Crowd interaction with SEEN-fruits of our labor

The project became a means to draw people out of their everyday routines and reflect on their aspirations and desires for the future. In a way, it was to inform them of why they did what they did. This is missed information, that when shared through the invisible IR spectrum becomes more poignant. SEEN-Fruits of our Labor provides a curious sight – a crowd of people looking at a blank screen (Fig. 10.5).

Like RRing, it engages the public through a protocol that requires little training and more importantly allows people to engage it through their own technology. This personalizes the information and the consequent capture and sharing moves the work from the public realm into more private communication channels. SEEN also forces the public to work for the information. Freedom of access is not to be taken lightly, and since the information is precious it cannot simply be displayed to simply become background visual noise. It is purposely hidden and slow paced to which the public is welcome to add their own fruit through a website.

Constructing the Public

What I have attempted to argue is a constructionist approach to designing interactive media and architecture for public spaces. The basic assumption of this approach is that the public and the content of the work do not exist a priori to its deployment. Both of these must be constructed through the work. The means to do so is by *underspecifying* the design of an interactive technology and allowing people to participate in developing it. What I would like to conclude with is how such systems can contribute to constructing unique publics and ultimately a more accessible public space.

As we witnessed in SEEN and speculated about in RRing, networked technologies facilitated a means for dispersed and remote participants to contribute to a collective endeavor. While the encounter with the technology may in some cases be brief, there was a personal investment made by each individual in developing the aesthetic experience of the public artwork. The private nature of this engagement; sharing a rumor, discussing personal aspirations, and allowing it to be broadcast and shared in a public forum points to a unique quality of deploying such pervasive interactive systems. The "private" is no longer an end in a gradient moving from public to semi-public to the private but as Dana Cuff argues "a nested metaphor in which publicity, has infected privacy in every conceivable context, and vice versa. Moreover, embedded networks undermine the pretense that we control our environment or our boundaries within it – a pretense that is fundamental to the construct of privacy" (Cuff 2003). While there are ample examples of how this conflation is eroding our privacy, I would like to argue for the opportunities it makes possible. In the first case we can take the opposite view that through these technologies it is privacy that is usurping publicity. This provides a means to empower the individual, the marginal, and the forgotten to act in a shared space. Unique publics and not the generic public of public space can emerge from the actions of individuals or groups, allowing for shifts in power structures. Second, the possibility for such marginal and private agendas to be represented and performed in the physical space of the city allows for what Adrian Forty in his analysis of private experience in postwar British public architecture calls *reflexive perception*. Borrowing the idea from Jean Paul Sartre's notion of a third dimension of being, where being occurs as "I am for others, the other is revealed to me as a subject for whom I am an object,"

Forty (1995) contends that only a truly public architecture can facilitate this. For it to happen, a space must be perceived by the subject as theirs, a conflation of the private into the public Words like *mine*, *yours*, and *ours* are continually to be negotiated as people confront one another in a dynamic public sphere. There is ample opportunity to exercise individual freedoms while constructing a collective public.

Acknowledgments I would like to thank the Department of Architecture at the University of Buffalo, and Cesar Cedano and Matt Zinski, graduate students who assisted in the research and implementation of SEEN-Fruits of our Labor. Also, Steve Deitz and the San Jose ZeroOne Festival for commissioning SEEN-Fruits of our Labor.

References

Ashby WR (1960) Design for a brain – the origins of adaptive behavior. Chapman & Hall Ltd., London

Barlow JP (1994) The economy of ideas. Wired Magazine, Issue 2.03.

Beer S (1974) Designing freedom. Massey Lecture Series. Canadian Broadcasting Corporation.

Besser H (2001) Intellectual Property: The Attack on Public Space in Cyberspace. http://www.gseis.ucla.edu/~howard/Papers/pw-public-spaces.html. Accessed 5 August 2008.

Brand S (1988) The media lab: inventing the future at M.I.T. Penguin, London

Buckland M (1991) Information as thing. Journal of the American Society of Information Science 42 (5): 351–360

Clarke R (2000) Information Wants to be Free…, Xamax Consultancy Pty Ltd. http://www.rogerclarke.com/II/IWtbF.html. Accessed 28 February 2009

Cuff D (2003) Immanent domain: pervasive computing and the public realm. The Journal of Architectural Education 57 (1): 43–49

Forty A (1995) Being or nothingness: private experience and public architecture in post-war Britain. Architectural History 38: 25–35

Hayles KN (1999) How we became posthuman. University of Chicago Press, Chicago

ITU Internet Reports 2005 (2005) The internet of things – executive summary. http://www.itu.int/osg/spu/publications/internetofthings/. Retrieved 10 January 2009

Mitchell D (1995) The end of public space? People's park, definitions of the public, and democracy. Annals of the Association of American Geographers 85(1): 108–13

Pask G (1969) The architectural relevance of cybernetics. Architectural Design 9.

Pointing JR (1973) Rumor control centers: their emergence and operations. American Behavioral Scientists 16: 391–401

Rosnow RL (1988) Rumor as communication: A contextualist approach. Journal of Communication 38: 12–28

Scott B (2004) Second-order cybernetics: an historical introduction. International Journal of Systems & Cybernetics 33: 9–10, DOI: 10.1108/03684920410556007

Shibutani T (1966) Improvised news: A sociological study of rumor. Bobbs-Merrill, Indianapolis

Weaver W and Shannon CE (1949) The mathematical theory of communication. University of Illinois, Urbana

Chapter 11
Encounters and Content Sharing in an Urban Village: Reading Texts Through an Archaeological Lens

Nicole Garcia, Marcus Foth, and Greg Hearn

Introduction

Archaeology can provide a theoretical lens to help understand "the ways in which past spaces were actively used to structure particular senses of place, forms of identity, social relations, and political power" (Giles 2007). This chapter discusses how this approach to reading of past spaces can be applied to a contemporary urban space, that is, a master-planned "urban village" in Australia. The urban village concept emerged in the United Kingdom in the late 1980s and gained popularity with developers and prominent advocates such as Prince Charles in the 1990s. With the support of Prince Charles, the first urban village was constructed at Poundbury in the United Kingdom (Franklin and Tait 2002). The urban village concept is closely associated with new urbanism, an urban planning movement in the United States (Biddulph 2000). Urban villages and new urbanism emphasize notions of neighborhood, community, and pedestrian-friendly urban design, and draw on urban design theories from the early twentieth century.

The case study for this chapter is the Kelvin Grove Urban Village (KGUV, www.kgurbanvillage.com.au), located 2 km from the central business district of Brisbane, Australia. The KGUV is a joint development between the Queensland State Government and Queensland University of Technology (QUT). Planning for the development began in 2000 and the first residents moved into the Village in 2006. The KGUV is a master planned development "... based on a traditional village design, with a vibrant town centre and a rich mixture of shops, cafés, restaurants and businesses"[1]. The development is of mixed tenure with a range of accommodation available including secure apartment blocks with resort type facilities, government subsidized housing, student accommodation (Fig. 11.1). Other uses include the

N. Garcia (✉)
Institute for Creative Industries and Innovation, Queensland University of Technology,
Creative Industries Precinct, Brisbane QLD, 4059, Australia
e-mail: picoloska@yahoo.com

[1] Department of Housing & QUT (2007). Kelvin Grove Urban Village (marketing brochure). Brisbane: Department of Housing & Queensland University of Technology.

K.S. Willis et al. (eds.), *Shared Encounters*, Computer Supported Cooperative Work, DOI 10.1007/978-1-84882-727-1_11, © Springer-Verlag London Limited 2010

Fig. 11.1 Aerial shot of the Kelvin Grove Urban Village master plan – courtesy of the KGUV development team

QUT Centre for Health and Physical Activity, the Australian Red Cross Blood Service headquarters, QUT's Creative Industries Precinct, and the Institute of Health and Biomedical Innovation. The entire KGUV is due to be fully completed by 2012, although a majority of lots and buildings have already been constructed and are being occupied by residential and commercial tenants and residents.

We deal with a discipline that is traditionally concerned with places in the past and uncovering hidden evidence of human society, and apply it to analyze an extant living space in order to produce insights into how encounters and content shape the operation of public spaces. The overarching interpretive frame is that of "reading texts." We direct our attention to three types of texts in the site in question: the space itself; content of an exploratory web application that is available to local residents called *HistoryLines*; and public documents that describe and record various aspects of the history of the urban village site and its present development. Put another way we read encounters and content across three media (space design; local encounters facilitated by a web application; public/oral history accounts produced in the context of digital storytelling workshops) to understand the operation of public space in an urban village. The archaeological lens can focus on both the physical and online space of such an urban site. What becomes apparent in our study is that in order to fulfill the intent of the design of the space – permeability, heterogeneous design, and social sustainability – not only the physical manipulation of the site, but also the construction and maintenance of the accompanying digital space is required. Archaeology is traditionally concerned with the artifacts of human culture and that now necessarily includes new media and digital content. This chapter introduces a contemporary urban village development, and argues for the application of the archaeological lens in this type of research environment. We discuss our findings in terms of three categories of readings, namely:

1. Our analysis begins with the section on "Readings of movement and places in between" that moves away from a conventional interpretation of explicit text and language. Three major features of the urban village are read via an archaeological lens in order to investigate the tension between the *design of space* and the *use of space*. Of note in this chapter is evidence for planned and serendipitous social encounters. Physical traces of movement within and between the features were recorded and analyzed using archaeological methods of reading the humanly constructed landscape as text. This study relies on a basic distinction between how space has been designed (and framed in an ongoing way via marketing, promotional, and neighborhood development strategies) and the actual uses people make of the space once it has been built. Utilizing an archaeological lens necessitates an intimate enquiry into the relationship between the material artifacts of a place and the socialities present there. Ordinarily, urban villages are studied within the disciplines of sociology and urban design (see for example, Biddulph 2003). However it is archaeology's "quest for sensuous knowing and corporeal knowledge" (Pearson and Shanks 2001) that makes the approach to this study relevant and innovative. Discontinuities between the *designed space*, as represented within the master plan and associated marketing material, can

then be tested against the *used place* as represented by the material culture and physicality of KGUV.

2. Our "Readings of the past for the future" explore the twofold significance of this chapter and the *HistoryLines* project. By utilizing archaeological theory and methodology, an integrated model of inquiry has been developed which can clearly analyze the boundaries – and the manipulation and permeability of those boundaries – of encounters that are shared within both place-based and new media domains. Communication, content sharing, and social encounters are experienced through a linking of the past with the present. Archaeology demonstrates that such social practices have always been an essential element of communication and a means of consolidating socialities in the present. We propose that our model of inquiry delves into how communication technologies can work to support and activate social encounters in certain urban settings, which has important implications for understanding the future.

3. "Readings between the conceived and perceived space" investigates the *Sharing Stories* project, whereby this textual artefact bridges the divide between the intent of the original design of the urban village and the use of place. The KGUV Master Plan proposes a site where links to the historical past are to be made explicit within the space. However, to enhance the relevance and social meaning of features such as storyboards and history plaques, the recording of personal accounts of history of the site represent content sharing, which activates static landscape features via digital storytelling.

Archaeology in a Contemporary Urban Setting

The fundamental theoretical basis to be utilized in this chapter is the assumed connection between the landscape and social realities (Gosden and Head 1994). Furthermore, material culture is understood as not only representative of social realities, but also as effective in the creation of those realities and social relationships (Pearson and Shanks 2001). The idea that material culture is not just a static representation of human activity is essential for this study. If the buildings, pathways, and artefacts of KGUV were just simply the material outcome of social processes at this particular urban site, then using an archaeological framework could be criticized as arbitrary because the social realities of the Village could have been more easily mapped using other methods such as ethnography (see for example Laurel 2003; Pink 2006) or space syntax (O'Neill et al. 2006). However, to reach useful empirical outcomes for future master-planned urban design projects, it is essential to view material culture as active and creative of social realities.

Of significance for this study is the criticism that archaeology's traditional "orientation towards depth, concealment, mystery and revelation is quite obstructive, for it enhances the belief that the past is entirely separate from the present: it is "somewhere else" that has to be accessed in a particular way" (Thomas 2004). The planning and development team of this urban renewal project has implemented strategies to link the past with the present and to engage new residents in the creation and interaction with these links in various social forms of creative expression. We argue that this is where the meeting between studying a contemporary and lived-in space within an archaeological framework becomes fruitful and meaningful. For the purposes of analyzing the space of this currently occupied urban village, sociali-ties are considered to have physical expression, and regardless of what social or economic requirements stimulated this expression, it can be studied and is retrievable as archaeological evidence (Perring 1991). The textual and physical evidence of the process of how *designed space* becomes *use space* is turned around and viewed archaeologically. Instead of viewing the site from the privileged position of the planner, the process can be understood from the "ground-up." The physical space and how people may or may not be using, contesting, and manipulating various features can be more precisely understood by the experiential and observational process of the archaeologist. (For an example of similar methods utilized by archaeologist Jonna Hansson in a contemporary urban locale, see Pearson and Shanks 2001) Data col-lected and analyzed within this framework can then render the design of future master-planned places as more critical and aware of the use of such places.

The idea of investigating the social and ideological significance of heterogeneous design and the urban village, and how the past and present are linked and utilized as a means of consolidating or enhancing this product for the benefit of the users and/or the producers, has been stimulated by research and interpretative accounts of particu-lar places and features in the prehistoric and early historical landscapes of Britain (for example, Bradley in Barclay 1994; Edmonds 1993; Giles 2007; Gosden and Lock 1998; Thomas 1997; Tilley 1994; Watson 2001). These interpretive accounts utilize theories about the relationship between landscape, movement, space, time, and human experience – thus providing the theoretical bases and assumptions for reading the culturally created landscape of the case study site in terms of social significance and impact. Beyond the theoretical aspects of utilizing archaeology in this study's reading of contemporary urban space are some direct correlations with past peoples' use of space that emerge from the archaeological literature (Gosden and Lock 1998), and how we are attempting to construct and design space now. One outstanding feature of the KGUV is the diverse range of historical links made to the past. The various ways in which users of the space are encouraged or directed to interact with these physical or conceptual links can be observed by a close reading of the space that looks not only at the design and physical shape of the KGUV, but also looks for remnants and evidence of how people are *choosing* to utilize and inhabit the space. Looking for such "remnants" is a typical form of evidence for the archaeologist; the original intent or design may be unknown.

Readings of Movement and Places in Between

The spatial analysis in this section focuses on three main features of the village: The Village Centre residential towers; the affordable housing at Ramsgate Street and Musk Avenue; and, Kulgun Park which runs parallel between these two major zones of residential accommodation. The two types of accommodation were chosen as they make up two of the original accommodation zones that were occupied early in life of the KGUV, and were designed and built for different socio-economic groups. Kulgun Park was chosen as an important feature of analysis because it is richly embedded with artwork, language, and symbols that link that past with the present of the KGUV. The physicality of the park's structure is also striking in that even at a glance it is clear that this structure effectively forms a boundary between the Village Centre and the affordable housing buildings (Fig. 11.2). Some of the key features of the site are intended to be its permeability, inclusivity, and social sustainability. One of the positioning statements in the Master Plan is that this urban village will be "A Connected Environment: A vibrant mix of activities and styles and places. Complete, liveable and sustainable, *achieving integration on line and in life*" (KGUV Master Plan 2004). So, the notions of permeability, inclusivity, social sustainability, and designing for heterogeneity can be tested for by this selection of data sources.

Biddulph's extensive critique of the urban village phenomenon highlights the marketability of the concept and how its popularity in part stems from how marketing and promotion and design and spatial organization give the impression of a traditional village layout and atmosphere (Biddulph 2000). The textual layering of marketing and promotion then enhances the design of the space according to Biddulph, and furthers in the creation of the other to consolidate and legitimize the new development. Is this the case at KGUV? Throughout this section, a range of archaeological theories and empirical research is drawn upon to help build a methodology for assessing the design and purpose of KGUV. Specifically, it is the potential for social encounters and how the design may operate and be experienced by those residing in and using the space.

Boundaries, walls, and gates have always had degrees of social significance historically and philosophically. Archaeology has long been concerned with boundaries and status markers that help to uncover the cultural and personal significance of how people lived. An archaeological interpretation therefore fits nicely with Ziller's assertion that "community is not a place" (Ziller 2004), but is more to do with relativities, and that differences in status are crucial for the health and well-being of a whole society (not just those who are disadvantaged). Archaeology traces networks and connections across time and space and often uncovers tensions and conflict as well. When presented with a site containing artefacts, buildings, human remains etc., a picture of life can be constructed which must include differences. Links and pathways between groups are often uncovered due to the spread and preservation of similar artefact types and styles. With this theoretical and methodological perspective in mind, we analyze the following three features of the KGUV.

The affordable housing buildings at Ramsgate Street and Musk Avenue, located within view of the café strip of the Village Centre, were built as residences for lower income earners, who meet certain financial and social criteria in order to be subsidized by the government. The external appearance of these apartment blocks blends with the rest of the site's architecture and they were built for environmental sustainability. Rainwater tanks are located on every floor and balconies and foliage ostensibly work together to provide ventilation and protection from heat.

Fig. 11.2 Kulgun Park between the Village Centre on the left and the Musk Ave affordable housing complex on the right

The four accommodation towers of the Village Centre form the pivotal residential zone for the whole village. As the name clearly suggests, this is located at the geographical and social centre of the site. The Village Centre also contains retail shops, the Community Hub, and a row of restaurants and cafés that form the active street life of the site. Clearly, residents of this accommodation zone are in a privileged position in that they can access facilities faster and more easily than any other group of residents. In fact, they do not have to even exit the complex to fulfill daily requirements or leisure activities in the main food outlets. Access to the accommodation towers is strict and security controlled as are the use of the facilities contained within the boundaries of the apartment blocks. Residents may enter and exit their home without ever meeting inhabitants from other accommodation zones as car parks are located within the basement of the structure and can be accessed via a lift system. The pathways between the Village Centre and the affordable housing buildings may conversely need to be utilized by the residents of the latter if they are to enter into and interact with the facilities located within and around the limits of the whole Village Centre complex. So, there is the potential for social flow *from* the affordable housing buildings, but not *to* them. Also, visitors are necessarily drawn to the Village Centre as this is the retail and social hub of the Village. They too are not required to leave the boundaries of the Village Centre and would effectively be discouraged from doing so due to the next feature to be discussed.

Kulgun Park forms what is in effect a border between the Village Centre and the two more visible affordable housing complexes. This long, narrow park is bounded by parallel footpaths (Fig. 11.3), which are embedded with small plaques relating historical content of the area's social, military, and educational past. In order to easily access either residential complexes from the other, the park would have to be crossed, not along the pathways which would greatly increase the distance travelled, but by cutting across the boundaries of the park. The artwork within the park, and indeed the name "Kulgun" reflects the area's indigenous history and what was once a waterway. The design and creative aspects of this park is richly embedded with ancient and historical pasts, but in reality acts as a boundary between different groups of residents and prevents visitors venturing beyond the Village Centre. Further, and quite the opposite to the Village Centre, the affordable housing complex is not a destination for anyone other than its own residents.

It is clear then that a boundary exists within the urban village that limits and defines certain socio-economic groups and the potential social encounters between them and visitors. Most notably in the theorization of boundedness is the work of anthropologist Mary Douglas in her book "Purity and Danger" (Douglas 2000). In her theorization of the boundaries of the body and the way in which they inscribe the borders or limits of the socially hegemonic, she makes the important link between the material and ideological or socio-political. Her analysis suggests that, "what constitutes the limit of the body is never merely material, but that the surface, the skin, is systematically signified by taboos and anticipated transgression: indeed, the boundaries of the body become ... the limits of the social" (Butler 1990). The archaeology of boundedness also rests on the assumption that, "the conceptual boundaries have their physical correlates and can, therefore, be recognized archaeologically"

Fig. 11.3   Tacit boundaries at the Kelvin Grove Urban Village

(Dark 1995). Just as it has been claimed that the boundaries of the body are "never merely material", we argue that the boundaries of the KGUV are not just physically manifested limits. Boundaries are a means of social classification, and are constructed within the context of societies' practices, ideals, beliefs, languages, and values (Lawrence 1996). This is a key insight for the design of digital media.

Boundaries operate culturally to produce and maintain identity through a logic of exclusion and the creation of the "other." The logic of this construction is that structures, such as walls, attempt to delineate and consolidate in opposition to a necessary, and excluded, disempowered group of others. This way of thinking about the production of identity draws on theorists such as Kristeva, whose work on subjectivity in particular utilizes the "structuralist notion of a boundary constituting taboo for the purposes of constructing a discrete subject through exclusion" (Butler 1990). Thinking about boundaries in this way is useful for this chapter, and how one of the key features of heterogeneous design – *inclusivity* – is constructed and experienced in both tangible and tacit ways. For example, clearly the KGUV is not just defined by its physical boundaries, but also exists and attempts to incorporate the socialities of the wider area in various ways. Viewing this urban place at the beginning of its development allows us to understand how the physical and symbolic boundaries put in place by development and marketing, are initially negotiated and possibly manipulated by the users and residents of the site. How people negotiate the space in its infancy provides a basis for projecting how the space and social encounters within it may develop in the future.

The recognition that boundaries can operate in both productive and prohibitive ways, or that they can simultaneously – indeed necessarily – produce structures of inclusion and exclusion is discussed extensively in anthropological discourse on spatial organization (e.g., Carlisle 1996; Lawrence 1996; Rodman and Cooper 1996). In her study of boundaries in France, Susan Carlisle recognizes how boundaries can establish specific social definitions. Specific to the interests of this chapter is the notion of *outsiders,* which is constructed on the basis of "I am not you; there is a line between you and me." Boundaries can also establish *possession* on the basis of "this is mine; there is a line around my belongings" (Carlisle 1996). Carlisle demonstrates, as does this study, how boundaries can function in these ways at different levels in society. For instance, the physical boundary can defend certain cultural values by "protecting" vertical hierarchical class distinctions (Carlisle 1996). At the outset, it would appear that the boundaries of the KGUV operate in very different ways due to the heterogeneous and inclusive nature of the planning and development of the built space. There is the construction of *presence* and *absence* as a means of dis-establishing certain social connections. The appreciation that boundaries can operate in this way is influenced by Rodman and Cooper's discussion of waterfront and housing co-op boundaries in Toronto (Rodman and Cooper 1996). Another key feature of this boundary of the KGUV is that it is not clearly permeable and easily negotiated. So, in one sense there is an attempt to enclose and define the space as containing buildings and zones which are separate and different, but to also create a space which invites visitors to explore – and attempts to maintain connections to – the spatial and temporal history of the area.

We find that the planners and developers of the KGUV have inscribed certain features in the space that appear to control and manipulate potential social encounters. What, at the point of its planned origins appears to be a place designed for social encounters is in fact a used space where shared encounters may largely be limited by the design of the place and its pathways of movement. Of interest for this chapter is Kulgun Park, and how this feature of public space and historical meaning forms a site of tension and lack of permeability. It is not only movement of residents between the two areas that is interrupted by this park, but also importantly it is the flow of visitor movement from the Village Centre that is also manipulated and controlled. So, Kulgun Park and the very nature of the organization of the village where visitor activities are centered within a complex that exclusively accommodates a specific group of people, work together to deactivate what was intended to be a heterogeneous place of inclusivity and permeability, where a range of serendipitous and organized social encounters could be expected to occur.

This spatial analysis demonstrates how the *use of the* space is operating quite differently from the intentions of the *design* of the space. Just like the ancient manipulations of landscape discussed earlier (Gosden and Lock 1998), the planners and developers of the KGUV have inscribed certain features in the KGUV urban landscape that would appear to prevent social encounters beyond the limits of individual buildings or spaces. It is not so much the distinctions between the two accommodation zones that mark boundaries or difference in this case. In fact, the appearance of the buildings themselves is similar architecturally. Both building types incorporate environmentally sustainable features such as large sun-shades, balconies, and rainwater harvesting systems. The materials used on the exteriors are different, but at a glance there is a homogeneous appearance throughout the village. In contrast to the criticisms discussed earlier with regards to the appearance of buildings in UK case studies, the residential buildings in this case study do not immediately indicate socio-economic difference. However, it is the tacit boundaries within the village, Kulgun Park in particular, that effectively mark as to who belongs where and how movement occurs between major zones within the landscape.

Readings of the Past for the Future

The text studied in this section is content produced through a local web application called *HistoryLines*. This component is part of a suite of new media tools we are developing to help us explore the use of narrative and new media in community engagement and urban planning processes (Foth et al. 2008). *HistoryLines* uses custom-designed Google Maps interface to illustrate residential history and migrational churn (Klaebe et al. 2007). It brings a cross section of new residents together to trace and map where they have lived in the course of their lives. When the longitude and latitude coordinates are collated and augmented with short personal narratives, overlapping and common lines become visible (Fig. 11.4). The stories at these intersections in time and space stimulate interest and offer opportunities for further personalized networking.

As a community-driven service, *HistoryLines* encourages people to participate in the content creation process. We employ recent Web 2.0 technology to allow KGUV residents to become authors and publish their personal history to a shared online community database. More specifically, we have created a custom-designed, content-management framework for KGUV residents to digitize their history by tagging places where they have lived in the past and attaching comments, multimedia content, and contact details. In order to provide an instinctive and user-friendly interface for the data input, we use a Google Maps mash-up application, so people can directly pinpoint places where they have lived in the past.

HistoryLines is an experiment to test how urban computing can be used to facilitate a social network of storytelling, themed around community history and place making. *HistoryLines* is a concept that allows individuals to leave their own "historical footprint" online and connect with others who they "cross paths with." By leaving narrative notes about the places contributors have visited using the categories: live, work, play, and study, others can connect and use the information to lessen the anxiety of their own transition from one community to another. The contributors are also able to visually see connections between their lines and those drawn by other residents and contact them if they wish with commonality to draw from. While still in early development, *HistoryLines* has the potential to visually

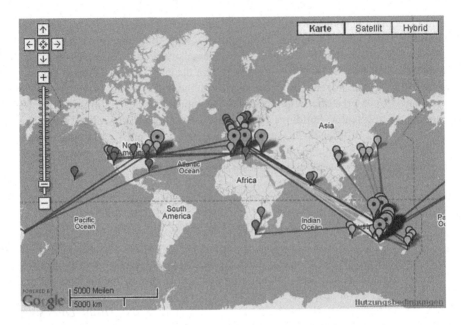

Fig. 11.4 HistoryLines

represent common themes using historical narrative, so as to foster a better understanding of our neighbors collectively and of community members individually. *HistoryLines* is thus an experiment to translate the "six degrees of separation" theory underlying global social networking sites such as MySpace and Facebook for local community engagement in a master-planned community site.

The associated *HistoryLines* workshops held locally at the KGUV not only allow residents to engage with each other's past, but it also provides means for serendipitous social encounters through content sharing of photos, annotations, and stories (Fig. 11.5). A typical scenario might be that a participant submits a range of previous locations to the application: He was born in Wagga in New South Wales. He then moved to Sydney to study. During his life, he also lived in Sydney in the suburb of Bondi Beach, then moved up to Queensland and spent most of his life in Brisbane's suburb of Fairfield before settling into the KGUV. Stories and anecdotes can be left at various points. Another participant might encounter crossovers of their shared *history lines*. She might be prompted to ask about his residency at Bondi Beach, because she, herself, or a family member lives down there. Shared experiences, previously unknown and without further significance, all of a sudden become the focal point for conversation and shared interests and exchange.

The outcome of the *HistoryLines* workshops was a richly constructed encounter between residents from different buildings within the site. Our interactions with study participants indicate that – except for serendipity – such social encounters would not have occurred without this initiative. However, the initial opportunity to get to know each other increases the chances for residents to encounter each other

Fig. 11.5 At the end of a HistoryLines workshop, participants share the results

again in a less anonymous manner, such as whilst shopping at the Village Centre, or walking the dog in the park. The manifold implications for the design of this heterogeneous site in terms of its physical and online/digital space centre around the quest to challenge and re-think traditional understandings of "community" and "village living." Social encounters in the urban village that go beyond personal friendship networks and advance the social fabric of the urban environment depend on the provision of public spaces – both physical and digital (Foth and Sanders 2008). What matters in this context is the quality of these spaces to foster social encounters as well as how well they bridge the physical and digital city.

This construction of part of the digital space of the Kelvin Grove Urban Village (2004) is a powerful link to the past: personal histories and serendipitous encounters within the digital mapping of those histories help to consolidate the present for the residents of the village whose pasts' are varied spatially and personally. As people in the past manipulated the landscape in different ways to help prescribe and consolidate certain social encounters (and possibly content sharing) so, too, do we now. The landscape has widened however and the digital horizon needs appropriate methods for interpretation.

Readings Between the Conceived and Perceived Space

Kelvin Grove Urban Village (2004) site has a rich and varied history, including its indigenous, military, educational, residential, and natural history. In a similar way to the *HistoryLines* project, the *Sharing Stories* project was a targeted community development initiative aimed at engaging members of the community. Whereas *HistoryLines* focused on the history of the new residents and where they came from, the goal of the *Sharing Stories* project was to preserve, honour, interpret, and publish the history of the site that is now home to the KGUV. Oral histories, visual art, photographs, archival information, and digital stories were collected, created, and shared from the past and the present by students and community participants who chose to share their memories, inspirations, and research about the KGUV site.

The workshops and related community engagement events such as openings and exhibitions that formed part of the *Sharing Stories* project provided an opportunity for members of the KGUV community to meet, interact, and encounter each other. The community in this context consists of historic witnesses that used to have a personal affiliation with the site of what is now the KGUV – from indigenous origins, to military, commercial, educational, and residential usage – as well as present stakeholders such as the urban planning and design team, members of the neighborhood, and students from local schools. Especially the digital storytelling workshops brought a diverse group of people together over a period of focused creative work.

Digital stories are short, personally narrated multimedia tales (Freidus and Hlubinka 2002; Lambert 2002; Meadows 2003). In a series of workshops led by Dr Helen Klaebe and run by specialist trainers from the Creative Industries Faculty at QUT, people from a wide range of age groups and experience levels worked together to produce digital stories related to the history of the Kelvin Grove Urban Village area. During the workshop the participants with the assistance of the trainers, developed their personal memories and stories into scripts, recorded voiceovers, and used professional video editing software to produce a personal documentary film of broadcast quality. The digital stories are made to a formula of around 2 min, 250 words, and a dozen images – but the results are as diverse as the individual participants who made them (Fig. 11.6). The public screenings of these digital stories provided further opportunities for creators to meet each other as well as for members of the audience to ask questions and interact with the participants with a view to honor and celebrate the history of the KGUV site.

The *sharing stories* project produced and published a comprehensive social history collection of the KGUV (Klaebe 2006). Klaebe and Foth also reported in detail on those processes involved in running the *Sharing Stories* project that utilize new media to engage with the community development strategies of the KGUV (Klaebe and Foth 2007). For the purpose of this chapter, we want to draw attention on the notion of ecology in the social production of space. In the context of the KGUV, we use Lefebvre (Lefebvre 1991) to distinguish between the phase of the *conceived* space when the designers and developers come together to plan the KGUV space; the *perceived* space that is communicated to a target audience of buyers and residents through marketing material, maps and plans, project websites; and the *lived* space consisting of the actual lived experience of tenants and residents that inhabit the KGUV (Klaebe et al. 2009). Whereas the *HistoryLines* project is positioned to connect the conceived space with the lived space, the *Sharing Stories* initiative was thought of and commenced much earlier with a view to build a bridge between the

Teresa Mircovich

Igor and Teresa Mircovich arrived in Australia from a WWII refugee camp.

Nigel Stevens

Nigel Stevens joined the National Service in 1951 and was stationed at the Kelvin Grove Barracks.

Ann Staples

Ann Staples lived on Victoria Park Road for 63 years.

Stephen Pincus

Stephen Pincus is the QUT Project Director for the Kelvin Grove Urban Village.

John Duncan

John Duncan has been associated with Kelvin Grove's military history since 1953.

Ailsa Skippen

Ailsa Skippen has a long association with Kelvin Grove.

Norma Mills

Norma Mills has had ties to Kelvin Grove and its surrounding areas since 1936.

Penny Somerville

Penny Somerville is the Department of Housing's Principal Project Officer for Kelvin Grove Urban Village.

Judith Cox

Kelvin Grove has featured prominently in Judith Cox's life.

Rex Kirkham

Rex Kirkham joined the National Service at Kelvin Grove in 1951.

Fig. 11.6 A selection of digital stories published on the Sharing Stories website at http://www. kgurbanvillage.com.au/sharing/digital/

conceived space and the perceived space. In a way, the project functioned as a research probe for the design and planning team in that it combines opportunities for research data collection and analysis with community development outcomes. It was funded at the planning and development stages as a vehicle to inform the representations of space, whilst preserving the history and heritage of KGUV. The local and historical content that *Sharing Stories* produced has informed the marketing material and the planning and design documentation of KGUV, but has also found its way into tangible representations of space in the form of for example, plaques embedded in the foot paths and other signage with historic anecdotes and citations.

Conclusions

In the section "readings of movement and places in between" we outlined a number of problems located at the point of the original design of KGUV which translate to a lack of permeability within the site where movement is restricted and controlled between different zones within the site. The hoped for inclusivity and social encounters presented in the master plan appear to be currently prevented by the physical shape of the site and the specific features of Kulgun Park and the Village Centre. Further developments on the other side of Kulgun Park opposite the Village Centre might change these dynamics if they create new destinations that attract residents and visitors to cross this tacit boundary and thus re-appropriate the park as a link and destination in its own right.

Essentially, a comparison of these levels of analyses reveals that certain social encounters may not occur within a master-planned landscape without themselves being "master-planned." In a heterogeneous space designed to include distinct groupings based on disparate geographical and socio-economic personalities and backgrounds, social encounters may not occur without support and facilitation. In the case of this urban village this is in part being carried out through the *HistoryLines* initiative and also within the digital place of *Sharing Stories*.

To an extent, content sharing is limited to those within certain zones – rather than between – of this heterogeneous public space. This formation of boundaries between different groups within the perceived space becomes more explicit within the spatial analysis where the lived-in space is explored. Barnes et al. neatly summarizes the interplay of actors in this process of urban (re)development and associated marketing: "The seductiveness of the urban village concept relies upon appealing to nostalgia for an ideal "community" linked to a main street with heritage architecture and lifestyle consumption. But, ultimately, such a vision is limited … in favour of a desirable, middle-class professional social group" (Barnes et al. 2007). So, what was conceived in the Master Plan is translated and narrated differently in the perceived space according to who is producing and reading the various marketing texts. The lived experience, yet again, can be quite different. Both *HistoryLines* and *sharing stories* are examples of attempts to bring these distinct spaces closer together. The sharing of creative content and the personal interaction between participants and community members are key elements of this strategy.

Other features in the landscape that serve to link the past to the present may in fact prevent encounters being shared between different residents and users of the space because of their physical organization. Clearly, these features also need support and associated cultural intervention in order to be activated and meaningful within the space. The landscape of the KGUV viewed through the lens of archaeology shows that social encounters in such a master-planned site can be enhanced and played-out in both constructed and serendipitous ways. The digital space where *HistoryLines* and parts of *sharing stories* are produced and accessed is an example of where the socialities and artefacts of a landscape have moved beyond the physical boundaries of the site. The workshops that facilitate these initiatives allow for present and hopefully future face-to-face encounters. The shared and recorded content links personal pasts and serendipitous encounters that may have occurred in the past. However, these encounters only have meaning because they are shared in the present with consequences for the future. The experiential cycles of the *HistoryLines* application have depth and meaning that could be applied to places of social fragmentation and isolation and where the "place" itself cannot function alone to fulfill the goals and desired outcomes of particular models of urban design. It will be exciting to see how people continue to negotiate this evolving space between the physical and the digital.

Acknowledgments This research is supported under the Australian Research Council's Discovery Projects funding scheme (project number DP0663854). Dr Marcus Foth is the recipient of an Australian Postdoctoral Fellowship. Further support has been received from the Queensland Government's Department of Housing. The authors would like to thank Helen Klaebe, Barbara Adkins, Jaz Choi, Aneta Podkalicka, Angela Button, Julie-Anne Carroll, and Jean Burgess for supporting this research project. The authors specifically thank Mark Bilandzic for developing the HistoryLines web application as part of his internship at QUT in 2007.

References

Barclay G (1994) Review of 'altering the earth' (Richard Bradley 1993, monograph 8). Proceedings of the Prehistoric Society 60: 456–58

Barnes K, Waitt G, Gill N & Gibson C (2007) Community and Nostalgia in Urban Revitalisation; a critique of urban village and creative class strategies as remedies for social 'problems'. Australian Geographer 37(3): 335–354

Biddulph M (2000) Villages don't make a city. Journal of Urban Design 5(1): 65–82

Biddulph M (2003) The limitations of the urban village concept in neighbourhood renewal: a Merseyside case study. Urban Design International 8: 5–19

Butler J (1990) Gender trouble: feminism and the subversion of identity. Routledge, New York

Carlisle S (1996) Boundaries in france. In: Pellow D (ed) Setting boundaries: the anthropology of spatial and social organization, 37–54. Bergin & Garvey, Westport

Dark KR (1995) Theoretical archaeology. Cornell University Press, New York

Douglas M (2000) Purity and danger: an analysis of the concepts of pollution and taboo. Routledge, London

Edmonds M (1993) Interpreting causewayed enclosures in the past and present. In: Tilley C (ed) Interpretative Archaeology, 99–142. Berg Publishers, Oxford

Foth M, Klaebe H & Hearn G. (2008). The Role of New Media and Digital Narratives in Urban Planning and Community Development. Body, Space & Technology 7(2)

Foth M & Sanders P (2008) Impacts of social interaction on the architecture of urban spaces. In Aurigi A & Cindio FD (eds) Augmented urban spaces: articulating the physical and electronic city. Ashgate, Aldershot

Franklin B & Tait M (2002) Constructing an image: the urban village concept in the UK. Planning Theory 1(3): 250–272

Freidus N & Hlubinka M (2002). Digital storytelling for reflective practice in communities of learners. ACM SIGGROUP Bulletin 23(2): 24–26

Giles K (2007) Seeing and believing: visuality and space in pre-modern England. World Archaeology 39(1): 105–121

Gosden C & Head L (1994) Landscape – a usefully ambiguous concept. Archaeology of Oceania 29: 113–116

Gosden C. & Lock G. (1998) Prehistoric histories. World Archaeology 30(1): 2–12

Kelvin Grove Urban Village (KGUV) Integrated Master Plan (2004) The Hornery Institute and Hassell for the Queensland Department of Housing and QUT.

Klaebe H (2006) Sharing stories: a social history of kelvin grove urban village. Focus Publishing, NSW

Klaebe H, Foth M, Burgess J & Bilandzic M (2007) Digital storytelling and history lines: community engagement in a master-planned development. Paper presented at the 13th International Conference on Virtual Systems and Multimedia (VSMM) Brisbane, QLD

Klaebe H & Foth M (2007) Connecting communities using new media: the sharing stories project. In Stillman L & Johanson G (Eds) Constructing and sharing memory: community informatics, identity and empowerment, 143–153. Cambridge Scholars Publishing, Newcastle

Klaebe H, Adkins B, Foth M & Hearn G (2009) Embedding an ecology notion in the social production of urban space. In: Foth M (ed) Handbook of research on urban informatics: the practice and promise of the real-TimecCity, 179–194. IGI Global, Hershey

Lambert J (2002) Digital storytelling: capturing lives, creating community. Digital Diner Press, Berkeley

Laurel B (ed) (2003) Design research: methods and perspectives. MIT Press, Massachusetts

Lawrence RJ (1996) The multidimensional nature of boundaries: an integrative historical perspective. In: Pellow, D (ed) Setting boundaries. The anthropology of spatial and social organisation, 9–36. Bergin & Garvey, Westport

Lefebvre H (1991) The production of space (D. Nicholson-Smith, Trans.). Blackwell, Oxford

Meadows MS (2003) Pause & effect: the art of interactive narrative. New Riders, Indianapolis

O'Neill E, Kostakos V, Kindberg T, Fatah gen. Schiek A, Penn A and Stanton Fraser D (2006) Instrumenting the city: Developing methods for observing and understanding the digital cityscape. In: Dourish P & Friday A (eds) Proceedings Ubicomp 2006, 315–332. Springer, Heidelberg

Pearson M & Shanks M (2001) Theatre/Archaeology. Routledge, London

Perring D (1991) Spatial organization and social change in Roman towns. In: Rich J & Wallace-Hadrill A (eds) City and Country in the Ancient World, 273–293. Routledge, London

Pink S (2006) Doing visual ethnography: images, media and representation in research. Sage. Thousand Oaks

Rodman M & Cooper M (1996) Boundaries of home in Toronto housing cooperatives. In: Pellow, D (ed) Setting boundaries. The anthropology of spatial and social organisation, 91–110. Bergin & Garvey, Westport

Thomas J (2004) Archaeology and modernity. Routledge, London

Thomas R (1997) Land, kinship relations and the rise of the enclosed settlement in first millennium B.C. Britain. Oxford Journal of Archaeology 16(2): 211–18.

Tilley C (1994) A phenomenology of landscape – places, paths and monuments. Berg Publishers, Oxford

Watson A (2001) Composing Avebury. World Archaeology 33(2): 296–314

Ziller A (2004) The community is not a place and why it matters – case study: green square. Urban Policy and Research 22(4): 465–479

Section 4
Social Glue

Introduction: Social Glue

Elisabeth F. Churchill

"Social glue" is a term that has increased in usage in the last few years. Although I cannot find the earliest use of or reference to the term, in its common use, "social glue" is central to the notion of "Shared Encounters," the title of this volume of research chapters. A brief review of results from an internet search suggests that the term is primarily used in contexts where people's feeling of social connection is strengthened through a shared experience which may or may not be facilitated by technology.

Much of the work in the area of Computer Supported Cooperative Work (CSCW) and related research areas has focused on the creation of such connections through video connections (Harrison 2009), blogs (Herring et al. 2004; Nardi et al. 2004), text and graphical virtual worlds (Churchill and Bly 1999; Churchill et al. 2001; Erickson and Kellogg 2000), and cell phones (Brown et al. 2001; Ito et al., 2005). More recently, public space displays have been used to provide possibilities for establishing connections and coordinating the use of space itself for facilitating and managing social encounters (Churchill et al. 2003; Churchill et al. 2004; Churchill and Nelson, 2009; O'Hara et al. 2003).

Stepping back, it may behoove us to think about what the term "social glue" actually means. The Princeton Wordnet[1] definition of "social" underscores relating to others, the establishment and maintenance of living with others, the fostering of communal activities, and the creation of assemblies and colonies. Definitions of "glue" emphasize joining, adhering and attaching, and the fixing and cementing together of things that would otherwise be separate.

Putting these words and their definitions together, we see that in order for communication technology to be considered as a "social glue," it must bring people together and hold them fast in some social dynamic. And, the experience of being together, of sharing something, should produce some "bond" (another word often

---

E.F. Churchill (✉)
Yahoo! Research, 2821 Mission College Blvd, Santa Clara, CA 95054, USA
e-mail: churchill@acm.org

[1]Princeton Wordnet: wordnet.princeton.edu/perl/webwn

used when adhering one thing to another) between people. We certainly know from psychology and sociology much about social bonds; a bond is a connection to another person or other people. Bonds imply certain forms of affiliation and are often strengthened by shared stories, reciprocal behaviors, and behavioral demonstrations of predictability, reliability, consistency and accountability, and adherence to social obligations.

Appropriately, in this section, all the chapters are focused on the intentional design of social activity to foster social bonds or connections and/or the therapeutic benefits of being so connected. All in some way describe technologies that orient around storytelling and around the orientation of people to known or imagined others. Central vehicles for the shared experiences or encounters are stories, and all the chapters in some way address the relationships between the mediated and digital connections that are fostered and their effects on people's physical, real-world activities. Assessments of success depend on evaluation criteria and on the metrics and measurements that are collected.

In addition to problematizing the words "social glue," I want to make a distinction that was also provoked by my reading of the chapters. The "social glue" can be the technology itself, where the technology is the glue that adheres people to each other and/or to social places. Here, the technology can be seen as the adhesive or the facilitation for strengthening the tie. Or, from another perspective, the "social glue" could refer to the actions people take toward each other, and it is these actions that cement their relationship(s). Such actions may be facilitated by the technologies that are discussed in these chapters, but they could also take place without the technology, where the participants collocated.

Of course, this is an artificial distinction; we know that technologies and human actors cannot be so completely separated (Bijker and Law 1992). But I find it a useful analytic stance. One implies that the removal of the technology may dissolve the connection between the people; the other suggests that the people will find other means to connect, should one technology be removed. One says "provide the channel and the connection will be made," but without it, it won't. Here, connections will be made when previously there were none. The other says this technology may be better than others, but some form of technology will be used to connect, because the volition, the desire, and the social connection exists, but has no form of expression.

This matters. Why? Because it dictates something about whether a technology will be successful or not, what criteria for success are established, the likely forms of uptake and adaptation of the technology, and ultimately the potential for personal transformation or for the transformation of the social connections overall. We should ask ourselves: Are we trying to make a bond where none existed, or are we trying to strengthen one that already exists? Are we aware that a technology designed as social glue can in fact be a solvent, can dissolve those bonds that exist socially as members become aware of the lack of locality, the lack of closeness and copacetic feelings, the conflict and clash of roles revealed?

Along these lines, in earlier work across many contexts, my collaborators and I have found that the introduction of new social technologies is fundamentally situated not only in the social relationships that already exist, but also the socio-technical infrastructure of place, the location of placement, that already exists. These affect how a technology is received, adopted, adapted, and ultimately owned (Churchill and Nelson 2009; Shamma et al. 2009).

These points are nicely reflected in the first chapter of this section, entitled Making Glue: Public Authoring in Urban Tapestries by Karen Martin. The author intentionally set out to build a system that would act as "social glue," to strengthen the relationships – or bonds–between members of a community. The author present two case studies; both take place in different communities in the London area of the United Kingdom. In one instance, the author felt the technology resulted in strong engagement and positive reactions from users. Martin makes the useful distinction between communities into which a technology is introduced and a community which is specifically convened for the research – that is, which is made up of people who are in some ways invested in, or bonded to, the research agenda or the research objects – in this case the mobile technologies and storytelling devices. The author illustrate how engagement and participation by members of the convened community involved subtle and explicit incentives to participate and disincentives for nonparticipation – you don't want to appear to be a nonteam player. By contrast, in a local community where no such convened and invested group exists, the author found considerably more difficulties in fostering uptake. The intended users represented members from different stakeholder groups; but also potential users did not necessarily see the obvious benefits of using the system and any potential benefit did not offset the costs of using the system (learning the technology, taking the time to contribute, and so on).

Andrea Grimes' chapter, Sharing Personal Reflections on Health Locally, deals with a somewhat different aspect of social glue – how reflecting on other's stories and the telling of one's own stories can bring about changes in someone's behavior. Grimes describes an application, EatWell, which was designed specifically to encourage healthy dietary practices by residents in low-income African American communities in Atlanta, GA. Participants can tell their own stories of healthy eating behaviors and can listen to stories told by others. The telling of personal stories brings out a notion of reputation and accountability – key ingredients for how humans orient to each other and how they determine whether or not to continue to feel part of, or members within a community. Interestingly, in this case, neither the narrator nor the listener is known to each other. This differs from the use of blogs, where the narrator is often known, while the audience is made up on unknown readers.

Turning to blogging, in the chapter entitled MoBlogs, Sharing Situations, and Lived Life, Connor Graham Mark Rouncefield and Christine Satchell describe a blogging study involving smokers. The authors studied four people trying to stop smoking, and addressed the ways their adoption of a technology for blogging about their smoking habit fits into their everyday lives. Curiously, while smoking cessation did not result from the exercise, the bloggers reported a sense of reaching out to others and sharing their experiences. The sense of being part of a group or community of people who smoke led to self reflection – both I am not alone, but also I want to hide because I failed to give up. This showed up in positive and negative ways – being happy to tell one's story and being ashamed that the attempt to cease smoking had failed.

In the fourth of the chapters in this section, Katharine Willis, Kenton O'Hara, Thierry Giles, and Mike Marianek discuss the importance of place structuring the ways in which we share experiences with others. The chapter addresses why people share knowledge about places. Following a detailed discussion of the literature on the synchronous and asynchronous sharing of place, the authors offer three case studies: a street game called Hide and Seek, where people follow comments created by others; an application for children to explore attractions in a zoo; and a study of geocaching. All these look at how digital annotations created by people can change others' experience of place – the sociality expressed in these scripted experiences may or may not entail, actually making a connection with the content authors, but in each case that which is transformed is the social space itself.

What is interesting about all four chapters in this section is that they reveal just how much the adoption and adaptation of a technology for social connection cannot be predetermined by the designers. They all also illustrate how much work it takes to make the system work – even in the most basic of ways. All the chapters reveal the sheer amount of work the researchers and system developers put into the creation of the technology, its introduction to the community in question, and to assessing its ongoing uptake and adoption. They also illustrate how difficult it is to conduct research that attempts to assess the impact of introducing strangers, bonding familiars, and precipitating personal and social journeys (addiction, diet; storytelling and co-present navigation through social space). A difference between the cases studied can be seen between the creation of connection in structured vs. unstructured ways (structured games vs. ad hoc encounters).

What holds these chapters together is that they all illustrate the complexity of the socio-technical emergence of connection and personal/group transformation. And, as the authors eloquently remind us through their case studies, one cannot script the transformation—one can only set the stage for its emergence.

References

Bijker WB & Law J (1992) Shaping technology / building society: studies in sociotechnical change. MIT Press, Massachusetts

Brown B, Harper R & Green N (Eds) (2001) Wireless world. Springer, London

Churchill EF & Bly S (1999) Virtual environments at work: ongoing use of MUDs in the workplace. In: Georgakopoulos D, Prinz W & Wolf AL (eds) Proceedings of WACC'99, 99-108. ACM Press, New York. DOI= http://doi.acm.org/10.1145/295665.295677

Churchill EF, Girgensohn A, Nelson L & Lee A (2004) Information cities: blending digital and physical spaces for ubiquitous community participation. Commun. ACM 47, 2 (Feb. 2004), 38-44. ACM Press, New York. DOI= http://doi.acm.org/10.1145/966389.966413

Churchill EF & Nelson L (2009 to appear) Information flows in a gallery-work-entertainment space: the effect of a digital bulletin board on social encounters. Human Organization 68(2), 206–217

Churchill EF, Nelson L & Denoue L (2003) Multimedia fliers: informal information sharing with digital community bulletin boards. In: Huysman M, Wenger E & Wulf V (eds) communities and technologies. Kluwer Academic Publishers, The Netherlands

Churchill EF, Snowdon D & Munro A (eds) (2001) Collaborative virtual environments: digital places and spaces for interaction. Springer Verlag, London

Erickson T & Kellogg WA (2000) Social translucence: an approach to designing systems that support social processes. ACM Transactions of Computer-Human Interaction, 7, 1 (Mar. 2000), 59-83. DOI= http://doi.acm.org/10.1145/344949.345004

O'Hara K, Perry M, Churchill EF & Russell R (Eds) (2003) Public and situated displays: social and interactional aspects of shared display technologies. Kluwer Academic Publishers, London

Harrison S (Ed) (2009) Media spaces: 20+ Years of mediated life. Springer, London

Ito M, Okabe D & Matsuda M (Eds) (2005) Personal, portable, pedestrian: mobile phones in japanese life. MIT Press, Massachusetts

Herring S, Scheidt L, Bonus S & Wright E (2004) Bridging the gap: a genre analysis of weblogs. In: Proceedings of HICSS 2004. 40101.2, January 05-08, 2004

Nardi BA, Schiano DJ & Gumbrecht M (2004) Blogging as social activity, or, would you let 900 Million people read your diary? In: Proceedings of CSCW 2004, 222-231. ACM Press, New York. DOI= http://doi.acm.org/10.1145/1031607.1031643

Shamma DA, Churchill EF, Bobb N & Fukuda M (2009) Spinning online: a case study of internet broadcasting by DJs. In: Proceedings of Communities and Technologies, June 25-27, 2009

Chapter 12
Making Glue: Participation in Everyday Computing

Karen Martin

Introduction

Within human computer interaction (HCI), there is increasing interest in how technologies can facilitate social interaction (Dunne and Raby 2002); (Borovoy et al. 1998). For these systems to act as social "glue," not only are technological developments required but these also need to facilitate social change (Pedersen and Valgårda 2004). While the field of Computer-Supported Collaborative Work (CSCW) has considered social collaboration for many years, Pedersen and Vallgarda suggest that social technologies located in an urban, public context face additional difficulties than those located in the workplace, as "urban life is arguably more difficult to grasp than work: it's less delimited; there is not necessarily a clear set of activities to support in a confined location, or any clear collaborative goals or partners." (Pedersen and Valgårda 2004). Understanding how technology might act as social glue relies on observation and analysis of people's interaction with the system in question. When technology is understood as only one stratum of a broader urban ecology that also includes social, spatial, economic, political, and cultural systems then this suggests that other factors may influence how participants engage with interactive systems, and the subsequent outcomes.

To explore this fact, this chapter analyses relationships between participants and researchers in two case studies. These case studies were carried out by Proboscis, an artist-based research studio (Proboscis 2009). As artists, Proboscis are free to explore weakly defined problems in a playful manner and their primary concern is to engage people with their work. Reflecting on their approach to constructing participation will, I believe, be of benefit to researchers exploring technologies to support social interaction. In presenting my reflections on these case studies, I describe how participants' social and cultural backgrounds, and the nature of the tasks and responsibilities they undertake, might affect their engagement with the technology and the underlying

K. Martin (✉)
The Bartlett School of Graduate Studies, University College London, 1-19 Torrington Place, London WC1E 6BT, UK
e-mail: karen.martin@ucl.ac.uk

K.S. Willis et al. (eds.), *Shared Encounters*, Computer Supported Cooperative Work, DOI 10.1007/978-1-84882-727-1_12, © Springer-Verlag London Limited 2010

concepts. I describe how assessing technologies in everyday settings may require collaboration with a third-party facilitator and identify ways in which this type of collaboration may impact on the perceived outcomes of the project.

Related Work

Interaction as Meaning-Making

The use of social science approaches to inform the design and evaluation of technologies began in CSCW before extending more generally to HCI (Dourish 2001). The adoption of ethnographic methods represents part of a strand that seeks to base the technological requirements upon an informed understanding of the intended users. Dourish describes how participatory design is similarly interested in considering the integration of technology into people's lives, yet it also emphasizes the importance of the user's voice in conversations around design of technologies (Dourish and Button 1998). More recent contributions within HCI consider interaction to be a process of meaning-making and co-construction. McCullough hints at the importance of shared understanding and negotiation to interaction, describing it as being 'deliberations over the exchange of messages' (McCullough 2004), while Harrison et al. are more explicit, stating that; "meaning derives from information, of course, but in this perspective cannot be summed up by mapping information flow; it is, instead, irreducibly connected to the viewpoints, interactions, histories, and local resources available to those making sense of the interface" (Harrison et al. 2007).

These themes of agency and participation in empowering social groups are echoed in Erickson and Kellogg's description of a co-created knowledge management system "if we could capture traces of this knowledge work, others with similar needs might find as much value in talking with users as with the original authors. Such a system would not be just a database from which workers retrieved knowledge, it would be a knowledge community, a place within which people would discover, use, and manipulate knowledge, and could encounter and interact with others who are doing likewise" (Erickson and Kellogg 2000).

They acknowledge, however, that achieving this is a significant social challenge. Quoting Grudin they ask; "Why should those who produce and use knowledge take the time to engage in such interactions? Why should they wish to? What benefits would they gain that might compensate them for their efforts?" Answering these questions involves understanding how technology fits into people's lived experience. Abowd and Mynatt suggest that in designing computing for everyday life, it is necessary to create technologies that are meaningful for their intended users. The purpose of this "compelling story," as they describe it "is not simply to provide a demonstration vehicle for research results. It is to provide the basis for evaluating the impact of a system on the everyday life of its intended population" (Abowd and Mynatt 2000).

In describing how technology acts as one element of the continual reconstruction of spatial experience enacted between humans, technology and the environment in which they are situated, Dodge and Kitchin suggest that this process of "transduction" shifts the focus of the relationship between these three elements "from meaning and narrative to operation and process" (Dodge and Kitchin 2004). When considered in relation to the design of social technologies, this brings issues of values, negotiation, and meaning-making to the fore raising questions about the effect that the context of a project may have on its outcome.

The Characterization of Participants

Barkhuus and Rode suggest that who is included or excluded from participant evaluations could affect future design decisions writing that; "feminist studies argue that technologies are created in the context of male culture and embody certain assumptions of female life. This in return means that women are alienated by technology and define their femininity in terms of rejection of technology rather than encompassing it. An obvious way of countering this trend would be to include more (or at least a proportion similar to the user population) females in technology evaluation. To date, this has not occurred in HCI, and we are perhaps perpetrating the design of a next generation of gender-biased technology" (Barkhuus and Rode 2007).

Eagle and Pentland's description of how the Gaussian mixture model for their Serendipity project was based on interpretation of survey data collected from participants at the end of a 2-month study suggests how these biases might occur (Eagle and Pentland 2005). Serendipity had around 100 test participants, 70 of whom were in technical school at MIT and 30 in the business school next door. While the use of students as participants is common - Barkhuus and Rode found this to be the case for half of the studies in their sample of recent CHI projects – this is probably not representative of any user population outside of a university. Yet the model was based on inferences such as "proximity at 3 p.m. by the coffee machines confers a much different meaning from proximity at 11 p.m. at a local bar" which appear to take a specific cultural and social perspective.

Preece notes how sociologists have redefined community over the past 50 years by stating that: "initially, communities were characterized mainly by their physical features, such as size, location and their boundaries. During and after the industrial revolution cheaper transportation made it easier for people to move from place to place and physical characteristics provided a less reliable basis for defining community. Instead definitions based on people's relationships were more promising"(Preece 2001). With regard to interactive systems, Friedman et al. suggest that two categories of stakeholder exist. These are described as direct and indirect stakeholders, where "direct stakeholders refer to parties – individuals or organizations – who interact directly with the computer system or its output. Indirect stakeholders refer to all other parties who are affected by the use of the system. Often, indirect stakeholders are ignored in the design process" (Friedman et al. 2001). Foth extends this notion, critiquing the conceptualization of community as a collective and proposing instead to define it as a group of networked individuals (Foth and Brereton 2004). He does, however, concede that technologies which conceptualize community as a collective succeed in facilitating social interaction in certain circumstances. Specifically, when the technology is introduced into a well-established residential community; when there is a common problem or issue for people to focus around; or when the project plan "contains preceding phases to initiate and sustain engagement and involvement of community members" (Foth and Brereton 2004).

The Evaluation of Everyday Technologies

While HCI has developed a variety of evaluation techniques[1], the evaluation of social interaction technologies raises new challenges. Abowd and Mynatt suggest that technologies for everyday computing have particular characteristics that should be considered during the design process. They describe these features of informal, daily activity as being; activities rarely have a clear beginning or end; interruption is expected; multiple activities operate concurrently. As a result, they argue, technologies for everyday computing should be evaluated in the context of authentic use. However they question how this can be achieved using task-centered evaluation techniques (Abowd and Mynatt 2000).

One approach, Preece suggests, is to make a distinction between "usability" and "sociability" (Preece 2001), while Friedman et al. propose that researchers might consider a project holistically through focusing on its conceptual, technical, and empirical aspects in turn (Friedman et al. 2001). Evaluation techniques exploring "multiple perspectives" of participants have been used to assess domestic technologies within the everyday context of the home (Gaver et al. 2008) (Dunne and Raby 2002), with each participant's interpretation of the project considered equally valid. This approach accommodates the outlook of different users and allows the work to be sited within everyday experience revealing the particular goals of the individual participants. This raises issues of value around whether the project is seen as desirable, achievable, and successful in turn giving rise to challenging questions for designers such as "Who is making the design decision?," "Who is paying for it?," "What is this saying about the user?" (Sengers and Gaver 2006).

The Case Studies

Urban Tapestries

Urban Tapestries is the name of a two-year research project (2002–2004) within which the Urban Tapestries' location-based software platform was developed.

---

[1]These range from usability testing and heuristic evaluation (Pedersen and Valgårda 2004) for assessing interface design to embracing social science techniques such as ethnomethodology which have proved useful for showing up the gaps between design intentions and situated use (Dourish and Button 1998).

Urban Tapestries was conceived and implemented by Proboscis in partnership with the London School of Economics, Orange, Hewlett Packard Research Labs, France Telecom R&D UK and Ordnance Survey.

Proboscis were interested in how the convergence of geographic information systems with mobile technologies might create new opportunities for people to share information and experiences of the places in which they live and work. They speculated that location-based services might be used for creating, collecting, and viewing stories, information, and experiences and that, by sharing these with others, this presented an opportunity for people to move beyond the consumption of content to become active authors. They call this approach "public authoring" (Lane et al. 2006).

The Urban Tapestries software ran initially on HP iPaqs, then subsequently on Sony Ericsson P800 mobile phones and enabled people to annotate locations on a map of Bloomsbury, central London, with text, photographs, audio, or video. By organizing these individual annotations (pockets) into themes and categories (threads), participants could build relationships between people, places, and things. Depending on participant's choices during authoring, these "pockets" and "threads" could be viewed and edited by other Urban Tapestries participants (Figs. 12.1 and 12.2).

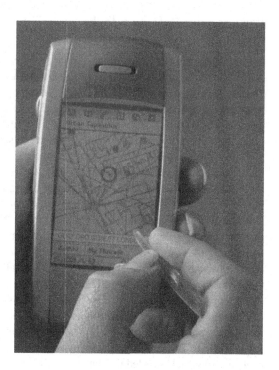

Fig. 12.1 Urban Tapestries interface (image courtesy of Proboscis)

Fig. 12.2 Participant during
first Urban Tapestries trial
(image courtesy of Proboscis)

Participants' Role and Tasks

Urban Tapestries aimed to gather people's stories and experiences of Bloomsbury, central London, and people's involvement with the project mostly took place in this area. In the early design phase, a series of bodystorming workshops were held (Buchenau and Suri 2000). Through storytelling and mapping activities, these workshops investigated the types of content individuals might choose to create and share using the Urban Tapestries system. Participants followed story "threads" on a large map by reading printed pages of iPAQ screens then authored their own content using post-it notes and stickers. Each newly created story was placed onto the map and walked through by its author, an experience generally lasting for around 3 hours. Four of these took place in Bloomsbury – three at the London School of Economics as part of larger "Creative Lab" events and one at the Marchmont Community Centre. Two further workshops took place outside of London at the City and Buildings Virtual Research Centre at Hewlett-Packard Research Labs, Bristol and in the Electrical and Mechanical Engineering Department at Trinity College Dublin.

An ethnographic study by Zoe Sujon and Roger Silverstone of London School of Economics (Silverstone and Sujon 2005) focused on respondents' "technological identities" (their relationship with media ranging from television to PDAs), their relationship to Bloomsbury, and the ways in which Urban Tapestries opened up the exchange of social knowledge. The study took place in Bloomsbury with nine subjects and was comprised of four data-gathering activities; (1) snapshots of relationships to ICTs (questionnaire); (2) relationship to place and technological identity (interview); (3) strategic walking tour; and (4) social knowledge, usability, and technological imagination (interview). Equipped with a disposable camera, a map, stickers for annotating places, a notebook and a rudimentary prototype of Urban Tapestries running on a PDA, participants were asked to find and explore nearby pockets. As the Urban Tapestries software had not yet been developed and no pockets actually existed, the researcher acted as a mediator, indicating verbally when the participant entered a pocket. Participants then created their own pockets by taking photographs, making notes, and recording the location on the map.

The first trial to explore how people might use the Urban Tapestries system took place on the streets of Bloomsbury between 6th and 14th December 2003 when around 100 participants responded to a call on the Proboscis mailing list and to notices posted around Bloomsbury. Participants met with researchers in Bloomsbury and were given an HP iPaq running the Urban Tapestries software. They then spent around 2 hours in Bloomsbury annotating locations, authoring content and uploading it to the system. When they returned, their feedback was captured on video and they were encouraged to write up their experience on the project blog (Urban tapestries/social tapestries: trial feedback 2009).

The second trial in June and July 2004 sought to understand how the use of Urban Tapestries might change over time with increased familiarity, and how it might fit into people's everyday lived experience. To address this, the project conducted a smaller trial with eleven participants. Each participant was provided with a mobile phone running the Urban Tapestries system for four weeks and asked to use the software as and when they desired. Participants were asked to complete several questionnaires, one before the trial and one at the end of each week. This required participants to reflect on their experience of using Urban Tapestries and to communicate these reflections to researchers.

Types of Participants

The two issues in participant selection raised by Barkhuus and Rode were gender and an over-reliance on students. Table 12.1 shows that participation in Urban Tapestries was almost equally balanced between male and female participants. Gender data from the first trial was obtained by analyzing the usernames of participants posting comments on the trial weblog (Urban tapestries/social tapestries: trial feedback 2009); six participants posting with nongender-specific names were excluded.

There was also a good balance of student and nonstudent participants with only the workshop at Trinity College Dublin in June 2003 consisting entirely of students. However, there are similarities in nonstudent participants' occupations. The first workshop at LSE included 16 participants from academia, the arts, design, government, and technology companies. Participants in the two further workshops at the same location had similar background augmented by professionals in community development and learning. The table (Table 12.2) shows a breakdown of the professional

Table 12.1 Breakdown of participants' gender in Urban Tapestries workshops and trials

Location	Total	Male	Female	Anonymous
LSE, May 2003	17	7	10	
LSE, April 2004	10	7	3	
LSE, Sept 2004	15	7	8	
Trinity college	12 (approx)	No data	No data	
HP labs	20 (approx)	No data	No data	
Ethnographic study	9	5	4	
First public trial	102	65	31	6
Second public trial	11	No data	No data	

Table 12.2 Breakdown of professional expertise in LSE bodystorming workshops

Date	Tech.	Design	Academia	Govt.	Arts	Learning	Community	Other
05/03	5	3	4	2	3	0	0	0
04/04	1	0	1	1	3	1	1	0
09/04	0	1	3	0	2	3	2	4
Total	6	4	8	3	8	4	3	4

background of these participants (note that there is some overlap between expertise areas, e.g., a researcher of technologies working in academia):

Links between Urban Tapestries and participants were more pronounced at the workshop in June 2003 at Hewlett-Packard Research Labs for researchers working in the City and Buildings Virtual Research Centre, an Urban Tapestries collaborator.

While the workshop at Marchmont Community Centre in Bloomsbury (Fig. 12.3), Central London in September 2003 brought together senior citizens (women from a mainly white working class background) and teenagers (mainly from the local Bangladeshi immigrant community) and the occupation of subjects in the ethnographic study varied widely (Silverstone and Sujon 2005), participants in the second trial were selected for their familiarity with mobile technologies and the concepts of public authoring, and they followed the trend of occupations observed in the LSE workshops.

Expectations and Outcomes

Researchers were pleased with people's perseverance and commitment in using the Urban Tapestries software during the trials (West 2005). Even participants who found the system frustrating continued to contribute to the research findings – an action which they recognized might not reflect real-world usage

> I have used the service – although I don't believe it has worked – I will try again as I want it to work – a customer might not bother though! (Lane et al. 2006).

Fig. 12.3 Participants at the bodystorming workshop at Marchmont Community Centre (image courtesy of Proboscis)

In using the software, participants' responses to Urban Tapestries varied greatly. During the first trial, some participants responded with delight:

> I think I was surprised at how useful I find Urban Tapestries. I found an amazing number of users, from the incredibly practical to the revealing and curious to the utterly pointless (Lane et al. 2006)

Less engaged responses were recorded during the second trial:

> I haven't wound it into my daily life of objects; I just haven't felt the urge to use it much. I guess I'm struggling with the device's mixture of latent utility and idle browsing pleasure (Hill 2004)

In the ethnographic study, Sujon and Silverstone questioned whether Urban Tapestries would be meaningful to all individuals "As a young, single, working mother, Mandy has strict limitations on her finances, her attention and her time. These constraints arguably instill a strict sense of responsibility (at least when it comes to spending large amounts of money) that prioritizes functionality, usefulness and direct applicability to one's personal life" (Silverstone and Sujon 2005) concluding that it would "require more than spontaneity if it's to have any meaning".

During the bodystorming workshops, however, the responses of some participants suggested that public authoring would have the capacity to facilitate social interaction. At the Marchmont Community Centre, content on the map triggered the following exchange:

One 80 year-old English lady pointed to the location of Camden Town Hall and told a story of her wedding there over 50 years ago. A young Bangladeshi girl, who had not spoken until then, responded to this story by saying her sister had only recently been married in the same place. Suddenly a location on the map became a catalyst for conversation between the two women (Jungnickel 2004)

Conversations and Connections

The second case study, Conversations and Connections, was part of Proboscis' Social Tapestries program. This was initiated in 2003 as Proboscis began to realize that working with people in situ led to a richer understanding of people's knowledge about the places in which they lived and worked. Social Tapestries aimed to work alongside community groups to understand how knowledge, experience, and information are communicated within specific communities, and how these communities might benefit from mapping and sharing these. Conversations and Connections sought to build on the experience and outcomes of Urban Tapestries by facilitating access to public authoring tools, techniques, and technologies (Lane and Harris 2005).

Conversations and Connections, was a series of events and activities that took place between 2005 and 2006 on Havelock Housing Estate in West London at the invitation of the resident management committee, Havelock Independent Residents Organization (HIRO) (Fig. 12.4). The project was carried out by Proboscis in collaboration with Kevin Harris of community development agency Local Level and funded by the Department of Constitutional Affairs Innovations Fund.

The project aimed at encouraging the conversations and connections that will engage residents to participate more fully in the democratic processes of managing their estate, relationships with the local authority and more broadly with other agencies (Lane and Harris 2005). HIRO invited Proboscis and Kevin to develop a project looking at civic participation because the committee was engaged in moving to tenant-management and wanted to develop greater resident support for this process. The activities sought to assist residents of Havelock Estate to document and share knowledge and experience about their community and local environment using public authoring tools including a cut-down version of the Urban Tapestries software, a blog for cataloguing estate maintenance issues, and Storycards for collecting residents' experiences of living on Havelock. Each month, Proboscis and Kevin Harris evaluated and reflected on the project, considering which activities were working and devising alternative approaches to the problems they encountered. In this way, they continuously adapted their approach to the context and situation of the residents.

Comprising 800 units, Havelock estate in West London, on which Conversations and Connections was set, has fallen into a poor state of repair with associated health problems and apparent crime and disorder. Originally managed by the local authority, housing management was transferred in 2004 to Ealing Homes, an Arm's Length Management Organization (ALMO) which now acts as landlord for the majority of residents. Ealing Homes provides a "community shop" for use by HIRO, and this is where the events of Conversations and Connections took place.

Fig. 12.4   Havelock estate (image courtesy of Proboscis)

During Conversations and Connections, five open events were organized, offering residents opportunities to record their experience of living on the estate, and access to tools and services that might improve that experience. Proboscis and Kevin began attending HIRO committee meetings in summer 2005 and the first event took place in November 2005. This was followed by an "IT Day" in March 2006 and Recording Havelock in June 2006. In October 2006, two open days were planned for successive Saturdays, with a "survey week" in-between to help residents capture information about their area.

Participants Roles and Tasks

The initial Open Day, IT Day, and Recording Havelock event took the form of drop-in sessions at the Community Shop. During the Open Day and Recording Havelock, a large-scale (five-foot square) map of the estate was placed in the shop onto which

Fig. 12.5 Bodystorming at the Community Shop (image courtesy of Proboscis)

people could add stories and notes (Fig. 12.5). The IT Day and Recording Havelock event both made technologies –the internet, digital cameras, digital video camera, and audio recorders – available to residents with researchers on hand to demonstrate their use.

Further activities took place outside of the community shop. During the IT day, the local authority computer training bus offering basic computer literacy courses was present on the estate; during the Recording Havelock event, two researchers went around the estate and recorded video interviews with 11 residents capturing different experiences of life on Havelock (Fig. 12.6); online, a new version of Urban Tapestries with a Macromedia Flash interface was introduced for people to annotate information about the estate.

In June 2006, A6 sized postcards with an aerial map of the estate on one side and space for residents to describe their stories and experiences of Havelock on the other were distributed. To trigger stories on the back of the card was written "What's the story? Help us collect stories about Havelock and where they happened. (mark the place or places on the map overleaf)." Residents were asked to

Fig. 12.6 Resident being interviewed during Recording Havelock (image courtesy of Proboscis)

return the completed Storycards to the community shop with the aim of building up a store of knowledge about the estate. In October 2006, the Storycard was recreated at A5 size and the text altered asking residents to identify the issues that mattered to them about living on Havelock (Fig. 12.7). This second set of cards was scheduled for delivery along with a HIRO newsletter to all residents of the estate.

Before the scheduled Open Days in October 2006, Proboscis created an internet service for residents to flag up maintenance issues (Fig. 12.8). This system required no specialist knowledge to maintain or set up and comprised various free services offering elements of public authoring – mapping, collecting data, sharing knowledge, images, audio, and video. An online spreadsheet[2] was used to catalogue individual entries that were linked to locations on Google Maps; images on Flickr were connected to spreadsheet entries and maps, and the whole was inserted into a blog. The aim was to build a picture of environmental conditions on Havelock and then to approach Ealing Homes to explore the potential use of this system to help improve delivery of services to the estate.

---

[2] http://www.editgrid.com/

Living on Havelock

What are the issues that affect **your** life on Havelock?
Please **tick** the boxes below if you think there is a *problem* or *need* and **mark** the place or places on the **map** overleaf.

	Problem or Need	Please describe
Garages		
Estate repairs		
Internal maintenance (flats, houses)		
Rubbish and flytipping		
Illness and overcrowding		
Anti-social behaviour		
Community spirit / neighbourliness		
Access, transport and traffic		
Activities for young people		
Shops		
Lighting		
Security and safety		
Local service points (health, police, housing, libraries etc)		
Other (please describe)		

Please return to the **Havelock Community Shop** at 39 Hunt Road

Fig. 12.7 Storycard (image courtesy of Proboscis)

HAVELOCK TAPESTRY

Monday, September 25, 2006

Havelock Lighting
A list of faulty lighting on the estate surveyed by M O Musani during April and May 2006.

Download as a PDF or Excel file.

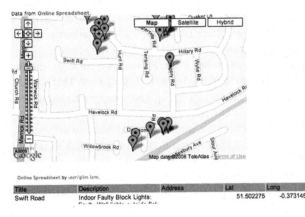

Data from Online Spreadsheet.

Online Spreadsheet by user/giles lane.

Title	Description	Address	Lat	Long
Swift Road	Indoor Faulty Block Lights:		51.502275	-0.373145

Fig. 12.8 Havelock maintenance blog (image courtesy of Proboscis)

Proboscis viewed the members of HIRO as project collaborators and as such expected them to undertake additional responsibilities such as following up contact with Havelock residents who expressed interest in participating further in the Conversation and Connections initiatives. For example, researchers expected HIRO to organize the distribution of the Storycards and newsletters before the open days and "survey week" and to facilitate access to the community shop and equipment for residents outside of the HIRO committee, who sought to engage with the Conversations and Connections initiative.

Types of Participants

Analysis of the participants in Conversations and Connections suggests that they might be characterized in ways other than by gender and occupation. Two distinct relationships between participants and researchers can be identified: members of HIRO and Havelock Estate residents. These two categories are not entirely analogous with the concept of direct and indirect stakeholders outlined by Friedman et al (Friedman et al. 2001) as both groups have direct contact with the project. Perhaps more useful analogies are Kevin Harris' conception of social connections as a series of concentric circles (Lane and Harris 2005) and Dan Hill's description of the social life of a broadcast (Hill 2004).

During Conversations and Connections, there was a direct relationship between Proboscis, Kevin Harris, and members of HIRO as events were planned and coordinated. The relationship between researchers and non-HIRO residents (children and teenagers, as well as adults) was primarily established at the Open Day events. The first open day in November 2005 attracted approximately 60 residents. This was seen as a sign of significant potential by researchers (Lane and Harris 2005), however attendance figures were lower at further events (Table 12.3).

The events and activities organized by Proboscis were resident's only contact with the project. Proboscis intended for these events to act as catalysts to increase residents' participation in the project

By bringing technologies for mapping and sharing information together and supporting residents and groups in combining their use, we sought to stimulate the recording of local issues, and hence participation in addressing those issues (Lane and Harris 2005)

Despite some residents expressing interest in participating further in various aspects of the project, this increase in participation did not take place.

Table 12.3 Participation in conversation and connections

	Open day Nov 05	IT day March 06	Rec. hav. June 06	Story Card I	Story Card II	Open day I Oct 06	Open day II Oct 06	Survey week Oct 06
Participants (approx.)	60	15	11	Unknown	7	6	1	Cancelled

Expectations and Outcomes

Proboscis believed that their initiatives on Havelock estate left no longer-term impact. In their report to the Ministry of Justice they state bluntly

> The project did not succeed. None of the innovations attempted under the project were adopted by the group with any lasting success (Lane and Harris 2007)

It is indeed difficult to find tangible evidence of participant's engagement with the various initiatives of Conversation and Connections. Attendance figures at events were low, falling steadily as the project progressed; over the 3 months following the launch of the online maintenance blog, only one member of the committee made entries; members of HIRO failed to deliver the redesigned Storycards to residents, and the two subsequent Open Days drew just seven attendees between them resulting in the planned survey week being cancelled. Proboscis' disappointment with HIRO members' lack of engagement is palpable in their final report. Writing about a proposal from a young resident of Havelock to take up an internship they say:

> The research team were delighted by his offer to gather and map local knowledge on the estate In the end the internship was abandoned as HIRO – deliberately or not – delayed so long in providing keys to the office in which the work was to be carried out that the volunteer resigned in disillusionment (Lane and Harris 2007)

The original proposal for Conversations and Connections outlines the expected outcomes of the project as follows:

> The tangible outcomes we anticipate will include engaging a diverse selection of the residents to participate in the knowledge mapping and sharing activities and processes, using and helping with the design of the tools we use. We intend to build a dynamic and vibrant database of materials about the area, and to assist the residents in understanding how they can add to this and access it in the most appropriate ways. We expect to see a wide range of issues and concerns being raised, solutions proposed and debate about how the residents' organization carries out its responsibilities (Lane and Harris 2005)

It appears that Proboscis' perception of the value of Conversations and Connections relied upon achieving a certain level of engagement and commitment from residents. Yet, Proboscis' contact with residents was mostly through the events organized in collaboration with HIRO, and while there is some evidence that residents began to engage in further activities,[3] Proboscis hoped HIRO would follow this up. However as one committee member admitted:

> We feel very sorry about not having the energies, our main objective was to get into the development stage [of the Right to Manage process] (Lane and Harris 2007)

The HIRO had other priorities and they failed to make further contact with residents regarding their interest in the project.

---

[3] For example, following the IT Day, researchers reported that a few people indicated their interest in developing their computer skills and participating in some of the project ideas (Lane et al. 2006).

Reflections and Conclusions

In presenting how participation was constructed in the two case studies, I identify three areas that may affect the outcome of studies exploring facilitation of social interaction:

First, a participants' social and cultural background, for example gender and occupation, may influence their response to the technology and the concepts under-pinning it, that is, whether it is meaningful to the participant. Urban Tapestries had a good balance between male and female, student and nonstudent, participants. However, the majority of nonstudent participants were employed in design, technology, academia, and the arts, and I suggest this may have affected the positive response to the Urban Tapestries concept and software recorded by Proboscis. A more accurate reflection of how participants would engage with the concept of public authoring during Conversations and Connections came from the ethnographic study and the second trial, both of which explored how Urban Tapestries might fit into everyday lived experience.

Second, the construction of participation in terms of tasks and responsibilities, and effecting meaning for participants, may affect the outcome. While participation in Urban Tapestries generally took place outside of the research lab, the structure of participation was closely controlled with participants understanding from the outset, the duration, tasks, and feedback techniques they were expected to undertake. Generally, participants were asked perform a time-delineated task, and on completion, to reflect on this and communicate their experience to researchers. One exception was the second trial: while the participants knew the duration and the feedback methods in advance, the task itself was open-ended. In contrast, the events and activities arranged for Havelock residents during conversations and connections were less formal, and the duration and range of activities on offer during Open Day events were specified in advance, participants were not assigned specific tasks to complete.

Third, access to an "authentic context of use" may require collaboration with a third-party facilitator and consequently researchers' relationship to some portion of the desired participants may be indirect. These organizations or individuals working in collaboration with researchers have their own agenda and may have different priorities to researchers. As a result, the parameters of the participation may be a result of negotiation with third-parties and participants rather than the a priori design of researchers. This requires careful consideration of how the outcomes of participation are measured.

In conclusion, I suggest that if spaces can be designed, but places can only emerge (Harrison and Dourish 1996), then the same might be said of technologies that aspire to facilitate social interaction; that is, the power to enable social change lies only partly with the research team and some portion of power is held by other agencies who are also required to take action for interactive systems to succeed in facilitating social change.

Finally, I understand that the computer training bus continues to visit Havelock. This suggests that the value of social glue projects might only become apparent a long time after the event – and possibly in unanticipated ways.

Acknowledgments I would like to thank Giles Lane, Alice Angus, and Orlagh Woods of Proboscis for sharing their experience of working on Urban Tapestries and Conversations and Connections. I would also like to thank Kristina Glushkova for her help in structuring this chapter.

References

Abowd GD & Mynatt ED (2000) Charting past, present, and future research in ubiquitous computing, ACM Transactions on Computer-Human Interaction 7 (1): 29–58. DOI= http://doi.acm.org/10.1145/344949.344988

Barkhuus L & Rode JA (2007) From mice to men: 24 Years of Evaluation at CHI. Alt.Chi ACM CHI 2007 Conference on Human Factors in Computing Systems

Borovoy R, Martin F, Resnick M & Silverman B (1998) GroupWear: nametags that tell about telationships. In: Proceedings of CHI 98, 329–330. ACM, New York. DOI= http://doi.acm.org/10.1145/286498.286799

Buchenau M & Suri J F (2000) Experience prototyping. In: Boyarsky D & Kellogg WA (eds) Proceedings of DIS00, 424–433. ACM, New York. DOI= http://doi.acm.org/10.1145/347642.347802

Dodge M & Kitchin R (2004) Code, space and everyday life. CASA Working Paper Series http://www.casa.ucl.ac.uk/working_papers/paper81.pdf Accessed 22 March 2009

Dourish P (2001) Where the Action Is: The Foundations of Embodied Interaction. MIT Press, Massachusetts

Dourish P & Button G (1998) On technomethodology: foundational relationships between ethnomethodology and system design. Human Computer Interaction, 13(4): 395–432

Dunne A & Raby F (2002) The placebo project. In: Proceedings of DIS02, 9–12. ACM, New York. DOI= http://doi.acm.org/10.1145/778712.778714

Eagle N & Pentland P (2005) Social serendipity: mobilizing social software, IEEE Pervasive Computing 4 (2): 28–34

Erickson T & Kellogg WA (2000) Social translucence: an approach to designing systems that support social processes, ACM Trans. Comput.-Hum. Interact. 7(1) 59-83. DOI= http://doi.acm.org/10.1145/344949.345004

Foth M & Brereton M (2004) Enabling local interaction and personalised networking in residential communities through action research and participatory design. In: Hyland P & Vrazalic L (eds) Proceedings of OZCHI 2004.

Friedman B, Kahn PH & Borning A (2001) Value Sensitive Design: Theory and Methods UW CSE Technical Report 02–12-01

Gaver W, Boucher A, Law A, Pennington S, Bowers J, Beaver J, Humble J, Kerridge T, Villar N & Wilkie A (2008) Threshold Devices: Looking out from the Home. Proceedings of ACM CHI 2008 Conference on Human Factors in Computing Systems

Harrison S & Dourish P (1996) Re-place-ing space: the roles of place and space in collaborative systems. In: Ackerman MS (ed) Proceedings of CSCW'96 . M. S. Ackerman, Ed. CSCW '96, 67–76. ACM, New York. DOI= http://doi.acm.org/10.1145/240080.240193

Harrison S, Tatar D & Sengers P (2007) The Three Paradigms of HCI. In Alt. chi. Proceedings of CHI 2007 Conference on Human Factors in Computing Systems

Hill D (2004) City of sound: urban tapestries: second trial: update 2. http://www.cityofsound.com/blog/2004/06/urban_tapestrie_1.html. Accessed 22 March 2009

Hill D (2004) City of sound: ripples, or "the social life of a broadcast" http://www.cityofsound.com/blog/2004/07/ripples_or_the_.html. Accessed 22 March 2009

Jungnickel K (2004) Urban tapestries, sensing the city and other stories, Proboscis Cultural Snapshots Number Eight

Lane G, Thelwall S, Angus A, Peckett V & West N (2006) Urban Tapestries: Public Authoring, Place & Mobility. Proboscis, London

Lane G & Harris K (2006) Application to the Innovations Fund, Department for Constitutional Affairs, UK Government. Provided by Proboscis

Lane G & Harris K (2007) Conversations and Connections. Ministry of Justice Report

McCullough M (2004) Digital ground: architecture, pervasive computing and environmental knowing. MIT Press, Massachsuetts

Pedersen J & Valgårda A (2004) Viability of urban social technologies. itu.dk/people/jensp/viability.pdf. Accessed 22 March 2009

Preece J (2001) DRAFT: Sociability and usability: twenty years of chatting online. Behavior and Information Technology Journal 20(5): 347–356

Sengers P & Gaver W (2006) Staying open to interpretation: engaging multiple meanings in design and evaluation. In: Proceedings of DIS06, 99–108. ACM, New York. DOI= http://doi.acm.org/10.1145/1142405.1142422

Silverstone R & Sujon Z (2005) Urban tapestries: experimental ethnography. In: Couldry N, Gill R & Pratt A (eds) urban space and communication technologies. http://www.lse.ac.uk/collections/media@lse/pdf/EWP7.pdf. Accessed 22 March 2009

West N (2005) Urban tapestries, the spatial and social on your mobile, Proboscis Cultural Snapshots Number Eight

Proboscis. http://proboscis.org.uk/. Accessed 22 March 2009

Urban tapestries/ social tapestries: trial feedback. http://urbantapestries.net/weblog/archives/cat_trial_feedback.html. Accessed 22 March 2009

Chapter 13
Sharing Personal Reflections on Health Locally

Andrea Grimes

Introduction

Nutrition-related health problems such as obesity and diabetes are a serious concern in the United States. Furthermore, health researchers have documented the disproportionate amount of health problems within the low-income African American population. This segment of the population faces most nutrition-related health problems more frequently than the majority groups in the population.[1] For example, diabetes, hypertension, and obesity are all much more prevalent in African Americans than they are in Caucasians. Thus, health researchers have advocated for a focused examination of how these health disparities can be reduced (Airhihenbuwa and Kumanyika 1996; Chesla et al. 2004). Furthermore, researchers advocate designing culturally relevant approaches that take into account the way in which health behaviors and attitudes are a reflection and reaction to one's cultural background (Campbell et al. 1999; Horowitz et al. 2004; Fitzgibbon et al. 2005). In this chapter, I discuss the work I have done to design culturally relevant technologies that promote healthy eating habits in low-income African American neighborhoods.

The construct of collectivism is one aspect of culture that is important to address when designing interventions to address African American health issues. Collectivism refers to a cultural orientation in which the emphasis is placed more on the well-being of the group than on the individual (Triandis 1995). In the African American population, the health needs of the larger group (family or community) are often seen as more important than simply the health needs of the individual. Researchers have thus found it effective to frame health interventions for this population such that they focus on the state of health within the broader African American population as opposed to just the individual (Kreuter and McClure 2004).

A. Grimes (✉)
School of Interactive Computing, Georgia Institute of Technology, 85, Fifth Street,
NW Atlanta, GA 30332, USA
e-mail: agrimes@cc.gatech.edu

[1] http://www.cdc.gov/nccdphp/publications/aag/reach.htm

While previous work has identified collectivism as an important construct and used it to design programmatic interventions (Kreuter et al. 2004; Kreuter and Haughton 2006), researchers have not investigated how to design technologies for low-income African Americans that incorporate the notion of collectivism. At the same time, computer-supported cooperative work (CSCW) research has shown the potential of collaborative technologies to address health issues in the general population, particularly through online health communities (Leimeister and Krcmar 2005; Rodgers and Chen 2005; Johnson and Ambrose 2006). To explore the potential of technology to address nutrition issues in low-income African American neighborhoods, I designed and evaluated a collaborative application called EatWell. This system allows people to record and share audio clips describing how they have tried to eat healthfully in their neighborhoods. EatWell incorporates the idea of collectivism because it focuses on harnessing community-held experiential knowledge, and helping people learn from the experiences of others.

I begin this chapter by discussing related research on the importance of collectivism in African American health and online health communities that support the sharing of experiential knowledge. I then discuss the EatWell system in more detail and the field study that I conducted to evaluate its use. I next describe the characteristics of the community that was created as people used EatWell, including (1) the users themselves (the *who*), (2) the context in which they used EatWell (the *where*), (3) the kind of content that they created (the *what*), and (4) the way in which they interacted with the content (the *how*). I conclude by discussing the design of nutrition-focused systems for local contexts, something that I call *deeply local health applications*. In doing so, I discuss the geographic and social boundaries that should be considered when creating deeply local information sharing applications. Through the work I describe in this chapter, I contribute to the field of CSCW by unpacking the implications of using technology to address health disparities by designing collaborative health applications for local contexts.

Related Work

There is a growing body of work within the medical community that examines nutrition-related health disparities in the African American community. In addition, researchers have argued that incorporating collectivism into health interventions is a promising way of addressing these problems. In the following section I provide an overview of this research and then describe CSCW-related research on the benefits of online health communities for the general population. While the online health community research has not focused specifically on the issue of health disparities, it provides a useful starting point for considering the design of collectivism-focused applications for low-income African American communities.

African American Health Disparities

Medical and public-health researchers have shown that some health problems affect ethnic minorities in the United States (such as African Americans and Hispanics) with greater prevalence than the rest of the population.[2] For example, African Americans are disproportionately affected by diet-related health problems such as diabetes, hypertension, heart disease, and obesity. As compared to non-Hispanic Whites, African Americans are 40% more likely to have high blood pressure, but 10% less likely to be adequately managing their high blood pressure. Similarly, African Americans are 40% more likely to be obese than Whites (African American women 70% more likely) and almost 2 times as likely to have diabetes. In addition, individuals living in low-income communities may face even greater challenges as poor neighborhoods are much less likely to have supermarkets than affluent neighborhoods, and these numbers are even further exacerbated when looking at poor African American neighborhoods (Morland et al. 2001).

Indeed, research has overwhelmingly shown that the African American community is facing a serious health crisis, as rates of many serious diet-related health problems remain significantly higher in this group than in other segments of the population. Because of these issues, health researchers have advocated for a directed research agenda that seeks to eliminate these health disparities (Karanja et al. 2002; Kreuter et al. 2003; Ahye 2006). Indeed, this crisis has become a part of the national health agenda as the National Institute of Health and the US Department of Health and Human Services have created specific offices in which the goal is to eliminate health disparities within minority populations such as the African American community.

Collectivism

Researchers have overwhelmingly come to the conclusion that understanding health is about more than examining the role of genetics and the biological nature of health practices (Plowden and Thompson 2002). Instead, to eliminate health disparities, interventions must be designed to account for the ways in which culture affects health behaviors and attitudes (Kreuter and McClure 2004). In the context of African American health, one aspect of culture that is particularly important to consider is collectivism (Kreuter and Haughton 2006). With respect to health, collectivist cultures focus on the well-being of the group as opposed to simply the individual. A collectivist orientation is manifested in the form of a sense of communal responsibility, interdependence, cooperation, and collective survival (Kreuter et al. 2003; Chesla et al. 2004; Black et al. 2005). While a few researchers have

---

[2] www.omhrc.gov/templates/content.aspx?ID=3018, www.cdc.gov/nccdphp/publications/aag/reach.htm

examined how to translate this concept into health communication materials and educational programs (Karanja et al. 2002; Kreuter et al. 2003, 2004), they have not examined how to do so in a technology designed to address African American nutrition. Thus, a contribution of my work is that I translate the concept of collectivism into a system design that helps people share their nutrition-related experiences and explore the implications of doing so.

Online Health Communities

Applications that support online health communities represent a class of systems that incorporate principles of collectivism (Kummervold et al. 2002; Leimeister and Krcmar 2005; Maloney-Krichmar and Preece 2005; Rodgers and Chen 2005). That is, by providing a venue through which people help one another manage their health, such applications focus on the values of cooperation, interdependence, and communal responsibility that are characteristic of a collectivist orientation. There are many online health communities in existence today such as those facilitated by website discussion forums and they focus on topics that range from breast cancer to diabetes to healthy cooking.[3]

Online health communities provide support for learning from experiential knowledge, help facilitate of a sense of personal empowerment, and provide mechanisms for social support (Kummervold et al. 2002). For example, Salem et al. (1997) found that in an online health community for individuals coping with depression, people were much more likely to share experiential knowledge than information learned from second-hand sources, and roughly half of the messages posted provided social support. In the online knee injuries community that they studied, Maloney-Krichmar and Preece (2005) found that the community empowered users to interact more effectively with healthcare workers because of the information they gathered from others in the online community. Thus, online health communities have shown the benefit of using technology to unite individuals who have a shared interest in health. In the following sections, I describe the approach that I took to helping individuals in low-income African American neighborhoods connect around the topic of nutrition.

EatWell

EatWell is a system for cell phones that I designed and implemented and, like existing online health communities, it helps individuals share experiential knowledge. I chose to build a cell phone application because the penetration rate of this

---

[3] For example, see http://www.revolutionhealth.com/community/index

device is high even in low-income communities. A Consumer Electronics Association (2005) Report survey showed that 74% of respondents with household incomes less than $25K per year owned cell phones. EatWell allows people to use their cell phones to create short audio memories describing how they have tried to eat healthfully in their neighborhood (e.g., at fast food restaurants or when cooking at home) and listen to the memories that others in their local community have created (Grimes et al. 2008). In contrast to most online health communities, EatWell supports individuals in sharing voice content (vs. text), using their cell phones to interface with the system (instead of a personal computer), and the user population is constrained to individuals living in the same geographic area.

In designing EatWell, I accounted for the importance of community in African American health by designing the system to support sharing personal experiences about health with members of one's local community. The system design thus leverages the existing and culturally situated knowledge of the community, and as such helps individuals to learn new culturally grounded strategies for healthy eating. EatWell reflects the three principles for designing culturally grounded health technologies that I identified in a previous synthesis of medical research (Grimes and Grinter 2007). Furthermore, EatWell incorporates many of the values of a collectivist orientation because by encouraging people to share their experiences for the benefit of others, it promotes a sense of communal responsibility, cooperation, and collective survival.

User Interaction

To access EatWell, users dial a number on their cell phone that connects them to the EatWell service. Once connected to the service, they are greeted by the following voice message: "Welcome to EatWell. You can Listen to or Record memories about eating healthfully in your neighborhood. Please choose what kind of memory you want to listen to or create." The user then chooses from the five categories of memories: (1) fast food, (2) restaurants, (3) cooking at home, (4) grocery stores and markets, and (5) other. Once the user chooses a category (by selecting the corresponding button on their keypad, (1)–(5), they are told that they can press (1) to listen to a memory or (2) to create their own. If they choose to record a memory, they are told to speak their memory into the phone after the tone. Once they have finished recording their memory, they can hear the memory played back and then keep it, re-record it, or delete it.

If a user wants to listen to existing memories, the newest memory is played first. The user can listen to the other memories created by pressing the appropriate keypad button to go to the next memory or the previous memory. All memories are played in chronological order. At any time, users can leave the memory category that they are in to listen to or record memories in a different category.

System Architecture

I developed EatWell by using the TellMe studio suite of tools for creating voice-based applications, VoiceXML and PHP. I stored memory information (e.g., file locations) and user-interaction information (e.g., the memories listened to and created by each user) in an SQL database. All this code was stored server-side, so no software was installed on the user's phone. To access EatWell, users only need to use their existing cell phone and service plan to dial the number to reach the system.

Field Study Method

I studied the appropriation of EatWell in an urban, low-income neighborhood in Atlanta, GA (Grimes et al. 2008). At the beginning of the study, I showed participants how to use the EatWell system, and then asked participants to complete a survey with questions related to three topics: demographics, nutrition-related attitudes and practices, and cell phone usage. Each participant had access to EatWell for at least 4 weeks, and during this time I collected log data about how they used the system (e.g., what memories they listened to). In addition, I interviewed each participant one to two times to gain deeper insight into how and why they used EatWell. (Three participants were unable to complete their second interview due to scheduling conflicts.) I used the survey responses together with the system usage logs and interview data to gain a rich picture of how my participants used and reacted to EatWell.

I recruited all participants at a YMCA[4] branch in a low-income, predominantly African American neighborhood in Atlanta. As the YMCA offers a number of health-related programs and facilities, recruiting participants there helped me find participants who had some interest in healthy living. In addition, as the YMCA is an organization that serves local communities, I was able to identify participants who spent time in the same general area. As I designed EatWell to help people share and gather strategies for eating healthfully in their local neighborhoods, it was important that I find participants who had a shared geographic frame of reference.

My analysis consisted of examining the system usage logs, survey responses, and interview data. I recorded participants' survey responses and generated descriptive statistics about their responses to the demographic, cell phone usage, and nutrition-related questions. Finally, I conducted a thematic, inductive analysis of the interview transcripts. More details regarding the analysis process can be found in an earlier article on this work (Grimes et al. 2008).

---

[4] The YMCA is a nonprofit organization in the United States that serves local communities by providing health-related resources such as exercise equipment and fitness classes.

Participant Overview

Twelve people participated in this study: four male and eight female. Participants were African American, and most were above 30 years old, though participants came from a range of age groups (from the 18–24 age range to the 46–54 age range). Four participants were married and eight had children. All participants had access to a cell phone, most used them three or more times per day, and they varied in how often they left and listened to voicemail messages (from a few times each week to multiple times in a day).

In terms of their previous nutrition-related behaviors, 11 participants had decided to stop eating certain foods in the past and eight people had experience introducing foods into their diet. This history of changing their diet meant that participants would have a body of experiences to draw from when creating memories in EatWell. In addition, seven participants indicated that they were unsatisfied with their current eating habits and all wanted to learn how to make changes to their current habits. Together, these health attitudes suggested that my participants might be particularly interested in a system like EatWell, as it allows users to learn from the healthy eating strategies of others.

Dimensions of Information Sharing in a Local Community

This study generated a number of interesting results. In this section, I discuss the characteristics of the community that was created as people shared their personal stories and reflections in EatWell.[5] In particular, I describe four aspects of this community: the users themselves (the *who*), the context of use (the *where*), the kind of content people created (the *what*) and the way in which they interacted with the content (the *how*). These findings provide insight into how technology can help people in low-income African American neighborhoods share health information.

Who? Strangers

For the most part, people did not know the other EatWell users and had very little information about the other participants. They knew that I recruited for the study at the YMCA, and a few people indicated that they suspected they knew another person who was participating. Beyond that, however, EatWell users did not know one another because they used the system anonymously (unless the person chose to self-disclose, which only one participant did in one memory).

---

[5] I discuss other aspects of participants' interaction with and adoption of EatWell in Grimes et al. (2008). EatWell: sharing nutrition-related memories in a low-income community. CSCW'08.

To understand the participants' reactions to receiving health information from strangers in EatWell better, I asked participants to complete a survey in which they indicated their current sources of food and nutrition-related information and their attitudes toward that information. In this section, I describe their responses to these surveys and in particular their relevant information gathering behaviors and attitudes prior to using EatWell. I then describe their reactions to receiving healthy eating information from strangers in EatWell. While my small sample of participants did not yield generalizable results, the findings do point to interesting directions for further examination of the phenomena that arose.

Current Sources of Eating and Nutrition Information

In the survey, I asked participants to indicate all of the sources from which they currently get nutrition information, recipe information, and advice on picking restaurants. Participants could choose from options such as friends, family, doctors, websites, magazines, radio, and TV shows. Second, I asked participants to look at the same list of information sources and indicate who they felt could give them useful and truthful information about healthy eating. The results indicate an interesting difference between two sets of information sources: (1) friends and family, that is, people that participants interacted with in their everyday lives and (2) websites and magazines, that is, print and digital media sources.

The survey results showed that for my participants, websites and magazines were popular healthy eating information sources and also considered useful and trustworthy. Participants noted that they considered Ebony, Good Housekeeping, and Vegetarian Times to be magazines with truthful information, and nutritiondata. com, fda.org, webmd.com to be examples of websites with truthful information. Most participants obtained nutrition information from websites and magazines. While half obtained recipe information from websites and magazines, most people did not obtain restaurant information from these sources.

While many participants also obtained recipe and restaurant information from friends and family, other interactions and attitudes toward family and friends were much different than for websites and magazines. In particular, *while websites and magazines were considered useful and truthful sources for healthy eating information and were utilized for nutrition information, most participants did not obtain nutrition information from friends and family and they did not consider them to be trusted sources of healthy eating information*. This suggests that the people who were close to my participants were not seen as the ideal sources of *healthy* eating information, while sources that participants did not have interpersonal relationships with were (websites and magazines).

These findings are important to consider in light of the fact that in EatWell, individuals were listening to healthy eating content that was created by strangers. Indeed, in analyzing the interview data, I examined whether participants considered the information in EatWell to be useful as they did with magazine and website content, or not useful, as they felt about information from friends and family.

EatWell users shared characteristics with both of these sources. Like websites and magazines, participants did not know EatWell contributors intimately. And yet like friends and family, EatWell contributors were everyday people who shared their personal opinions and experiences.

Reactions to EatWell Content

In the interviews, participants indicated that they found the information in EatWell to be useful, even though they did not know the content creators personally. Some participants said that they were comfortable because before using EatWell they already felt that they got useful information from strangers. This comfort with receiving information from strangers is consistent with participants' survey responses, which indicated that they considered content from websites and magazines to be more useful than that from friends and family (people that participants had interpersonal relationships with). P4 described his comfort in this way:

> I think about it in this context: some of the things I've learned about health, I've learned from people I don't know. Via books they've written or via some other form of media... Some of the people I know most well, I would not necessarily take health advice from them

P12 had similar feelings about receiving information from strangers

> Oh, I was fine with that because of the fact that um, I didn't know anybody but I figured that everyone has something positive to contribute

In summary, participants were comfortable overall with gathering information from people they did not know. They felt that the memories in EatWell were useful because they contained interesting ideas that most participants tried out or planned to try out (Grimes et al. 2008). In addition, the memories were useful because they helped a couple participants to get back on track with eating healthfully. As P8 said,

> You know uh, sometimes especially when I'm getting ready to eat certain things, you know I'll kinda remember EatWell and I'll think you know I really need to be changing up my diet, I'm supposed to be doing something else myself and other people right now. Kinda just is a reminder to me to not overdo certain things and uh, just to watch my health habits

Two participants did note that a challenge in getting information from others was assessing the quality of the content, saying that one has to take the opinions of others with a grain of salt. This is a common issue with virtual health communities (Johnson and Ambrose 2006). However, on the whole, participants found the content that they obtained from the strangers in EatWell to be useful.

Where? Local

EatWell users were not simply strangers, however. More specifically, they were what I have termed *local strangers*, because while they did not know who was using the system, all users were united by their locality. All participants lived, worked in, or frequented the southwest area of Atlanta, an area that is characterized by high rates of poverty, low income, and mostly African American residents. All participants frequented a YMCA branch that serves a particular southwest Atlanta neighborhood. In 2004, the average adjusted gross income for this area was 37% lower than the state average, and 21.8% of residents in this area are below the poverty line (compared to a state average of 14.3%).[6] My goal in recruiting participants with this shared orientation was that they would have a common experience of eating in this context. Participants knew that I recruited people for the study from their YMCA branch and they were informed that through EatWell, they would be sharing experiences with others in their community.

In Grimes et al. (2008), my colleagues and I describe the enjoyment people felt in using EatWell because they could identify with other system users, even though they did not know them. People felt this sense of identification in part because people were local strangers, that is, they lived in the same neighborhoods and had a shared cultural background. As P8 noted:

> You know, the types of food that was talked about when I listened to messages and also the ones that I did leave in regard to myself, kinda fits the community and the area where I live

The fact that EatWell users were familiar with eating in the same local context meant that some memories in the system were reflective of the economic and cultural realities of eating in that particular neighborhood. For example, some memories discussed low-cost ways of eating healthfully and foods common in traditional African American cuisine (Grimes et al. 2008). For some participants, the local flavor of memories made it particularly useful. P3 said that she did not know if broadening the scope of EatWell to people from other geographic contexts would be as useful

> You know if it was from a wider source, I don't know… I mean, if you talk about restaurants, I don't need to hear about restaurants in New York City

This quote shows how users' shared geographic context meant the content in EatWell had an added practical usefulness. EatWell thus stands in contrast to many other online health communities who often note the benefit of bringing together people from all over the world and thus helping people to "bond without being in close proximity" (Johnson and Ambrose 2006). While this is certainly a positive attribute of such communities, EatWell offers the complimentary benefit of supporting a community in a more local context.

What and How? Listening in on Individual Reflections

Common models of information exchange in online health communities involve members asking questions or sharing their problems and other members subsequently providing answers or solutions to those problems (Johnson and Ambrose 2006).

---

[6] http://www.city-data.com/zips/30311.html

The design and appropriation of EatWell reflected a different model of information exchange. To contribute content in EatWell users created an audio memory that was stored in a repository, which was browseable by other users. That is, unlike the question and response model common in many online health communities, each person in EatWell effectively shared a single reflection that was rarely followed-up by other users. If a user did want to reply to an existing memory, he or she would have to do so by creating a new memory that was not linked to the memory that they were replying to. Thus, the design of EatWell was much more conducive to people creating one-off clips describing their experiences.

In summary, as people used EatWell, for the most part they listened to the individual reflections posted by users, or created their own reflection. There was little two-way interaction between users, save for the few memories that referenced other memories. And yet still, by hearing the stories of people in their community, people felt a sense of community empowerment. As discussed in Grimes et al. (2008), the sense of empowerment was rooted in the fact that through the stories in EatWell they saw that there were other people who were trying to eat healthfully in their community. The glimpses into the lives of others allowed them to see their community in a new light. By sharing their personal reflections on eating and nutrition, community members demonstrated that even though there exist extreme health disparities in these communities, there are people who are trying to eat healthfully. Furthermore, participants were encouraged when they saw that there were other people who cared enough about the community to take the time to share experiences that might help others.

Deeply Local Health Applications

In this chapter, I have discussed the nature of sharing information about health amongst local strangers through EatWell: the who, where, what, and how. Each of these dimensions has implications for the design of *deeply local health applications*, a concept that I introduced in Grimes et al. (2008). Such systems are applications that are designed for individuals within a constrained geographic context. In the remainder of this chapter, I expand upon this idea and I focus my discussion on designing deeply local health applications that facilitate information sharing in communities. In particular, I discuss the importance of considering where to place geographic and social boundaries.

My results showed that there was great benefit in gaining information from individuals within a shared local geographic context. Going forward, when designing deeply local health applications for information sharing it is important to consider *how local* such systems should be. That is, designers should reflect upon where the geographic boundaries for such applications should be placed. With EatWell, I recruited participants at the YMCA, an organization designed to serve local communities. Thus, many participants lived within the same zip code, and were likely to frequent some of the same neighborhoods. However, I could have restricted participation even further such that I, for example, only recruited participants who lived within a set number of miles of one another. An alternative approach would have been to relax the participation criteria and expand the user population to people who had experience with eating in the southern United States more generally. The scope of what it means to be "local" is important to consider, as it may have implications for how relevant the shared experiences are. If the scope is too broad, then systems risk losing some of the benefits of supporting community building amongt people within a local context. As I mentioned earlier, the fact that participants could identify with other EatWell users was an important aspect of the system. Furthermore, the local nature of EatWell helped to facilitate the sense of community empowerment as individuals saw that there were others like them trying to eat healthfully and who cared about improving the state of health in the community. Defining "local" too broadly may affect the sense of community empowerment that individuals feel. Alternatively, scoping too narrowly may limit the potential impact and reach of such systems and the diversity of content that is shared.

In addition to geographic boundaries, there are social boundaries to consider as well. That is, there are social considerations that should be made regarding to what extent system users should know other users, and to what extent social interaction should be facilitated amongst system users. First, designers should consider *whether the application should support information sharing with people that individuals already know or with strangers.* EatWell was made up of a community of local strangers, but it could easily have been implemented as an information sharing utility amongst friends and family. Indeed, a number of researchers in CSCW-related fields have created systems that allow people to share information about their health behaviors (e.g., exercise history) with friends (Consolvo et al. 2006; Anderson et al. 2007; Toscos et al. 2008). For my participants, this may not have been considered useful, as most indicated that they did not feel they could get useful and truthful information about healthy eating from these individuals. Alternatively, one could argue that a different set of benefits would arise from sharing health information amongst friends and family. For example, information sharing in this context while perhaps not as educational may help foster deeper social bonds. In either case, it is clearly important to examine the relative benefits and drawbacks of supporting information sharing amongst strangers and people with interpersonal relationships.

Second, it is important to consider *to what extent interaction should be facilitated amongst users of deeply local health applications.* EatWell exemplified how even with very little interaction, a sense of community empowerment was facilitated. Providing users with mechanisms to respond more directly to the reflections left in the system might further strengthen the feeling of community. However, this design feature might also make users feel pressured to have more extended interaction with EatWell, and subsequently feel less positive about the system. Since EatWell is primarily a venue for sharing reflections and not, for example, for seeking answers to questions, adding support for more extensive interaction might not mesh with the system's primary goals. Future work should unpack the benefits, challenges, and drawbacks afforded by different levels of social interaction in deeply local-health applications.

Conclusions

There is great potential in examining how researchers can design health applications for specific, local contexts. By describing the initial work I have done in this area, my goal is that researchers will continue to explore new and exciting ways of creating deeply local health applications. I have described the importance of considering the geographic and social boundaries of such systems and future work should examine these and other dimensions of the deeply local health application space further. The results of my exploratory field study of EatWell indicate that the local nature of the system helped people to share eating experiences that are reflective of their particular socio-cultural context. Furthermore, the system facilitated a sense of community empowerment, showing that in the face of extreme health disparities, there are people in the community trying to improve their own health and that of others. Going forward, these results suggest that designing deeply local-heath applications may be a particularly fruitful approach to addressing health disparities by empowering people to address locally relevant issues.

References

Consumer Electronics Association (2005) Handheld Content: Measuring Usage and Subscription Service Opportunities. see http://www.marketresearch.com/product/display.asp?productid=11 98102&xs=r&g=1&kw=&view=toc&curr=USD

Ahye B, Devine C & Odoms-Young A (2006) Values expressed through intergenerational family food and nutrition management systems among African American women. Family & Community Health 29(1): 5–16

Airhihenbuwa CO & Kumanyika S (1996) Cultural aspects of african american eating patterns. Ethnicity & Health 1(3): 245–260

Anderson I, Maitland J, Sherwood S et al. (2007) Shakra: tracking and sharing daily activity levels with unaugmented mobile phones. Mob. Netw. Appl. 12(2-3): 185-199. DOI= http://dx.doi.org/10.1007/s11036-007-0011-7

Black AR, Cook JL, McBride Murray V M et al. (2005) Ties that bind: implications of social support for rural, partnered African American women's health functioning. Women's Health Issues 15(5): 216–223

Campbell MK, Honess-Morreale L, Farrell, D et al. (1999) A tailored multimedia nutrition education pilot program for low-income women receiving food assistance. Health Education Research 14(2): 257–267

Chesla, C. A., L. Fisher, et al. (2004) Family and disease management in African-American patients with type 2 diabetes. Diabetes Care 27(12): 2850–2855

Consolvo S, Everitt K, Smith I et al. (2006) Design Requirements for Technologies that Encourage Physical Activity. In: Grinter R, Rodden T, Aoki, R et al. (eds) Proceedings of CHI 2006, 457–466. ACM, New York. DOI= http://doi.acm.org/10.1145/1124772.1124840

Fitzgibbon ML, Stolley MR, Ganschow P et al. (2005) Results of a faith-based weight loss intervention for black women. Journal of the National Medical Association 97(10): 1393–1402

Grimes A, Bednar M, Bolter JD et al. (2008). EatWell: Sharing nutrition-related memories in a low-income community. CSCW'08, 87-96. ACM, New York. DOI= http://doi.acm.org/10.1145/1460563.1460579

Grimes A & Grinter R (2007) Designing Persuasion: Health Technology for Low-Income African American Communities. Persuasive Technology (2007): 24–35.

Horowitz CR, Tuzzio L, Rojas M et al. (2004) How do urban African Americans and latinos view the influence of diet on hypertension. Journal of Health Care for the Poor and Underserved 15(4): 631–644

Johnson GJ & Ambrose PJ (2006) Neo-tribes: the power and potential of online communities in health care. Communications of the ACM 49(1): 107-113. DOI= http://doi.acm.org/10.1145/1107458.1107463

Karanja N, Stevens VJ, Hollis JF et al. (2002) Steps to soulful living (steps): a weight loss program for African-American women. Ethnicity & Disease 12: 363–371

Kreuter MW & Haughton LT (2006) Integrating culture into health information for African American women. American Behavioral Scientist 49(6): 794–811

Kreuter MW & McClure SM (2004) The role of culture in health communication. Annual Review of Public Health 25: 439–455

Kreuter MW, Skinner CS, Stegar May K et al. (2004) Responses to behaviorally vs culturally tailored cancer communication among African American women. American Journal of Health Behavior 28(3): 195–207

Kreuter MW, Steger-May K, Bobra S et al. (2003) Sociocultural characteristics and responses to cancer education materials among African American women. Cancer Control 10(5): 69–80

Kummervold PE, Gammon D, Bergvik T et al. (2002) Social support in a wired world: use of online mental health forums in Norway. Nordic Journal of Psychiatry 56(1): 59–65

Leimeister JM & Krcmar H (2005) Evaluation of a systematic design for a virtual patient community. Journal of Computer-Mediated Communication 10(4), article 6

Maloney-Krichmar D & Preece J (2005) A multilevel analysis of sociability, usability, and community dynamics in an online health community. ACM Trans. Comput.-Hum. Interact. 12(2): 201–232. DOI= http://doi.acm.org/10.1145/1067860.1067864

Morland K, Wing S, Roux AD et al. (2001) Neighborhood characteristics associated with the location of food stores and food service places. American Journal of Preventive Medicine 22(1): 23–29

Plowden KO & Thompson LS (2002) Sociological perspectives of black American health disparity: implications for social policy. Policy, Politics, & Nursing Practice 3(4): 325–332

Rodgers S & Chen W (2005) Internet community group participation: psychosocial benefits for women with breast cancer. Journal of Computer-Mediated Communication 10(4)

Salem DA, Bogat GA & Reid C (1997) Mutual help goes on-line. Journal of Community Psychology 25(2): 189–207

Toscos T, Faber A, Connelly K et al. (2008) Encouraging physical activity in teens: can technology help reduce barriers to physical activity in adolescent girls? In: Proceedings of Pervasive Health'08, 218–221

Triandis HC (1995) Individualism & collectivism. Westview Press, Boulder

Chapter 14
MoBlogs, Sharing Situations, and Lived Life

Connor Graham, Mark Rouncefield, and Christine Satchell

Introduction

"Shared encounters" take various forms and embrace various technologies. In "Smart Mobs" Rheingold (2002) presents some provocative thoughts on the ways in which a simple technology – the mobile phone – can impact on a wide range of shared encounters; from the simple process of meeting friends on an evening out, to the possibilities for orchestrating political demonstrations. While not necessarily sharing Rheingold's interest in the political and the dramatic, we are interested in exploring empirically the ways in which mobile phones (and applications that run on them) can impact on a variety of meaningful shared encounters and shared experiences and the insights we may thereby gain into how people live their everyday lives. Our concern is to explain and understand (mobile) blogging practices involving digital content sharing and what this achieves in people's lives. How meaningful can it be to write and display content for an unknown audience while "being mobile?" (Nardi et al. 2004). Our contention here is that this question can only be answered through a profound understanding of what it is to "be mobile" and the associated technologies and practices. These concerns, we believe, are important when trying to understand "modern" shared encounters variously tethered to physical places.

In this chapter, we also address more specific questions about mobile blogging and encounters: does mobile blogging simply capture encounters or does it support further encounters? How does this actually play out in people's lives? We also explore the extent of the physical trace and involvement of self in "shared encounters": how much physicality is necessary for an encounter to be meaningful? How important is that real, physical aspect of the encounter? How is the self enacted through these same encounters? How important is it to share the original moment? We explore these questions by drawing on a study that intimately involves the self

C. Graham (✉)
Computing Department, Lancaster University, Lancaster, LA1 4YW, United Kingdom
e-mail: c.graham@lancaster.ac.uk
Department of Information Systems, University of Melbourne, Parkville, Victoria 3010, Australia

K.S. Willis et al. (eds.), *Shared Encounters*, Computer Supported Cooperative Work,
DOI 10.1007/978-1-84882-727-1_14, © Springer-Verlag London Limited 2010

and digital contents in encounters. The compelling narrative thread here is participants' actions and opinions with regard to sharing digital content. We believe this "thread" informs the notion of "encounter" itself. Our suggestion here is that notions of "being in a place" and "sharing an encounter" are actually being challenged through technologies such as mobile blogging.

We explore these questions by utilizing Urry (2000) mobilities paradigm – an appealing approach to understand "shared encounters" and the role of digital content, given its coverage of both physical and virtual travel. Urry suggests that different forms of travel are no longer "exceptional" but an inherent aspect of modernity (Urry 2000), an aspect that is artfully accomplished through "various practices of networking" such as emailing, texting, sharing gossip, making 2 min bumping-into-people conversations, chatting over a coffee, traveling many hours to meet people (Larsen et al. 2006). Urry's (2004) "five interdependent mobilities" (Larsen et al. 2006) are a useful way of characterizing how shared encounters are enacted today: physical travel; travel of objects; communicative travel; imaginative travel and; virtual travel.

Like Sheller and Urry (2006), our interest includes how these mobilities are related to other things like the physicality of being located in a place and the digital flows in the environment (Sheller and Urry 2006). To explore this and the digital aspects of shared encounters, we review relevant literature which informs us on the various aspects of mobile blogging – blogging itself, pervasive image capture and sharing (PICS), mobile blogs, and video blogs. Our concern in doing this is to draw out themes and problem areas to be investigated through the study of the particular technologies we consider here. We are suggesting that "shared encounters" are evolving across different media to form a new kind of "mobile life" where personal relationships can persist and even flourish despite the "tyranny of distance" (Blainey 1966). To explore this, we present an empirical study of smokers' use of blogs through a quit attempt. This provides insights into various aspects of encounters as this "life goal" involved physicality – acutely felt bodily addiction – "temporal stretch" – quit attempts tend to extend over time – and particular locations – smoking is often associated with particular places. The smokers' attempts, both documented and variously "supported" by their (mo)blogging, allowed us to gain insights concerning "…what their affairs consist of as locally produced, locally occasioned, and locally described, locally questionable, counted, recorded, observed phenomena of order*[1] …". At the end of this chapter, we reflect on sharing digital content and its relationship to real people, places, and time. Finally, we consider future directions in blogging technologies and how these might shape shared encounters of the future.

---

[1]Garfinkel and Wieder (1992) describe this as "locally produced, naturally accountable phenomena, searched for, findable, found, only discoverably the case, consisting in and as "work on the streets.""

Blogs, PICS, Moblogs, and Vlogs

We begin with a review of some studies of moblogs and aligned technologies. Our concern in this review is to consider the questions posed earlier regarding the relationship between moblogs and encounters and the physicality and involvement of self in encounters lived through blogging-related technologies.

Weblogs

Herring et al.'s (2004) study of web blogging suggests that there are three primary types of blogs; individually authored personal journals, "filters" (because they select and provide commentary on information from other websites), and "knowledge logs" and that the majority of blogs are the personal journal "online diary" type (Herring et al. 2004). Nardi et al.'s (2004) study of 23 Californians and New Yorkers blogging their everyday lives for individuals or small groupings discuss how blogging is a social activity beyond diary-keeping. They describe how it can be used for a number of objects including updating others, expressing opinions to influence others, seeking others' opinions and feedback, thinking through writing to an audience, and the release of emotional tension. Both Schiano et al. (2004) and Nardi et al. (2004) describe how blogs do not "stand alone" – they are interlinked to other sites on the Internet and coexist with a multitude of media and devices, including email, other blogs and talk.

Nardi et al. (ibid) also note, with regard to Weblogs, that "Consciousness of audience is central to the blogging experience." However, this awareness of and relationship with the audience is a curious one; "a third-order experience" that involves writing for the unknown (Dix 2006) and often celebrates the trivial and mundane detail of people's lives. Thus, blogs are both "personal" (Herring et al. 2004) and intensely impersonal and "phatic" (Gibbs et al. 2005) supporting digital "prods" and snippets of information exchange that form "touch work" for the known, less known, and anonymous. As Nardi et al. (2004) note "Maybe we are ready to hold each other at arm's length." More recently, Cheok et al. (2007) "BlogWall" system suggests, at least for the authors, that the most salient aspect of blogging is that it comprises some kind of "public" message. The suggestion from their work is that blogging is still blogging if it is directly solicited and if the content gathered is transformed in some way and then displayed.

PICS

Studies of PICS technologies such as cameraphones also provide insights into the shared encounters, enabled through new digital content sharing technologies. When members of a social network cannot be together physically, images captured and shared in real time via mobile phones not only can provide an authentic way to share the experience, but also, ultimately, reinforce real-life friendship networks and social connectedness (Van House et al. 2005). The introduction of image capturing and sharing into the social stream brings with it a lightweight visual communication, "an intimate visual co-presence," which ideally, acts as an extension of SMS (Ito 2005). Emerging systems supporting digital content sharing also suggest how the link between the physical and digital in shared encounters is changing. Sarvas et al.'s (Sarvas et al. 2004) MobShare allows for the management of images via shared digital albums within a individually controlled group (e.g., by leveraging an individual's address book). Jacucci et al. (2005) describe how spectators can actively contribute to an event through a field study of a car rally through mGroup, a content sharing mobile messaging system that converts "the mobile terminal into both a powerful means of expressing and learning supportive group experiences." Salovaara et al. (2006) report on a messaging application, Media Stories, that supports the immediate, collective construction of a blog, again shared within a particular group. They describe how this allows users who are co-present at an event to have an enhanced feeling of "being there," creating a sense of "shared space." These PICS systems challenge the notion of a mobile phone (and by implication the blogging it supports) as supporting only individual authorship and reimagine the participant in an event as someone who is active through interaction with people there and the generated media both during and after the event as opposed to simply the event itself (Sellen et al. 2007; Harper et al. 2007; Khalid and Dix 2006). Interactions also extend beyond the event through post-hoc viewing via these technologies, sometimes provoking realizations and even feelings of strangeness about their own lives (Harper et al. 2007).

Moblogs

As PICS technologies can reconfigure the physical and digital aspects of encounters through changing the nature of membership and the experience of time, so mobile blogging potentially reconfigures personal social space (Wang et al. 2005) and the construction of a "digital narrative" as it unfolds (through SMSes for example). This kind of technology also supports instantaneous sharing through a peer-to-peer network. Visions of blogging in the future extend to attaching digital memories to particular places that can be shared and act as a form of personal memorial after death (Hall et al. 2006). A recently reported prototype (Cheng et al. 2005) reconfigures space through exploiting a hybrid architecture (peer-to-peer and client-server), RFID tag readers in Wi-Fi enabled phones, and RFID tags in place to enable tagging of particular things in the real world (e.g., a restaurant). Beale (2006) suggests an important additional function which allows for mobile blogs to support the development of user-defined labels or "categories" allowing blog entries to be clustered and viewed according to topic, not only according to their temporality. Bamford et al. (2007) describe LocoBlog[2]: "a mobile phone application and web site which supports location-based mobile photo blogging." LocoBlog facilitates posting "blog-like" entries – a photo with various text tags – from a GPS-enabled phone to a Website which superimposes the entry on Google Maps[3] using the GPS coordinates. They describe three kinds of entries – (1) "travel blogging" (mapping out (a) particular trip(s)); (2) "mash-ups" (a concentrated set of postings around one area); and (3) "location-based life blog" (day-to-day activities "stamped" with location information). They also report a general lack of concern among participants concerning privacy. These findings suggest both that the "personal journal" type of blog identified by Herring et al. (2004) is developing different forms and that notions of privacy are being reconfigured through new mobile blogging technologies.

Vlogs

Studies of video blogging (vlogging) suggest the potential blogging has for supporting transformation. Lange (2007a), in a study of 17 female video bloggers, describes how these women shared intimate moments in order to "connect with others and raise awareness." She argues that such practices can be "socially transformative," even if such intimate sharing involves risk (e.g., embarrassment, using the material in unintended ways). In another study of 54 "YouTubers," Lange (2007b) describes how participants exhibited "publicly private" (identifying content with restricted circulation) and "privately public" (anonymous content with high circulation) behavior when sharing videos. She also reports that participants used video sharing to negotiate membership of particular social networks. However, it should be noted that Cheng et al.'s (2007) study of YouTube videos showed that "People and Blogs" (one of 12 self-selected categories for YouTube videos) only accounted for 7.4% of over 2.5 million YouTube videos analyzed in early 2007. Despite these concerns, Lange's (Lange 2007b) findings are both important and relevant to the study reported here.

Ways Forward

In summary, these studies have indicated that the term "shared" is not a straightforward one when digital technologies are considered in any detail – it can involve both intentional and unintentional sharing, effortful and effortless sharing, authored

[2] http://www.locoblog.com/

[3] http://www.google.com/maps

(e.g., writing a blog post) and unauthored (e.g., sharing a picture taken by someone else) sharing. As with online communities, there are varying levels of participation and different roles in "sharing" – from active contributor to reader (Baumer et al. 2008) to "lurker" (Khalid and Dix 2006). The studies have also shown the importance of considering the relationship between the author and the readership and how that is managed through different "modes" and technologies deployed in sharing. The role these technologies have in managing relationships with others and "the self" and how they are woven together to help achieve these relationships is also an important concern.

The following study responds to these issues through the use of a "personal journal" type of blog (Herring et al. 2004). We were particularly interested in the opportunity blogs offered to think about things through and release emotional tension (Nardi et al. 2004) through them and the role they could play in transformation (Lange 2007a). Given that blogs do not "stand alone" (Nardi et al. 2004), we also thought it important to consider them in connection with and relation to other technologies. Broadly, the study explores the public-private dichotomy in people's relationship to digital content they had generated. Although we were constrained by our desire to protect participants' right to privacy, the study also explored the nature of the spectatorship that people engaged in concerning their own lives and if, as Harper et al. (2007) suggest, such technologies can actually facilitate reflection about the self and everyday routines. The study also considered that digital content sharing technologies such as moblogs are "carried" through time and place, during an encounter and after an encounter, with others and alone. Studying something in people's lives that can provide a persistent presence through these times and places, challenge notions of privacy and the self-adequacy, and involvement of digital and physical aspects of encounters is difficult. Quitting smoking seemed to be such a persistent, personal and at times public activity that occurs over time, across all sorts of places, and over a variety of encounters.

A Blogging Study

This study was conducted in 2007 in Melbourne, Australia. It intended to examine the real, every day practices around Nokia's Lifeblog: mobile blogging software designed for Nokia phones. What it ended up examining was people's Weblogging and digital photo-sharing practices. It was an exploratory case study (Yin 2003) conducted using rapid ethnographic (Millen 2000) approaches – it was a relatively "quick and dirty" ethnography (Hughes et al. 1994). It drew on Probes as an approach (e.g., Gaver et al. 1999) and Mobile Probes in particular (Hulkko et al. 2004) – we regarded the mobile phone itself as a data collection tool and a generator of digital "documents of life" (Plummer 1983): key (auto) biographical accounts potentially providing us with deep, personal insights into people's lives.

Study Background

In earlier work (e.g., Graham et al. 2006, 2007), the potential role of "social technologies" (e.g., gaming, Wikis, blogs) in smoking cessation support emerged. Broadly, we believed that blogs could potentially provide social support as well as enable temporal and geographic reach and self-awareness. Examining the use of the N-series Nokia mobile phone over a period of several weeks seemed to offer the opportunity to explore this social support. Thus, we wanted to explore the relationship between blogging with a mobile phone and quitting smoking, although, we were also interested in evaluating different kinds of moblogging software in a real-world setting.

Participants

Participants were aged between 26 and 32. They were all educated to at least tertiary level, spanned professions, and, broadly, they fitted into the category of "professional." All participants already owned a mobile phone. "Benji" continued to use his existing mobile phone in parallel with the phone we issued him throughout the study and the other participants used the phones we issued them as their primary mobile phone. We have used pseudonyms instead of participants' names to protect identities and asked permission to include participant-specific media.

Blogging Technologies

We encouraged participants to use Nokia's LifeBlog 2.00.23, providing them with an N-series Nokia phone – three received an N93 and one received an N80. The phone already had the LifeBlog software installed and we provided participants with the PC version of the software. Nokia's Lifeblog (http://www.nokia.com/lifeblog) has a strong sense of temporality at the heart of its design (Fig. 14.1a) – it supports the seamless import and display of phone content (i.e., SMSes, MMSes, images, sound and video files, notes and blog posts) into a timeline that can be searched and scrolled either through a mobile phone or a PC when the phone content is synchronized with a PC running Lifeblog (Fig. 14.1b). It also, in theory, supports mobile publishing through sending it across a network connection (e.g., GPRS, Wi-Fi) to a Weblog.

Having similar software across different devices potentially allowed us to explore the affordances of different kinds of blogs – Weblogs, PC blogs, and mobile blogs. Lifeblog supports synchronization across PCs and mobile phones (Fig. 14.2), thus enabling the exploration of how different technologies "fit together" in the personal change process.

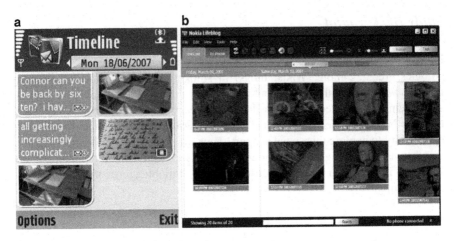

Fig. 14.1 (a) Mobile LifeBlog timeline. (b) PC LifeBlog timeline

Fig. 14.2 Synchronising LifeBlog across an N80 and Windows (Mac)

Process

Figure 14.3 presents an overview of our process. First (Fig. 14.3, Step 1), we recruited four smokers who wanted to quit, had access to the Internet, were broadly early adopters of technology, and were known to at least one of the investigators: as this study explored personal change, this seemed an advantage, not a difficulty.

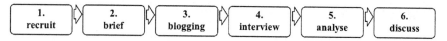

Fig. 14.3 Overview of research process

We briefed the four participants concerning the study (Fig. 14.3, Step 2) – the aims of the work, the steps involved, what was required from them, and the incentive we offered (a cash payment for completion of the study and SIM card credit). During this briefing, we told participants: "Please use Lifeblog to document your attempt to stop smoking. We are interested in your experience, but cannot guarantee that Lifeblog will help. You can use your phone to blog other things of course as well." We also referred them to a phone help line and Web site for additional cessation support, as we were unable to provide expert quit counseling. During the same session, we showed them: how to use Lifeblog on the N-series phone we issued them; and how to synchronize their phone with a PC using the Nokia PC Suite and the PC version of Lifeblog. We provided them with some instructions – a form of minimalist user manual documenting how to perform basic tasks. We then encouraged participants to blog their quit attempt using what we had provided them at that stage, that is, the multimedia phone and Lifeblog.

We contacted all participants after a few days to ask them about their progress, to discuss their use of the technology and to help them troubleshoot problems if necessary (Fig. 14.3, Step 3). After a period of several days (the time lapse depended on the availability of the participants), we arranged for a semi-structured interview asking them about their use of the phone, the PC Suite, and how the technology introduced to them was being "fitted into" their lives (Fig. 14.3, Step 4). At the same interview, we introduced them to their Weblog, providing a set of instructions concerning how to use it (Fig. 14.3, Step 2). After this they blogged, or collected images specifically for their blog, for at least seven days (Fig. 14.3, Step 5). We periodically checked what they had blogged through accessing their Weblog – they were aware that we had access to their blog, but otherwise all participant blogs were protected from others accessing them via passwords. At the end of their period of blogging, we conducted a session to discuss individual participants' blogs (Fig. 14.3, Step 6) with one of us, asking questions around predetermined themes (e.g., phone and blog usage, relationship with quit attempt), and issues determined from examining their blog data (e.g., if blogging had been used as a replacement exercise for smoking). Finally, we conducted a focus group with participants (Fig. 14.3, Step 7) discussing their blog and phone usage and how this fitted into their lives, strengths and weaknesses of the technologies introduced to them, and possible improvements to the blogging software itself. Some discussion also focused on the design of future "personal change" or smoking cessation services. We used findings from this research process to inform the design of some new screens (Graham et al. 2007).

Data and Findings

In all, we collected two Weblogs, one PC blog, five interviews, three collaborative data analysis sessions, and focus group data – a video recorded, 1-h session with the four participants. We also collected the participants' mobile phone content including images, videos, and sound bites. A description of the data and digital life documents collected from individual participants generated is provided in Table 14.1. Significantly, none of the participants provided us with their SMS messages since they regarded these as private.

A general comment about Table 14.1 is: participants did not adopt the technologies in the way we expected. They predominantly used the digital photo, not the mobile blogging functionality and found the Weblog easier to use than LifeBlog. Their blogs were also kept private for the duration of the study and so, while they discussed their blogs in a focus group and shared their blogs with known others, they did not actually choose to share them with unknown others. Despite this, they had particular opinions on sharing their digital content.

The first finding was that there was a palpable desire to connect, to have some form of encounter, through communicative travel – this was difficult given the blogs were private. Benji described how it was:

> Better to reach out to everyday man to see they have the same problem and find out how they dealt with it.

Veronica noted:

> I want to be able to share the content

Both the participants are referring to digital sharing here – there was nothing to stop them sharing the content physically – but how the technology was configured made digital sharing difficult. Veronica also noted how the need to synch the phone with her PC first was an impediment:

> By waiting to synch with PC I'm making it artificial

Table 14.1 Overview of data collected from the participants

Participant	Phone	Involvement	Media	Blog	Postings
Benji	N80	3 months: 2 interviews (1 h), analysis (2 h), focus group	320 images, 15 videos, 43 sound bites	PC LifeBlog	None
Alexandra	N93	3 weeks: 2 interviews (1 h), analysis (2 h), focus group	23 images, 3 videos	Wordpress Weblog	8
Veronica	N93	2 weeks: 1 interview (12 min), analysis (1.5 h), focus group	30 images	Wordpress Weblog	3
Fleur	N93	1 week: 1 interview (10 min), focus group	50 images	None	0

Here, the lack of simple publishing from the phone was an impediment to spontaneous sharing. Yet, there were limits and boundaries to this desire to engage in communicative travel. Fleur noted how:

> I've got a reason not to use the technology anymore because I'm still smoking. Blogging – why would I want to share this with the world?

In this case, Fleur had failed to quit and did not want to celebrate this fact and thus her motivation dissipated. Fleur's comment highlights three issues concerning the sharing of digital content through communicative travel. First, particular modes seem more private than others: Benji noted that he was inherently reluctant to share his video diary; he also noted with concern that LifeBlog "just dumps it all in there – text and all"; no participants shared their SMS messages with us. Thus, just as there are modes of "corporeal travel" such as "walking, travelling by rail, driving, and air travel" (Urry 2000) with particular affordances, so there are modes of communicative travel with particular affordances, at least with regard to privacy. Second, sharing brought with it awareness. In Veronica's case, this awareness was of her own glorification of her smoking habit through the taking of pictures like burning cigarettes which resulted in a volte face concerning her blogging practices. Third, with sharing came an awareness of the audience. In Alexandra, this awareness concerned the audience of her blog: "Seeing as my Mum never knew I smoked." This awareness relates to the mobility of objects too and the perceived difference between their portability and therefore their "publicness." Veronica noted:

> On Friday night I was able to show people the pictures that I had taken in my phone gallery…I'm not going to be able to do that on my computer. There is a wider audience I got access to via my blog but that doesn't happen here and now – the people that I am smoking with are there at the time

The issue here is that the digital content supported a physical encounter because it was portable. The suggestion here is that physical sharing is both more intimate and less embarrassing, but that it need not support any transformation.

Despite LifeBlog being portable, communicative travel was not necessarily coupled with physical mobility and shared physical encounters. Indeed, in Veronica's explanation of how she would share digital photos, neither physical nor communicative mobilities were involved. Participants largely decoupled their physical and communicative travel through LifeBlog – they did not use LifeBlog to publish while on-the-move (this was likely due to technical constraints). Instead, two participants used their more "tethered" Weblog (they could not access their Weblogs from their mobile phones) to publish: Alexandra and Veronica transferred images (e.g., by BlueTooth) from their phones to their PC's and then published them on their Weblogs. Benji, on the other hand, used his USB key as a kind of "digital library" and as a way of sharing images physically with his girlfriend. The suggestion here is that mobilities are multiple and dependent. Veronica's communicative mobility depended on her physical mobility, that is, if she was close to an Internet access point. Benji was on-the-move most of the time, thus his physical travel could impede his communicative travel (at least with regard to blogging).

In addition, he carried certain things with him – his USB key and his mobile phone – and thus his physical travel was closely tethered to these objects' travel.

Three further points seemed important after analysis: concerning granularity, time, and translucence (Erickson and Kellogg 2000). First, there are different granularities of mobilities and this is more salient with some mobilities than others. In physical travel for both objects and people traveling, the scale of bodily movement (e.g., reorientation) is important – from one hand to another, from room to room, from city to city etc. In communicative travel, this "tyranny" is ended and instead the mode becomes important. With regard to time, Veronica expressed frustration concerning the "unsophisticated" temporal view her Weblog provided:

> The blog narrative means the update comes to the forefront…It's scrolling rather than linear

> The way the phone picture gallery is organized is much more sophisticated than the way Weblog is organized. I would use this phone as a visual diary

This sense of "temporal sequence" was important for her, yet it should be noted that no participants could actually publish while physically traveling, that is, leverage the extensive possibilities for "simultaneity" (Jaureguiberry 2000) of mobilities (at least via blogging). Thirdly, the blog offered varying views – to others, to themselves – on participants' mobilities – communicative travel, physical travel, object travel. This "viewing" had different implications. It could mean reexamining moments with others. Veronica noted how:

> The blog says this is how I live my life…You take a picture; every time you relook at it or tell that story to a different person it gains new meaning

This could mean a dialogue with self. Benji noted:

> Whether or not they actually share it it becomes their own internal blog, it allows them to become more comfortable with displaying their emotions by being able to communicate, first and foremost, with themselves

Thus the suggestion here is both that the encounters supported by blogging need not have any physical or social aspect, but instead can be both more personal and reflexive. The notion of encounter here is almost even solipsistic both at the moment and after the moment. The nature of these "reflexive encounters" permitted surveillance by researchers who were keen to get insights into people's lives.

What People Do When They Share Digitally

Sharing personal situations and aspects of life to an audience sometimes known, sometimes unknown, may seem rather unusual in an era of identity theft and online fraud. It seems close to a charming naiveté mixed with a desire to get attention through putting oneself on display. Yet, the findings of this study point to a new and developing form of social encounter that, like Lange's (2007a), indicates both a willingness to "reach out" via blogging and an acute awareness of and caution (as opposed to deep concern) concerning privacy issues.

What we have seen in the study reported here is a characterization of digital and physical encounters that different forms of blogging support, how digital content is involved in people's lives, and the kinds of preferences people have regarding sharing and self-portrayal. The report on the study, as we have presented it here, may seem to have little to do with smoking (cessation). However, there are various ways in which our analysis of the moblogs might proceed that are relevant to smoking cessation behaviors. Examining the various photographs of smoking and smoking paraphernalia suggests aspects of Urry's (2002) "the tourist gaze" of idealized and stereotypical representations, of "fixing" an ephemeral view and of ways in which taking a picture and posting it on a blog impacts on the experience of smoking. Such an analysis also leads into the possibilities of a therapeutic analysis of moblogging practices where blogs may be considered a form of "writing therapy" through a process of "personal translucence" (cf. Erickson and Kellogg's (2000) "social translucence"); putting the self "on view," providing some kind of (admittedly distorted) mirror on the self, so that individuals might think about, reflect on, themselves. We suggest three aspects of personal translucence: *visibility of change*; *awareness of actions*; *longitudinal accountability* and thereby indicate some temporal characteristics of the reflexive encounter suggesting that blogging, particularly in the case we document, but also more generally; enables the individual to see *the difference* between distinct time periods, of phases in their ongoing biography; supports an ongoing awareness of *pertinent actions* as they traverse through everyday life; and engages the individual in, and make them accountable for, an *ongoing process of contributing* to their visible biography. Through the notion of "personal translucence" moblogs become a form of "facework" (Goffman 1967; Kato and Shimuzu 2005).

In this chapter, we also argue that taking these "generic" blogging findings and placing them in the context of Urry's mobilities has enriched our understanding of the "mobile" component of the blogging. It has shifted focus away from movement alone to how certain mobilities are more "coupled" than others, for example, communicative travel and travel of objects. In fact, this study does not suggest that people are coupling blogging with physical travel or the travel of objects at all. Instead, it has drawn attention to how the nature of the objects carried – particular form, factor, mode, and service "convergences" (Howard et al. 2004) potentially affect communicative mobility differently. This perspective, because it considers objects, places, and resources, brought into focus what it is and is not to blog. As Baumer et al. (2008) point out, readership is a neglected aspect in blogging research. Blogging, as we have portrayed it here, involves authoring, publishing, and (awareness of) reading and these can be distributed across time and space – publishing may be done in particular places (e.g., the home) where particular resources (e.g., Wi-Fi) are more readily available for example. However, there seems to be a question regarding whether sharing and/or publishing are necessary conditions for blogging.

However, the findings of our study indicated the importance of asynchronous interaction stretched over time. This issue was critical – people rarely seemed to "blog" on the move (at least author, share/publish and read), perhaps because the technology we issued did not facilitate that "instantaneity," but instead authored and crafted entries after the fact – they separated the different aspects of blogging. The suggestion here is that blogging may be inherently asynchronous and that there is little point in developing technologies that enable it to be otherwise. Thus, as with global informational workplaces, so mobile blogging is "characterized not by the disappearance of time and space as realities of…life, but by their increasing importance and intensification" (Ó Riain 2000). How these concerns affect and play out with regard to social networks we can only speculate concerning as participants blogs were kept private. Despite this, we found an acute awareness of audience and a desire to configure privacy across modes.

Challenges and Opportunities

The literature we have reviewed and the study described in this chapter suggest challenges and opportunities for blogging (particularly mobile moblogging) technologies. Broadly, we consider these to be: the mobile self; the new digital life document, and digital content sharing practices.

The "Mobile Self"

The accounts of moblogging we present here, though inevitably restricted, resonate with many ideas about the prevalence of "mobility" in a (post)modern society. In "Sociology Beyond Societies: mobilities for the twenty-first century" Urry (2000) suggests ways in which "automobility" has transformed modern civil society, forcing people into "intense flexibility," in the various ways in which we are obliged to juggle our everyday lives. This is certainly reflected (experienced and commented on) by our mobloggers, who would evidently concur with Urry's (2000) comment that:

> Automobility entails instantaneous time that has to be juggled and managed in a complex, heterogeneous and uncertain fashion. Automobility…involves a more individualistic time-tabling of one's life, a personal timetabling of these many instants or fragments of time. There is here a reflexive monitoring not of the social but of the self…Automobility coerces almost everyone in advanced societies to juggle tiny fragments of time in order to put together complex, fragile and contingent patterns of social life, which constitute self-created narratives of the reflexive self

Our findings, although from a rather different tradition, resonate with the thoughts of Bruce Chatwin who in "Songlines" (Chatwin 1987) describes how Australian aboriginals couple traditional songs and stories with places to the extent that they can be used to navigate the continent. He also makes a somewhat surprising suggestion to those of us who talk of the need for local "roots" and "community": that a singularly located home, garden, car, and local club membership are all a relatively recent phenomenon in human history and that we are more nomadic by nature than we admit. The "mobile self" is presented across time and space, both digitally and in person, across different media with different affordances. This "self" is then connected to others with ties of various strengths. Posting can become a form of "touch work" or "face work" (Kato and Shimuzu 2005), maintaining and renegotiating these ties. Readership and how this material is used and misused is something bloggers have little control over, although there is an opportunity to develop more sophisticated awareness mechanism or mechanisms that can work redundantly with other media (e.g., talk). Such considerations reconfigure privacy as a mutual, collective, and somewhat recursive concern for both digital content creators, readers, and lurkers where being aware of who is aware of personal digital content becomes important.

As one's biographical trajectory (Strauss 1993) progresses, managing online identity and representation (Mynatt et al. 1997) becomes complex as the various fragments of identity can become disconnected and untethered as the body ages and eventually dies. Satchell et al. (2006) describe how management of this "digital identity" is becoming more nuanced, noting that "the digital generation" can artfully "create, manipulate, control, and even play with digital representations of themselves." However, even for this generation, the management of new phases and transitions in everyday life – moving from adolescence to adulthood, entering a stable relationship, becoming a parent – may prove problematic. As with the concern over privacy, this suggests the importance not only of boundaries to readership and how the relationship with readers and the awareness of this readership, but also the inevitable change that comes with time (Mynatt et al. 1997).

The New "Digital Life Document"

Plummer (1983) describes different kinds of life document (e.g., diaries, vox populi) that can be used to gain insights into particular people's lives. Blogs can have aspects of many forms of these personal documents: they are part life history, part diary, part letter, part guerrilla journalism, part "literature of fact" and they support media elements, such as photographs, videos, and voice recordings. The digital content we have considered here, far from being overly individualistic, can generate a humanized, contextualized, and richly personal perspective on experience:

> Experience is a stream, a flow; social structures are seamless webs of criss-crossing negotiations; biographies are in a constant state of becoming and as they evolve so their subjective accounts of themselves evolve

Plummer's (1983) points can be applied to various forms of digital content, with the difference that these evolving, changing accounts are immediately (and highly) visible as they evolve, as are the crisscross connections among different biographies.

The kinds of digital documents we have described here seem to offer considerable potential in this regard with particular modes offering us particular insights. Two particular challenges are evident. First, how can we make sense of someone's mobilities (e.g., physical, communicative travel) that is, not only to get insights into their life, but the embodied character of their experience? This is clearly not simply an issue of data collection (which is difficult enough – our participants didn't return text messages), but of how analytical work can be done. The process we adopted did not simply involve digital documents, but digital document *exchange* and *discussion*. In this discussion, it seems important to regard the assemblage that a blog marks as a particular view through particular modes. Second, practically how can we sensitively investigate their lives through these life documents without engaging in surveillance? The potentially "live," "as it happens" nature of moblogs seems to threaten personal privacy. Yet, we have shown that the ephemeral nature of shared digital photographs via blogs can easily be exaggerated – for participants sharing and publishing seemed quite distinct from capture with time, practices, and particular communicative travel separating the two.

Digital Content Sharing Practices

The technologies we describe here afford the sharing of digital content concerning the nature of everyday life as well as a less-regulated form of journalism (personal news) and new forms of activism (O'Brien 2007) through various mobilities. Blogs, and other "social software" have the potential to present poignant accounts of unfolding events that, in turn, unfold with events, as which occurred in the case of the chilling events at Virginia Tech in 2007 (Mayerowitz 2007). These events remind us that technologies such as blogs can be appropriated for good or for ill: they allow us again, if in a different medium or technology, "people's nastiness and niceness" (Sacks 1992); to remain connected to loved ones when in danger; or to celebrate and commemorate perverse acts. Thus, we have to be careful that our expectations around these technologies are neither too utopian nor anti-utopian (Kling 1996).

We are unwilling to peer too speculatively into the future. We prefer to make a few, we hope grounded, observations. First, we note that today physical travel can much more easily reinforce and even replace imaginative travel and that communicative travel can be variously coupled with "real" encounters. Thus, we would expect to see more artfully achieved social ties managed through these different mobilities in the future. Second, we note that the various mobilities – physical, object, and communicative in particular – and their interdependencies work together to manufacture particular views on the world and the self (Urry 2002). Digital content sharing practices are an expression of both these mobilities and these interdependencies. These practices often produce material that focuses on the trivial aspects of life in an attempt to offer particular perspectives – journalistic, self-critical, confessional, hedonistic, malicious, perverse, pornographic, "green," autobiographical etc. Thus, these "gazes" on the world and the self are put on display and made consumable for a readership (Urry 2002). In doing so, both the sharing technologies (e.g., camera phone, broadband Internet) and practices will become an important component of "network capital" (Larsen et al. 2006) comprising and sustaining everyday relationships. Finally, "life" is, to some extent, staged through these practices, but as Rojek and Urry (1997) point out perhaps this "inauthentic staging" is little different from the process of cultural remaking that happens in cultures anyway. Blogging in particular may become a central part of this response to change during the passing of time (if it isn't already), and rather than being ephemeral and momentary mark the slowing of time and the production of mundane history.

Conclusions

In "The Presentation of Self in Everyday Life" (Goffman 1967) Goffman famously presents a dramaturgical analysis of social interaction drawing attention to the relationship between every day, "real world" events and theatrical performances. It would, of course, be easy to present, or rather re-present, our data along familiar Goffmanesque lines of "front stage" and "back stage," impressions "given" and impressions "given off" etc. But, we are not interested in merely fleshing out Goffman's analysis with exemplars from a different setting. Whilst, such comparisons can be amusing, our interest carries a rather different analytic and practical purpose and concerns whether such an approach, and the rich descriptive vignettes it provides, adds much to our understanding of the accomplishment of everyday encounters since such dramaturgical analogies seriously misrepresent most people's (and certainly our people's) approach to the serious business of everyday life and the extent to which people occupy rather than merely "play out" social roles.

In this chapter, we have explicated a series of "reflexive encounters," people's encounters with their addiction and their efforts to document aspects of their encounter. Blogs potentially present the opportunity to become more self-aware. While for our smokers, the quit attempts failed, blogging seems to promise some support for aspects of the self-encounters involved, perhaps even necessary, in life change. Like with graffiti, the blogging moment itself is an intensely personal, momentary encounter largely decoupled from the audience eventually consuming it (Ferrell 1993). However, we acknowledge it as merely a claim that "social technologies," particularly blogs, actually support quitting at all, and agree with Nardi et al. (2004) that "the affordances of blogging are currently being worked out by millions of users, and tool-makers are adapting blog features to this use." Nevertheless, and as part of that "working out," we have tentatively explored how blogs become embedded in people's lives, and their role in facilitating one particular kind of encounter – with addiction and the possibility of life change. However, we would not want to advance any crude characterizations of life change or even cruder, hyped, understandings of the impact of technology. Instead, we are trying to point to and develop more subtle understandings both of what a life change might be and what a "persuasive" technology might achieve. We consider this a preliminary attempt to engage with some of the subtleties required for understanding both these kinds of encounters and "persuasion" as a process designed to involve the user. Our data also clearly highlight some of the more emotional features of social encounters – in this case reflexive social encounters – addressing Williamson's (Williamson 1989) critique of the social sciences and their attempts to document and understand such encounters:

> The fact that people are alternately happy and sad, full of optimism or disappointed, envious, jealous, despairing, proud, self righteous, angry or composed hardly seems to matter… the people whose lives are charted in the annals of social science are incapable of hate or of sympathy for their fellow men

In terms of explicating some characteristics of the nature of encounters, our work suggests that quite ordinary social technologies, familiar devices like mobile phones or cameras, can enable both extraordinary and very ordinary things. Far from radically transforming the world, novel technologies, are fitted into, made "at home" in, people's everyday lives (Sacks 1992). In this sense, they afford everyday features of social encounters, and, in the case of the reflexive encounters documented here, effectively enable people to see (again) their own niceness and nastiness' through a process of what we have termed "personal translucence" (cf. Erickson and Kellogg's (2000) "social translucence"). However, while our emphasis has been on some of the characteristics of "reflexive encounters," quitting smoking, as with dealing with any addiction, can also generate particular kinds of social encounter supported and enacted through different media: ad hoc chats with friends and loved ones about photos on a mobile phone depicting aspects of addiction; concerted conversations with fellow addicts about Weblogs describing addiction. In this sense, we believe our data on the use of blogging technologies also points to the importance of considering the particular topologies of emerging social networks in general and the patterns of extensive, variously maintained weak ties that may generate "small worlds" (Watts 1999), stretching across time and space amongst those apparently unconnected except for their addiction or passion (Buchanan 2002; Granovetter 1983).

References

Bamford W, Coulton P & Edwards R (2007) Space-time travel blogging using a mobile phone. In: Proceedings of ACE'07, ACM Press 1–8.

Baumer E, Sueyoshi M & Tomlinson B (2008) Exploring the role of the reader in the activity of blogging. In: Proceeding of the Twenty-Sixth Annual SIGCHI Conference on Human Factors in Computing Systems, 1111-1120. ACM, New York. DOI= http://doi.acm.org/10.1145/1357054.1357228

Beale R (2006) Mobile Blogging: Experiences of Technologically Inspired Design. In: CHI '06 Extended Abstracts on Human Factors in Computing Systems, 225-230. ACM, New York. DOI= http://doi.acm.org/10.1145/1125451.1125498

Blainey G (1966) Tyranny of distance: how distance shaped australia's history. Sun Books, Melbourne

Buchanan M (2002) Small world: uncovering nature's hidden networks. Wedenfeld Nicholson, London

Chatwin B (1987) The Songlines. Elisabeth Sifton Books, Viking, New York

Cheng X, Dal C & Liu J (2007) Understanding the characteristics of internet short video sharing: YouTube as a case study. Technical Report arXiv:0707.3670v1 [cs.NI], Cornell University, arXiv e-prints. July 2007.

Cheng YM, Yu W & Chou TZ (2005) Life is sharable: blogging life experience with RFID embedded mobile phones. In Proceedings of Mobile HCI'05, ACM Press, 295–298. ACM, New York, NY, 295–298. DOI= http://doi.acm.org/10.1145/1085777.1085837

Cheok A, Fernando O, Wijesena J, Mustafa A-u-R,d, Barthoff A & Tosa N (2007) BlogWall: displaying artistic and poetic messages on public displays via SMS. In Proceedings of MobileHCI'07, ACM Press, 483–6. ACM, New York, NY, 483–486. DOI= http://doi.acm.org/10.1145/1377999.1378058

Dix A (2006) Writing as third order experience. Interfaces 68: 19–20

Erickson T, Kellogg W (2000) Social translucence – an approach to designing systems that support social processes. In: ACM Transactions in Computer-Human Interaction, 7, 59-83. DOI= http://doi.acm.org/10.1145/344949.345004

Ferrell J (1993) Crimes of style: urban graffiti and the politics of criminality. Garland Publishing, New York

Garfinkel H & Weider L (1992) Two incommensurable, asymmetrically alternate technologies of social analysis. In: Watson G and Seiller RM (eds) Text in context: contributions to ethnomethodology, 175-206. Sage Publications, London

Gaver W, Dunne A & Pacenti E (1999) Design: cultural probes. Interactions: New Visions of Human-Computer Interaction, 6(1): 21–29

Gibbs M, Vetere F, Howard S & Bunyan M (2005) SynchroMate: a phatic technology for mediating intimacy. In: Proceedings of DUX'05, AIGA, Article No. 37

Goffman E (1967) Interaction ritual: essays on face-to-face behaviour. Pantheon, New York

Graham C, Benda P, Howard S, Balmford J, Bishop N & Borland (2006) "heh – keeps me off the smokes...": probing technology support for personal change. In: Proceedings of OZCHI'06, 221–228. ACM Press, New York. DOI= http://doi.acm.org/10.1145/1228175.1228214

Graham C, Satchell C, Rouncefield M, Balmford J & Benda P (2007) Lessons from failure: re-conceiving blogging as personal change support. In Proceedings of DUX'07, Article No. 22. ACM Press, New York. DOI= http://doi.acm.org/10.1145/1389908.1389937

Granovetter MS (1983) The strength of the weak tie: revisited. Sociological Theory 1: 201-33

Hall A, Bosevski D & Larkin R (2006) Blogging by the Dead. In: Proceedings of NordiCHI'06, 425–428. ACM Press, New York. DOI= http://doi.acm.org/10.1145/1182475.1182528

Harper R, Randall D, Smythe N, Evans C, Heledd L & Moore R (2007) Thanks for the memory. In Proceedings of British HCI'07, British Computer Society 10

Herring S, Scheidt L, Bonus S & Wright E (2004) Bridging the gap: a genre analysis of weblogs. System Sciences, 2004. In: Proceedings of the 37th Annual Hawaii International Conference, 101–111

Howard S, Hartnell-Young E, Shanks J, Murphy J & Carroll J (2004). When the whole is less than the sum of the parts: humanising the convergence of interactive systems. In: Proceedings of OZCHI'04. Narrabundah, Australia: CHISIG, 1–10

Hughes J, King V, Rodden T & Andersen H (1994) Moving out of the control room: ethnography in system design. In Proceedings of CSCW'94, ACM Press, 429–438

Hulkko S, Mattelmäki T, Virtanen K & Keinonen T (2004) Mobile probes. In: Proceedings of NordiCHI'04, 43-51. ACM Press, New York. DOI= http://doi.acm.org/10.1145/1028014.1028020

Ito M (2005) Intimate visual co-presence. In: Ubicomp 2005 Workshop on Pervasive Image Capture and Sharing: New Social Practices and Implications for Technology. http://www.spasojevic.org/pics/papers.htm. Accessed 3 March, 2009

Jacucci G, Oulasvirta A, Salovaara A & Sarvas R (2005) Supporting the shared experience of spectators through mobile group media. In: Proceedings of the 2005 international ACM SIGGROUP Conference on Supporting Group Work, 207–216. ACM Press, New York. DOI= http://doi.acm.org/10.1145/1099203.1099241

Jauréguiberry F (2000) Mobile telecommunications and the management of time. Social Science Information 39(2): 255–268. DOI: 10.1177/053901800039002005

Kato F & Shimuzu A (2005) Moblogging as face-work: sharing a 'community-moblog' among project members. In: Ubicomp 2005 Workshop. Pervasive Image Capture and Sharing: New Social Practices and Implications for Technology. http://www.spasojevic.org/pics/papers. htm. Accessed 3 March, 2009

Khalid H & Dix A (2006) From selective indulgence to engagement: exploratory studies on photolurking. In: Proceedings of British HCI'06. British Computer Society. 17–20

Kling R (1996) Hope and horrors: technological utopianism and anti-utopianism in narratives of computerization. In Kling R (ed) Computerization and controversy, 40–58. Academic Press, San Diego

Lange PG (2007a) The vulnerable video blogger: promoting social change through intimacy. The Scholar and Feminist Online, 5(2). http://www.barnard.edu/sfonline/blogs/index.htm. Retrieved 8 June 2008

Lange PG (2007b) Publicly private and privately public: social networking on YouTube. Journal of Computer-Mediated Communication, 13(1): article 18. http://jcmc.indiana.edu/vol13/ issue1/lange.html. Retrieved 8 June 2008

Larsen J, Urry J & Axhausen K (2006) Mobilities, networks, geographies. Ashgate Publishing Limited, Aldershot

Mayerowitz S (2007) Students turn to social networking sites for info. ABC News, April 17, 2007. http://abcnews.go.com/Business/story?id=3046434&page=1. Accessed 3 March, 2009.

Millen DR (2000) Rapid ethnography: time deepening strategies for HCI field research. In: Boyarski D & Kellogg W (2000) Proceedings of DIS '00, 280–286. ACM Press, New York. DOI= http://doi.acm.org/10.1145/347642.347763

Mynatt E, Adler A, Ito E & O'Day V (1997) Design for network communities. In: Proceedings of CHI'07, 210–217. ACM Press, New York. DOI= http://doi.acm.org/10.1145/258549.258707

Nardi BA, Schiano DJ & Gumbrecht M (2004) Blogging as social activity, or, would you let 900 million people read your diary? In: Proceedings of CSCW'04, 222–231. ACM Press, New York. DOI= http://doi.acm.org/10.1145/1031607.1031643

O'Brien V (2007) Visible voices, shared worlds: using digital video and photography in pursuit of a better life. In: Graham C & Rouncefield M (eds) Proceedings of SIMTech'07. http://www.mundanetechnologies.com/goings-on/workshop/melbourne/program.html. Accessed 3 March 2009.

Ó Riain S (2000) Net-working for a living: Irish software developers in the global workplace. In: Buraway M, Blum JA, George S, Gille Z, Gowan T, Haney L, Klawiter M, Lopez SH, Ó Riain S & Thayer M (eds) Global ethnography: forces, connections and imaginations in a postmodern world, 175–202. University of California Press, London

Plummer K (1983) Documents of life. George Allen & Unwin, London

Rheingold H (2002) Smart mobs: the next social revolution. Perseus Publishing, Massachusetts

Rojek C & Urry J (1997) Transformations of travel and theory. In: Rojek J & Urry J (eds) Touring cultures: transformations of travel and theory, 1–22. Routledge, London and New York

Sacks H (1992) A single instance of a phone-call opening. In: Jefferson G (Ed) Lectures on conversation volume II, 542–553. Blackwell, Oxford

Salovaara A, Jacucci G, Oulasvirta A, Kanerva P, Kurvinen E & Tiitta S (2006) Collective creation and sense-making of mobile media. In: Grinter R, Rodden T, Aoki P, Cutrell E, Jeffries R & Olson G (eds) Proceedings of the CHI '06, 1211–1220. ACM Press, New York. DOI= http://doi.acm.org/10.1145/1124772.1124954

Sarvas R, Viikari M, Pesonen J & Nevanlinna H (2004) MobShare: controlled and immediate sharing of mobile images. In: Proceedings of Multimedia'04, 724–731. ACM Press, New York. DOI= http://doi.acm.org/10.1145/1027527.1027690

Satchell C, Howard S, Shanks G & Murphy J (2006) Beyond security: implications for the future of federated digital identity management systems. In: Proceedings of OZCHI'06, 313–316. ACM Press, New York. DOI= http://doi.acm.org/10.1145/1228175.1228231

Schiano D, Nardi B, Gumbrecht M & Swartz L (2004) Blogging by the rest of us. In: Proceedings of CHI '04, 1143–6. ACM Press, New York. DOI= http://doi.acm.org/10.1145/985921.986009

Sellen A, Fogg A, Aitken M, Hodges S, Rother C & Wood K (2007) Do life-logging technologies support memory for the past? an experimental study using SenseCam. In: Proceedings of CHI '07, 81–90. ACM Press, New York. DOI= http://doi.acm.org/10.1145/1240624.1240636

Sheller M & Urry J (2006) Introduction: mobile cities, urban mobilities. In: Sheller M & Urry J (eds) mobile technologies and the city, 1–17. Routledge, London

Strauss A (1993) Continual permutations of action. Aldine de Gruyter, New York

Urry J (2000) Sociology beyond societies: mobilities for the twenty-first century. Routledge, London

Urry J (2002) The tourist gaze. Sage Publications, London

Urry J (2004) Connections. Environment and Planning D: Society and Space 22: 27–37

Van House NA, Davis M, Ames M, Finn M & Viswanathan V (2005) The uses of personal networked digital imaging: an empirical study of cameraphone photos and sharing. In: Ext. Abstracts CHI'05, 1853–1856. ACM Press, New York. DOI= http://doi.acm.org/10.1145/1056808.1057039

Wang H, Deng Y & Chiu S (2005) Beyond photoblogging: new directions of mobile communication. In: Proceedings of MobileHCI'05, 341–342. ACM Press, New York. DOI= http://doi.acm.org/10.1145/1085777.1085856

Watts D (1999) Small worlds. Princeton University Press, Princeton

Williamson C (1989) Witchcraft and winchcraft. Philosophy and Social Science 19: 445–460

Yin, R. K. (2003). Case study research, design and methods, 3rd ed. Newbury Park: Sage Publications.

Chapter 15
Sharing Knowledge About Places as Community Building

Katharine S. Willis, Kenton O'Hara, Thierry Giles, and Mike Marianek

Introduction

There are many ways of sharing place-based experience with others, as highlighted by Brown in his ethnographic study of a project in a UK city, where he points out that "tourists already put considerable effort into sharing their visit with distant others – such as through travelogues, or sending photos home from their holiday" (Brown et al. 2005). The travel photograph is a good example of how media are used to facilitate sharing place-based experiences. Apart from being a personal memory device, a holiday photograph is often used as a way of capturing a personalized experience such as a beautiful view or an event as a moment in time, where in the process of capturing the image we have in mind the person or group we will show it to and the narrative it will reveal. In viewing an image of place we effectively imagine ourselves in that place and in doing so seek to construct an experience of the place with which to empathize with another person.

In terms of sharing experience, a number of applications seek to find ways to capture the personalized experience of space and create platforms for exchanging such knowledge. These enable users to upload their own annotations for specific locations which others find later as they pass by and some even enable them to locate physical items that have been hidden as part of a treasure hunt, for example

K.S. Willis (✉)
Locating Media Graduate School, University of Siegen, US 236, 57072, Germany
e-mail: willis@locatingmedia.uni-siegen.de

K. O'Hara
Microsoft Research Cambridge, 7 J J Thomson Avenue, Cambridge, UK
v-keohar@microsoft.com

T. Giles
K3 The School of Arts and Communication, Malmö University, SE-205 06 Malmö Sweden
e-mail: thejimiworld@gmail.com

M. Marianek
Bauhausstrasse 7b, Bauhaus University of Weimar, 99423 Weimar, Germany
redmike@spiritofspace.com

K.S. Willis et al. (eds.), *Shared Encounters*, Computer Supported Cooperative Work, DOI 10.1007/978-1-84882-727-1_15, © Springer-Verlag London Limited 2010

as demonstrated by the emerging sport of geocaching. Although geocaching may appear to be popular due to its gaming format, it has been noted that the rich combination of social aspects of the geocaching game are often the key motivators for those who participate (Willis 2009; O'Hara 2008). Brown et al. (2005) created a system called George Square that allows visitors to a particular open public space to share their experiences with others both far and near through tablet computers that share photographs, voice, and location. In this study, the researchers found that the taking of photographs was a powerful sharing practice, alongwith other activities such as geo-referencing pictures on a map and the persistent display of photographs on the map or in a timeline or "filmstrip." The project Urban Tapestries worked on similar metaphors, but sought to become more embedded in a specific community setting. It provided the basis for a series of engagements with actual communities, such as social housing and schools, to play with the emerging possibilities of public authoring in real-world settings. A participant of the system recognized the value of social capital derived from sharing place-based knowledge by relating that "it made me realize I had information that other people might find useful – much more than I had at first realized" (Lane and Thelwall 2006). In a study by Ludford et al. (2007) of everyday sharing practices, in an application called Sharedscape, participants reported the value of bookmarking of place recommendations and the subsequent potential for social matching of shared interests. In one example, a participant explained that he "wanted to meet others who had bookmarks for the same lesser-known places that he does. He took this as an indicator of shared interests and he wanted to use this information for social matching."

Oulasvirta (2008) describes an application; Comedia, and discusses the role of cues in media sharing. They found that of all cues available, location was of fundamental importance and it supported a feeling of mediated companionship, mainly through their use as weak signals of another's situation and presence. The author reports that the reasons for this are not just practical, but that "awareness cues became a sort of proxy for another person, particularly in the way they can act and be used in the place of a distant person, like having that someone somehow 'with you.'" Urry (2002) also highlights how travel to places is motivated not by the desire to be distant from people or places, but rather to experience a form of co-presence in what he terms a compulsion to "co-proximity." This shows that sharing information about place does not need to be explicit, but can instead act as a way of signaling background presence, since individuals use location cues to infer situations, actions, and intentions and as a proxy for companionship. Similar findings were also reported by Stapel et al. (2008), who studied a gaming environment, with the hypothesis that becoming aware that you are often at a similar location induces affinity. They found that when a player received more information about the location of another player it made the game more challenging and gave the game a better flow. They also found that social presence was higher for explicit location cues, but only if cueing was frequent.

These studies underline the fact that sharing knowledge about places, whether this is formally through applications specifically designed for sharing of information or through a simple awareness of the location of another person, is a rich social practice. Although, many applications and media, which support the delivery of spatial information have been developed, an understanding of how sharing takes place and whether it can contribute to a wider understanding of community building still needs to be developed. In this chapter, we initially discuss some issues with knowledge sharing in community frameworks and then continue to describe three case studies and the sharing practices that derive from the use of the media. Drawing from these examples, the final stage of the chapter proposes some more general practices that support sharing of place-based information and how these can facilitate a sense of community or the bonds that create "social glue."

Sharing Knowledge About Places: Motivations and Roles in Community Building

This section is divided into two stages in order to understand the frameworks in which sharing spatial knowledge can help develop community relationships. First, how can we understand the role of spatial knowledge in the creation of community or social glue? Second, what are the motivations and effects of the sharing of this knowledge within the community?

Community is a Sense of Spatial Co-Presence

The concept of community is deeply interwoven with the shared physical setting in which a group exists. Traditionally, one of the key concepts of community is proximity in a topographical sense, but it is actually a far more differentiated social framework that does not simply relate to a physical setting. Bell and Newby (1976) distinguish between three types of community. First, the aspect of physical concentration, that is, living in one geographical area is the key (Minar and Greer 1969). This refers to settlement based upon close geographical propinquity, but where there is no implication of the quality of the social relationships found in such settlements of intense co-presence. Second, there is the sense of community created from a localized set of relationships centered around tightly-knit social groups and organizations. Third, there is a sense of belonging or communion created by strong personal ties and a feeling of belonging amongst the members of the group. The last of these is what is conventionally meant by the idea of "community" relationships (Putnam 2000). These characteristics are underlined by the growth in online social communities. Donath reviews social network websites and highlights the way that users of such sites employ signaling to ensure co-operation and that "the public display of connections is one of the most salient features of the social sites."

Knowing that someone is connected to people one already knows and trusts is one of the most basic ways of establishing trust with a new relationship (Donath 2004). Such sites increasingly include location information about the user so that the signaling described by Donath is performed by the either the current location of the user, or their location preferences. If this sharing of locational information becomes meaningful within a group of people then it can support the creation of community ties. According to Harrison and Dourish (1996) "many collaborative and communicative environments use notions of 'space' and spatial organization to facilitate and structure interaction." Since the motivation to share experiences about places is strong, it can easily extend from simply person-to-person exchange of information into a stronger linking factor between individuals.

Sharing Knowledge Creates Social Capital

In the field of HCI, to date there has been a strong focus on developing a new source of spatial information; online maps, GPS co-ordinates, Wi-fi access points etc. The result is that people have access daily to a wealth of spatial data. Yet, despite this abundance of information, it is questionable as to whether this data is actually contributing to people acquiring knowledge. Thus, we propose that when information is transformed into knowledge, it can really become valuable as social capital and when knowledge is shared it can support the development of a community of practice.

How can information be transformed into knowledge? According to Brooking, knowledge is "a fluid mix of framed experience, values, contextual information and expert insight that provides a framework for evaluating and incorporating new experiences and information" and can be defined "as information in context with understanding to applying that knowledge" (Brooking 1999). Thus, knowledge is information that is by definition contextualized information and so requires the holder to offer their insights into the relevance of the information through communicating it in some way to others. In what form is this knowledge about place shared? The act of traveling to a place, or of discovering it requires some form of effort, either in the travel itself or in the process of finding a particular place. This hard-earned knowledge can be seen as social capital and it is for this reason that there is a strong motivation to communicate it to others. Thus, the experience of place becomes a body of knowledge which at the top of the hierarchy is held by one individual and in the next level is exchanged directly to another person and this exchange becomes third-hand as the information is spread among a chain of others. This reflects the approach of Lave and Wenger (1990), who, in their work on learning highlight that knowledge acquisition normally occurs as a function of the activity, context, and culture in which it occurs and as such, is situated. They further emphasize that "social interaction is a critical component of situated learning and it is vital that learners become involved in a 'community of practice' that embodies certain beliefs and behaviors to be acquired" (Lave and Wenger 1990). Such communities of practice are the key structures through which technologies can become integrated with activities in a way that the technology ceases to be external to the task, but, rather, is bound intimately to it.

In order to understand the way in which social relations are developed and extended through sharing of place-based knowledge, we investigate three case studies. These case studies were chosen because they represent three contrasting approaches to the sharing of place-based knowledge, but they also have some significant common threads. The first is a prototype mobile street game that seeks to enable the exchange of knowledge about places through a narrative format. The second study is a mobile location-based application aimed at children with fixed information points installed in a specific setting. The third case study reviews the way in which a location-based game; geocaching enables users to find and share experiences about places through following GPS co-ordinates listed on a web-based information platform.

Case Study One: "Hide and Seek"

Hide and Seek as described in Giles et al. (2007) is a street game experience, which creates opportunities for place-based knowledge transfer. The game narrative is based on the concept of sharing place-based knowledge where participants assume the role of either "Guest" or "Host" of the story. The host creates a personalized adventure route through a known space and publishes it to a specific person (Fig. 15.1). The guest then has the opportunity to explore an unknown place through unraveling of a series of clues, which lead them through a particular spatial experience. The treasure at the end of the game is not a material reward, but rather the construction of a shared social experience; the exploration and revealing of a place known to the host and initially unknown to the guest developing as a valuable artifact in the memory of both game participants.

Accessible from any normal internet connection, the game web application records the Host's story and organizes it into an exportable package. This package is stored in the application ready to be downloaded by the guest. When the adventure package is completed, a notification is sent to the chosen guest inviting him or her to play the game. The notification, in the form of an e-mail, contains the instructions of where to start the game and a URL of where to download the adventure. As an alternative, a link to a printable document is also given for guests to download a paper version.

Hide and Seek consists of an exchange of mapped challenges between the host and the guest. In traditional treasure hunt activity, puzzles or riddles are created with a time intensive and singular reproducible format which is then used to find a real treasure hidden somewhere in the physical world. However, in this game, a Web-based application is used by the host to create and share an "Adventures Map" which the guest then uses to locate stories and interact through the game mobile game interface. When a guest accepts the host's invitation, the game package con-

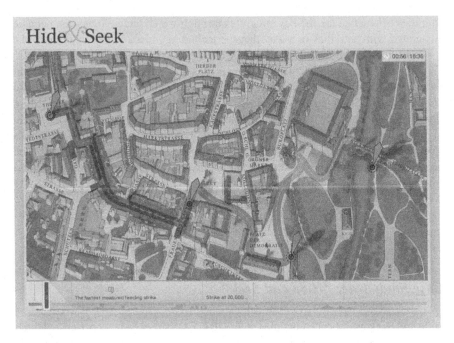

Fig. 15.1 Adventure route

taining the game interface plus the personal host adventure is saved direct onto their mobile device, ready to be played. Once activated, the interface, which is included in the downloaded package, displays the host's personal description of how to reach the starting point of the game. When the guest confirms his physical presence at the starting point by answering the first clue, the adventure then begins. Additionally, both the guest and host can reload, print, and review their adventures in Hide and Seek web archives that stores discoveries and perceptions, and whose resources can be accessed over time.

Although the game platform assumes that there will be no communication between guest and host once the challenge has been sent to the guest, we found that some participants initiated direct contact during the game. This happened particularly when the participants were unknown to each other prior to taking part in the game. The game then became an opportunity to discover not only a place, but also a person. It was observed that the host, in some cases, participated remotely in the guest's progress through the game by literally observing them and their actions from a hidden location. The host only chose to reveal their position when the guest had successfully completed the game. In this case, the host is then himself or herself revealed as the treasure that is discovered at the end of the game. For example:

> In the light under the tree, that's where I've seen you, in the dark, that's where I'll be. Go back
> to the bridge, on the other side of the river, close to the tree, that where you will find IT

It was also observed that guests and hosts used SMS interaction during the gameplay. These messages were not only used by the host to help the guest orientate themselves when they were lost (e.g., "Wrong way! Go back 2 the Sternbrücke"), but also to enrich spontaneous moments lived along the way:

"Felsentreppe" translates into "stone staircase" in English

In general, many hosts admitted to being curious about how their guest would interpret the space of the game. This curiosity also reflected the desire of the host to share their knowledge and to continue the exchange through real-time conversation. These interactions over a third communication platform added another level of more direct interaction and feedback in the game. The unexpected usage of the Hide and Seek game lies in the interaction between the participants. The motivation for the participants was not simply to create an interesting and challenging experience for the game player, but also to participate in the gameplay as it happened. This included offering additional place-base knowledge to enhance the player's experience.

Case Study Two: "London Zoo"

The system deployed at the London zoo comprised a number of key components: First, a mobile application, second a series of situated signs (Fig. 15.2), and finally a personalized web page. The situated signs were distributed at 13 animal enclosures around the zoo, and included a data matrix sign encoded with media content. Participants would then use a mobile phone to retrieve content from the signs, which was a mixture of audio, video, and text files. This information was also available for review and was displayed in the phone interface as icons indicating different animals that had been collected by the participant. Participants were children visiting the zoo, who were either part of organized trips or on individual trips. The participants were then observed whilst using the system, and following their visit they were asked to fill out a questionnaire or were interviewed.

In order to find the signs, placed around the zoo site, the children need to search to find them. As described in O'Hara et al. (2007), the researchers observed that for many of the children, there was excitement bound up in this search behavior, which again is consistent with the findings from the literature. Discovering a sign with a data matrix code was usually accompanied by animated utterances such as "There's one" and "You guys – a sign post" and then running up to the sign to read the code. The exclamations at discovery are indicative of this act of discovery being a social act. Being the one to find the signs bestowed kudos on the individual shouting out the exclamation. The key here was also the time and effort that went into the search. In this particular application, because the content was bound to location, the collected items embodied the fact that the collector had actually been to the place or seen the real-life counterpart of the collected item. It became proof of the visit to the location – a digital souvenir.

Fig. 15.2 Situated sign at London zoo

Much of the value of collected content is bound up in the narratives that can get told around the objects. We saw several instances where such narratives were being told around the content that had been collected and at locations away from the initial collection points. A good example of this was an episode in which a young boy was visiting the zoo with his mother and grandmother. As DeVault has argued, family is something that is actively constructed through such activities as the family visit to the zoo (Devault 2000). What was also important was for the parent to demonstrate their interest in their child's behavior and performance. Parents sitting down with their children to watch the collected video content was a way of them demonstrating their interest in the child and encouraging their engagement. This is not exclusive about location-based content, but rather that location-based content which has been collected comes to acquire additional meaning and significance through these kinds of narratives that get told as it is shared with others beyond the actual trigger location (O'Hara et al. 2007). In this way, the opportunities for sharing a place-based experience are enhanced since the value of location-based content extends beyond its in situ value.

Case Study Three: Geocaching

Geocaching is an outdoor treasure-hunting game in which the participants use a GPS receiver or other navigational techniques to hide and seek containers, called "geocaches" or "caches" anywhere in the world (see Fig. 15.3).

Currently, there are 356,759 registered members, based all over the world. The quick take-up of the idea underlines the attraction and subsequent popularity of the activity. It also highlights the fact that people may use the Internet to gain guidance on places of interest; but the real interest is in visiting the physical location, rather than reading about it. It sounds deceptively easy to seek a cache; all that is required is to enter the coordinates of the destination into the GPS and follow it to the destination. However, while it is one thing to know where a location is on a map, it is quite another to actually attempt to arrive at that location. The main problem is that the abstract space between two coordinates hides a wealth of topographical information, which means that it is not possible to navigate directly to a cache by going straight in the direction to which a GPS receiver

Fig. 15.3 The contents of a geocache

points. The coordinates give no indication of the relationship of the "theoretical" point in space and the physical properties of the location. It is precisely this complicated relationship between location-based elements and on-line elements that makes geocaching of interest to study. According to O'Hara "within the domain of location-based computing geocaching represents an interesting and important object of study" (O'Hara 2008).

In Willis (2008), the life of one particular "cache" is discussed in detail; and a series of key practices are described that characterize the geocaching experience, which may provide insights into the sharing of local place-based information. In the study, 17 visits were logged as specifically being found by either two or three people; six identified themselves as a "team"; and three as "family." When geocachers choose to identify themselves as "team XXX" or "family XXX," it suggests that within the group there is a clear division of roles and aims for the game. Typically, each member of the group writes a separate log, outlining his or her role in the search. The logs also indicate that the people who participate in geocaching form a community and recognize their membership. There is a specific language used and non-geocachers are labeled as "muggles." (The word is taken from the popular children's book series, Harry Potter). Geocachers do not use their real names, but instead have usernames and some even have specially-printed stickers bearing their username, which they inscribe with the particular date and time of a cache find. In addition to the actual hiding and finding activities, people arrange social gatherings to meet others who geocache. In this manner, geocaching supports a whole social structure complete with distinct roles and hierarchies. For instance, despite the superficially flat social hierarchy, geocachers have developed sophisticated ways of distinguishing status. This is primarily achieved by the number of caches a member is listed as having found, with more caches indicating expert knowledge and therefore a higher status. Additionally, there are two or three "gatekeepers," or key members per county, who are responsible for checking each cache before it is authorized. It is clear that geocachers value these status "levels," and that the social aspect of the activity is an important quality that they choose to develop over time. In this manner, the spatial aspect of geocaching provides not just a basis for the sharing of experience about places, but also supports and stimulates a rich social framework.

O'Hara's study involved 14 participants who were required to keep a diary over a 3-week period and also took part in in-depth interviews (O'Hara 2008). The researchers found a range of intensity of geocaching activities; from those who took part only rarely to those who participated avidly. These enthusiastic geocachers often monitored the arrival of new caches and new log entries for their own caches and built up an awareness of the cache landscape in their local area, around their home, their work, or other places where they visited on a regular basis:

> I just do half an hour to quickly go through – just to see what is happening locally – any new ones I put into my Garmin so that they are all on there – so that if we happen to come here I can look at it to see what is local to here

I am conscious of where they all are in Cheltenham. So if ever I am passing them I will
probably have a nose around

But the key motivation underlying participation was its use as a way of discovering
new places. In this respect, it was not so much the finding of a cache that was primary,
but where it led to as a consequence of participating in the treasure hunt.

That's the reason I do it – new places – because we go out with the dog we are always
looking for new places to go. The same place gets boring

Interestingly, in the study, some geocachers remarked that geocaching had
sometimes opened their eyes to everyday places that they were familiar with.
The appreciative comments left by other geocachers in the log of a place
well-known to one participant enabled the "local" to reassess his own experience
of the place described and revalue it. The social aspect of gaining feedback about
your local area from a stranger cannot be undervalued. However, the researchers
found that the challenging aspect of some geocaches created opportunities for
social action in terms of reputation among an existing community. Solving the
geocache puzzles was at times a collective effort in which participants solved them
with friends, family, or work colleagues. The puzzle solving activities thus created
an opportunity for social engagement and play among the immediate social groups
such as family and caching friends. This aspect is particularly highlighted by the
making of a cache, which was usually motivated by the desire to share with others,
a place of significance or natural beauty (mirroring the earlier motivation for doing
caches to find out about new places).

There is one over in Wales by the side of a reservoir – this reservoir is so beautiful that I
thought well I've got to take people there

The geocachers derived great satisfaction from helping others find these
"hard-earned" places that people would otherwise not know about. However,
there was importance of reputation and the geocacher was also aware that their
cache had social capital. This is reflected in the fact that geocaching was not
seen as a one-off event, but rather an ongoing practice that develops over time.
The reputation and standing of the geocacher in the community is seen as
something that can be cultivated, and geocaching creates the opportunity for a
rich and sustainable participation.

Discussion: Practices

The three case studies describe different ways that place-based knowledge is shared
in social settings. However, despite their differences, there are some key practices
that underpin the activities. We term these aspects of behavior, practices in line with
Wenger's definition, where practice "is a process by which we find the world and
our encounters with it meaningful" (Wenger 1999). Although these practices that
are discussed here are each different in approach and participation, it is possible

that they can offer some insight into the broader issue of how to create meaningful structures for sharing spatial information. In particular, we focus on how these practices may contribute to the strengthening or cohesion within a community framework. First, we outline how learning is facilitated through the individual examples, through the creation of what we term a "technology narrative" and also through knowledge collectives. Second, we focus on the particular aspects of sharing practices, such as the development of social roles, membership, and even competitive practices.

Knowledge in Context

Creating a Technology Narrative

Although all the case studies are focused around particular technologies, they do not "live or die" based on these technological frameworks. In all the cases, the technology may suggest a fixed outcome or goal, but actually it simply creates a point in space to which people weave their own practice of the use of technology. This is in line with Suchman et al.'s concept of technologies (1999) as reconstructing social practices since "as practice, technologies can be assessed only in their relations to the sites of their production and use." This is also reflected in Star and Ruhleder (1996), who highlight the fact that "an individual is often a member of multiple communities of practice which use technologies differently and which thus have different demands on their flexible-standard requirements." The narrative as a format creates a way of making the personal, hard-learned information of one person or group accessible to another person or group. In fact, there are many formats where information about a place is woven into a narrative structure. According to David Turnbull, the narrative format creates such possibilities since "storytelling is how a particular piece of technology becomes seamlessly integrated into our cultural practices" (Aedy et al. 2002).

For example, with geocaching, the publishing of raw GPS data apparently leaves little room for participants to construct their own narrative. However, it is the way in which this method of publishing data leaves people free to plan the way they choose to act on it in the searching or finding activities that distinguishes its application. They are offered simply a piece of location data that is the "goal" and many of the means of reaching this outcome are left open to the geocacher to define themselves. People create and publish caches with particular meanings and motivations so that it is not simply in creating a treasure hunt, but rather through the social meaning expressed through their particular choice of location, route, destination, and theme. Additionally, all the case studies showed that the mobile device used in each case to receive and gather information is often only one part of a selection of technology interactions available. In all three case studies the web site provides a key starting out and returning point (e.g., through the log or feedback) for the activity, but the ability to engage with a range of media formats seems to be a critical aspect of the success of the activity. The use of photography and analogue media formats, such as an analogue feedback system, enables participants to negotiate their own narrative through the technology. A further critical aspect is that media is used before, during, and after the activity, which means the interaction with the technology is not limited within the frame of the activity, but becomes an open-ended system.

Inbuilt Learning

A key aspect of sharing place-based information, in the case studies described here, is that instead of the destination or places visited existing purely as information, it gains meaning through social exchange. In addition, they all required some work or effort on the part of the participant. For instance, a teacher in the zoo study described how:

> The kids hate being force-fed with information – it makes them feel like they are at school. This [application] gives them more independence. They can read the signs and go "look what I have found" (O'Hara 2008)

Geocaching has difficulty levels designed into the system that provides a further level of motivation to undertake more challenging tasks. In fact, the cache log almost always includes some reference to the difficulty of finding the cache, such as "found the cache quickly" or

> the cloudy sky meant I couldn't get a good fix with my GPS and spent a long time looking[1]

The fact that each cache requires a slightly different approach to finding the correct location means that the search is meaningful. In the Hide and Seek case study, the exchange between the guest and the host also enabled the host to add in new layers of information as the guest visited a specific location. For instance, explaining the meaning of the description of a place in the guest's native language:

> "Felsentreppe" translates into "stone staircase" in English (Giles et al. 2007)

In this manner, information is transformed into knowledge since people learnt about places in way that was memorable. This can help contribute to the creation of a broader sense of learning that can be described as "knowledge collectives" (Saveri et al. 2005). These are personal knowledge structures aggregate to form broad-based knowledge communities. Thus, it is not only the individual or group in which the knowledge is shared at first hand, but a wider social milieu that participates in learning about places.

Social Roles and a Sense of Co-Presence

Role-taking

In order for social exchange to occur, it is important that there are frameworks for people to understand the modes of communicating. This necessitates the establish-

---

[1] http://www.geocaching.com/seek/cache_details.aspx?guid=2

ing of roles and a common language so that the sharing activities operate on some form of commonly agreed upon and understandable format. A key aspect of this social framework is that it is facilitated by commonly understood and simple rules for communicating and must also allow for individuals to define their role. Thus, in the London zoo case study it was differentiated into the seekers (the children), those who became the recipients of information (parents, relatives), and those that were holders of the information (the zoo staff and BBC staff). Within this social framework, it is not necessary to spend a great deal of time negotiating the appropriate role to take and the subsequent patterns of interaction. Similarly, in the Hide and Seek case study, the participation is divided into the "hiders," who are the holders of knowledge and the "seekers" who have to work to learn about a place. However, in all the case studies, the projects seem to benefit from a fairly flat hierarchy and thus a very open exchange between those with different roles.

In order for them to maintain sustainable ties, social relationships require objectification, that is, a process by which subjectively shared meanings become objective to the individual and, in interaction with others become common property and thereby massively objective (Berger and Luckman 1967). This shared objectification can be achieved through common memories or shared vocabulary and are grounded in shared experiences. The retelling of an experience to a third party ensures that the experience becomes knowledge that exists beyond the memory of the original participants, and also contributes to a sense of holding shared knowledge.

Feedback, Recognition, and Reputation

All three case studies exhibited mechanisms that showed an inherent awareness of others beyond the participants' immediate social setting. The processes of feedback and of reputation building allowed people to both recognize and respond to the presence of unknown others. In fact, many participants in interest-driven communities are motivated by knowing that their achievements in the system will be available to others or by being part of an appreciative community. For instance, in O'Hara (2008), one geocacher reported the importance of creating an experience that will be appreciated by others:

> I try to think up new angles all the time – only so that people will go wow that was a good idea and you will go yes that's cool – that's probably why I put my own caches out

Another participant in this study acknowledged the importance of such practices in geocaching by pointing out how the logs are expected to have feedback that places the experience in a clear and subjective social context.

> For a while Pam was doing just "Found it thanks." But now that she has set some of the own she is realizing what pleasure you get from seeing other people's logs… they are looking for "Cor we suffered with this and we fell in the stream and here is a picture of us getting wet – it makes people seem real then"

A further aspect of this feedback is the degree to which the efforts of the participants are recognized by the community in terms of their reputation. A participant in the zoo study noted that:

> I like the ones that are hard to find because there is a bit more of a reputation to be gained from doing a hard one

Beyond the more immediate aspect of feedback on single events, the ability to develop a social status within the experience, as reputation provides a strong motivation for many people.

Being the Best

Within a social framework, individuals enjoy the challenge of comparing their behavior with others. For example, a participant in the O'Hara (2008) geocaching study explained that:

> When we first-to-find. The email went off as we were going out to a school play and it was on the Downs a few 100 yards from the front door. I couldn't let Gore-Tex beat me to that one and then we went out. That was the closest to the geekiness I had got to going out to find the geocache with a torch. It was dark. It was 8.15 in the winter

This was also noted as a key motivation in the London zoo case study, where the children saw one of the key aspects of the system to be the competitive nature of the collecting activity. This also highlights a potential disadvantage with competitiveness for sharing of knowledge about places, due to the tendency to become so involved in "being the best" that the actual experience of the place is subjugated.

Within a social group, the challenge of "being the best" was directly related to gathering or acquiring knowledge. However, the motivation to gather "places" is also an important aspect to be acknowledged. Participants were often quite goal-oriented and the perceived difficulty of reaching a remote place or of solving a complex spatial clue was highly valued. Discovering or revealing places and sharing this knowledge with others affords social status that is heightened depending on the difficulty of gaining this knowledge. Although competitive comparisons of performance do not initially appear to be a positive sharing experience, it is in fact an indication of a desire and ability to recognize and reward the achievements of others within a social group. Sharing knowledge is part of a system of motivation by incentive that is related more to the worth of the incentive to someone as opposed to the type of incentive. In this way, it is possible to understand competitiveness within a framework of knowledge donating and knowledge collecting, an interdependent system that requires some form of reward structure for it to function in a social network. The incentive legitimizes the practice since that person feels fairly compensated for sharing the knowledge and is reassured that everyone else had also completely shared their knowledge.

Co-Presence through Membership

In addition to developing roles within the practice of participation, a further aspect is the potential for the system to initiate membership or a sense of belonging. As described by Nahapiet and Ghoshal (1998), shared languages and codes are used to facilitate common understanding and the combination and exchange of knowledge. In geocaching, this is achieved through aspects such as the use of specialized language and the adoption of customs, in particular, the practice of thanking the owner of the cache. For example, the practice of leaving the message "TFTC" in the cache logbook means "Thanks for the cache" and there are further examples such as the fact that nongeocachers are referred to as muggles (i.e., outsiders) in the log. In the Hide and Seek game case study, participation is not available to all, but instead is dependent upon the "seeker" being individually invited by the host, which creates a heightened sense of membership. Similarly in the London zoo example, the children's use to specific technology enables them to gain a higher level of access to information in the space. In this example, the ability to read and decode the signs in the space grants them entry to a sense of exclusive use and interaction with the space. This shows that feelings of membership may also be created through access in an informational sense, rather than more traditional access in a social sense.

Summary and Future Directions

In this chapter, we reviewed some of the ways that knowledge about places is shared within social groups. We proposed that sharing spatial knowledge whether implicitly or explicitly can facilitate a sense of co-presence, and can support a collaborative learning process. However, to date, the focus in fields such as LBS and guiding applications has tended to be on delivering mobile information at the location where it is required. This information push has sometimes neglected the vital social aspects of location-based information and in particular the key aspect of sharing within the experience of place-based knowledge. Future applications should focus more on the way that knowledge can be shared among a community, whether this is within an existing social framework or a more temporal set of social associations.

A further and perhaps critical factor is that the enormous wealth of web-based information systems on place has tended to focus on information about remote locations, for example, holiday destinations. This creates communities of remote individuals that tend to be temporally quite transient. This could in part be due to the very nature of the system in which the information is shared, since web-based place information can be created or retrieved independently of where the information is created or references. Although, this has benefits of enabling access to a much wider audience, it also fails to capitalize on the valuable process of the local exchange of knowledge. A focus of future work should be on re-localizing web-based databases of information and binding them into located social structures.

There must also be a note of caution in aspirations for future work, since there are many problems inherent in studying an intangible concept such as community, and in particular how to evaluate whether a design has succeeded in supporting or improving notions of community (Cheverst et al. 2008). A desirable outcome is for the sense of co-presence realized through sharing of place-based knowledge to have some tangible impacts on the everyday lives of people such as improving maintenance of hitherto "forgotten" places or supporting social matching of like-minded individuals who share the same attachment to a particular place.

Conclusions

In this chapter, we introduced the concept that sharing knowledge about places can help develop social glue. In order to understand in more detail how this process can occur, we discussed three case studies, the first a location-based game with a guest and host component. The second was a series of situated signs and a corresponding web page in a zoo environment. The third was the established activity of geocaching; a GPS based game. Each of these examples revealed practices where knowledge about place was exchanged within a social framework. Finally, there was a discussion on the implications of these issues on the way in which place-based information can be a catalyst for both developing and reinforcing existing relationships within a community.

References

Aedy RK, Evans K & Turnbull D (2002) The thing about string. The Buzz: 27 May, http://www.abc.net.au/rn/science/buzz/stories/s568986.htm. Accessed 4 December 2008

Bell C & Newby H (1976) Communion, communalism, class and community action: the sources of new urban politics. In: Herbert D & Johnston R (eds) Social areas in cities. Wiley, Chichester

Berger P & Luckman T (1967). The social construction of reality: a Treatise in the society of knowledge. Anchor, New York

Brooking A (1999) Corporate memories, strategies for knowledge management. Thompson Business Press, London

Brown B, Chalmers M, Bell M, Hall M, MacColl & Rudman P (2005) Sharing the square: Collaborative leisure in the city streets. In: eds. H. Gellersen et al (eds) ECSCW, 427–447. Springer, New York

Cheverst K, Taylor N, Rouncefield M, Galani A & Kray C (2008) The challenge of evaluating situated display based technology interventions designed to foster sense of community. In: Proceedings of USE '08, South Korea

DeVault ML (2000) Producing family time: practices of leisure activity beyond the home. Qualitative Sociology 23(4): 485–503

Donath J and Boyd D (2004). BT Technology Journal, Vol 22 No 4, October 2004. MIT Press, Massachusetts

Giles T, Marienek M, Willis KS & Geelhaar J (2007) Hide&SEEK: sharing cultural knowledge. In: Proceedings of ACM Multimedia '07 ACM, New York. DOI= http://doi.acm.org/10.1145/1291233.1291351

Harrison & Dourish P (1996) Re-placeing space: the roles of place and space in collaborative systems. In: Ackerman MS (ed) Proceedings of ACM CSCW 96, 67-76. ACM, New York. DOI= http://doi.acm.org/10.1145/240080.240193

O'Hara K, Kindberg T, Glancy M, Baptista L, Sukumaran B, Kahana G & Rowbotham J: (2007) Social practices in location-based collecting. CHI 2007: 1225-1234. ACM, New York. DOI= http://doi.acm.org/10.1145/1240624.1240810

O'Hara K (2008) Understanding geocaching practices and motivations. In: Proceedings of CHI 2008: 1177–1186. ACM, New York. DOI= http://doi.acm.org/10.1145/1357054.1357239

Oulasvirta A (2008) Designing mobile awareness cues. In: Proceedings of MobileHCI '08, 43–52. ACM, New York. DOI= http://doi.acm.org/10.1145/1409240.1409246

Lane G & Thelwall S (2006). Urban tapestries: public authoring, place and mobility. Proboscis Report, London. http://urbantapestries.net/. Retrieved 3 January 2009.

Lave, J. and E. Wenger. 1990. Situated learning: Legitimate peripheral participation. Cambridge, UK: Cambridge University Press.

Ludford PJ, Priedhorsky R, Reily K & Terveen L (2007) Capturing, sharing and using local place information. In: Proceedings of CHI '07, 1235–1244. ACM, New York. DOI= http://doi.acm.org/10.1145/1240624.1240811

Minar DW & Greer S (eds) (1969) The concept of community; readings with interpretations. Aldine Publishing Company, Chicago

Nahapiet & Ghoshal S (1998) Social capital, intellectual capital and the organizational advantage, Academy of Management Review 23 (2): 242–356

Putnam RD (2000). Bowling alone: the collapse and revival of american community. Simon & Schuster, New York

Saveri A, Rheingold H & Vian K (2005). Technologies of cooperation. Institute for the Future report, Palo Alto. http://www.rheingold.com/cooperation/Technology_of_cooperation.pdf. Retrieved 10 October 2007

Stapel JC, de Kort YA & IJsselsteijn WA (2008) Sharing places: testing psychological effects of location cueing frequency and explicit vs. inferred closeness. In: Proceedings of MobileHCI 08, 399–402. ACM, New York. DOI= http://doi.acm.org/10.1145/1409240.1409298

Star SL & Ruhleder K (1996) Steps towards an ecology of infrastructure: design and access for large information spaces. Informations Systems Research 7 (1): 1047

Suchman L, Blomberg J, Orr J & Trigg R (1999) Reconstructing technologies as social practice. American Behavioral Scientist Journal 43 (3): 392–408

Urry J (2002) Mobility and proximity. Sociology 36 (2): 255–274

Wenger E. (1999) Communities of Practice. Learning, meaning and identity, Cambridge: Cambridge University Press

Willis (2009 to appear) Hidden Treasure: Sharing Local Information. In Thielmann, Tristan (ed.): Locative Media and Mediated Localities, (Aether. The Journal of Media Geography, Vol. 6), Northridge, CA

Index